MANAGER'S GUIDE
TO COMPUTERS
AND INFORMATION SYSTEMS

MANAGER'S GUIDE TO COMPUTERS AND INFORMATION SYSTEMS

Larry E. Long

PRENTICE-HALL, INC., Englewood Cliffs, N.J. 07632

Library of Congress Cataloging in Publication Data

Long, Larry E. (date)
  Manager's guide to computers and information systems.

  Bibliography: p.
  Includes index.
  1. Management information systems. I. Title.
T58.6.L664 1983   658.4'0388   82-21403
ISBN 0-13-549394-3

Editorial/production supervision
  and interior design: *Lynn Frankel*
Cover design: *Miriam Recio*
Manufacturing buyer: *Gordon Osbourne*

Printed in the United States of America

10 9 8 7 6 5 4 3 2

ISBN 0-13-549394-3

Prentice-Hall International, Inc., *London*
Prentice-Hall of Australia Pty. Limited, *Sydney*
Editora Prentice-Hall do Brasil, Ltda., *Rio de Janeiro*
Prentice-Hall Canada Inc., *Toronto*
Prentice-Hall of India Private Limited, *New Delhi*
Prentice-Hall of Japan, Inc., *Tokyo*
Prentice-Hall of Southeast Asia Pte. Ltd., *Singapore*
Whitehall Books Limited, *Wellington, New Zealand*

*To those managers
with the vision to seize opportunity
and the sense of purpose to act decisively*

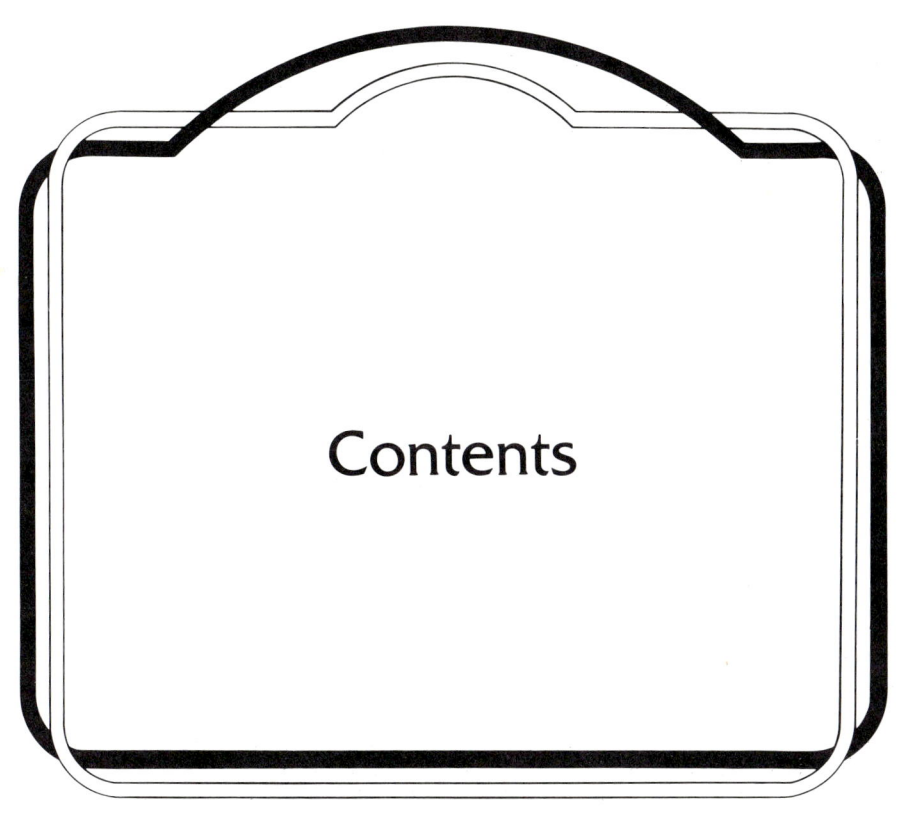

Contents

PART II
COMPUTERS AND DATA MANAGEMENT

PART III
MANAGEMENT INFORMATION SYSTEMS

Preface

BACKGROUND

For the past three decades, many functional area managers and executives have adopted an isolationist attitude toward data processing and computers in general. Data processing (DP)/information services (IS) personnel have perpetuated this attitude by refusing to communicate in terms the user (one who "uses" the computer) can understand. This lack of interest and inability to communicate has slowed the development of needed computer-based systems and encouraged autonomy and redundancy in others.

No organization can expect a 100% efficiency in communication between user and IS personnel, but some have experienced reasonable success. Those that have a good user/IS interaction attribute this success to the user community having mastered a basic body of knowledge in the area of computers and information resource management. This knowledge is assumed of an IS professional, but it must be acquired by user managers through formal study, reading, and experience.

The user/IS interaction is enhanced by a compromise of respect. Each must respect the other's willingness to produce and maintain a quality information system. The level of system quality is directly proportional to the effectiveness of the interaction between user and IS personnel.

User managers and executives who are not willing to acquire a basic understanding of computers and information resource management will be left behind. This is particularly true with the recent and growing trend of encouraging direct user involvement in the information system development process. Historically, user managers have relied heavily on IS personnel to suggest, develop, and implement systems to the benefit of the functional areas. With the continuous and diverse demands placed on information services, the responsibility for system identification and enhancement now rests with the user—and so it should. This trend toward greater user involvement began in the mid-1970s and has gathered momentum since then. Information services has now entered an era of partnership. Who knows better what they would like from an information system than the end users?

The personification of user involvement in information resource management (IRM) is distributed data processing (DDP). In the DDP environment, the user is not only involved during systems development, but ultimately assumes responsibility for the hardware and personnel required for ongoing production.

Only in recent years have corporations recognized and accepted information as a resource. This valuable resource must be managed or it is wasted. In this competitive environment, managers and executives must use information effectively or lose ground to the competition. In the past, managers viewed the computer as a tool to save money. Now the computer is viewed as a tool to make money. Every corporation has abundant untapped potential for the use of computers and the information resource. The level of computer/information processing understanding required to tap this potential is well within the grasp of most managers and executives. This book was written with the intent of providing this requisite level of understanding.

AUDIENCE

This book will produce the greatest benefits for managers, executives, and those aspiring to these positions. They can develop a knowledge base that will enable them to do the following:

1. Better articulate functional area requirements to information system development teams.
2. Be proactive in identifying new and better uses for computers and information systems.
3. Manage an information system development project or, perhaps, an IS department within the functional area.
4. Realize the benefits of computers and the information resource.

The manager or potential manager who absorbs the material in this book will acquire the necessary technical background and management insight to fulfill his or her role in the age of information.

CONTENTS

Computer-based information systems are not only bigger and better than they were a decade ago, they are different. The entire complexion of corporate information services has changed. This book contains material that will enable management personnel to gain the awareness and knowledge necessary to use computers effectively for data processing and managerial decision-making. A secondary objective is to provide some insight into why one approach is superior to another and what actions the user manager and executive can take to improve the quality of corporate information services. The contents were carefully chosen to eliminate material which is superfluous to these objectives.

The editorial philosophy embodied in the text of this book is to be candid and forthright. There is nothing to be gained from sugarcoating or oversimplifying a critical concept. The book is written for managers in the "real world"; therefore, the contents reflect the "real world." IS, user, and top management shortcomings and strengths are equally and openly portrayed.

ORGANIZATION

The book is organized to be equally effective either as a managerial introduction to computers and information resource management or as a reference manual. It is divided into four parts: PART I—Corporate Information Services; PART II—Computers and Data Management; PART III—Management Information Systems; and PART IV—Strategic Planning for Information Services.

PART I—Corporate Information Services presents an overview of information services and the role of the user manager in the information services function.

PART II—Computers and Data Management presents those hardware, software, and data management concepts that are important for effective communication between user and IS personnel.

PART III—Management Information Systems presents an overview of computer-based information systems and the system development process.

PART IV—Strategic Planning for Information Services discusses approaches and strategies for cultivating the corporate information resource to its fullest potential.

Data processing (DP) is still a popular term; however, most computer centers have transcended batch data processing and now provide management information to aid in the decision-making process. While the term *data processing* has tremendous momentum and will be used for years to come, it does not reflect the treatment of information as a corporate resource or the expanded role of the information services function. In this book, the term DP will be used sparingly (and then only when appropriate). A more contemporary and accurate terminology will be used in its place. For variety, the corporate entity that performs the information services function will be referred to as *information services, management information systems,* or *MIS. Information resource management* (IRM) will be used to refer to the concept of treating information as a corporate resource.

Terms that are regularly used interchangeably in casual conversation are introduced and identified as synonyms. In keeping with the "real world" editorial philosophy, such terms are interchanged throughout the book to familiarize the reader with computerese.

Throughout the book, important computer/information processing terms are presented in boldface type, then followed by an explanation. Others are introduced in context, without separate explanation; these terms appear in quotes. Italicized words are used for emphasis. The glossary may be used both as a general reference and as a tool for reviewing terms. With a little practice, the reader should become proficient in computerese.

To maintain a consistency of presentation, all organizational references are to the "corporation," "corporate entities," "corporate managers," and so on. The contents of this book are equally applicable to state, local, and federal government agencies; educational institutions; and nonprofit agencies.

ACKNOWLEDGMENTS

I would like to acknowledge my wife and partner, Nancy, whose contribution to this book and my career in general goes far beyond a mere expression of appreciation. I am grateful to Mrs. Elsie Hamel, Mrs. Barbara Wilson, and Miss Lynn Frankel for our association and their professionalism. I would like to thank my tennis partners, Art, Brad, Charles, Drew, Gene, John, and Sandru, who exhibited patience and understanding when my thoughts were on chapters rather than forehands. I owe a debt of gratitude to Mr. Karl Karlstrom, Senior Editor at Prentice-Hall, Inc., who, for two decades, has been a continuing inspiration to me and other authors in computer-related areas. I would also like to thank my computer, Vector, for without Vector's help, this book would probably still be in the making.

Larry E. Long, Ph.D., C.D.P., P.E.

About the Author

Larry Long is an internationally known lecturer, writer, and consultant in the field of information services. He has presented a variety of MIS seminars in the United States and abroad and is a frequent speaker at professional conferences. He has authored books on MIS strategic planning, system documentation and procedures, and information resource management for user managers. He has also written numerous articles on management, computers, and information services. Dr. Long's "Turnaround Time" column appears bi-weekly in *Computerworld* and in several sister affiliates throughout the world. His consulting practice has enabled him to interact with all levels of management in virtually every industry type.

Dr. Long is President and founder of Long and Associates, a management consulting firm. He is also an Adjunct Professor at Lehigh University. Dr. Long received B.S., M.S., and Ph.D. degrees in industrial engineering from the University of Oklahoma and holds certification as a C.D.P. and a Professional Engineer.

MANAGER'S GUIDE
TO COMPUTERS
AND INFORMATION SYSTEMS

Part I

CORPORATE INFORMATION SERVICES

CHAPTER 1

Managers, Computers, and Information Systems

Consider the following scenario. A systems analyst is assigned the responsibility of responding to a service request submitted to the information services department for the development of a computer-based cost accounting system. This analyst has advanced through the ranks by working exclusively on personnel systems and has little knowledge of the principles of accounting, much less cost accounting. To be consistent with the corporation's top-down design policy, the analyst schedules a meeting with two vice-presidents, one of whom submitted the service request. The objective of the meeting is to obtain an overview of corporate objectives relative to cost accounting and to set the tone for the development project.

This all-too-familiar scenario has very little potential for an efficient exchange of information. With limited knowledge of cost accounting, the systems analyst will not know what questions to ask; nor the significance of the responses and statements made by the vice-presidents. The analyst may grasp, at most, half of what is being said. Without knowledge

3

of computers and information processing, the vice-presidents will have the same lack of ability to ask intelligent questions and to understand responses and statements by the analyst. System quality is directly proportional to the effectiveness of this and subsequent interactions between users and analysts.

The moral here is that users and potential users should have a working knowledge of computers, and information processing and information services (IS) professionals should have a knowledge of the functional areas in which they work. Each should acquire this knowledge or suffer the consequences—both individual and corporate.

The objective of this book is to provide managers and potential managers with a foundation of computer/information processing understanding that will result in efficient communication with IS personnel and quality information systems. The computer-wise manager can realistically anticipate peripheral benefits: increased mutual responsiveness between the user and IS organizations; increased productivity in operations, both in the functional area and in information services; an overall better working environment; and, for the individual, greater career opportunities.

THE USER MANAGER DEFINED

The target reader for this book is the user manager or executive. *User* is applied to any person who uses the computer or information services, either routinely or periodically. The *user manager* is the manager of a non-IS corporate entity (e.g., accounting, marketing, engineering, and so on) or any officer with corporate-wide responsibilities. The user manager manages a *functional area* (synonymous with *corporate entity*). These commonly used terms have specific meaning and are a part of the computerese vocabulary.

SCOPE OF INFORMATION SERVICES

Information services encompasses all the events and activities affected by or under the control of information services. Users who are not appraised of the scope of IS responsibilities may have a limited perspective, associating IS only with those events and activities affecting their specific functional areas. In fact, IS activities are corporate-wide. Today the functional area *not* employing the use of corporate data processing and information services is the exception rather than the rule, even in small companies.

This broad scope can best be illustrated by discussing some of the ways IS serves the functional areas of a typical company. A manufacturing company is used in this example. Figure 1-1 illustrates the organizational structure. By supporting major systems throughout the company, IS has made significant developmental and operational commitments to each of the major corporate entities.

Computerization of the **accounting and finance** division functions have proven very cost effective; therefore, accounting systems are among the first to be automated in almost every corporation. Receivables, payables, general ledger, and payroll have been used to cost-justify the purchase of the initial computer in many corporations.

Production divisions use information services for such applications as inventory control and production scheduling.

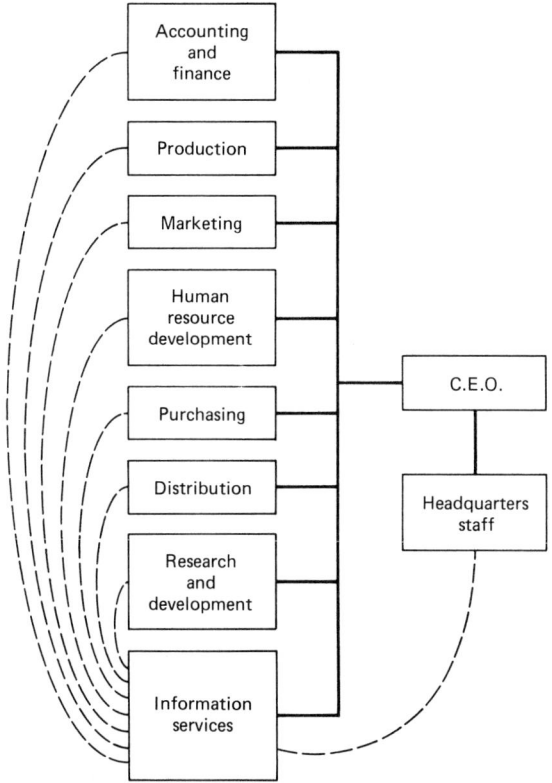

FIGURE 1-1 Functional area interaction with information services in a manufacturing organization.

Many manufacturing resource planning (MRP) systems have been implemented in recent years. The continuity and integrity of the production function is highly dependent on accurate, timely output from information services.

As competition becomes keener, **marketing** divisions have turned to information services for aid in fine-tuning marketing efforts through market analysis systems, and as a means of providing better services to the customer via on-line order entry systems. Market analysis systems have proved invaluable in determining marketing strategy. Among other benefits, an on-line order entry system provides up-to-the-minute inventory status for salespeople.

Most **human resource development** divisions have automated the basic personnel accounting functions. Computer-based systems encourage more effective utilization of personnel via skill matrices that match employees to the jobs that best fit their talents. In one instance, a disenchanted engineer was actively seeking employment elsewhere when a technical sales opening was automatically routed to him by the company's computerized upward mobility system. As vice-president of marketing, he is now a staunch believer in using the computer for career development.

Agents in **purchasing** divisions are quickly replacing cumbersome manual systems with computer-based systems. Not only do these systems provide agents with the information necessary to extend their buying power, but they also generate the necessary paper work. As a result of the implementation of an information system, a purchasing agent of a 50 million dollar corporation spent 1 million dollars less to purchase essentially the same items as the year before.

Distribution divisions receive output that usually is generated in production or marketing. A computer system can integrate these functionally adjacent areas and optimize the load, mode, and distribution points for finished goods.

Research and development divisions typically rely on data centers to support a variety of technical software packages, including models, scientific languages, graphics, statistics, and in some cases, special-function hardware. R&D demands on IS are more acute because of their special characteristics. First, demands for resources are usually ad hoc and are difficult to schedule. Second, most R&D-type programs are processor bound, requiring large amounts of primary storage and processor capability. In these cases, R&D processing may require a dedicated computer, precluding any other processing.

Headquarters staff, or those with corporate-wide responsibilities, depend on computer-produced output for routine and strategic decision making. An embarrassed president of a small manufacturing company was unable to respond when asked his fixed cost for production. He immediately authorized the purchase of a small computer and the hiring of a programmer/operator. After 20 years the department now numbers over 100 IS professionals and the president attributes much of the corporation's success to the judicious use of the computer as a tool.

Although a department's budget share is a poor indicator of its contribution to profit, it does serve to make a point in the case for recognition of information services. With budgets between 1% and 4% of sales, information services is in the same category as other, more traditional corporate entities. Note that in Figure 1-1 information services is included as a major corporate entity. Unfortunately, most corporations have not recognized IS in their organizational structure and in some corporations IS is as much as four levels removed from the president. As user and corporate managers recognize the scope of information services, it will be afforded appropriate functional and organizational status, but for now this problem remains.

When IS is viewed from a corporate perspective, the perceptive user will recognize the significant demands placed on information services from all corners of the corporation. As a rule, problems or deadlines facing marketing, accounting, or any other corporate entity also become problems and deadlines for information services. The user manager should temper the extent and critical nature of service requests with this understanding.

MANAGEMENT CHALLENGE

The challenge to management is to increase productivity and thereby profitability. Managers have used work-simplification techniques, employee motivation, and data processing systems as means of enhancing productivity. These and other approaches have proven successful.

However, the manager of the 1980s is further challenged to view information as a resource and to make judicious use of this corporate information resource.

Information resource management (IRM) encourages the treatment of information as a *major* resource. Managers can do this by:

1. Using information more effectively through decision support systems and other aids to managerial decision making;
2. Using information services in support of transaction-based systems;
3. Participating in and encouraging the integration of functionally adjacent systems.

Functionally adjacent systems feed each other, have functional overlap, and share all or part of a data base. The majority of installed information systems were implemented in a crisis environment and with a single functional objective in mind. For this reason, the typical corporation has massive system, procedural, and data redundancy that could be eliminated through computer-based integration.

CRITICAL BUZZ WORDS DEFINED

The computer and information processing industry has an amazing affinity for introducing new words and acronyms into the computerese vocabulary. Much of this book is devoted to simplifying and clarifying this terminology. The functional area manager and corporate executive may be led to believe that all professionals in information services share a common understanding of these terms. This simply is not true. When conceived, these terms are seldom clearly defined and are subject to a variety of interpretations and misinterpretations.

There are hundreds of IS terms and concepts with which user managers should be familiar. These will be discussed and illustrated in context throughout the book. Since the following terms are a continuing source of confusion to user managers (and IS professionals), they are presented at the outset.

Data processing (DP), as the name implies, encompasses the processing of manual or automated transaction-based systems.

Electronic data processing (EDP) was coined to distinguish manual data processing systems from those that are electronic (unit record or computer).

Automatic data processing (ADP) is an alternative term for EDP and is more common in the public sector.

Information system describes a computer-based system that provides both data processing capability and information for managerial decision making.

Information processing is actually a misnomer since information is produced, not processed. It is, however, a commonly accepted term that is used in two contexts. First, it references the processing of data and the production of information. Second, it is used to refer collectively to the people, procedures, systems, and hardware associated with the information services function.

Computer-based information system (CBIS) is equivalent to *information system.*

Management information system (MIS) was coined to highlight the integration of functionally adjacent systems, data bases that are corporate-wide, and the elimination of system redundancies. After it became apparent that initial MIS objectives were unattainable in most corporations, the term remained popular and is used interchangeably with *information system.*

Decision support systems (DSS) was recently introduced as a new concept in information processing. It is not. What is new are the technical innovations, models, user-oriented query languages, and advanced hardware (e.g., color graphics) that enhance the capability not only to produce, but to present information to support the decision process. An information system is developed and implemented in degrees. A DSS is that component of an information system that uses available data and technology to enhance the decision-making process.

Each of the above terms is also used to refer to that corporate entity which accomplishes the information services function (e.g., a DP department).

Information resource management (IRM) is a concept advocating that information is a resource and should be managed accordingly. IRM can also be an individual, the **information resource manager**. In theory, the information resource manager is appointed to a high-level position, presumably vice-president, and charged with managing the corporation's information resources. This position should not be confused with the traditional manager of the information services function (services, programming, operations, and so on).

Office automation and word processing (WP) have been given enormous media attention and are therefore included in this initial list of critical terms. All of the notoriety surrounding office automation is unwarranted. Office automation is simply using the computer and information services in the traditional manner in the office environment. Office automation is an important application of the computer, but far from a revolutionary new concept, as some have touted. Word processing refers collectively to the hardware and software required to manipulate text, and it is generally considered to be a subset of office automation. Office automation is discussed in detail in Chapter 14.

It is not uncommon for a group of systems analysts and programmers to use four or five of the above terms interchangeably during a functional specification interview with a user manager. This is unfortunate, but nevertheless a daily occurrence. Although subtle differences exist between most of the terms, they are, for the most part, interchangeable. Ask for clarification if the term is used in a context that implies a deeper meaning.

Information services will be used in this book as the primary term for the corporate entity or entities that develop and maintain information systems. However, in order to accustom the reader to other commonly used terminology, "MIS," "information systems," and the "computer center" will be used in the same context as "information services."

LACK OF COMMON UNDERSTANDING

Ask any five executives to define a management information system. Invariably, the only commonality between these definitions is that there is no agreement. Considering the widespread use of the term by management and information services professionals, this is indeed a paradox.

It is economic heresy to think that an executive committee (C.E.O. and V.P.s) would approve the introduction of a new product line without an in-depth understanding of the product, the cost of production, and the market potential. This same group of executives will approve the development of a million dollar management information system that is ill-defined in purpose, scope, and objectives. This lack of common understanding and, in some cases, the lack of desire to understand, place severe constraints on the system development process, thereby minimizing the probability of successful implementation.

Even though each member of the executive committee renders enthusiastic approval for a proposed MIS, each may have different expectations for the system. Invariably the "hit and miss" development strategy produces ill-defined information systems. This approach to development begins with a superficial set of functional specifications and proceeds slowly, often requiring backtracking to make major modifications. This backtracking can be avoided if those involved have a common understanding of what is approved in the first place. Ultimately these systems are implemented, but only after it is apparent that the marginal returns for further modifications do not merit the expenditure of resources. Seldom is anybody satisfied.

It is not critical that the entire industrial/computer community share a common working definition of management information systems. Information services professionals have called MIS a method, a function, an approach, a process, an organization, and a system. What is important is that managers and executives within one organization reach a common understanding of the purpose, scope, and objectives of a particular information system or MIS. To facilitate efficient communication between reader and author, the following working definition of an MIS or information system is proposed:

> *Given a multilevel organization having component groups which perform a variety of functions in order to accomplish a unified objective, an MIS (or information system) is an integrated structure of data bases and information flow over all levels and components, whereby information collection and transfer is optimized to meet the needs of the organization.*

The above definition was formulated to represent the ideal. In reality, an organization can only strive for optimization and total integration. Even if a finished product falls short of the above definition, user and information services personnel are shooting at the same target. Time spent by executives, user managers, and IS managers to formulate a working definition of an information system is easily justified. A well-conceived definition can provide guidelines for making resource commitments for system development projects.

GROWTH PATTERNS FOR CORPORATE INFORMATION SERVICES

Computer centers, like people, have a rather standard pattern of growth during the first 5 to 20 years. Some people mature earlier than others— and so it is with computer centers. The general information services growth pattern follows the "S" curve first described by Gibson and

Nolan.[1] They first defined four stages; Nolan later identified six distinct stages of growth.[2] The number of stages is academic. What is important is that the user recognize the existence of the information services growth patterns.

The S-shaped growth pattern, which is repeated in each cycle of Figure 1-2, is in reality an accumulation of subordinate growth patterns combined to illustrate overall information services growth over time. Each of these subordinate growth patterns may take a variety of forms, as illustrated in Figure 1-3. These subordinate patterns may represent growth in:

♦ Number of data processing and information systems
♦ Sophistication of information systems
♦ Management techniques
♦ Attitudes toward information services

Growth in organizational attitudes may lag behind growth of sophistication by as much as 10 years, and vice versa. Since the S-shaped growth pattern is repeated in cycles (see Figure 1-2), differences in the shape of subordinate growth patterns ultimately affect when information services enters the next cycle.

[1] Cyrus F. Gibson and Richard L. Nolan, "Managing the Four Stages of EDP Growth," *Harvard Business Review,* January–February 1974.

[2] Richard L. Nolan, "Managing the Crisis in Data Processing," *Harvard Business Review,* March–April 1974.

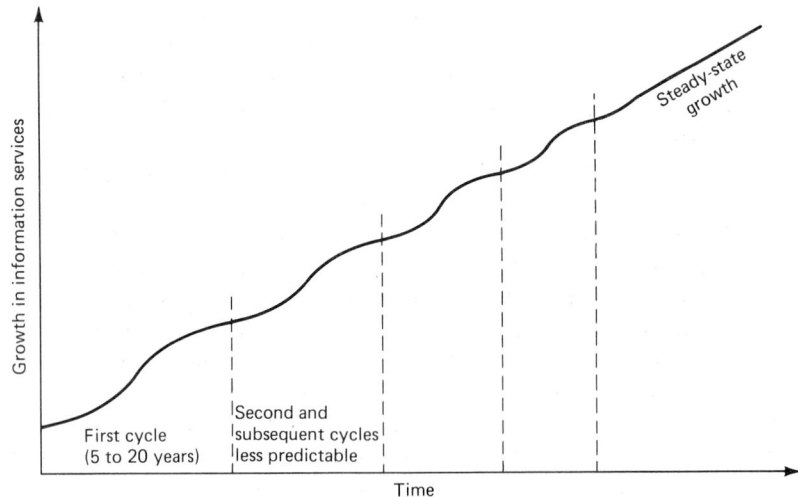

FIGURE 1-2 Long-term growth pattern for information services.

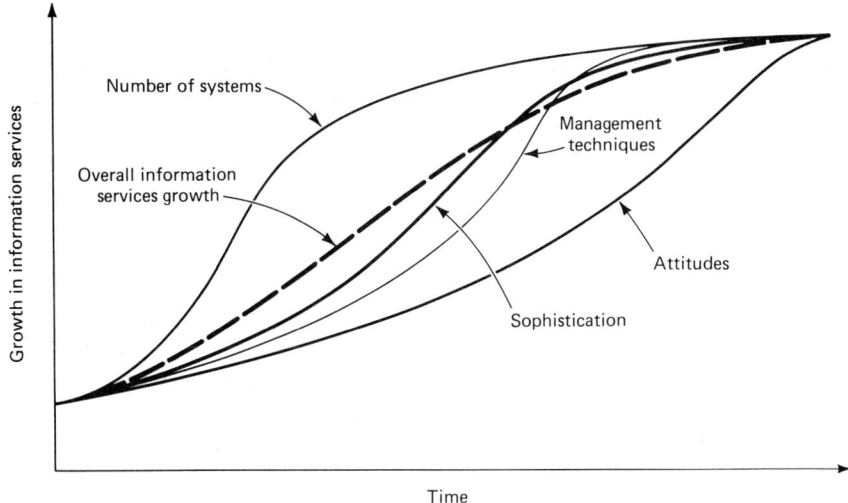

FIGURE 1-3 First-cycle subordinate growth patterns for information services.

Growth in the Number of Data Processing and Information Systems

Data processing and information systems with a readily identifiable potential for contribution to profit are given the highest priority when a computer is first installed. A typical corporation would first computerize such application areas as payroll, accounts receivable, and general ledger. Those with specialized functions, like beverage distribution centers, might opt for a route-accounting system, or in a hospital, a patient billing system. As computer-based systems become operational, managers in areas not using the computer see potential to use the computer for their immediate purposes. The second wave usually includes such systems as inventory control, order entry and processing, and market analysis. At this point in the growth pattern, the typical organization has installed a wide variety of basic and autonomous computer-based data processing systems. Once these basic systems are operational, user managers begin to see ways that the computer can be used to enhance operation of the basic system. A comptroller might request an enhancement that provides cash flow analysis. A plant manager might wish to combine several functionally adjacent systems into a manufacturing resource planning (MRP) system.

As corporate officers and user managers become more sophisticated in the application of the computer to their areas of responsibility, it becomes apparent to the knowledgeable manager that continued emphasis on autonomous systems will build in greater redundancy. The planning for future systems is dictated by the need to integrate not only corporate operations, but the computer-based information systems themselves. (Strategic planning for information services is covered in detail in Part IV.)

Sophistication in Information Systems

Unlike the late 1950s and early 1960s, high levels of sophistication in hardware, software, and personnel are available to the entry-level corporation. Although not a prerequisite, most corporations entering the computer age will follow the paths of their predecessors with batch-oriented data processing systems. Those with the patience and perseverance to do it right the first time can actually make a quantum jump in sophistication to an on-line, data base environment. However, the typical progression is from batch-oriented data processing to enhanced batch systems (which tend to inundate managers with vast quantities of unusable information). At this stage of sophistication, the years of system patches (minor and major modifications to the basic system) have taken their toll, and systems begin to approach the end of their life cycle. Systems often can no longer meet functional area requirements for data processing and information. Those systems are redesigned, incorporating the latest technological innovations in the new design (data communications capabilities, appropriate specialized hardware, data base, and so on). In the next level of sophistication, a shared data base environment is created allowing functionally adjacent systems to be integrated for a more efficient and effective corporate operation.

Management Techniques

A corporation's initial DP manager is usually more concerned about programming than about good management. The mode of DP operations is totally reactive, with the manager often responding to ill-conceived demands and, in some cases, the whims of corporate executives. Typically there are no standards, controls, planning, or regularly revised budget.

Inevitably, computer centers grow in the size of their staff, providing management with more flexibility to implement management tools and techniques. Manuals are compiled that reflect standard approaches, conventions, and procedures. But written and mandated documents are seldom followed during the first five years. During this period, the prevailing management philosophy appears to be every person for himself or herself.

The ever-increasing number of demands placed on information services causes management to emphasize production work and de-emphasize documentation and, sometimes, quality. However, perceptive corporate management will ultimately call a halt to uncontrolled and nondirectional growth. This turnaround happens in every computer center. IS management then develops and adopts a systems development methodology, a project management and control system, and an equitable personnel evaluation system, and establishes an organization that can be more responsive to user requests. Strategic planning for corporate information services is very much dependent upon the growth of corporate attitudes towards information services and is not accomplished with any level of sophistication and corporate-wide cooperation until the end of the first growth cycle.

Growth in Organizational Attitudes

Organizational attitudes are usually the critical factor in determining rates of growth in the number of systems, in sophistication, and in management techniques. The initial user and IS communication is usually inefficient and sometimes nonexistent.There is a resentment, more perceived than real, that data processing is impinging on the unwritten proprietary rights of the functional areas. A lack of knowledge creates a distrust among the user community that persists to a lessening degree throughout the first growth cycle.

Only after computer-based systems have proven that the computer and information services professionals are an asset to the corporation does the overall attitude change from distrust to reluctant acceptance. This acceptance results in a period of rapid growth in a number of applications of the computer. With virtually every manager demanding top priority from information services, a crisis-oriented environment is created that persists for 3 to 10 years. During this period, system quality is forsaken for rapid implementation.

After this period of rapid growth, user and corporate management develop an attitude of respect for the potential of information services to contribute to the corporation. This respect becomes acceptance. This acceptance opens the door for a coordinated plan for growth in information systems. Managers at all levels of the corporation accept direct and continued involvement in computer and information processing matters. The corporate attitude becomes that of a team with user managers, executives, and information services all working toward a common goal.

Long-Term Information Services
Growth Pattern

After a computer center has completed the initial cycle of the growth pattern, the cycle is repeated beginning with rapid growth and followed by a cleanup period. The cleanup period necessitates the allocation of resources to nonproductive activities such as planning and documentation. Therefore, the corporation must accept a moratorium or, at the minimum, a slowdown in number of service requests during new systems development. These cycles are repeated with ever-increasing frequency until IS growth is smooth and under control (see Figure 1-2).

A major technological innovation provides the impetus and capability to advance to the next cycle. For example, inexpensive hardware and software have made **distributed data processing (DDP)** a reality for many corporations. The implementation of DDP has resulted in these corporations entering the second cycle. A controlled, steady-state growth of the information services function cannot be realized until a corporation has passed through several cycles. Certainly, no information services department enjoys such a steady-state growth at this writing.

Speeding the Growth
of Information Services

The end of each cycle will not be reached until each of the subordinate growth patterns has matured. There is no law that precludes knowledgeable executives or user managers from using the experience of others to take action and circumvent roadblocks that impede smooth and rapid growth of information services. Although the user has little control over the internal information services management process, the user manager can significantly influence acceptance, recognition, and degree of integration, and can be sympathetic to a moratorium on new systems development. Proactive thinking on the part of corporate executives and user managers can hasten progress towards a more efficient and effective information services operation.

It is implied that information services management also has an obligation to take action to effect a smooth and steady growth. Since this book is oriented to users, these actions are not discussed. But foremost among these actions is establishing a meaningful liaison with functional area managers and corporate management.

Corporate and Information Services Growth

In 17 years one data processing department grew from 5 unit record operators to over 300 information services professionals. It is not uncommon for information services to grow rapidly both in budget share and numbers of persons. This growth can be attributed to IS under-taking and assisting in more and more of the operational tasks of the functional areas. For example, purchase orders are now machine pro-duced. In a university, classes are scheduled using a computer-based algorithm. In a hospital, the pharmaceutical inventory is built into the drug delivery system.

COMPUTER MYTHS

For whatever reasons, certain myths have evolved around computers. Unfortunately, these myths have served to create erroneous impressions that have made development and operation of computer-based systems unnecessarily difficult.

The Computer Did It

Seldom a week goes by that a major newspaper or magazine will not carry a headline to the effect that a major error is attributed to the computer: "The computer did it." The computer, of course, is inani-mate, with no feelings, and is the perfect scapegoat. Unfortunately, this trite excuse for human failure still holds water.

Computers do fail, but with proper system safeguards and restart procedures, the only thing lost is a little time. Ninety-nine percent of the time errors can be directly attributed to a breakdown in procedures (or human error). For example, a program logic error was undetected for over five years and a unique set of circumstances occurred that were not accounted for in the program logic. The computer did only what it was told.

Computers Cause Loss of Jobs

Computers create jobs. The computer may cause the elimination of jobs dedicated to certain routine and mundane tasks, but invariably the people holding these jobs are retrained and moved to positions with greater opportunities. The computer industry is experiencing enormous growth, and that growth creates jobs.

Computers Are Too Complex

To be sure, the complexity of communications network design and operating systems software cannot be overestimated. However, these and other complex areas are either transparent to the user manager or require only an easily attainable overview knowledge. Many people avoid any attempt to understand the computer and information processing for fear that the material is beyond their capabilities. To achieve an effective interface with IS personnel, the user manager needs only a general knowledge that is well within the capability of someone achieving the position of manager.

The body of knowledge concerning computers and information processing is built on successive levels of detail. Figure 1–4 illustrates graphically that body of knowledge recommended for user managers. The user manager should have a working knowledge of virtually every aspect of information services and then depend on specialists to achieve particular objectives. This book contains the material necessary for the user manager to acquire the skills for an effective interface with IS personnel.

Information Services Professionals Develop Information Systems

The information systems development process is a 50/50 proposition. Some users like to phase out of the development project soon after the initial interviews. Some IS professionals prefer limited user involvement, even if the end product is unsatisfactory. Quality systems

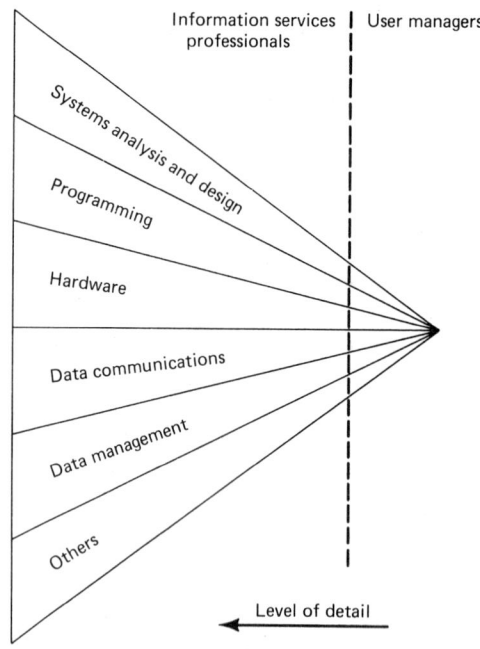

FIGURE 1-4 User/information services knowledge requirements.

are the result of continuous and frequent interaction between user and information service personnel.

A recent trend has been to encourage more and more participation by users during development. Some companies are encouraging user managers to serve as IS project managers.

Computers Mean Programming

Depending upon the approach to system development, the programming effort may comprise 15% to 30% of the development effort. Considering information services as a whole, programming takes on an even lesser significance. Educational institutions are at fault for perpetuating this myth. Too often business students are given one course on computers and 95% of it is devoted to COBOL or BASIC programming, with little or no emphasis on the system life cycle, hardware/ software alternatives, or a dozen other equally important facets central to effective utilization of the computer.

Mathematical Expertise Is a Prerequisite to Understanding Computers

Another myth is that one has to be a mathematician to understand a computer. This myth had its origin in the early 1960s, when computer science and information systems curriculums were scarce and employers began looking to graduates of mathematics curriculums for their DP programmers. This is ironic because invariably, the mathematician's first assignment was to learn the principles of accounting.

Anyone with the ability to synthesize and think logically can contribute to the industry and to successful information systems. Musicians, engineers, sociologists, and people from every discipline have been active contributors.

Computers Are a Panacea

A newly appointed vice-president of administration and finance of a medium-sized corporation was shocked to find that his predecessor had left him with virtually no budget information. After trying in vain to sort out existing budget data and establish a budget for the coming year, he gave up and turned to the computer as if it were a panacea. During the two months remaining before the budget deadline, the vice-president fully expected information services and their computers to bail him and his staff out of this dilemma. A bare-bone system to meet his minimum requirements was estimated at three persons and eight months elapsed time.

The computer has the potential to serve every facet of corporate operation, but time is always a constraint. The computer is seldom, if ever, a short-term panacea.

POLITICS AND COMPUTERS

It is often said that information is power. Power and politics go hand in hand. Every organization, no matter how small, has a political infrastructure that is always highly active in attempts to influence the role and plight of information services.

Each user manager has a proprietary interest and must vie for limited computer information services resources. It is not uncommon, therefore, for the computer center and its personnel to become and remain the center of corporate controversy. Information services is sometimes used as a pawn in a political game played by corporate executives desiring top priority for their special interests and information services needs.

Internal politics are a fact of life, but the wise executive will harness the power and influence of the political infrastructure to effect cooperation and integration. In the long run, special interests are best served through system integration. Self-serving efforts to expedite the implementation of autonomous systems tend to maintain the status quo and impede progress.

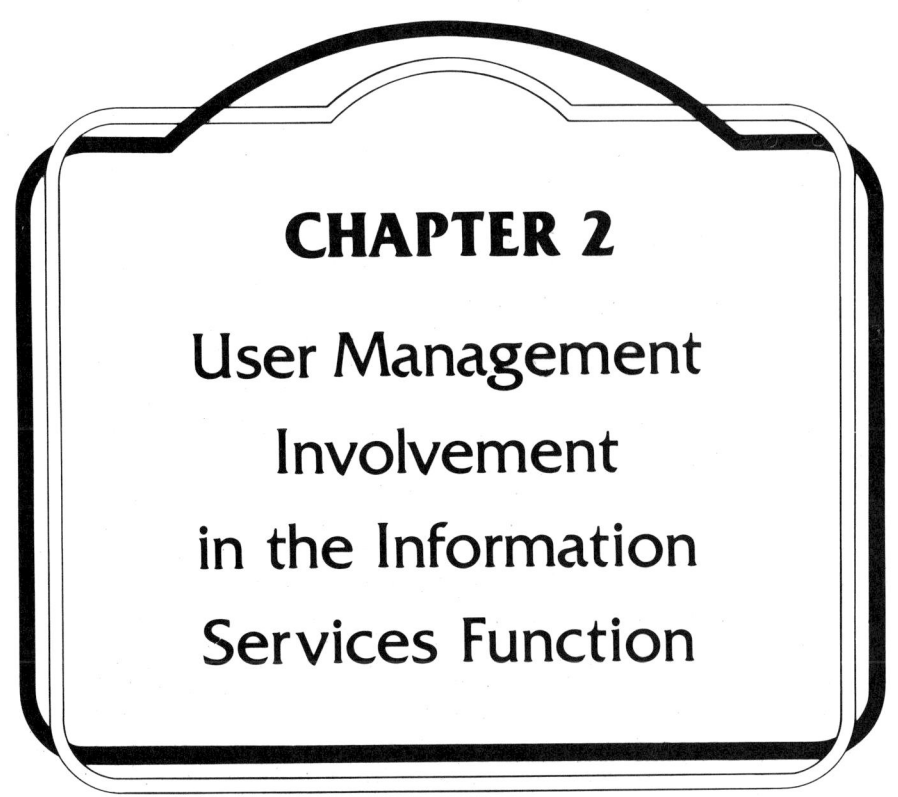

CHAPTER 2

User Management Involvement in the Information Services Function

The intent of this chapter is to give the reader an *overview* by highlighting how the user is involved or affected by the various facets of the information services function. This overview will make it easier for the reader to assimilate the material contained in the remaining chapters and to appreciate more detailed coverage of these facets in later chapters.

For the purposes of this discussion, the information services function can be divided into seven categories:

♦ Information services environment
♦ Personnel and organization
♦ Strategic planning
♦ Management and administration
♦ The information system life cycle
♦ Control
♦ Operations

Italicized words and phrases are included to highlight the pertinent responsibility areas within each category. These responsibility areas (e.g., word processing, the system life cycle, IS organizational structure, data management, quality assurance, and so on) are discussed in detail in later chapters.

INFORMATION SERVICES ENVIRONMENT

Policy relating to computers and information processing will affect some or all of the functional areas. For example, policy relating to access of personal information, user chargeback systems, and priority criteria will affect users at all levels of the corporation. Implementable policies require continuous and direct interaction with those involved. In fact, managers have an obligation to provide input on all computer/information processing policy that affects areas within their scope of responsibility.

The successful computer center has well-defined *roles and responsibilities* for information services. The potential exists for IS personnel to accomplish those activites best suited for users, and vice versa. Users should not only have a say in identifying roles and responsibilities, but should be aware of these roles and be responsive to their demands.

Education is a two-way street. As information services is responsible for user education, the functional area managers are responsible for providing the opportunity for IS personnel to learn the intricacies of the functional area activities. This can be done through formal in-house seminars, individual consultation, or by providing appropriate books, articles, and programmed instruction materials.

Although information services may not be recognized as the center of corporate operations, when one considers the scope of responsibility and the areas affected, it comes very close. For this reason user managers must respect the information services manager's desire for neutrality in *internal politics.* User managers should resolve computer-related conflicts between functional areas before making conflicting requests to the IS department.

DP and IS departments have traditionally been very unpopular. Because services extend to most operational entities, information services has become not only the workhorse, but the whipping boy of the corporation. It is the rare IS department that does not have *image* problems. User managers can help improve the IS image by sharing responsibility for failures and successes, extending full and continuous cooperation, and generally working as a team with the IS personnel. The chief executive can improve IS image by moving the IS department to an organizational level commensurate with its scope of responsibilities.

PERSONNEL AND ORGANIZATION

The *IS organizational structure* should be designed to be responsive to the user community and should encourage effective interaction between IS and users. The appointment of a full-time user liaison and assignment of users to information services are two of many organizational alternatives proven effective.

The average turnover rate for IS professionals fluctuates between 20% and 30% per year. This high rate of turnover causes constant problems in IS *staffing*. Many IS departments operate with less than the authorized number of personnel because the demand is greater than supply. User managers can alleviate staffing problems by providing IS managers with as much lead time as possible for IS resource requirements.

Consultants are retained to offer specialized expertise and, in some cases, for work force augmentation. IS managers should include affected user managers in communications with consultants.

STRATEGIC PLANNING

The information services function has essentially two *goals*. The first relates to those matters internal to IS and the other parallels the goals of the corporation and the various functional areas. Since achievement of these corporate goals requires the expenditure of IS resources, user managers and corporate officers should make such requirements known to IS planners as soon as possible.

The user plays a significant role in the *growth* of information services. As discussed in Chapter 1, corporate attitudes toward information services and user demands determine the rate and direction of growth. Rapid advances in technology are constantly opening new horizons for computer usage.

IS managers make *estimates* of resource requirements (personpower, time, dollars, and materials) with the understanding that the user managers want what they request and are willing to make the necessary commitments of their functional area resources over the term of the project. Unfortunately, user revisions to so-called "frozen functional specifications" have become commonplace. Once an information system development project gets underway, functional area personnel tend to give priority to routine activities, forsaking commitments to the IS project. IS managers are well aware of this historical pattern and tend to pad project estimates accordingly. This can become a vicious circle. With a little forethought on system requirements and judicious internal personnel planning, user managers can cooperate with IS management to realize better estimates. Reliable estimates benefit all concerned.

Inaccurate estimates cause shortcuts and ultimately affect the quality of the resultant system.

The information services manager should not be charged with *setting priorities* for development projects. The choice between allocating limited IS resources to an on-line order entry system or a manufacturing resource planning (MRP) system should be made by corporate officers, not information services management. These decisions should be based on corporate need, not political pressure. One vehicle for achieving corporate-wide concensus on priorities is a high-level information services steering committee (see Chapter 3).

Distributed data processing and data communications have encouraged the placement of computing hardware at the user site. The user manager is usually responsible for these remote *facilities* and works with IS personnel to select equipment, design the work space, plan for the installation of communications channels, and make arrangements to accommodate any environmental, power, and security requirements.

What happens when the computer center ceases to be operational? This could happen as a result of a natural disaster or some other extraordinary occurrence. Because these disasters can and do happen, user managers must work closely with information services to develop a *contingency plan*. The objective of contingency planning is to keep the corporation operational. The plan defines duties, responsibilities, logistics, and security for various possible occurrences.

Word processing (WP) and office automation are computer applications that can be implemented at the user level with little or no interaction with information services personnel. Simple, inexpensive, stand-alone word processing systems are an economic reality that has encouraged many user managers to purchase word processing hardware without guidance from information services. User managers can better serve their areas of responsibility and the corporation by coordinating such purchases through a central group (IS is one of several alternatives). The key is compatibility. Uncontrolled growth in word processing has resulted in many corporations purchasing a variety of incompatible stand-alone systems that cannot be integrated with the corporate data base. The user manager has an obligation to the corporation to ensure that any WP system purchased is compatible and can be integrated with other corporate information systems.

MANAGEMENT AND ADMINISTRATION

User management has everything to do with IS *budget preparation and cost management*. In corporations with internal IS chargeback systems, the IS budget is directly proportional to the level of use. When the IS budget is allocated in the same manner as that of the functional areas, the user must realize that IS is taking on certain functional area operational responsibilities and, therefore, can be expected to grow in budget share more rapidly than most other functional areas.

This is a period of rapid technological development. IS personnel are constantly in the process of *evaluating and selecting hardware and software*. These are major decisions which require significant input from functional area management. For example, most user managers in the corporation would be affected by the selection of a proprietary software package for finance and accounting. Although the user would be only peripherally involved in the selection of high technology support hardware, the selection of end-user terminals should be a joint decision.

With thousands of vendors marketing computer hardware, software, and services, the user manager should be keenly aware of corporate policy toward *vendor relations*. User managers can and do purchase or lease these items without any input from information services. The danger is that an inexperienced buyer of computer hardware/software or services may be unaware of an important operational compatibility and contractual consideration. The best approach is to establish a corporate policy towards vendor relations.

Since functional area personnel are almost always involved in both one-time and on-going IS projects, the user manager is in continuous contact with the IS project manager. A recent trend is to release users from functional area responsibilities and to make them project managers. Some companies have experienced considerable success with this approach to project team organization. The obvious advantage is that the user has control over the project and is, therefore, responsible for its success or failure.

Productivity seems to be the key word of the 1980s, and effective communication between user and IS personnel is the key to increased productivity in information services. Studies[3] have shown that it takes approximately *50* times the effort to rectify errors found after implementation than those found during the design phase. This highlights the importance of user managers identifying systems requirements accurately and completely and carefully scrutinizing the system development effort. User managers and their staff can also contribute to productivity by providing timely feedback on operational systems. This feedback should not be delivered in the form of complaints, but as suggestions on how the system can be more effective and responsive. In one instance, a clerk was asked what she did with the report that was delivered to her every Friday for the last seven years. She responded by

[3] B. Boehm, "Software Engineering," IEEE Transactions on Computers, Vol. C-25, December 1976.

saying that she usually threw it away but on occasion it provided good coloring material for her kids. This is just one of thousands of situations where the user can take the initiative and provide feedback to enhance system effectiveness.

THE INFORMATION SYSTEM LIFE CYCLE

The four stages of computer-based information system are represented by the *system life cycle* (see Figure 2-1). The cycle begins with the "birth" stage, or the conceptualization of the system. Once approved for development, the system becomes a reality during the system "development" stage. The "production" stage is the period for which the system is operational. The "death" stage occurs when the system has ceased to be economically or operationally effective and is subsequently discarded. Thus, the cycle repeats itself. The system life cycle, and information services in general, are discussed in more detail in Part III of this book.

Ironically, the computer/information processing area is labor intensive. Any user manager is aware of the high demand for information services and the limited resources to service those demands. Out of this situation has surfaced an awareness of the importance of investigating the possibility of *technology transfer*. The user is generally the primary participant in the identification, evaluation, and selection of existing technology. Technology transfer from a user's perspective takes the form of applications software (i.e., packaged information systems). User managers should be advised that substantial revisions to packaged systems software may actually defeat the purpose of technology transfer. Some companies have actually channeled more resources into revising a packaged system than would have been required for in-house development of the system.

The continuous and direct involvement of user managers and their staff throughout the system development process is discussed in detail in Chapter 12.

Some information services organizations have a *quality assurance* group. Whether an explicit or implied function, system quality is the responsibility of both user and IS. The user should call attention to any violation in established standards for system quality.

Traditionally, *documentation* (including user manuals) has been an information services responsibility. Unfortunately, poor documentation has plagued DP/information services for decades. User managers should be aware of the existence of user manuals which cannot be understood and are easily misinterpreted. Therefore, these manuals should be operationally tested by functional area personnel prior to system acceptance.

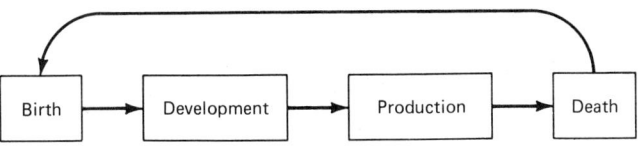

FIGURE 2-1 The system life cycle.

Data are the source of corporate information, and *data management* is the responsibility of everyone in the corporation. IS is responsible for storage, update, manipulation, and retrieval of data. However, the functional areas are responsible for triggering the update and for the integrity of those data items under their control.

Since computer-based information systems are "owned" by the functional areas, user managers are responsible for evaluating the *social impact and legal implications* of their respective system, both within the company and external to the company (customers, creditors, clients, and so on).

User and information services personnel must cooperate to provide the necessary system *security*. Logical security should be built into the system design. Physical security for remote facilities in the user environment is usually a functional area responsibility.

CONTROL

The critical nature of the end product demands that the development and operation of any information system be tightly controlled. Information services use *standards* and *standardized procedures (methodologies)* to achieve this control. The affect of these standards and procedures extends into the functional areas. For example, the system service request and the system development methodology are just two of many standardized procedures that users and IS personnel follow for the good of the company.

Although *information systems auditing* is not usually a function of the information services department, it is an area in which the user is involved. The audit function is usually performed by a neutral group that places special demands on functional area personnel for data verification, information, and, in some cases, procedural assistance.

OPERATIONS

In the past, the actual *data reduction* task (transcription from source document to machine-readable code) has traditionally been an IS responsibility. With the advent of on-line systems and intelligent terminals, the trend has been to move the data reduction function to the user office, eliminating a transcription step and reducing the possibility of error. One company which once had over a hundred keypunch operators in the data processing department now has no keypunch machines or operators. Data reduction was transferred to the functional area departments.

A computer center can be likened to a miniature manufacturing environment with functional area requirements as input and information as output. The user is involved in both directions. The *input/output (I/O) distribution and control* function is actually a cooperative effort. Users are primarily responsible for data integrity and clearly stated specifications on the front-end, and information services is responsible for accurate reports and physical distribution on the back-end.

Scheduling is a function of available resources and user requirements. Routine operational systems are "givens" and automatically included as input to the scheduling algorithm. But like so many data centers, one time requests, reruns, and other demands on the computer system jeopardize the timely completion of scheduled "jobs." To help schedulers, user managers can be both responsive and sympathetic to overall organization needs by providing appropriate lead time for ad hoc requests.

SUMMARY

The italicized words and phrases in this chapter represent the basic areas of responsibility of information services. Depending on the type of corporation, some will have other responsibilities not specifically noted. The purpose of this chapter is to acquaint the reader with the scope of responsibilities of the corporate information services function and to provide an overview of user involvement in each responsibility area within the information services.

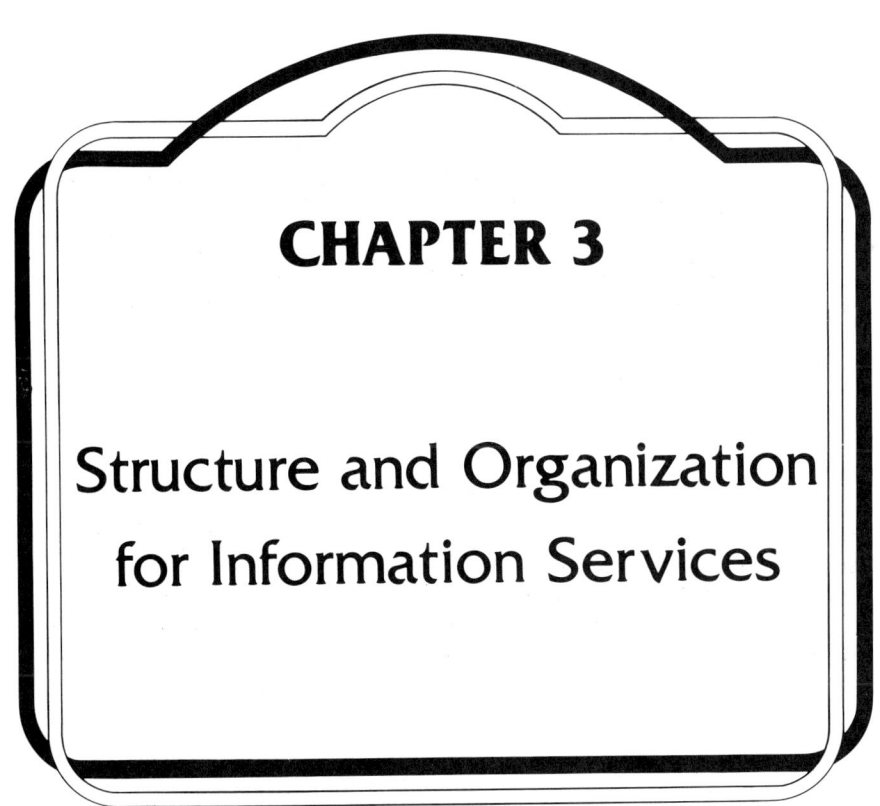

CHAPTER 3

Structure and Organization for Information Services

The purpose of this chapter is to present the organizational considerations and structure for information services, both within the corporation and within the information services department. The titles and functions of IS personnel and IS-related committees are also discussed.

BACKGROUND

Applications which give a high payback are usually the first to be automated. Consequently, the first three or four major computer efforts are most often concerned with accounting systems. Originally, in most companies, the DP function was organizationally located in a line position, one or more levels down from the chief corporate financial officer. Although the scope of computer-based systems has expanded to other organizational entities, finance and accounting remains the largest single user in most companies.

For the most part, centralized computer organizations are either under the jurisdiction of the chief financial officer or have achieved organizational neutrality. It is human nature for a manager to put proprietary interests before those of others. This sometimes happens when the IS department is part of a functional area organization. As a result, IS requirements of other functional areas are given priorities that conflict with the overall corporate good. Several organizational strategies have been used successfully to counter this dichotomy of interest.

UNIQUE CHARACTERISTICS
OF INFORMATION SERVICES

Most corporate executives feel their organizational problems are unique. Usually the problems are quite similar, it is the people who are unique. Since information services must be organizationally located to render service to all areas of the company, organizational alternatives will invariably reflect emotions, biases, prejudices of corporate executives, and the politics and traditions of the corporation.

Information services has some unusual characteristics that set it apart from other organizational entities:

1. Information services, as a service organization, is at the beck and call of any person or department of the corporation.
2. Information services is shrouded with a technical, almost mystical veil.
3. Information services engages in ongoing interaction with most other corporate departments.

ORGANIZATIONAL LOCATION
WITHIN THE CORPORATE HIERARCHY

There is no standard or traditional location for an information services department. This is also true within any given industry. There are three basic approaches to locating IS within the corporate hierarchy.

1. The largest user of information services has IS responsibility and provides support to other organizational entities.
2. Each major functional area maintains its own computer and IS staff.
3. Information services is centralized under a high-level neutral office, usually the president.

Other approaches are variations and combinations of these. The second alternative is extreme and seldom found in practice without the influence of the first and/or third alternatives. The advantages of the first approach are skewed to the largest user. The second embodies the advantages of decentralization and the third, the advantages of centralization and neutrality. The advantages and disadvantages of each are discussed in more detail below.

Under the Largest User

As earlier noted, the largest user is usually the top financial officer or comptroller. This organizational approach realizes the advantages of centralization and provides superior service to the parent department. However, the disadvantages are overwhelming. This structure causes conflict in corporate information services priorities, promotes a low level of support to smaller users, and makes strategic IS long-range planning almost impossible.

This organizational alternative is still the most popular, not because of its effectiveness, but because decades of tradition have developed such tremendous momentum. Figure 3-1 illustrates this type of organizational structure.

Functional Areas Support
Their Own Information Services Function

In theory, decentralization provides each functional area with a totally responsive IS organization. In practice, this does not happen. The corporation opting for this alternative forfeits the flexibility to develop specialized expertise and, therefore, higher levels of IS sophis-

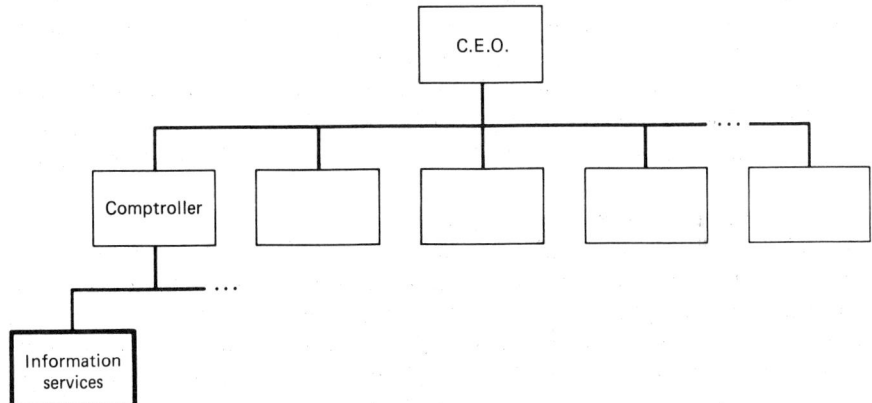

FIGURE 3-1 Centralized information services located under the largest user.

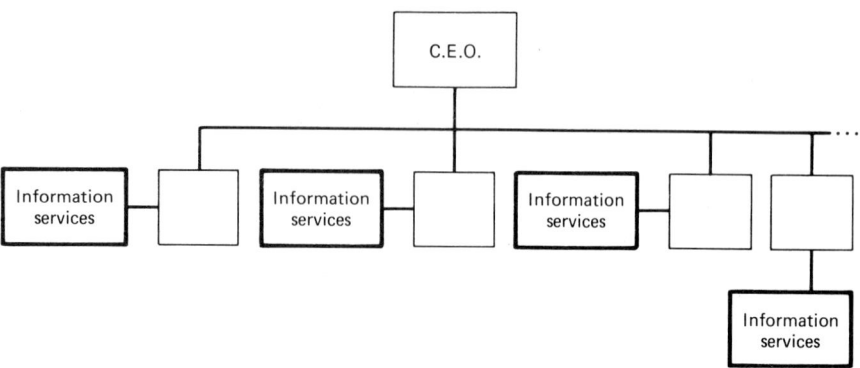

FIGURE 3-2 Totally decentralized information services organization.

tication. A totally decentralized IS function has little flexibility to respond to general corporate needs. Without central control, systems integration is extremely difficult. Figure 3-2 illustrates this organizational alternative.

Under a High-Level Neutral Office

This structure has advantages over the other two because of information services' unique charge to be responsive and responsible to all segments of the corporation. It is still inferior, however, to a well-conceived combination of all three. In theory, this type of organization can be responsive to corporate needs that are prioritized with the corporate good in mind. The information services manager is on an equal level with managers of functional areas. Neutral centralization makes possible the integration of information services and the preparation of realistic strategic plans for information services.

The disadvantages cannot be overlooked. A centralized operation, whether neutral or under the largest user, can significantly affect corporate operation if the computer system goes down (downtime). The largest user will complain of the lack of priority service. Centralized environments are more complex and require a higher level of expertise among IS managers and technicians. Without this expertise the probability of having a successful installation is low. Figure 3-3 illustrates how IS can be organized under a high-level neutral office.

DISTRIBUTED DATA PROCESSING (DDP)

Through the mid-1970s, the prevailing thought was to take advantage of the economies of scale and strive for total integration of corporate information services by centralizing the IS function. With increase in

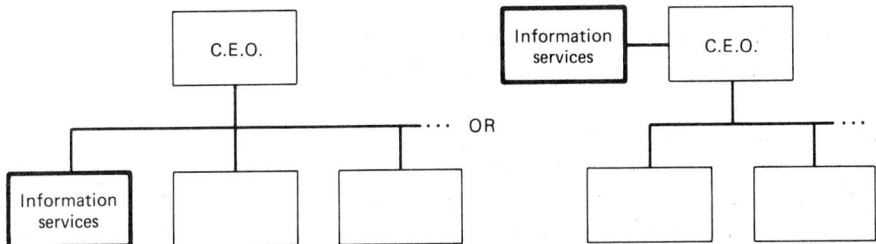

FIGURE 3-3 Centralized information services located under a high-level neutral office—line (left), staff (right).

size came increases in complexity that reduced the capability of IS departments to be responsive. This lack of responsiveness was a major factor in reversing the trend to centralization. Another factor was the rapid decrease in the cost of hardware, especially for small computer systems.

The alternative to decentralization is **distributed data processing (DDP)**. DDP is not only a technological concept, but it is also an organizational concept. The concept is built around a philosophy which, if implemented correctly, will render the benefits of both centralized and decentralized information services.

The centralization/decentralization question boils down to a trade-off between service to the user and the potential to provide integrated information systems. Economy of scale is no longer an issue. In theory, DDP combines the best of both worlds. The computer systems are not only physically distributed to the functional areas, they are dedicated to functional area applications. Since all distributed systems are linked together in a network, information systems can be integrated.

A company should realize a higher percentage of uptime because the failure of one computer system does not jeopardize the operation of the entire company. In fact, in a well-designed DDP system, other computing resources can be used to keep all systems operational.

In DDP, computers are arranged in a network, with each computer being connected to one or more of the other computers. A DDP network is usually designed around geographical and/or functional considerations, with most networks reflecting a combination of both.

Distributed data processing is another of many oft-used terms that do not have a common meaning and are easily misinterpreted by both user and IS personnel. This lack of common understanding often leaves unresolved the question of "what to distribute" and "what degree of distribution would best serve the needs of the company." Any or all of the following facets of information services can be distributed:

- Input/output
- Processing
- Data storage
- Personnel (including management)
- Audit and control
- Planning

Which facet and to what degree each facet is distributed should be resolved before any IS reorganization effort is considered.

Satellite computer systems and centers in a DDP environment can be controlled through either a centralized IS department, by the functional area served, or via a matrix organization where user and IS share the management responsibilities. In either case, in order to maintain corporate compatibility, consistency, and integration in information processing, a centralized group is usually charged with:

- Evaluating and selecting hardware
- Establishing standards, procedures, and documentation policy
- Short- and long-range IS planning
- Recruiting and hiring of IS personnel
- Maintaining a corporate data base (that data used regularly by several remote sites)
- Establishing corporate-wide IS priorities (usually through an IS steering committee)
- Staying current on available technology
- Supporting IS and user education programs

The trend toward DDP is visibly encouraged by the type of hardware and software being developed and offered by vendors. The available technology and the advantages of DDP have resulted in many unsuspecting functional area managers taking on the responsibility of managing an information services group and/or a computer center. Figure 3-4 illustrates an IS organization for DDP.

THE INFORMATION CENTER

Some user managers and executives felt that an alarming precedent was being set by IS taking on more and more of the operational duties of the functional areas. Had the trend continued, there would indeed be cause for alarm. However, user managers of the 1980s are much more willing to become directly involved, not only in the information systems

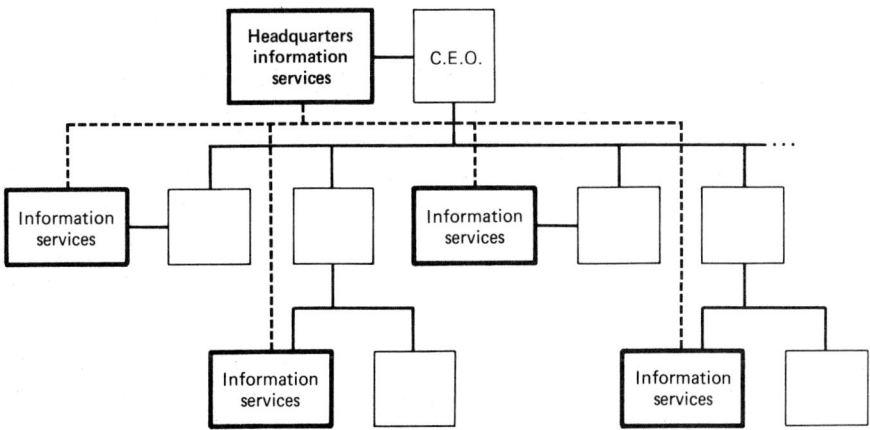

FIGURE 3-4 Distributed data processing organization.

that affect their immediate operation, but in other facets of corporate information services. This positive attitude is the key to successful decentralized IS operation.

To realize direct user involvement effectively, the corporation must provide facilities, technical support, and education to the user community. This is accomplished with an **information center**. The information center is a concept that is complementary to the implementation of DDP.

The theory behind the information center is that a user has a place to go, not necessarily to request information services, but to help himself or herself. The purpose of the information center is to provide the user with the opportunity to be a direct participant in accomplishing his own request for IS services. This eliminates several steps in the handling of a typical service request. Instead of having to submit a formal service request, obtain approval, communicate requirements to a systems analyst, and so on, the user simply uses the information center to do it himself. Given this opportunity, the users have shown an intense desire to become an active part of the information services function. Existing information centers have experienced user acceptance and utilization far beyond initial expectations.

The operation and management of an information center is typically a responsibility of corporate information services. The center offers convenient location(s), the appropriate hardware (video display units, printers, and possibly a graphics terminal), and the expertise of IS professionals. The IS personnel are there to answer questions, and to provide guidance and occasional assistance. They should never be asked to engage in production work. Depending on the complexity of user involvement, one IS professional would be assigned to the information center for every 5 to 10 regular users. Information center personnel regularly conduct courses and seminars in a variety of technical and user oriented topics.

STRUCTURAL ORGANIZATION OF THE INFORMATION SERVICES DEPARTMENT

The purpose of this section is to acquaint the user manager with the basic components, personnel, and committees integral to the information services function, and with how they are structured to meet the information needs of the corporation. The principles discussed are equally applicable to small and large corporations. Depending on the degree of distribution and the specific activities distributed, a user-managed IS function may have only a subset of the basic IS components, with the remaining components being centralized.

Components of Information Services

Prior to 1970, data processing directors were content to organize their departments into three groups: systems, programming, and operations. Many elected to combine the systems and programming functions and have only two groups. As the information services function expanded and as the complexity of hardware and software increased, group and individual specialization became a necessity. A new area of specialization has evolved almost yearly since 1970. Therefore, directors of IS have engaged in frequent reorganizing to include such specialty groups as technical support, data base administration, standards and procedures, and the information center.

There is no "best" way to organize for effective information services. Circumstances surrounding IS in any given corporation have caused 10 similar companies to implement 10 unique organizational structures. However, each of the following components is embedded either implicitly or explicitly in every IS organization.

Operations. Operations encompasses machine room activities, the running of routine production systems, and other nonscheduled system requirements. The term "operations" is often used to refer collectively to all of those components that support the basic operations function (data entry, control, and so on).

Systems. Although the primary function of the systems component is to design, enhance, and implement computer-based information systems, systems analysts are often asked to perform those functions not logically a responsibility of any of the other major components of information services (e.g., feasibility studies, work place design, and so on).

Programming. The programming component translates design specifications into instructions that can be read and interpreted by computers. There are actually two types of programming: applications programming and systems programming (see *technical support* below). A reference simply to "programming" refers to applications programming or the programming effort associated with a specific information system (e.g., standard cost, patient billing, deposit administration, and so on).

Technical Support. Technical support is responsible for the design, development, and maintenance of applications-independent (generalized) software or systems software. "Systems" programming cannot be associated with a specific information system and is used in support of all information systems. For example, the operating system and data base management system are classified as system software. Categories of programming and software are discussed in detail in Chapter 9.

Control. The control component is responsible for ensuring the integrity of the input to and the output from production information systems. In support of this function, the control group maintains status logs for all I/O and is responsible for the distribution of computer produced output.

Administration. Administration is a support function that handles the paper work and administrative details associated with the operation of an information services department. These functions include stenographic services, ordering supplies, and other clerical tasks associated with records administration. The management function is purposely not included under administration because it is embedded in the other components of information services.

Data Base Administration. With the trend to integration and data base management systems, the data base administration component evolved to maintain order and data integrity in this complex environment. This group designs and maintains the corporate data base.

IS Audit. The purpose of the IS (or EDP) audit component is to audit both the information services department and information systems. It is, therefore, not organizationally attached to information services. The IS audit group is either part of an internal audit group or chartered as a separate organizational entity which reports to the president. The audit group performs operational audits, application audits, and systems development audits. Operational audits involve such areas as physical security and procedures for program change documentation. Application audits ensure the accuracy and integrity of production systems (payroll, inventory management, and so on). System development audits ensure that adequate audit controls are embedded in the initial system design.

Career Development and Education. Information processing technology and techniques are constantly changing, requiring IS personnel periodically to update their skills. Promotions are often dependent on personnel mastering a certain level of skill. This group provides opportunities for in-house education (programmed instruction, multimedia courses, and in-house seminars). Quality and status information is maintained on external sources of IS-related education. The career development and education component serves as the administrative arm of personnel career development.

Data Entry. The purpose of the data entry component is to transcribe source data into machine-readable format. In past decades this has been accomplished on a keypunch (card punch) machine from a source document (e.g., time sheet or order form). The data entry function is quickly disappearing from the information services organization. With remote data entry an economic reality, more and more users are eliminating the manual transcription step by entering data directly into the computer. Devices and approaches for data entry are discussed in Chapter 7.

Planning. The productivity benefits derived through integration and judicious allocation of limited resources have made strategic planning for information services a necessity. Although planning is considered a management function, the complexities of information services planning demand that an individual in a medium-sized installation, or a group in larger installations, be dedicated to the IS planning function. Strategic planning for information services is discussed in detail in Part IV.

User Liaison. Information services, as the name implies, is a service organization. In order to be more responsive, many organizations have identified an individual, or established a group, whose primary function is to interface with users. The rationale for the user liaison is that there should be a single contact point for all users having ·

problems or requesting services. The user liaison group assists users with service requests and either attends to their problems or directs them to the IS section that can.

Business Analysts. This group is made up of functional area analysts who are organizationally attached, usually temporarily, to the information services department. A number of companies are experimenting with the potential of this kind of arrangement. Members of the group become active project team members and serve as functional area advisors.

Quality Assurance. The quality assurance component encourages the do-it-right-the-first-time approach to system development. Studies have shown that it takes approximately 50 times the effort to rectify errors found after implementation than for those found during the design phase. Quality assurance is a separate group assigned the task of monitoring the quality of every aspect of the design and operation of information services, including system efficiency and documentation.

Standards and Procedures. In any automated environment, adherence to standards and procedures is critical to operational efficiency and effectiveness. The standards and procedures component establishes the standards for such areas as programming conventions, communications protocols, and hardware acquisition. Computer centers have dozens of written procedures. Such procedures include preventive maintenance, service request submittal, performance evaluation, and user chargeback. This group is also responsible for developing and maintaining methodologies. For example, most IS departments maintain a system development methodology.

Security. With the trend to decentralized operation and large centralized data bases, security is becoming a high-priority item. However, at this writing only a few large installations have formed security groups. These groups are responsible for periodic evaluation of the security of hardware, systems, data bases, and facilities.

Since no computer system or information system can be totally free of the risk of a security violation, the question becomes "How much risk is the corporation willing to accept?" With this in mind, the group identifies and analyzes vulnerable areas and, through a risk assessment process (see Chapter 13), establishes a level of acceptable risk for each of these areas. The group then sets up a risk-reduction program to address those areas with unacceptable risks. This is an ongoing activity that has a yearly cycle.

Information Center. The information center concept is discussed in detail earlier in this chapter.

Process Control. Many companies are presently debating the organizational plight of process control. Process control can include numerically controlled (NC) machines, computer-aided design (CAD), robotics, and computer-aided manufacturing (CAM), all of which are discussed in Chapter 6. Process control activities have proliferated in information services and functional area departments. For purposes of compatibility and standardization, some companies have elected to place process control applications under the umbrella of information services.

Documentation. The documentation group provides a service to other areas of information services by assisting in the compilation of written documentation. Members of this group are skilled in technical writing and documentation techniques. They produce user manuals from system and programming documentation. They compile the system development methodology from guidelines set forth by the standards and procedures groups. Information services produces dozens of manuals and directives which must be easily understood by any reader. Technical IS professionals have not shown an affinity for this facet of the information services function. The introduction of the documentation specialty is an attempt to streamline the information services function.

Specialist Functions. Information services must adapt to the environment and accommodate special industry requirements by establishing specialty groups. As an example, a highly technical systems-oriented company has an ongoing requirement for a full-time operations research (OR) group. Another has taken on the corporate printing function because it became so highly automated. One IS department that receives hundreds of new development and major enhancement requests for service each year has established a group that does nothing but feasibility studies.

IS PERSONNEL AND FUNCTIONS

The following is a discussion of the functions of commonly accepted information services positions. The order of presentation is not meant to be indicative of level of importance. There are usually several levels and a manager associated with each position type (e.g., apprentice programmer, programmer, senior programmer, and chief programmer). Of course, it is implied that those persons occupying the higher levels of a given position receive more complex and demanding assignments. A position description for an apprentice programmer in a given company, for example, may be markedly different from that of a senior programmer. The differences, though, are primarily in the level of complexity and not in the basic function; therefore, only the basic function is presented. The positions listed below should not necessarily be associated with one of the previously discussed IS components. For example, a documentalist could just as well be assigned to the systems section to compile user manuals or a systems analyst could be assigned to the operations section to help in work flow analysis.

Director of Information Services

The director of information services (often called the data processing manager) has responsibility for all corporate information services activities. The managerial duties are similar to those of the functional area counterpart. The primary difference is that the director of IS will spend 50% or more of the time interfacing with user managers and corporate executives.

An interesting characteristic of information services directors is that their technical orientation varies (or should vary) with the size of the company. This is consistent with the requirement for specialization in larger companies. Figure 3–5 illustrates the relative importance of management and technical skills as a function of company size. For

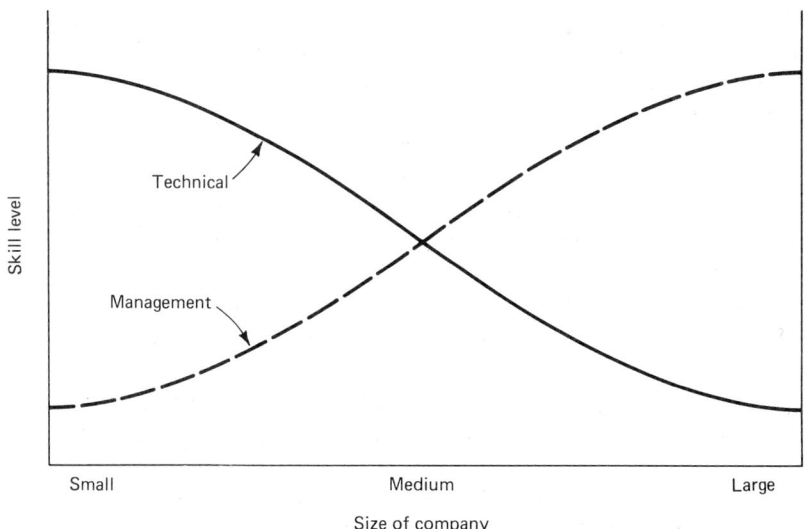

FIGURE 3-5 Technical/management skill mix for directors of information services as a function of company size.

ease of comparison, a small company is arbitrarily defined as one with a professional information services staff of 25 or less, a medium-sized one with between 26 and 175, and a large one with more than 176.

The IS director is the catalyst for new systems development and corporate-wide systems integration. This task is directed not only to the user community, but to IS staff as well.

Systems Analyst

The primary function of the systems analyst, or simply "analyst," is the analysis, design, and implementation of information systems. In most companies the analyst is also assigned a wide range of other systems-related tasks (e.g., feasibility studies, periodic system reviews, hardware evaluation and selection, capacity assessment, and others).

The systems analyst is the primary interface with the user during the systems development process. The analyst is especially active during the analysis and design phase and again during the conversion and implementation phase. Systems analysts usually provide operational training for users prior to system implementation.

Programmer (Applications)

In theory, the applications programmer, or simply "programmer," receives detailed system and input/output specifications from the systems analyst. The programmer then translates these design specifications into machine-readable instructions (programs or software). The programmer designs the logic, then codes, debugs, and tests the programs.

Some companies distinguish between development and maintenance programmers. The former work only on development of new systems and the latter on maintaining existing systems.

Until only a few years ago, programmers anticipated and were expected to advance to systems analysts. Unfortunately, this attitude still prevails in many companies and is even supported through the salary structure. The two positions require different skills and a programmer position is not necessarily a stepping stone to systems analyst and career advancement. The industry will see more and more programmers making careers out of programming and programming management.

Programmer/Analyst

Those IS directors desiring a more vertical approach to systems development have adopted the programmer/analyst position. As the position title implies, persons holding these positions perform the functions of both programmer and systems analyst.

Programmer/analysts are not found in every IS department. Some companies use the programmer/analyst position as an intermediate step between programmer and systems analyst. The programmer/analyst position is sometimes created as a compromise in response to programmers' desire to do systems analysis and systems analysts' desire to do programming. The effectiveness of the programmer/analyst role is still a matter of considerable debate. Many would argue that two specialists, one a systems analyst and one a programmer, can accomplish more and higher-quality work than can two programmer/analysts.

Systems Programmer

The systems programmer is concerned with applications-independent or generalized software. A computer is usually accompanied by vendor-supplied systems software (see Chapter 9). This software is fundamental to the general operation of the computer and includes such software modules as the operating system, I/O scheduler, hardware utilization accounting system, and utilities (e.g., sort routines, disk-to-tape dump). The systems programmer installs the various modules and selects appropriate software options. Vendors periodically send customers enhancements to the various modules in the form of "software updates." Systems programming responsibilities include the installation of the "latest version" of the updates. Systems programmers are also responsible for making any required modifications to vendor-supplied systems software and for developing in-house systems-oriented software.

Project Leader

The position title of project leader is not unique to information services. In IS, the project leader is assigned a staff and the responsibility for the development and implementation of a new system or for implementing a major enhancement to an existing system. Primary responsibilities include managing the project, meeting assigned deadlines, and periodically reporting on progress. The project leader has traditionally been selected from the ranks of systems analysts; however, as previously mentioned, some organizations are experimenting successfully with users as project leaders.

An IS project leader is unique in that there is an implied, and sometimes explicit, element of matrix management. A project team leader may be assigned four users from two different departments, two systems analysts from the systems section, and three programmers from the programming section, all part-time. This creates a situation where each team member has at least two and possibly more immediate supervisors. The key to success in this matrix environment is for each supervisor to respect all personnel commitments to projects not under his control. For example, the sales manager cannot commit the assistant sales manager for 50% of his or her time to a major development project, then revoke that commitment once the project is underway. On the surface, this appears a minor problem, but invariably this happens and has disastrous effects on team progress toward meeting deadlines. A typical project team and the relative commitment of its members is illustrated in Figure 3-6.

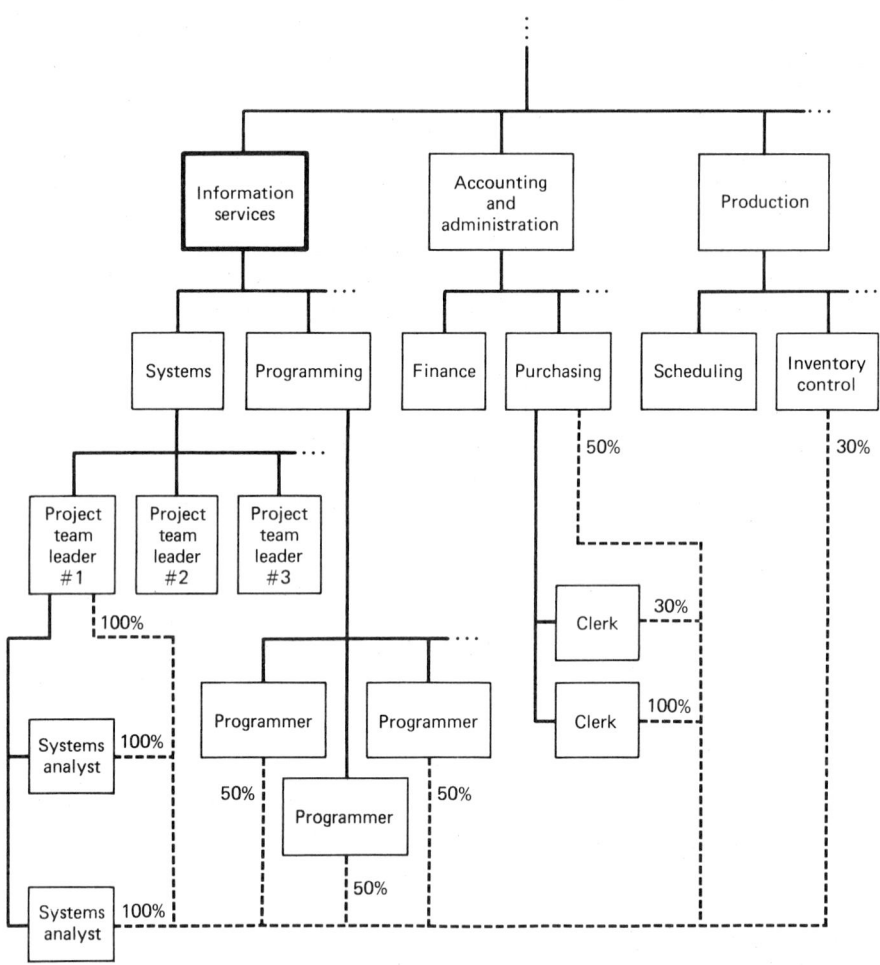

FIGURE 3-6 Project team makeup and personnel commitments for one project (noted by dashed line).

Chief Programmer

During the programming phase of the systems development process, intensity of effort shifts to the programmer members of the project team. Since the project leader has responsibilities that preclude intimate involvement with the programming effort, a chief programmer is designated for teams with two or more programmers. The chief programmer is a product of the chief programmer team concept that encourages the hierarchical modular development of programs.

The chief programmer identifies program modules (usually of no more than three person-weeks each) in a hierarchical manner, writes the job control and driver program(s), and assigns and supervises the development of subordinate program modules.

Data Base Administrator

The data base administrator (DBA) position evolved with data base management systems software and the integrated corporate data base. The DBA designs, develops, and maintains the corporate data base, and is responsible for its accuracy and security.

Control Clerk

The control clerk accounts for all input to and output from the computer center. Persons assigned control responsibility use standard procedures to validate the accuracy of output before it is distributed to user departments.

Education Coordinator

The education coordinator is responsible for monitoring IS educational (user and IS personnel) needs and for identifying or providing a source for this education. The coordinator may maintain a historical file on commercial seminars and their availability and quality, multimedia educational packages, and a resource library of books and journals.

Technical Writer/Documentalist

Technical writers/documentalists assist in the compilation of IS-related manuals and text-oriented documentation (systems documentation, user manuals, etc.) The technical writer/documentalist is one of the most recent specialty areas introduced to information services.

Librarian

The "tape librarian" position originated during the era of the second generation of computers when most computer systems were tape-oriented. In this tape environment, even small systems had hundreds of active magnetic tapes, half of which would be used during any given week. The tape librarian readied tapes for processing and kept track of the processing status on each tape.

As tape systems evolved to disk systems and disk systems to on-line systems, the "tape librarian" became simply the librarian. The librarian is now charged with status monitoring and storage of tapes, disks, microfiche, documentation, and, in the absence of an education coordinator, IS-related books and journals.

Operator

The operator performs those hardware-based activities necessary to keep production systems operational. This includes mounting appropriate tapes, disks, paper, and initiating software routines.

Larger computer installations may have one operator designated as a console operator. The console operator is in constant communication with the computer while monitoring the progress of a number of simultaneous production runs, initiating ad hoc jobs, and troubleshooting. If the computer system fails, the console operator initiates checkpoint/restart procedures to "bring the system up."

Scheduler

Given certain equipment constraints and criteria for system prioritization, the scheduler strives to utilize the valuable hardware resource at optimum efficiency. Along with production systems, the scheduler allocates and schedules computer time for program development and testing, system quality assurance testing, data and file conversion, one-time and ad hoc jobs, preventive maintenance, general maintenance, and system downtime for hardware upgrades and additions.

Data Entry Operators

The data entry operator, sometimes called key operator, uses key-to-tape, key-to-disk, and card-punch devices to transcribe data into machine-readable format. The latter is economically inferior to other alternatives and is disappearing quickly. Data entry operators enter data received verbally and via hard-copy source documents. Key operators are found both in information services and user departments. The current trend is to move the data entry function close to the source.

Information Services Planner

The information services planner is a recent entry into the list of IS professionals. The planner develops and maintains the strategic information services plan on a yearly cycle. This process is described in detail in Part IV.

Information Systems Auditor

The IS auditor is an information services-related position that is not part of the information services department. The IS auditor performs those IS auditing functions described earlier in this chapter.

INFORMATION SERVICES COMMITTEES

Information services-related committees can be classified in two categories. The first category encompasses corporate committees dealing with the information services function, such as the high-level MIS steering committee. The other category includes those committees that are established and function within the information services department structure. The committees are of two types: standing and ad hoc.

Standing committees are permanently established and usually have regularly scheduled meetings.

Ad hoc committees are appointed for more immediate purposes (e.g., investigations and feasibility studies).

Corporate Information Services Committees

The primary corporate IS committee is the high-level information services steering committee. The names and charges given this committee vary widely from one company to the next. Common names include: Computer Advisory Committee, Executive DP Steering Committee, MIS Advisory Council, Information Services Priorities Committee, and the Information Systems Policy Committee. To maintain consistency throughout the book, this high-level steering committee will be called the Information Systems Policy Committee or ISPC. Members typically are user managers and executives. An effective ISPC is an essential ingredient to the success of any corporate information services function.

During the past decade the ISPC has been a popular addition to many corporations' organizational structures. Unfortunately, many of these committees were founded because it was the "in" thing to do and they were not given a definitive charge; consequently, they were ineffective more often than not. In these cases, the committee is established and the committee charge and responsibilities tend to evolve, usually in the wrong direction. To establish an ISPC properly, corporate policy makers must address questions regarding the committee's responsibilities, membership, meeting frequency, scope of involvement, and, in some cases, attendance.

The charge of the ISPC should be well defined and formulated in writing, then distributed to those with a need to know. The following ISPC charge has proven successful in a number of organizations:

Support the use of information services for an effective and efficient corporate operation. The ISPC should be visible in its encouragement of information services.

Periodically present a report and recommendations on information services to the chief executive officer and the board of directors.

Approve and reject requests for major information services. Corporate policy should delineate major and minor service requests based on estimated resource requirements, usually personpower and/or cost. For example, a medium-sized corporation might designate major projects as those requiring more than one person-year of effort or a 30 thousand dollar expenditure.

Set priorities among approved information systems development projects. A typical committee would have a queue of approved projects for which priorities are continually evaluated and updated, depending on corporate needs.

Monitor the progress of major information services projects and the performance of ongoing production systems. On occasion, the committee will have to evaluate the merits of allocating additional resources to projects that are expected to run substantially over budget. The committee might also make go/no-go decisions when it becomes apparent that the finished project will fall short of expectations. Many corporations are adopting the policy of not pressing the doomed projects to an untimely completion (throwing good money after bad). The ISPC should also monitor the performance of ongoing production systems in order to assess their contribution to corporate goals. In essence, the committee is charged with signing the official death certificate for information systems that have outlived their usefulness.

Arbitrate differences between user departments and/or divisions arising from IS operations and/or proposed operations. For many years, the director of data processing was placed in a position of having to choose between two or more functional area alternatives. Major procedural conflicts should be resolved by the ISPC and those departments most affected by the decision, not by IS management.

Set policy that relates to information services and affects all departments. IS policy areas are discussed in detail in Chapter 4.

Develop short- and long-range plans for information services growth. The information services planning function is a tedious task. An IS functionary would normally be assigned to accomplish the mechanics of the planning process. The committee provides major input to the plan and ultimately renders final approval.

The above are suggested responsibility areas and would vary considerably depending on the type of industry and committee emphasis. It is implied that the full capabilities of the information services department are available to the ISPC to assist in carrying out these responsibilities.

The ISPC is an arm of the corporation, not of the information services department. The committee should be chartered and given authority by the chief executive officer and the board of directors. The committee normally reports to the chief executive officer. The committee's contact with the information services department is the director of IS.

The membership of the ISPC should be established by corporate policy. To do this, the president, executive committee, and possibly the board of directors must answer the following questions:

1. Who should serve on the committee and/or how should they be selected?

For the ISPC to be operationally effective, its members should be at the policy-making level. Members could be high-level functional area managers and/or other high-level corporate managers, preferably vice-president or higher. Historically, IS steering committees whose members are more than one level removed from the chief executive officer have not been successful. At best, these have caused no undue hardship, and at worst, they have been counterproductive. To work, the committee must have power to make decisions and follow up on these decisions. An ISPC at any level demands that considerable IS resources be channeled to support the committee. Without the authority to act decisively, a lower-level committee tends to operate in a circle, wasting valuable resources as well as the time of its members.

2. How many should serve on the committee?

A committee dealing with such complex and politically sensitive topics can become sluggish with more than eight or nine members. Too many members make the decision-making process unnecessarily difficult. A body of six or seven voting members is recommended.

3. What is the duration of the appointment of the individual members?

Because most major projects span more than a year, the appointment should be a minimum of one year, with two or more years preferred. Permanent appointments are possible with corporations that have only six to nine potential members. Other larger or more horizontally organized corporations need to rotate this important responsibility. The appointments should be rotated in such a manner that the nucleus of the committee is retained after each appointment period.

4. Should the director of information services be a member?

Whether the director of information services is a member of the ISPC is a matter of corporate preference. Ironically, some consider it a must, others think it is ridiculous. The rationale for appointing the information services director to the ISPC follows this line of thought: The trend is to create organizational neutrality for information services by making the director a vice-president. The director is then at the appropriate level for the ISPC. Perhaps the most compelling reason is that the data center and information services are major users of their own services and should have input on long-term direction, projects, and priorities.

Those who feel the IS director should not be a part of the committee argue that his or her presence would introduce too much bias into the decision-making process. Executive committees unable to resolve this issue have opted for a compromise that makes the director of IS a nonvoting member. Some have even made the director a nonvoting chairperson.

5. Who should be the chairperson and how is he or she selected?

Perhaps the best approach to selecting an ISPC chairperson is to allow the membership to nominate and elect their own. A minimum term for the chairperson is two years. When the chairperson is appointed by the chief executive officer, the committee neutrality is compromised by an often subtle but very real pressure from the top management. Another alternative is to designate a specific corporate position, (e.g., president, executive assistant to the president, director of IS, comptroller, or others).

6. Should the chairperson's position be rotated?

If elected, the position of chairperson should rotate among the membership. If designated, the chairperson would change only if the person holding the designated position is promoted or transferred.

7. How often should the committee meet?

The committee must meet often enough to stay abreast of project progress and to fulfill the charges of the ISPC. Information services utilization and progress is more volatile in some corporations than in others. It is recommended that the committee meet no less than once every two months and no more than once per month. This range of meeting frequencies has been proven effective. Special meetings should be arranged during periods of high IS activity.

8. Should there be an attendance policy?

To be an effective working body, each voting member must be actively involved in ISPC activities. It is recommended that attendance at all meetings be highly encouraged by the chief executive officer and further encouraged by an attendance policy. As an example, policy might require a voting member to maintain a cumulative attendance record of at least 75%, and the member and a designated representative to maintain a cumulative attendance record of at least 90%. Failure to participate should result in loss of the committee seat. A policy could be established that a new committee member is automatically appointed when a member's cumulative attendance falls below minimum requirements. Membership in the ISPC should be an appointment that every high-level person with a special interest would like to receive. Any recommendation for an attendance policy will not be well received, but past experience has shown that one inactive member breeds committee inactivity and, therefore, must be avoided at all costs.

Another corporate IS-related committee is the **user committee**. The purpose of the committee is to encourage a continued positive liaison between IS and the user community. The committee is made up of functional area managers who are closely associated with a computer-based information system. The committee meets periodically to provide verbal and written feedback on information systems operation.

Committees Within the Information Services Department

Properly chartered committees play an integral role in the day-to-day routine of the corporate information services department(s). In some organizations the informal network is the only vehicle for obtaining concensus opinions and soliciting external input. In contrast, other companies make liberal use of the committee. The following are typical standing or ad hoc committees within information services.

The **hardware selection committee** is responsible for the evaluation and selection of all computing hardware. Knowledgeable users are often invited to participate in the selection process, especially if they are paying the bill.

The **software selection committee** evaluates and selects all software products (systems and applications). Functional area representatives are always involved in the selection of packaged applications software (proprietary software).

The **project steering and review committee** is responsible for monitoring and/or reviewing the progress of major ongoing information services projects. This function overlaps with responsibilities assigned the ISPC, but the project steering and review committee examines projects in greater detail. This committee's function does not encompass the management of these projects; however, one of the primary functions of the committee is to provide meaningful feedback to project managers.

The **information services long-range planning committee** may consist of the information services management team, an operative (perhaps a senior systems analyst who doubles as the information services long-range planner), and one or two knowledgeable users, not necessarily managers. The purpose of this committee is to provide ongoing feedback on the feasibility and value of IS planning strategies and to the planning process in general.

This list of committees is not exhaustive. It is presented to provide user managers with some insight into the makeup of IS committees.

INFORMATION SERVICES
ORGANIZATIONAL STRUCTURE

The importance of a responsive information services organization cannot be overestimated. Unfortunately, most IS organizations evolve without much thought to optimizing internal effectiveness and external interaction. Each of the operational areas described earlier must be incorporated in the organizational structure, if not in name, then in function. There exist thousands of one-, two-, and three-person "shops." In these shops the director serves as chief cook and bottle washer, performing the tasks required for each operational area. The large IS organization will be specialized and have virtually all of the operational areas and position types represented in the organizational structure.

Figure 3-7 illustrates how the operational areas of information services can be organized for a medium-to-large corporation. A different thought process and circumstances would render a substantially different organizational structure. The chart illustrates traditional patterns and recent innovations, such as the information center.

A typical organizational structure for a small corporation (25 or less IS professionals) is illustrated in Figure 3-8. Although specialty areas are not specifically noted in the organizational chart, they do exist. For example, the director of information services also serves as the user liaison. The operations manager is the scheduler, and a senior systems analyst is assigned a part-time duty as data base administrator.

There are a variety of ways to subdivide each operational area. For example, Figure 3-9 illustrates that the systems and programming sec-

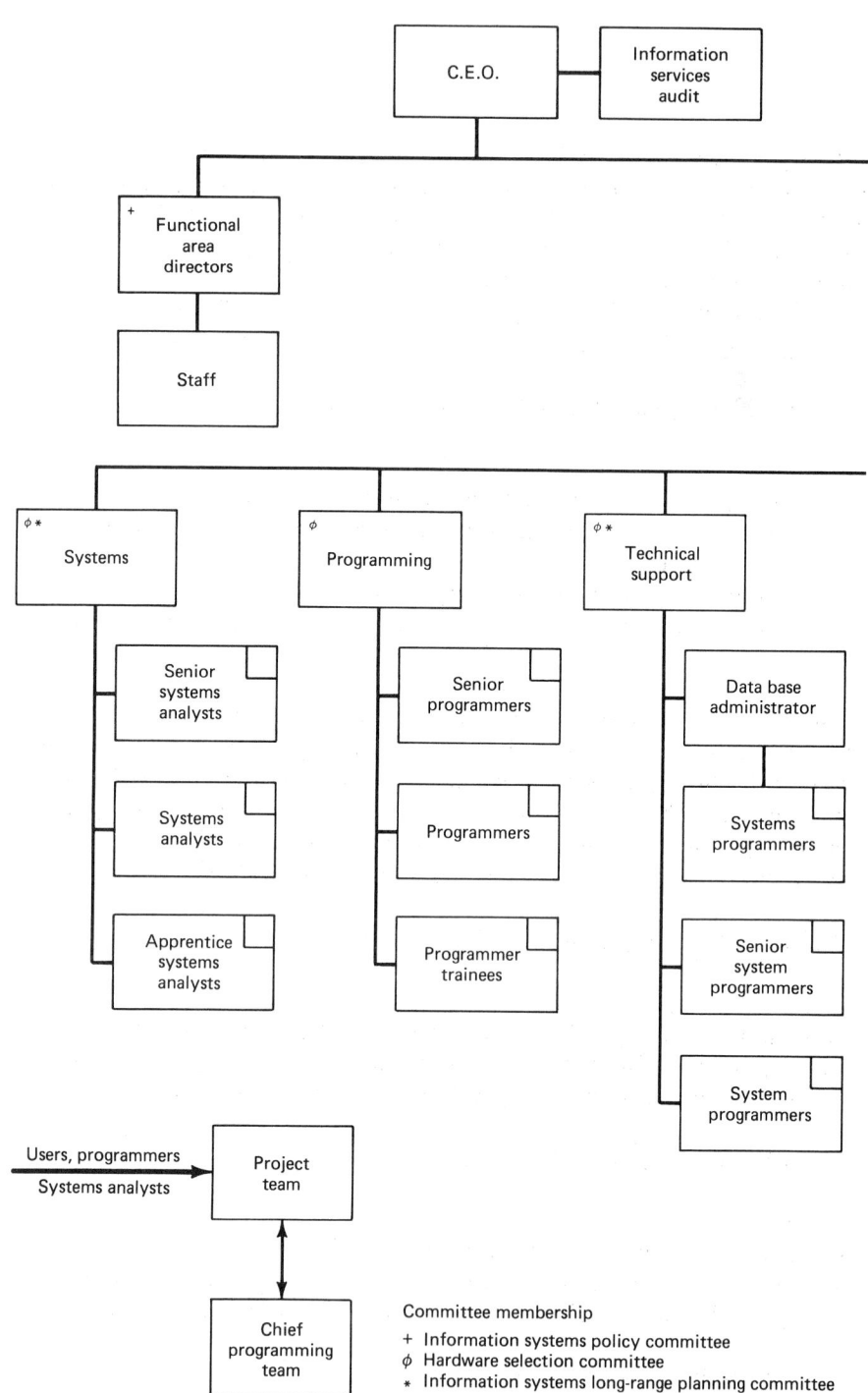

FIGURE 3-7 Example organization chart for medium and large information services departments.

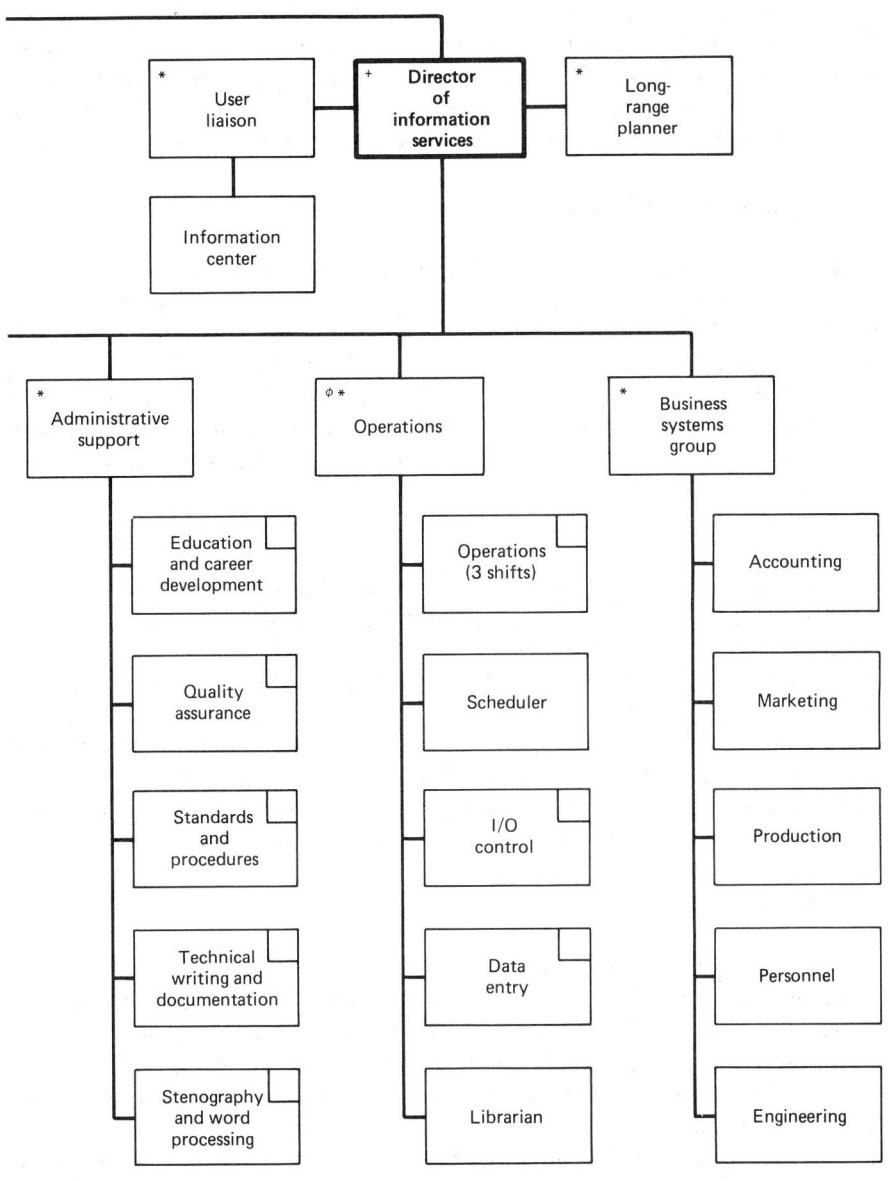

Note: Boxes in upper-right corner provide
space to include number of persons
in that position.

FIGURE 3-7 Continued.

55

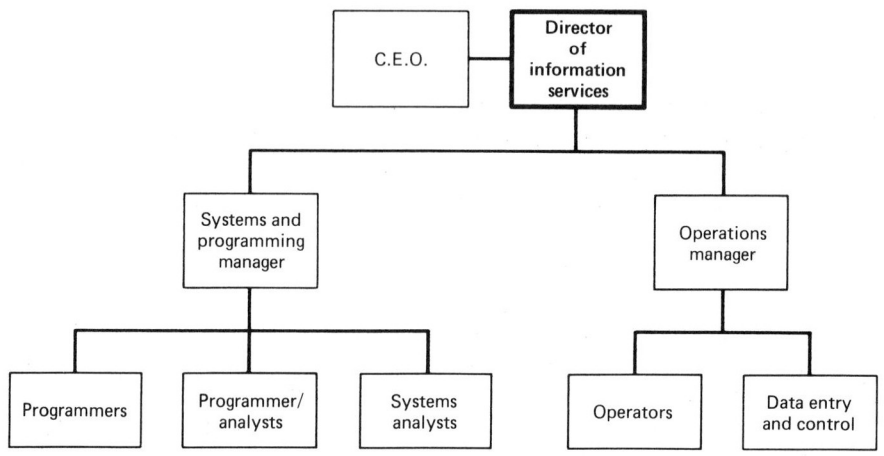

FIGURE 3-8 Example organization chart for a small information services department.

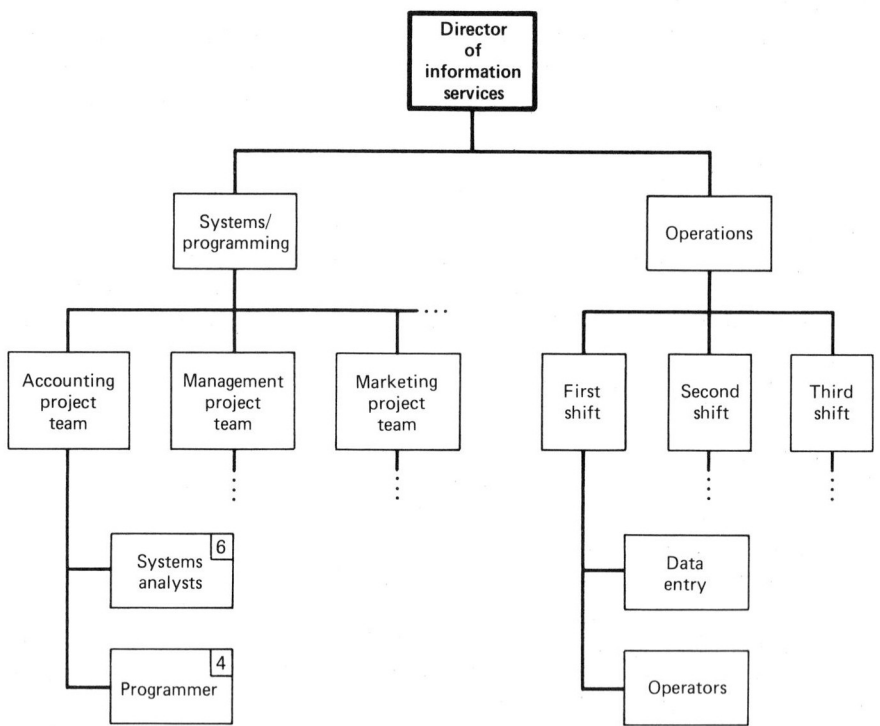

FIGURE 3-9 Functional area project team organization and shift organization.

56

tions can be combined and organized into functional area project teams or the operations section can be organized by shifts.

USE OF CONSULTANTS
AND CONTRACT PROGRAMMERS
AND ANALYSTS

The peaks and valleys of IS resource requirements and the lack of internal expertise in specialty areas have made the use of outside consultants and contract programmers and analysts an economic necessity.

Consultants

Information services consultants are retained by both user and IS management. An IS consultant is most effectively utilized

1. To provide specialized expertise (strategic IS planning, networking, and so on).
2. To render new insights and different perspectives.
3. To confirm or refute a decision.
4. To aid in a specific decision-making process.

Contract Programmers and Analysts

The IS consultant should not be confused with contract programmers and systems analysts. Contract programmers, analysts, and other MIS professionals are important primarily for work force augmentation and not because they have unique skills. They may be hired to develop a high-priority information system for which in-house resources are not readily available, or to work side by side with corporate programmers and analysts in system development and enhancement projects.

User managers and executives with projects that have a low corporate priority and a high departmental priority often seek help from outside companies. To achieve the best results, this should be closely coordinated with IS management.

Pitfalls in the Use of Consultants

Consultants are underutilized by some companies and overutilized by others. The company struggling to maintain the status quo will invariably benefit greatly from the recommendations of a competent consultant. Unfortunately, many companies have a written or implied policy that precludes retaining consultants. Such policies can be stifling to corporate productivity. In this volatile industry, no computer center can hope, nor would they want, to maintain up-to-date expertise in all facets of information services.

At the other end of the spectrum, some companies call in IS consultants to assist in routine decisions and in certain less-desirable, but important, activities. These companies are developing an unhealthy dependence on consultants and are forfeiting the opportunity to gain valuable internal expertise.

Another common pitfall in the use of consultants is forcing the consultant to work in isolation by not cooperating to achieve an effective interaction. Perhaps the most common, and the worst, pitfall is to retain a good consultant, give full cooperation throughout the engagement, and then ignore the advice.

CHAPTER 4

Information Services
Policies and Procedures

IS departments are, by definition, service organizations and must establish written procedures that formalize the interface between corporate departments and IS. The importance of IS policy and procedures is highlighted by the need for systems integration and coordinated information systems planning, and by the potential legal ramifications of not having an IS policy. IS and user managers and the information systems policy committee are responsible for establishing appropriate policies and procedures.

All IS-related policies and procedures discussed in this chapter involve or affect the functional areas. A typical IS department will have dozens of policies and procedures that are transparent to the user community and are, therefore, not presented.

JUSTIFICATION FOR IS POLICY

Every corporation confronts essentially two types of situations: common ones and unusual ones. Fortunately, the routine user/IS interface deals primarily with common situations. Good IS policy is directly applicable to common situations and indirectly applicable to unusual situations. By establishing guidelines for most common situations, IS policy will provide a framework by which IS and user managers can better cope with exceptional situations.

Too many IS decisions are based on individual rather than corporate criteria. Four functional area managers asked to rank proposed IS projects for the corporate good may use individual criteria that are unacceptable to the other three. A policy with stated criteria would structure the decision-making process for the good of the company.

Corporate managers, especially in crisis-oriented environments, are forced to make quick decisions before sufficient information can be gathered. Appropriate IS policy statements will, at a minimum, reduce the potential for managers to make bad decisions.

The absence of IS policy leaves the door open for user and IS managers to make their own interpretation of what they perceive IS policy to be. Without policy, conflicts between IS and user personnel, among users, and within information services are a foregone conclusion.

POLICY AREAS

Information Services Charter

The IS department, as a service organization, receives its authority and its charge from top management and the people and organizations it serves. With the expanded scope of information services and the trend to decentralization, user and information services responsibilities become confused and, therefore, must be carefully delineated. An IS charter can be used to identify responsibilities for such areas in input/output control, hardware selection and acquisition, data base integration, word processing, and so on. When no corporate-approved IS charter exists, the responsibilities for these and other areas become fragmented.

The uncontrolled proliferation of small computers and word processing equipment is a classic example of what can happen when IS responsibilities become fragmented. This proliferation can cause serious compatibility and integration problems. The IS charter may overlap with established IS policy, but it would not contain the detail found in policy directives. The charter should contain a written list and a concise explanation of the responsibilities of the information services department. A typical corporate IS department might be charged with the following responsibilities:

- ◆ IS standards and procedures
- ◆ Data base management

- Development, ongoing operation, and maintenance of production information systems
- Maintenance of backup capabilities
- Control of accuracy (after the source document has been completed)
- Physical and logical security
- Corporate advising on issues involving computers and the use of computers
- Long-range planning for IS and information systems integration
- User education
- Hardware/software evaluation and selection (with input from user)
- All physical facilities containing computer equipment (including user facilities)
- IS compliance with federal, state, and local laws
- Primary contact for all vendor interaction
- Word processing and office automation
- Process control (numerically controlled equipment, computer-aided manufacturing, and computer-aided design)
- Catalyst for new systems development

Once a formal IS charter is approved, responsibilities for user departments are implied. Although not specifically written into IS charters (but perhaps this is a good idea), the following activities are generally user responsibilities:

- Completing the source document (accurately and legibly)
- Data entry (recent trends have been to push data entry as close to the source as possible)
- Completing service requests according to standardized procedures
- Informing the data base administrator of data element and record changes
- Educating IS personnel in the functional areas
- Assisting in the system development process as designated in the systems development methodology
- Participating in and evaluating acceptance tests
- Periodically reviewing production systems (in cooperation with IS personnel)
- Establishing priorities and other high-level steering committee responsibilities (see Chapter 3)

Although the above charter areas have a solid logical foundation, circumstances may cause some companies to delete, add to, and change these lists for the good of the corporation.

Personal Information

Most companies maintain data bases on company personnel and/or customers. Such data bases could contain sensitive data and information. Whenever personal information is concerned, the individual has certain implied rights of privacy. Hence, a minimum personal information policy would outline access and disclosure guidelines (see Chapter 11).

Personal information is controlled on a "need to know" basis. Policy on disclosure should detail to whom, when, and how often personal information is released within the company and externally.

Hardware Acquisition

With the advent of inexpensive, full-function computers and stand-alone word processing computers, forward-thinking corporate officers have had to act quickly to establish a hardware acquisition policy that ensures hardware compatibility. The selection of hardware influences the design of the system and has the potential to introduce not only hardware, but system and data base incompatibilities. Uncontrolled proliferation of computing hardware will inevitably cause delays in progress towards the realization of integrated information systems.

High-Level Information Services
Steering Committee

The president, executive committee, and possibly the board of directors should establish a written policy (or charge) directing the efforts of and providing authority for a high-level information services steering committee. The format and charge of such a committee (the ISPC) is discussed in detail in Chapter 3.

System Priorities

Allocation of corporate information services resources is now primarily a user manager responsibility. The IS director is more concerned with "how" to allocate resources and not "where" to allocate resources. For this reason, user managers and the ISPC should establish and adhere to guidelines (corporate criteria) when establishing system priorities. The following priority guidelines are listed for consideration, with the highest priority first.

- Systems that have ceased to be operational (for whatever reason)
- Legal or regulatory requirements
- Management requests for service that are necessary to make *significant* decisions
- Level of savings/earnings
- Intangibles

The above suggested priorities cannot be applied without regard to extenuating circumstances. Decision makers must also consider: economic risk, technical risk, operational risk, degree of uncertainty in obtaining benefits, urgency, equipment capacity, available expertise, duplication of requirements, system dependencies, personpower availability, dollar availability, and length of project.

PROCEDURES APPLICABLE TO USERS

In the information services environment, procedures are the bottom line. A typical computer center will have dozens of written procedures, but three are particularly important to user managers. These are submittal of the system service request (SSR), the system development methodology, and the information system review.

System Service Request

The system (or user) service request is the formal vehicle by which a user manager requests any kind of service from the IS department. The system service request is a formal written request that is compiled by the user, submitted to the IS department, and evaluated according to specific corporate-approved procedures.

The purpose of the service request is twofold. First, the service request procedure encourages the user to submit a well-conceived and properly documented request for service. Second, the director of IS and/or the information system policy committee will require certain information in order to make an informed decision on the service request.

To establish procedures for a systems service request, several questions must be resolved. For example:

- Who approves service requests?
- Should there be an appeal procedure for rejected service requests?
- What are the possible decision alternatives?
- What information should be included on a service request?

Once these and other questions are resolved, the systems service requests procedure can be established.

The service request procedure of Figure 4-1 illustrates how one company resolved the above questions.[4] The numbers outside the upper left-hand corner of the "activity blocks" correspond to the following numbered discussion.

1. The user manager submits a suggestion for a new or enhanced computer-based information system. The service request could also be for a service that is not directly related to an information system, such as internal consulting. The requestor, usually a functional area manager, compiles the system service request to include the following:

    ♦ Title of the system

    ♦ Date of completion of the service request

    ♦ Names, positions, and affiliations of those who prepared the service request

    ♦ General description of the system to include the following: (1) a statement of the objectives of the proposed system; (2) a general word picture of the fundamental operation of the proposed system; and (3) the scope of the proposed system, covering all organizational interfaces, volumes, frequencies of activities, complexity of the system, and a gross estimate of personnel requirements

    ♦ Identification of problem areas in the present system

    ♦ Justification: how the proposed system will solve present problems, increase services, upgrade management reporting, save money, and so on

    ♦ Identification of source of funds

    ♦ Expected date to begin system development, expected implementation date, and any explanation if timing is critical

    ♦ Identification of all external corporate documents that contain pertinent information

    ♦ A list of other similar successful systems, including the name of the organization and division heads responsible for the similar system

    ♦ General long-range objectives of the proposed system

    ♦ Other pertinent information

---

[4] This user service request procedure is a modified version of one that was originally presented as part of a standardized system development methodology in L. Long's *Data Processing Documentation and Procedures Manual* (Reston, VA: Reston Publishing Company, 1979), pp. 20, 22–24.

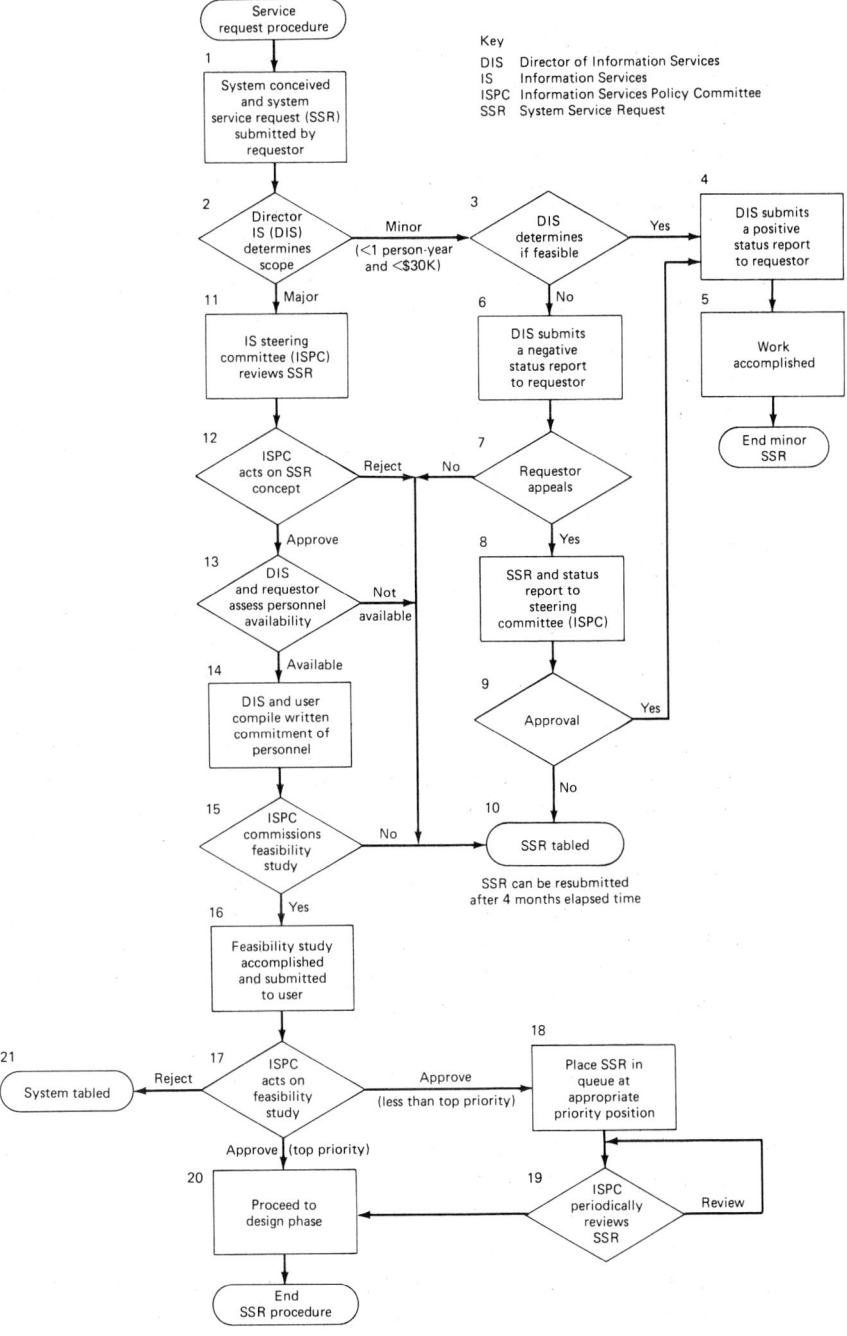

FIGURE 4-1 Example system service request procedure.

65

The services request is submitted to the director of information services. A completed service request is illustrated in Figure 4-2.

2. The information services director is authorized to render the decision on projects that he or she estimates to require less than one professional person-year and less than $30,000 expenditure (these figures are arbitrary and would vary according to the size of company). All other service requests

SYSTEM SERVICE REQUEST	June 1, 198X
EROS (Efficient Residence Operations System)	

SUBMITTED BY: Carla Rothlisberger, Director Residence Operations

GENERAL DESCRIPTION OF SYSTEM

OBJECTIVES FOR PROPOSED SYSTEM

Primary Objectives:

1. To automate the room assignment procedure.
2. To automate the inventory record-keeping task.

Supporting Objectives:

1. To provide the staff of Residence Operations with an instrument to use in making more efficient and effective decisions.
2. To integrate existing procedures.

FUNDAMENTAL OPERATION OF PROPOSED SYSTEM

The basic work flow of the present system will be followed. Areas to be computerized include:

1. Freshmen roommate and room assignment procedure
2. Upperclass room lottery (to be on-line)
3. Inventory control
4. Student billing to include damage billing
5. File updates (to be on-line)
6. Report generation including:
   - On-campus population by building and room number
   - Off-campus population
   - Home address labels
   - File folder headings by academic class and name
   - Statistical reports of residence halls population
   - Room assignment notification
   - Waiting list update

SCOPE OF PROPOSED SYSTEM

Other Organizational Interfaces:

1. Bursar and Registrar—to supply student information
2. Campus maintenance—for general repairs and upkeep on residence halls
3. Dining Service—to inform them of the number of students on the various meal plans
4. Admissions Office—to handle housing assignments

FIGURE 4-2 A completed service request in a university environment.

are routed to the ISPC (IS steering committee) for further action.

3. The IS director either accepts or rejects the request based on availability of resources.

4. The IS director submits a status report to the requestor reflecting acceptance and an estimated completion date and cost, if appropriate.

Volumes

The proposed system must be able to process approximately 2,100 students in the residence halls and about 1,000 additional students through the lottery process. The general student files will include approximately 4,000 students. Most residence forms will be restricted to the students in the system; many will be sent to approximately 1,000 incoming freshmen who will not be involved in the lottery with other students. Most forms (excluding maintenance forms) will be generated only once during the yearly cycle.

PRESENT SYSTEM PROBLEMS

There are a number of problems with the present system:

1. A tremendous amount of paperwork is generated.
2. A considerable amount of time is necessary to assign rooms and roommates.
3. There is no cross reference between room inventory and occupancy (i.e., lack of inventory control).
4. In regard to maintenance, there is no way systematically to isolate recurring problems.
5. It is not immediately known when and where a room vacancy has occurred.

JUSTIFICATION

The proposed system should eliminate those problems noted above, as well as provide information for better decisions. Better service will be rendered through a more efficient lottery program and a faster notification of eligibility for a room.

FUNDING SOURCE

The system development and ongoing operation will be funded out of the Residence Operations budget.

TIME FRAME

If the feasibility study begins immediately, implementation will be scheduled for approximately two years from the present time. The timing of the start of parallel operation is critical. It must begin at that part of the cycle when the lottery process is about to begin (end of January).

ADDITIONAL INFORMATION

University policy guarantees housing to freshmen. The University Forum has provided for the use of in-class lotteries to distribute housing fairly among upperclass students.

By University discipline policy, residents are held responsible for damage to residence halls.

OTHER SIMILAR SYSTEMS

Heferdine University has a computer-based lottery system. Phillip Deutsch is Director of Housing.

LONG-RANGE OBJECTIVES

The proposed system will ultimately be incorporated into the proposed student information system, scheduled for implementation in three years.

FIGURE 4-2 Continued.

5. The work is accomplished without further evaluation.

6. The IS director submits a negative status report to the requestor relating the reasons for rejection of the proposed project.

7. The requestor has the option to appeal the IS director's decision to higher authorities (the ISPC).

8. The service request and the negative status report are routed to the ISPC for review.

9. The ISPC can override the IS director's decision or allow it to stand.

10. The service request is tabled without further action. The request can be reactivated by the requestor after four months' elapsed time (an arbitrary figure).

11. Copies of the service request are distributed to ISPC members two weeks prior to the scheduled ISPC meeting. Each member reviews the service request and should be prepared to discuss advantages and the disadvantages from his or her perspective.

12. The ISPC acts on the merits of the concept and the need for the proposed system (an approval is not possible at this point). The request is either tabled as being inconsistent with the needs of the company and/or deficient in applicability, or it is approved for further study.

13. The IS director and the appropriate user manager(s) assess the availability of personnel. A lack of personnel availability and/ or commitment on the part of IS or the functional areas causes the request to be tabled.

14. Both the IS director and the appropriate user manager(s) complete a written commitment of personnel.

15. A feasibility study involves a considerable commitment of personnel, time, and company money; therefore, the ISPC must make a decision on whether to expend resources on further study.

16. A detailed feasibility study on the systems service request is compiled and submitted to the ISPC for evaluation.

17. The ISPC reviews the feasibility study. For clarification purposes, a brief verbal summary is presented at the ISPC meeting. The ISPC directs the proposed project to be either tabled indefinitely, approved and given the go-ahead for development, or approved but placed in the appropriate priority position in a queue of approved systems.

18. The service request is approved and placed in a queue at the appropriate priority position.

19. The ISPC periodically reviews a list of approved projects and their priorities and renders go-ahead decisions according to corporate needs.
20. Periodically the ISPC gives the go-ahead for certain projects to be initiated.
21. The feasibility study is rejected and the service request is tabled (see activity 10).

The above procedure for submitting and evaluating a system service request contains two decision levels, an appeal process, a requirement for a feasibility study on large projects, and alternative actions on completed feasibility studies. The procedure was presented in detail to illustrate these options.

System Development Methodology

The system development methodology describes activities and responsibilities during the development and implementation of an information system. Chapter 12 is devoted to the system development methodology.

Information System Reviews

The post-implementation system review is incorporated into most system development methodologies, but subsequent system reviews are usually not accomplished unless a formal procedure is established to initiate these reviews periodically. Periodic system reviews are the best way to maintain a proactive environment and effective information systems. These periodic reviews encourage user and IS personnel to identify and rectify system shortcomings before they become a burden on system effectiveness. It is more expensive to react to changing corporate needs than it is to anticipate these needs.

The System Review Schedule[5] form shown in Figure 4-3 can be used both to plan periodic reviews and to initiate these reviews as the review time approaches. The review schedule is completed after the post-implementation review. The circled numbers on the various items of Figure 4-3 cross-reference the following explanations:

1. **System title:** the title of the application system (payroll, general ledger, and so on).

[5] Taken from L. Long's *Data Processing Documentation and Procedures Manual* (Reston, VA: Reston Publishing Company, 1979), pp. 170-71.

System title_____ ① _____

System review cycle_____ ② _____

Review date	Review coordinator	Dates reviewed	Action
③	④	⑤	⑥

FIGURE 4-3 System review schedule.

2. **System review cycle:** a set period of time that elapses between reviews (e.g., quarterly, semiannually, and so on). The review cycle should not be less than three months or more than one year.

3. **Review date:** the beginning date of each review. The review dates should be consistent and in support of the IS long-range planning cycle.

4. **Review coordinator:** the name of the person expected to do the review or the person who did the review.

5. **Dates reviewed:** the beginning and ending dates during which the system was reviewed.

6. **Action taken:** Put either "none" or "revised." If the review coordinator recommends that the system be revised in any way, a description of the revisions should be attached to the System Review Schedule. The description should contain appropriate remarks by user and IS personnel about timeliness, clarity, applicability, format, response time, turnaround time, procedures, reports, documents, and/or displays. The description would also contain the recommended actions based on the results of the periodic review and the benefits to be derived from these actions.

INFORMATION SERVICES
MANUALS AND DIRECTIVES

An information services department will distribute and maintain as many as 20 manuals and formal directives detailing standards, policies, procedures, and methodologies for use both internally and throughout the corporation. The user manager would either be on the distribution list or be responsible for the contents of the following manuals or directives:

User manuals. A user manual is compiled for each production information system (e.g., MRP, order entry). It describes work flow, input/output, and operational procedures for the system.

System development methodology. The development or enhancement of any computer-based information system is a cooperative effort between user and information services personnel. This methodology is described in detail in Chapter 12.

Hardware/software evaluation and selection procedure. Since computer hardware and software represent a substantial corporate budget item, many companies have adopted a rigorous standardized evaluation and selection procedure.

Strategic IS planning methodology. Like systems development, planning is a cooperative effort between user and IS personnel. A strategic IS planning methodology is described in Chapter 16.

IS policy. The IS policy manual is the written documentation of some or all of those policies discussed in this chapter.

Security guidelines. This document presents security guidelines for development and operation of information systems (see Chapter 11).

Contingency plan. The contingency plan is a detailed document describing events, activities, and responsibilities of user and IS personnel during or following a disaster or an extraordinary event that has caused IS operations to be terminated (see Chapter 16).

Word processing. This manual describes the technical aspects of using IS-supported word processing systems.

Part II

COMPUTERS AND DATA MANAGEMENT

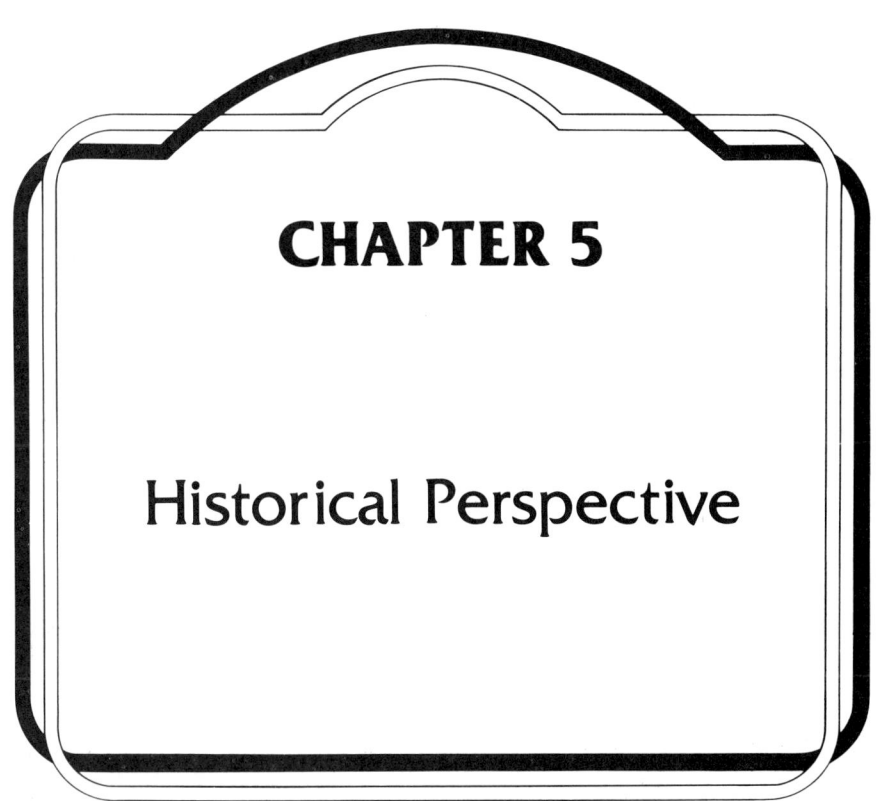

CHAPTER 5

Historical Perspective

The development of computers is of particular significance to the readers of this book because they will have lived through virtually all of the short but glorious history of the electronic computer. Many will have had a working association with all three generations of computers.

In terms of effect on the way people live and work, Dr. John V. Atanasoff's invention (1942)[6] can be considered one of the more significant events in history. But only after numerous technological improvements and 20 years' elapsed time did the computer experience a widespread acceptance. In retrospect, the acceptance and utilization of the computer in the late 1950s is small compared to what it is today. Any knowledgeable forecaster would say that the current level of acceptance and utilization is small compared to what it will be a decade from today.

Rather than present a detailed chronology of technical innovations, the history of computers is presented in a way that will provide the reader with a historical perspective and a feel for the "roots" of the

[6] The reader desiring more detailed information on significant figures and events in the history of computers is referred to M. Zientara's 12-part series on "The History of Computers," *Computerworld*, Vol. XV, Nos. 26, 28, 30, 32, 34, 36, 38, 40, 42, 44, 46, and 48. The series is also available as a reprint through *Computerworld*.

modern computer. An appreciation of the trials and successes of the past encourages one to be positive about the future.

EARLY HISTORY

The history of modern electronic computers may have begun in 1942, but there were significant events prior to that date that merit mention.

The Abacus

The abacus was probably the original mechanical counting device and has been traced back at least 5,000 years. Its effectiveness has stood the test of time. The abacus is still used to illustrate the principles of counting to school children and for modern business applications. When a Chinese restaurateur was asked why he used an abacus for computing the bill rather than a hand calculator, he simply stated that the abacus was faster. (See Figure 5-1.)

The Pascaline

Blaise Pascal, a 17th century philosopher and mathematician, invented the first calculator (see Figure 5-2). The Frenchman's calculator, called the Pascaline, was not that much different from the mechanical calculators of the early 1960s. The numbers for each digit position were arranged on a wheel such that the adjacent wheel was turned a one-tenth revolution for each complete revolution of the neighbor wheel.

Although Pascal was praised for his accomplishments throughout Europe, the Pascaline was a dismal financial failure. Businessmen considered the Pascaline too complex, and besides, human labor was less expensive.

FIGURE 5-1 An Abacus. (*Courtesy of IBM.*)

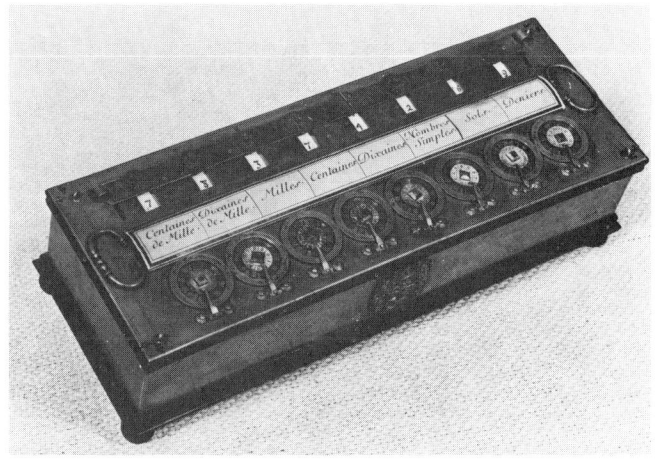

FIGURE 5-2 The Pascaline, the first calculating machine. (*Courtesy of IBM.*)

Babbage's Folly

An English visionary named Charles Babbage (1792–1871) could have hastened the development of computers had he been born a hundred years later. He advanced the state of computational hardware by inventing a difference engine capable of computing mathematical tables. In 1834, while working on advances to the difference engine, Babbage conceived the idea of an analytical engine. This was, in essence, a general-purpose computer. Skeptics nicknamed his machine "Babbage's Folly." Babbage worked on his analytical machine until his death.

Babbage's detailed drawings described the characteristics of the modern electronic computer. Had Babbage been born in an era of more advanced technology, the electronic computer might have been invented 50 years earlier. Ironically, some early pioneers in the development of the electronic computer were not aware of his ideas on memory, printers, the punched card, and sequential program control.

PUNCHED-CARD EQUIPMENT

The First Punched Card

The Jacquard weaving loom, invented in 1801 and still in use today, is controlled by punched cards (see Figure 5-3). Holes are strategically punched in the card to indicate the weaving design.

Babbage wanted to employ the punched-card concept of the Jacquard loom to his analytical engine. In 1843 Lady Ada Augusta

FIGURE 5-3 Jacquard's weaving loom used punched card technology in the early nineteenth century. (*Courtesy of IBM.*)

Lovelace suggested that cards could be prepared that would instruct Babbage's engine to repeat certain operations. By implementing her idea, Lady Lovelace became the first programmer.

The Emergence of Electronic Data Processing

The United States Bureau of the Census did not complete the 1880 census until almost 1888. Bureau management concluded that soon the 10-year census would take more than 10 years! The Census Bureau commissioned Herman Hollerith, a statistician, to apply his expertise in the use of punched cards to assist in taking the 1890 census (see Figure 5-4). With punched-card processing and Hollerith's tabulating machine, the census was completed in 2½ years. Thus began the emergence of electronic data processing (EDP). (See Figure 5-5.)

FIGURE 5-4 Hollerith's tabulating machine. (*Courtesy of IBM.*)

FIGURE 5-5 Card punch machine used for data entry at the Census Bureau during the 1890s. (*Courtesy of the United States Department of Commerce, Bureau of the Census.*)

Hollerith's machine was in demand all over the world. Russia's first census was taken in 1897 and was recorded with Hollerith's machine. In 1911, Hollerith's Tabulating Machine Company merged with several other companies to form the Computing-Tabulating-Recording Company.

Electronic Accounting Machines

Tabulating machine results had to be posted by hand until 1919, when the Computer-Tabulating-Recording Company announced the printer/lister. The printer/lister revolutionized the way companies did business. To better reflect the scope of their business interests, the company was renamed International Business Machines (IBM) in 1924.

Through the mid-1950s, **punched-card technology** improved with the addition of more punched-card devices and more sophisticated capabilities (see Figure 5-6). Since each card usually contained a record (e.g., an employee's name and address), punched-card processing also became known as **unit record processing** (one card = one record). Although interactive programming and on-line data entry (both discussed later) have made punched-card devices economically obsolete, one can still find isolated occurrences of these devices in today's computer center.

The **electronic accounting machine (EAM)** family of punched-card devices includes the card punch, verifier, reproducer, summary punch, interpreter, sorter, collator, calculator, and the accounting machine (see Figure 5-7). These devices were "programmed" to perform a particular operation by inserting a prewired panel. A different panel was "wired" for each type of operation to be performed.

Punched-Card Processing

A machine room operator in an electronic accounting machine installation had a physically demanding job. Some machine rooms resembled a factory. Handtrucks loaded with cards and printed output were moved from one device to the next. The noise was no less intense than an automobile assembly plant. Today's machine room operators use their brains rather than their backs. Ask one of them about the "old days." Many of them are former EAM operators.

In order to prepare punched-card files for processing, the cards had to be **sorted** (sequenced by employee last name, part number, and so on) and **collated** (two or more files combined for processing—e.g., name and address file with payroll file). Because electronic accounting

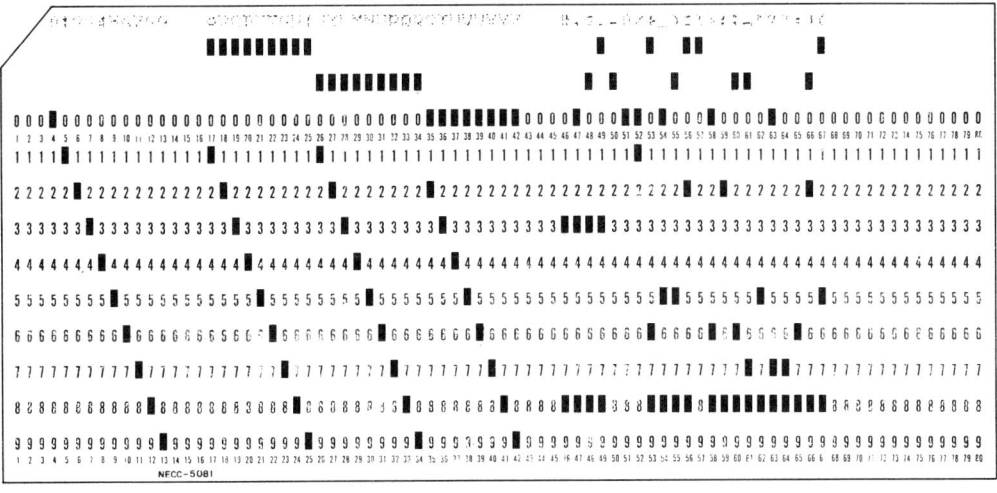

(a)

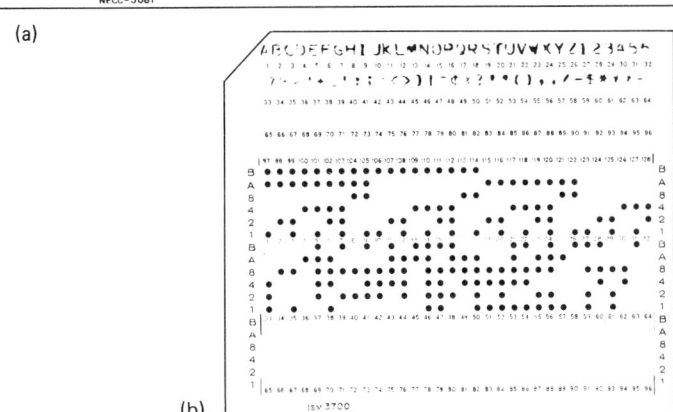

(b)

FIGURE 5-6 The 80-column card used by EAM equipment and most computers. The 96-column which was used only by IBM's small business computers.

machines operate independently, several steps called **machine runs** are required to produce a given output. In each run the entire file is "read" one card at a time. In most modern information systems, only that portion of the data base that is needed is processed, usually in one run.

For over 30 years electronic accounting machines were the mainstay of administrative data processing. Until only recently the punched card was the primary means of entering data into the computer. For the most part, electronic accounting machines have worn out. Nevertheless, the punched-card concept of **batch** sequential processing (processing all transactions during one machine run) has a half century of momentum and is dying slowly.

FIGURE 5-7 An electronic counting machine (EAM) installation. (*Courtesy of IBM.*)

EARLY COMPUTERS

Computer pioneers Dr. John W. Mauchly and J. Presper Eckert, Jr. secured a patent on a device that most people thought to be the first electronic digital computer. A generation of people were led to believe that Mauchly and Eckert were the inventors of the computer. But, in 1973 a Federal court ruled that the patent was derived from the work of Dr. Atanasoff and was invalidated. Dr. Atanasoff was officially credited with the invention of the electronic digital computer. During the years from 1937 to 1942 he developed the first electronic digital computer—the Atanasoff-Berry Computer, or the *ABC* (see Figure 5-8). A graduate student, Clifford Berry, assisted him.

After talking with Dr. Atanasoff, reading notes describing the principles of the ABC, and seeing the ABC, Dr. Mauchly collaborated with Mr. Eckert to develop a machine that would compute trajectory tables for the United States Army. The end product, a large-scale fully operational electronic computer, was completed in 1946 and called the *ENIAC* (see Figure 5-9). A thousand times faster than its electro-mechanical predecessors, the ENIAC was a major breakthrough in computer technology. It weighed 30 tons, occupied 1,500 square feet of floor space, and had over 18,000 vacuum tubes. Lore has it that the ENIAC, built at the University of Pennsylvania, dimmed the lights of Philadelphia when it was activated.

The imposing scale and general applicability of the ENIAC signaled the beginning of the first generation of computers.

FIGURE 5-8 Dr. Atanasoff's ABC computer, the first electronic digital computer. (*Courtesy of Iowa State University*.)

FIGURE 5-9 The first large-scale fully operational electronic computer, the ENIAC. (*Courtesy of Sperry Univac, division of Sperry Corporation*.)

COMPUTER GENERATIONS

The First Generation of Computers
(1946 through 1959)

The UNIVAC I. The **first generation of computers** was characterized by the most prominent feature of the ENIAC: **vacuum tubes.** Through 1950, several other notable computers were built, each producing significant advancements in the development of computers. These advancements included binary arithmetic, random access, and the concept of stored programs.

They say history repeats itself, and so it did with the installation of the first commercial computer in the United States Bureau of the Census in 1951. The computer, called the Universal Automatic Computer (*UNIVAC I* for short) was developed by Mauchly and Eckert for the Remington-Rand Corporation. This put what is now the UNIVAC Division of Sperry-Rand years ahead of the competition. The federal government got its money's worth out of the UNIVAC I. The Census Bureau used it for 12 years.

By 1951 other manufacturers, primarily in the punched card and electronics industries, were beginning to enter the commercial computer market. This group included Burroughs, Honeywell, International Business Machines (IBM) and Radio Corporation of America (RCA).[7]

IBM Enters the Computer Market. The first electro-mechanical computer was the result of IBM-sponsored research. The product of the research, the *Mark I*, was completed in 1944 by Howard Aiken, a Harvard University professor. At the time, IBM held a virtual monopoly on punch-card data processing equipment (EAM equipment). IBM's management did not feel that computers could replace punched-card equipment and were reluctant to enter the market. Not until the success of the UNIVAC I did IBM make the decision and commitment to develop and market computers. IBM quickly became a formidable competitor to UNIVAC.

IBM's first entry into the commercial computer market was the *IBM 701* in 1953. However, the *IBM 650* introduced in 1954 (see

---

[7]To avoid confusing the reader by alternately referencing a dozen manufacturers of computers, the IBM product line is used as a point of reference in the following historical development of the computer generations. This is done with a realistic recognition that IBM has been a dominant force in the worldwide computer market for three decades. It should not be construed as an explicit or implicit recognition that "IBM is best." Dozens of computer vendors manufacture comparable computer systems. The competition is, and always has been, very intense.

Figure 5-10) is probably the reason IBM enjoys such a healthy share of the market today. Unlike some of its competitors, the IBM 650 was designed to be a logical upgrade (similar type operation) to electronic accounting machines. Current electronic accounting machine users were much more willing to accept a computer that was similar to EAM. If not for the IBM 650, what is affectionately known as the "IBM card" would probably have been called the "UNIVAC card." IBM management went out on the limb and estimated sales of 50. This was more than the installed number of computers in the United States at that time. They actually leased (computers were seldom sold during the first and second generation) more than 1,000. The rest is history.

The Computer Industry Comes of Age. By the end of the late 1950s a number of other manufacturers, including Control Data Corporation (CDC), General Electric (GE), and National Cash Register (NCR), had decided to commit resources and test the water. Each new entry to the computer business made significant contributions to the state of the art of computer technology.

Scores of other companies entered into other facets of the computer/information processing industry (such as punched cards, printout forms, machine room accessories). By 1960 the computer industry was established and was beginning to influence the direction of industry in general.

FIGURE 5-10 The IBM 650 computer was the most popular of the first generation computers. (*Courtesy of IBM.*)

The Second Generation of Computers
(1959 through 1964)

To most people, the invention of the **transistor** meant small portable radios. To those in the data processing business, it signaled the start of the **second generation of computers**. The transistor meant more powerful, more reliable, and less expensive computers that would occupy less space and give off less heat. The expense item should be emphasized. The cost of a computer during the first, second, and part of the third generation represented a significant portion of a company's budget.

Computers were expensive. Cost per instruction executed can be used to compare the cost of computers over time. Significant innovations spurred by intense competition have resulted in enormous increases in computer performance and substantial reductions in price. This price-performance trend, established with the introduction of second-generation computers, continues today. Figure 5-11 graphically illustrates this trend.

IBM's announcement of the transistor-based 7000 series computers was paralleled by announcements from other computer manufacturers. The IBM 1400 series, the data processing workhorse of the early 1960s, was announced shortly thereafter (see Figure 5-12).

The dominant characteristics of the second generation were:

1. The transistor.
2. Limited **compatibility** within a manufacturer's line of computers (programs written for one computer cannot be run on another without modification).
3. No compatibility between manufacturers.
4. Continued orientation toward tape sequential processing (good for processing transactions but cumbersome for providing information for decision making).
5. Low-level, symbolic programming languages (discussed in Chapter 9).

Limited compatibility meant that any computer system upgrade would be accompanied by a myriad of conversion woes.

The Third Generation of Computers
(1964 through ?)

Characteristics of Third-Generation Computers. What some computer historians consider to be the single most important event in the history of computers occurred when IBM announced their *System 360* line of computers on April 7, 1964. The System 360 ushered in the

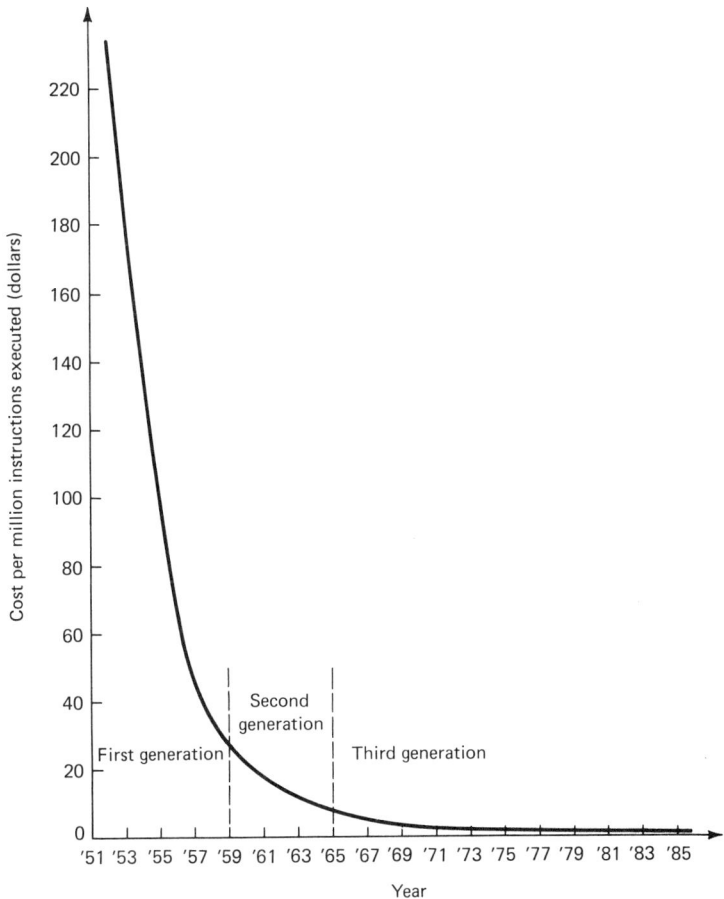

FIGURE 5-11 Decreasing cost of computers.

third generation of computers. Integrated circuits did for the third generation what transistors did for the second generation. The System 360s (shown in Figure 5-13) and third generation computers of CDC, UNIVAC, BURROUGHS, GE, and other manufacturers made all previously installed computers obsolete.

The compatibility problems of second-generation computers were almost eliminated in third-generation computers. However, third-generation computers were radically different from second generation equipment. The change was revolutionary, not evolutionary. This caused conversion nightmares for thousands of computer users. In time, this was written off as the price of progress.

By the mid-1960s it was apparent that almost every computer installation could expect rapid growth. An important characteristic of

FIGURE 5-12 During the second generation the IBM 1401 computer led the way to new vistas for data processing. (*Courtesy of IBM.*)

the third generation of computers was **upward compatibility**. This meant that a company could buy a computer from a particular vendor, then upgrade to a more powerful computer without having to redesign and reprogram existing information systems. Unfortunately, compatibility between computers of different vendors was and is still a problem.

Third-generation computers provide the capability to run more than one program simultaneously (**multiprogramming**). For example, at

FIGURE 5-13 The IBM System 360 series of computers formed the cornerstone of the third generation. The IBM 360 Model 50 was one of the more powerful in the System 360 series. (*Courtesy of IBM.*)

any given time the computer could be printing payroll checks, processing orders, and testing programs. Although third-generation computers continued to provide tape processing capabilities, the computer systems were developed to encourage the use of random processing and rotating magnetic disks. Random processing and magnetic disks enabled computers to process only that portion of the file that was needed. Multiprogramming and disk processing set the stage for the introduction of data communications and "on-line" systems (around 1966).

The Race Was On. Most third-generation computers were conceived and designed to be responsive to the needs of both the business and scientific communities. The name of the IBM 360 computers was derived from the "all-encompassing" 360 degrees of the circle. However, it soon became apparent to IBM and other vendors that certain market demands were not being met by their line of computers—and the race was on. There were "holes" (product demands) in the computer market when the System 360 series was introduced in 1964 and there are holes in the market now. Vendors are continually developing new and better computers to meet these demands.

As an example, after the first round of third-generation computers was introduced, small colleges and universities, scientific groups, and engineering firms were still left without a computer capable of handling their applications and priced within their budgets. They needed a small, inexpensive scientific computer. IBM saw this market need and developed a small scientific computer (see Figure 5-14). Unfortunately, it was not compatible with the System 360 line of computers and the

FIGURE 5-14 The IBM 1130 was first introduced as a relatively inexpensive scientific computer. Later the plotter (left) was replaced with a printer and the 1130 was marketed as a small business computer also. (*Courtesy of IBM.*)

naming of the computer was not as simple as assigning it a model number. Having difficulty conceiving a good name, one member of IBM's board of directors noted that it was 11:30 and time for lunch. The *IBM 1130*, as it was eventually named, not only fulfilled its initial objective, but surfaced another market need. There was an enormous market for inexpensive computers for business data processing. As an interim step, certain modifications and enhancements were made to the 1130 software so that it could be used as a data processing computer until another computer could be developed specifically for this market. Today, even though hundreds of different computers are available, vendors are still identifying requirements that are not adequately met by existing computers.

The Minicomputer. The demand for small computers in business and for scientific applications was so great that several companies manufactured only small computers. These computers became known as **minicomputers**. Data General Corporation and Digital Equipment Corporation (DEC) took an early lead in the sale and manufacture of "minis."

The 1970s. During the 1970s the most prolific line of computers was the IBM *System 370*. Each 370 computer could deliver two to five times the power of its 360 counterpart, at only a slight increase in cost. The same price/performance was evident in subsequent third-generation upgrades by other vendors (e.g., CDC's Cyber series). Getting "more bang for the buck" has become a tradition in the computer industry and is not only anticipated, but expected.

The Fourth Generation of Computers

A number of computer vendors have announced a "fourth generation of computers." This is more a marketing ploy than a reality. This is not to say that almost two decades have passed without any significant technological advances in computers. Advances have been made in the further miniaturization of circuitry, data communications, computer architecture, software, and peripheral devices. However, the fourth generation has not arrived. The fourth generation is emerging slowly in the form of computer components and in sophistication in software. Only in retrospect will the emergence of the fourth generation be pinpointed.

One of the most significant contributions to the emergence of the fourth generation of computers is the **microprocessor**. The microprocessor is a product of the micro-miniaturization of electronic circuitry. The entire computer is contained on a single silicon chip. The first fully operational microprocessor was demonstrated by Texas Instruments in 1971. Today the microprocessor is integrated into virtually every computer system component. It can be purchased for as little as a few dollars and can be found in everything from soft drink vending machines to satellites.

The **microcomputer** is a result of microprocessor technology. A small, reasonably priced computer, it opened the door to entirely new markets. Hundreds of thousands of homes and small businesses use microcomputers for personal computing and general business applications.

THE HISTORY OF SOFTWARE

Hardware and software are interdependent. Therefore, a historical perspective on one should be accompanied by a historical perspective on the other. **Software**, also called **programs**, refers to the machine-readable instructions that direct the activities of the computer.

Programming

The Stored Program Concept. The quantum leap in technology brought about by the ENIAC was offset by the cumbersome method by which the machine was programmed. The ENIAC was programmed to perform a particular set of operations by setting switches and by strategically inserting wires into a series of panels. The panels were similar to those used by the telephone operators of that period. Each time a different program was to be run, the switches would have to be reset and the wires would have to be repositioned. This task usually took several hours.

Realizing that a better method of programming was necessary to make the computer a truly general-purpose machine, Mauchly and Eckert worked with a mathematician named John Von Neumann to develop a computer that would store a program in the same manner that it stored data. The "stored program" concept enabled a computer to execute one program, then electronically load and execute another program within a matter of minutes.

Programming Languages. Today, computer operations are directed by a *program* that is written by a *programmer* in a particular *programming language*. Early programs were written in **machine language** and consisted entirely of 1's and 0's. Imagine the difficulty in keeping track of the sequence of program instructions made up entirely of 1's and 0's, not to mention the eye strain. The next language, called **assembler language,** used symbols to represent a series of 1's and 0's. Both of these languages required the programmer to write a program instruction for every operation to be performed.

The next level of languages, called **procedure-oriented languages,** allowed the programmer to write instructions that combined a number of computer operations. One instruction could direct the computer to perform several operations. Dr. Grace Hopper, a pioneer in computer programming, has been instrumental in advancing the state of the art of programming from the Mark I and the ENIAC to today. Dr. Hopper, a Navy captain, was at the helm during the development of what is now the most popular procedure-oriented language—COBOL.

Since COBOL was introduced in 1959, many languages have been developed or proposed. The trend in program language development has been to make each new language easier to use and to reduce the number of programming instructions required. The hierarchy of programming languages is discussed in detail in Chapter 9.

Programming Efficiency. The astonishing improvement in the performance of computers, coupled with an equally impressive decrease in price, has diminished the concern of programmers about being efficient in software design. When the third generation of computers was first introduced, programs had to be written and rewritten in order to fit into the very limited computer memory.

Programmers and analysts are still concerned about efficiency, but in a different way. Programs written in procedure-oriented languages can be lengthy and complex, even for the simplest programming task. Recent developments in programming languages place much of the burden of "how to do it" on the computer and other generalized software. The programmer has only to designate "what to do," not "how to do it."

This type of programming has a high **overhead** (memory and processing capacity requirements) and does not utilize the computer efficiently. It does, however, allow the programmer to make efficient use of his or her time. With hardware costs decreasing and programmer salaries increasing, computer efficiency will continue to be sacrificed to save the time of the programmer.

The Emergence of the Software Industry

Prior to the late 1960s, virtually all generalized software was supplied by the hardware vendor. Generalized software is software that is not oriented to any particular application, such as inventory management or payroll. It is designed to support *all* applications and, at the time, was included as part of the purchase price or lease agreement for the hardware. Also during this era most applications software was developed in-house, without regard to **portability** (potential to be used by another company). Consequently, the programmers and systems analysts in a typical computer center were concerned almost exclusively with applications software.

During this period there was an implied understanding that the software supplied by the vendors could not be improved. This myth quickly faded as several independent companies developed software that increased **throughput**: the amount of work that can be done by a computer per unit time. This was done through judicious scheduling of input and output. At the same time, information systems professionals and user managers realized that their problems and system needs were shared by others. **User groups** were formed to foster the sharing of ideas and software.

About this time IBM announced the **unbundling** of their products (1970). Simply stated, *unbundling* meant that previously "free" education, software, and services would be billed separately from the hardware. Prior to unbundling, IBM and other manufacturers provided software as part of the purchase or lease agreement for the hardware. Therefore, companies had little incentive to produce and market software. IBM's unbundling was the incentive the software industry needed. Overnight, the software industry was born. Today, over 1,500 software vendors market more than 10,000 products.

A CASE HISTORY—
THE HAPPY COW MILK COMPANY

The following case history of the Happy Cow Milk Company is presented for the benefit of those readers who may not have had the opportunity to experience firsthand a conversion from a manual to a computerized environment. The experience inevitably includes the depths of depression as well as the ecstasies of a maturing corporate data processing installation. The Happy Cow conversion took place over 30 years ago. A comprehensive case history would easily fill a book, but the intent of this case history is to highlight the hardware upgrades and significant activities.

The Happy Cow Milk Company was founded with five employees in a large metropolitan city in the southwestern part of the United States. Over the next 20 years the company expanded its service and became the largest milk and milk products producer in the state.

Recognized for their quality products, Happy Cow continued to grow. In 1949 the company decided to automate their manual bookkeeping procedures. They purchased an IBM 402 Electronic Accounting Machine (not a computer) and other associated unit/record equipment (sorter, card punch, and so on). The founder and president had hoped to use the EAM equipment to do the company's payroll, accounts receivable, accounts payable, and the general ledger. The IBM salesman trained four bookkeepers to wire the boards. The logic functions of all unit/record equipment were controlled by wired boards, called panels. Therefore, the logic was "hard-wired" and any change in function required a change of the panel. Three of the bookkeepers failed to grasp the art of wiring boards; however, all three eventually became excellent keypunch operators. One inexperienced person was not sufficient personpower to complete all of the panels before the arrival of the EAM equipment. The IBM saleman and several systems engineers (SEs) assisted the new DP manager at no cost, and the panels were completed on time. The boards were designed and wired during the day and tested at night at a local bank. Six months elapsed from the time the training started until the time the 402 was installed.

The president was satisfied with the relatively slow progress made towards implementing the four applications. The last of the four, the general ledger system, was finally completed in 1953. During that year the IBM 402 was upgraded to an IBM 407 Electronic Accounting Machine.

The biggest administrative headache had still not been addressed. This was route accounting, a manual system that maintained daily load, delivery, and sales information for over 200 delivery routes. The equipment required to handle the route accounting system would, in effect, double the size of the installation. The DP manager hired two more people with unit/record experience and began designing the system. Another IBM 407 arrived in 1958 but the route accounting system was never made to work properly. The DP manager told management that the route accounting system was too complex for unit/record equipment. Since all other applications were operating satisfactorily, the owner reluctantly accepted the DP manager's statement, even though he had seen an operational punched-card route accounting system in another state.

Happy Cow had a medium-to-large unit/record installation. The only way to increase their capabilities was to acquire more of the same type of equipment. This, however, was not the answer. The IBM salesman sensed a reluctance on the part of the DP manager to discuss the possibility of converting to a computer and focused his efforts on the president. The DP manager deeply resented this approach to marketing and being left out of the decision process. The IBM salesman had talked often about upgrading to a computer, but all of his arguments for justifying a computer had fallen on deaf ears until the president was told that route accounting could not be handled with existing EAM equipment. IBM had just announced the IBM 1401 computer. Happy Cow, like thousands of other unit/record users, had completely ignored the first generation of computers. The president ordered the IBM 1401 and it was scheduled for delivery in late 1961.

The DP manager was informed that he and his staff had one year to convert all existing unit/record systems to the computer. An IBM marketing representative and an IBM systems engineer helped the DP manager set up a schedule for training, systems design, programming, testing, conversion, and implementation. The schedule assumed that Happy Cow had three knowledgeable programmers. This proved to be an erroneous assumption. The DP manager and the two other people, formerly responsible for system design and the wiring of boards for U/R equipment, attended training sessions on the IBM 1401 and its programming language, AUTOCODER, at the local IBM branch office. The difference in skill requirements for wiring boards and programming was apparent when only one of the three (not the DP manager) completed the training with sufficient understanding to begin the conversion. Ironically, the two who did not understand programming had resisted the proposed conversion to a computer from the start. Experienced programmers were hard to come by and the owner was forced to go with one inexperienced programmer and two still in training.

The design of the magnetic tape-based systems fell well behind schedule and the delivery date slipped 6 months. Two more people were hired and trained as programmers, bringing the total number of data processing employees, including key punch and machine room operators, to 14. All systems were designed similarly to existing unit/record systems. Tape records remained in card image, 80 characters in length. One of the two new programmers proved to be surprisingly effective and all U/R and several new minor systems were installed in early 1963, but the route accounting system was still manual. The actual conversion took place over a period of two months with all computer systems being paralleled on the unit/record equipment. Almost a year elapsed before all major systems were operating smoothly.

In 1964, design of the route accounting system began in earnest and was completed in mid-1965. The IBM 1401 was already operating close to capacity and the data processing center had a backlog of systems to be developed. Happy Cow was about to enter the third generation.

An IBM System 360 Model 30 was installed in 1966. Since the 360 series computers did not use the AUTOCODER programming language, IBM supplied an **emulator** that, in effect, made the 360 Model 30 function like an IBM 1401. With the emulator, the new computer lost some of its efficiency, but the purpose of the emulator was to buy time for programmers to convert AUTOCODER programs to COBOL programs. With one exception, the Happy Cow DP department could not, by any stretch of the imagination, be considered a quality department. Only one of the seven programmers had exhibited a true facility for computers. For this reason, the DP staff was content to use the emulator and existing AUTOCODER programs rather than work towards converting existing systems to more efficient COBOL programs. However, the staff used COBOL for all new systems development.

Happy Cow began to outgrow the 360 Model 30 six months after installation and they ordered an IBM System 360 Model 40. It arrived in late 1967 and most of the systems were still using the 1401 emulator. The founder retired, his son took over the business, and the data processing manager was released. The new president hired a new director with eight years of computer experience (a real veteran at the time) and authorized the hiring of three more experienced programmers. The new DP manager used an IBM-supplied AUTOCODER-to-COBOL translator (a system software package that converted AUTOCODER source code to COBOL source code; less than 100% efficient, the conversion still required considerable revision and testing) to convert all 1401 systems and do away with the emulator. This process took six months.

The new president, a dynamic individual, established a four-year plan that called for expanding the Happy Cow's product line and building plants in the other two major cities in the state. The opening of plant number two coincided with the arrival of an IBM System 360 Model 50. The Model 50 was purchased to support data processing at both sites. The selection of the Model 50 followed a rigorous evaluation process in which four other vendors submitted proposals. This was the first time that Happy Cow had ever considered another vendor. The president gave serious consideration to three of the proposals before awarding the contract to IBM. The reason IBM was awarded the contract was because the other vendors did not have local service in two of the three cities in which Happy Cow also hoped to install computers.

The remoteness of the second plant (70 miles away) made daily processing difficult and untimely. The decision was made to install a 360 Model 30 at plant number two and install the route accounting and several other systems locally. Accounts receivable, accounts payable, and payroll were still handled at the home office.

With the opening of plant number three in 1971, the president and the data processing manager, also a dynamic individual, decided to draw up a five-year plan for information systems. The data processing manager was made a vice-president and the department was renamed the Management Information Systems Division. The plan called for an immediate upgrade of computers at all sites. This included an upgrade to an IBM System 370 Model 155 at the home office and System 370 Model 135s at the other plants.

The vice-president of MIS decided to take advantage of the benefits of data base software and made the decision to develop a corporate data base and convert all existing systems to IBM's IMS (Information Management System) data base system. The decision was prompted by: (1) the president's desire to go on-line with order entry, and (2) the fact that many of the existing production systems had outlived their usefulness and needed to be scrapped and completely redesigned. The 40 systems analysts and programmers at the three sites were given assignments to learn IMS and to integrate a dozen autonomous DP systems that now required over 800 programs. The commitment to IMS and integration was complete, but because of the magnitude of the task, the conversion took four years to complete.

In 1979 Happy Cow had three rather sophisticated, but nevertheless, autonomous DP centers. Enormous duplication existed between the operation of the three computer centers. The method of communication between computers was physically to exchange magnetic tapes via courier vehicle. Since the plants produced complementary products and some delivery routes overlapped, a decision was made to emphasize a larger central facility and provide data communications links to the two smaller installations. About half of the staff of each of the two smaller plants were transferred to the headquarters facility.

In 1982 Happy Cow had an IBM 3032 computer at the central site that was linked to two IBM 4331 computers. Most systems were on-line and required 112 terminals at the three sites. Two of these terminals were dedicated to exclusive use by the president, with one in his office and one at home.

Happy Cow had many hardware, conversion, people, and operational problems over their 30-year association with unit/record equipment and computers, but they and thousands of other companies with similar histories have survived and prospered.

Happy Cow is now entering the retail business and has acquired options on 50 sites in three states with the intention of opening ice cream parlors. They recently formed a hardware selection committee.

THE HISTORY OF VENDOR STRATEGIES

The driving force behind significant events in the history of computers was not innovation in new applications for computers. Nor was it innovation in software or system development techniques. It was and still is hardware. The history-making decisions born in the board rooms of the major computer systems manufacturers revolve around hardware.

Computer manufacturers have a difficult task. While responding to the needs of the industrial community, they must keep one eye on the need to turn a profit and the other on the competition. Make no mistake about it, hardware/software vendors are in a highly competitive business. To respond properly to industrial computer needs and the competition, vendors must be aware of the importance of marketing and production strategy. This strategy has been the steering wheel of the events of the past.

Survival

Throughout the first and second generation of computers, the prevailing vendor strategies were straightforward—recoup the initial investment and survive. By the mid-1960s the competition had eliminated some major and formidable vendors of computing hardware. Several of these companies gave up because of serious errors in strategy. RCA severely limited the scope of their marketing effort. GE made a tactical error by investing too much money in an idea whose time had not yet come.

The survivors developed reputations that paralleled their strategies. For example, the **architecture** (internal hardware logic) of the CDC computers was designed for scientific applications first and business applications second. On the other hand, IBM architecture was designed for business applications first and scientific applications second. DEC was content to stay in the small computer end of the market.

Trends

Through the mid-1970s vendor strategy seemed to reflect the trend to large, centralized information systems departments. Each vendor sought to provide hardware that would enable an entry-level customer to grow indefinitely. By the mid-1970s a number of computer centers had reached a size and complexity in systems and procedures that made further growth almost impossible.

In a positive response to a dead-end direction (total centralization), vendors began producing hardware and software that reflects the current trend to decentralization and distributed data processing (DDP). This strategy is designed to increase the role of the user departments (e.g., personnel, accounting, and so on) in information services activities (e.g., system design, programming, data entry, and so on).

THE TECHNOLOGY GAP

Although technological innovations will continue to dominate the direction of vendor strategies, users of this technology are becoming aware of an alarming trend. The state of the art of hardware and software technology is growing exponentially. The ability of user and IS managers to cope effectively with this technology, and thereby realize its potential, is not keeping pace. The rate of growth in management techniques is somewhat less than that of the technology. The ever-widening "technology gap" between the technology and management's ability to cope with that technology is graphically illustrated in Figure 5-15. It is uniformly recognized by executives in most corporations that, overall, the information services function is not realizing its potential. More and better hardware does not necessarily guarantee a more capable and responsive information services function.

When computers were introduced, management had several techniques that were applicable to any project-oriented environment. At that point management was actually ahead of computer technology through the first generation of computers. Since that time, amazingly little effort has been made by either the vendor or the user community to narrow the ever-widening gap between computer technology and management techniques. The technology gap was one of several reasons that vendors have adopted a strategy to manufacture and support hardware for distributed data processing. Large, centralized information services departments can become so complex that existing management techniques are not sufficient to cope with the technology.

Corporate executives and directors of information services departments may not visualize the problem as illustrated in Figure 5-15. There is, however, a growing awareness that a technology gap exists and that something must be done before the technology can be used effectively. For example, end-user involvement is a prerequisite to DDP success. An

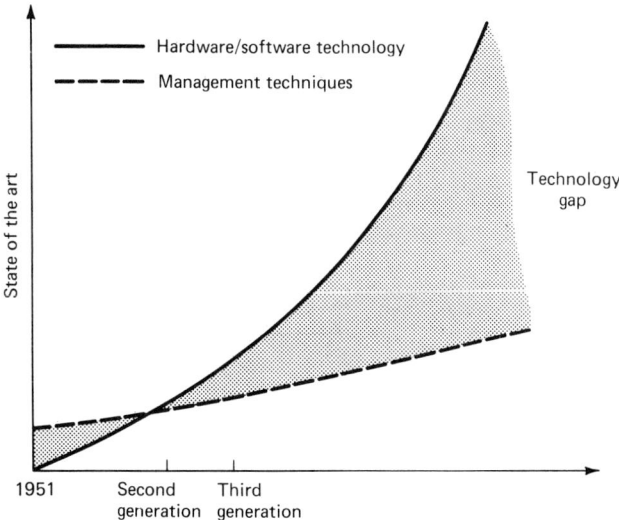

FIGURE 5-15 The technology gap.

ongoing user education program, a high-level IS steering committee, and a user-oriented system development methodology are management tools that can be used to encourage user involvement and to realize the potential of DDP. To help narrow the gap internally, IS management can integrate project management with systems development, provide for adequate and up-to-date documentation on all aspects of the IS function, and implement a vehicle for measurement of programmer/ analyst productivity. The above are just a few of the many management tools and techniques that can be used to take advantage of the benefits derived from a rapidly changing technology.

One reason that industry is 5 to 10 years behind in utilization of state-of-the-art technology is that very basic management techniques are simply not used. As awareness of the technology gap gathers momentum, industry and vendors will begin to commit their resources to narrowing the gap. The fourth generation may be realized when the technology gap disappears (see Figure 5–16).

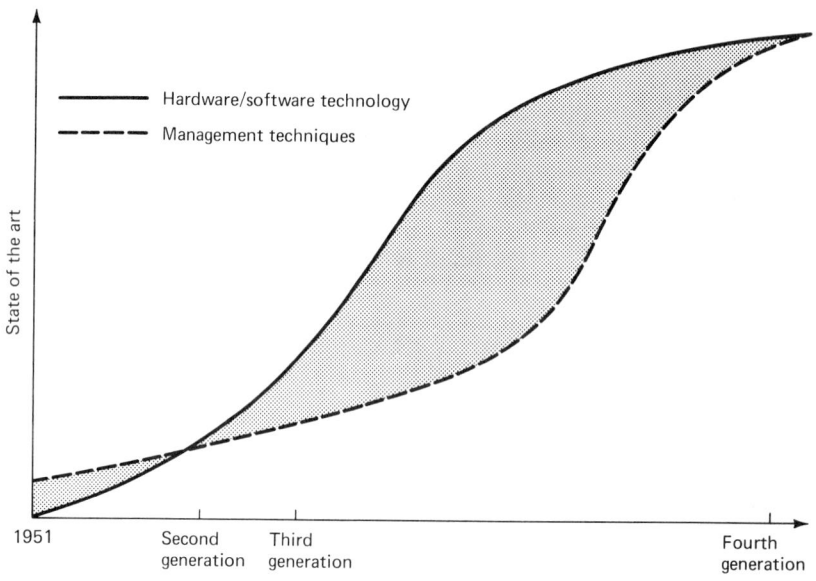

FIGURE 5-16 The technology gap extrapolated to the fourth generation.

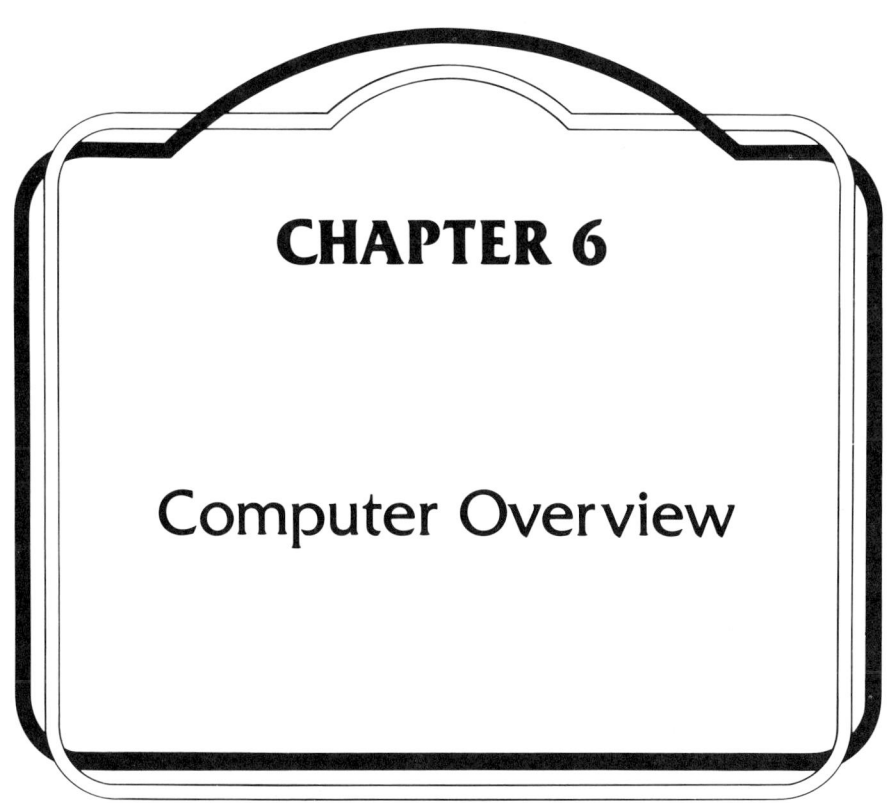

CHAPTER 6

Computer Overview

The purpose of this chapter is to provide the reader with an overview of the types of computer systems, their uses, their capabilities and limitations, and the various segments of the computer/information processing industry. Components of a computer system are discussed in detail throughout Part II, Computers and Data Management.

USES OF COMPUTERS

For the purpose of discussion, the uses of computers are presented in five categories:

1. Data processing/information services
2. Science and research
3. Process control
4. Education
5. Personal computing

These categories are not necessarily independent and will overlap when there is an opportunity for more efficient computing. For example, a process control computer may compile production data for input to a production scheduling system.

Figure 6-1 illustrates the approximate relative usage of computers by category. Process control, personal computing, and education are all expected to gain momentum and comprise a bigger share of the computer pie.

Data Processing/Information Services

The bulk of existing computer power is dedicated to data processing/information services. This category includes all uses of computers for administrative purposes. Examples include payroll systems, airline reservation systems (see Figure 6-2), university job placement systems, hospital patient billing systems, vehicle maintenance systems, office automation systems, and thousands of others. Tens of thousands of computers are dedicated to DP/information services applications and, in

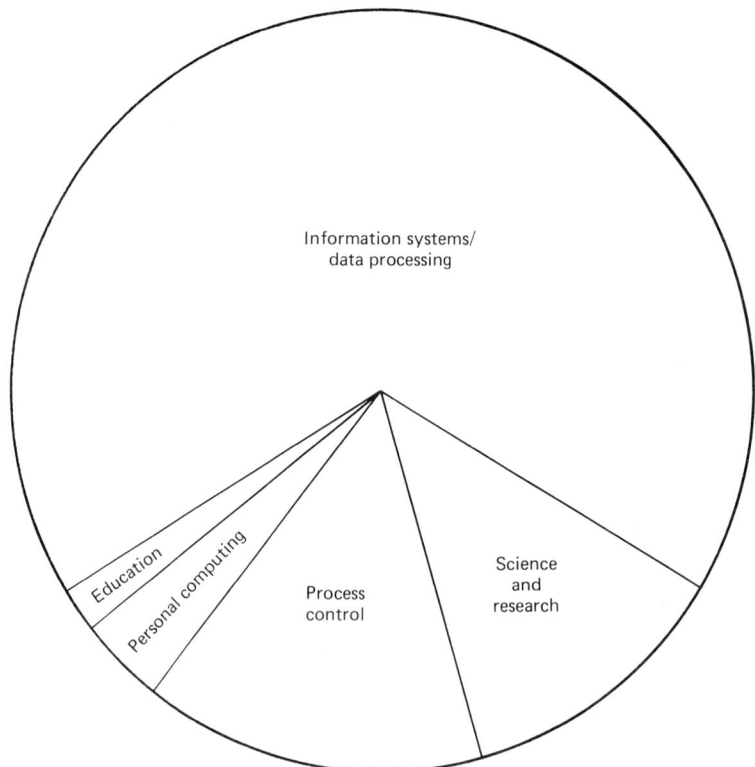

FIGURE 6-1 Approximate relative use of computers by category.

FIGURE 6-2 An airline service representative interacting with an airline reservation system. (*Courtesy of Pan Am.*)

some cases, to a single application system. The functional area manager identifies most closely with this category of computer usage.

Science and Research

Engineers and scientists routinely use the computer as a tool in experimentation and in design. Such uses might include: a chemical engineer solving a set of simultaneous differential equations to compute a rate of flow; a civil engineer analyzing the stress points in a bridge; an industrial engineer using a statistical package to investigate the interactions between number of defects and level of lighting; an operations research analyst using linear programming to optimize the location of a proposed warehouse; a physicist generating random numbers for experimental input; a draftsman using computer graphics to draw a part explosion, and so on. As computers become "user friendly," the science and research use of computers is expected to increase substantially. The accessibility problem that persisted through the 1970s has been overcome with inexpensive, dedicated computers and with remote terminals.

Process Control

Computers used for process control accept discrete and analog data in a continuous feedback loop. As the data are received (output from the process), the computer takes appropriate action to control

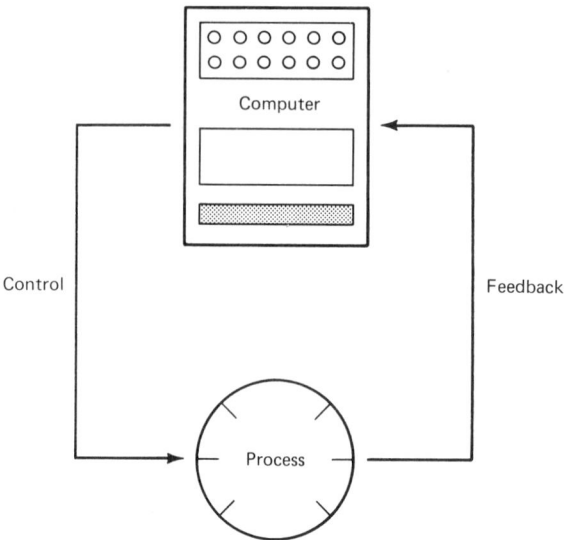

FIGURE 6-3 Process control feedback loop.

the process (see Figure 6-3). Computers used primarily for information systems can also be used for process control applications. However, vendors tend to manufacture and market computers designed specifically for process control. General-purpose process control computers can be programmed and equipped for a variety of applications. Special-purpose process control computers are manufactured for a specific application. For example, the computers used in inertial navigation systems are manufactured specifically for that application. The general-purpose process control computer can be used to monitor and control the temperature of buildings, city traffic, automobile ignition systems, machine tools (robotics), and power distribution for utility companies (see Figures 6-4 and 6-5). The number of process control applications is limited only by one's imagination.

Since process control applications are extremely cost effective, they are experiencing widespread acceptance. Even so, the use of the computer for process control is still in its infancy. Basic applications such as temperature and lighting control have yielded substantial returns on investment, but front-end costs and limited knowledge of process control have precluded potentially profitable applications from being implemented.

Education

The education category encompasses all applications where the computer is used as the vehicle by which to communicate with the learner. Figure 6-6 shows a classroom computer application. Early

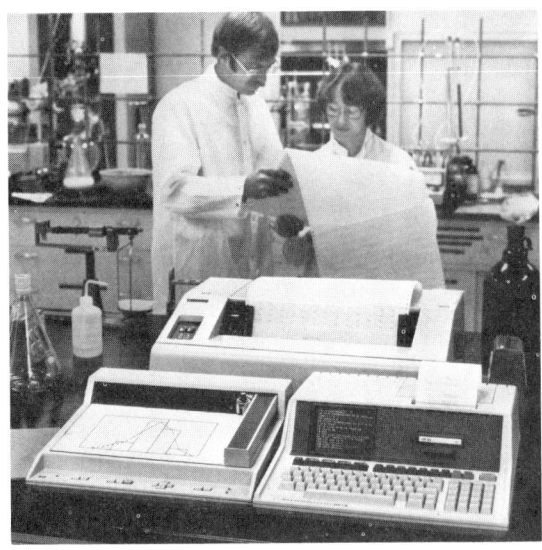

FIGURE 6-4 A small computer in a laboratory environment with a plotter, printer, and soft copy output that can be used for process control and for data collection and analysis. (*Courtesy of Hewlett-Packard Co.*)

attempts at computer-assisted instruction (CAI) were met with resistance, primarily because of the expense of the required equipment and its limited capabilities. With the advent of inexpensive hardware capable of

FIGURE 6-5 A computer at the National Meteorological Center can be used to control the temperature and humidity inside and to forecast it outside. (*Courtesy of the National Oceanic and Atmospheric Administration—NOAA.*)

FIGURE 6-6 The microcomputer is a proven learning tool and is often found in the classroom environment. (*Courtesy of Apple Computers, Inc.*)

multidimensional communication (sound, written, graphic and color) and an almost immediate response time, there is a renewed interest in CAI.

Although hardware is an important item in CAI, the ability of the person who designs the educational program is the critical factor. A good classroom teacher may not be adept at developing computer-based educational programs.

Remote terminals are becoming commonplace in the offices of users and user managers. These terminals are, of course, used primarily for production systems, but they can just as well be used as tools for education. IS personnel in many companies are developing interactive instructional programs that provide education on operational systems (as a replacement or supplement to the users manual), high-level user-oriented programming, and fundamentals of information systems. Commercial multimedia educational services companies are also developing computer-based products directed at users.

Personal Computing

Personal computing is a small but rapidly growing computer usage category. Individuals are purchasing small, inexpensive computers for fun and domestic use (see Figure 6-7). A personal computer system can

FIGURE 6-7 The microcomputer has become a common site in the home and in the office and is used for a variety of applications. (*Courtesy of Radio Shack, a division of Tandy Corporation*.)

be configured for such sophisticated business applications as general ledger and inventory management; however, most personal computer systems have a minimum configuration and are used for such basic applications as checkbook balancing, computer games, and education.

COMPUTER SYSTEMS OVERVIEW

The terms used to describe a particular class of computer systems are a point of confusion to users and IS professionals. Ask any two seasoned IS professionals to describe a minicomputer and compare their responses. Terms like microcomputer, desk-top computer, minicomputer, midicomputer, maxicomputer, and supercomputer are no longer appropriate because what may have been distinguishing characteristics in the past no longer exist. Yesterday's supercomputer may be today's minicomputer. These terms have lost their meaning since most computers can be considered full function (except special-purpose computers). A full-function computer is one that can accommodate most common peripherals (printers, disk drives, and so on) and multiple remote stations.

Even though it is relative and somewhat ambiguous, perhaps the best general classifications for computing systems are small, medium, and large. Gertrude Stein said it best: "A computer is a computer is a computer . . ." The quote may not be exact, but it is close enough.

Computers versus Computer Systems

A distinction should be made between a computer and computer systems. The computer is that portion of a computer system that interprets instructions, performs arithmetic and logic operations, and controls input from and output to the other components of the computer system (input, output, and storage devices). The computer is the "guts" of the computer system. In casual conversation, a reference to the computer is actually a reference to the computer system. A computer system is "configured" by selecting a computer and appropriate "peripheral" devices. Computer system configuration is discussed in more detail in Chapter 8 after all computer system components have been presented.

Small Computer Systems

Desk-top computers, so called "microcomputers," and stand-alone word processing systems make up the low end of the small computer classification. These are physically small (all can fit comfortably on the top of a desk) and are also relatively small in capabilities. These and all entry-level computers are called small computers. Depending on the manufacturer, some second and third-level computers are also classified as "small." For larger computers, it becomes a matter of personal preference as to whether to classify a computer as small or medium. The large computer of the late 1960s had about the same power as a "high-end" small computer of today.

The desk-top computer literally applies to any computer that can be conveniently placed on a table or desk. Microcomputers are desk-top computers. In most desk-top computers, the computer is combined with the memory, video display unit, and keyboard in a single unit. Some manufacturers combine the diskette(s) and even the printer in the same unit.

The microcomputer derived its name from the fact that the entire computer was contained on a single circuit board (a silicon chip called a microprocessor). Because many "micros" have expanded functions and require several circuit boards, the "micro" label is somewhat misleading.

Stand-alone word processing systems are simply single-application, small computer systems. Word processing is just another application of computer technology. It has been presented as a revolutionary new concept in office automation by those who stand to gain from not having it associated with information systems and computers. A typical stand-alone word processing system consists of a small computer, one or two diskettes, a video display unit, a high-quality printer, and a software package for text processing.

Other than being slower, small computers have most of the operational capabilities of computers a hundred times faster. Small computer systems can be used as stand-alone computer systems or as terminals in computer networks where they are linked to a larger "host" computer. A small computer may support one, or even several, on-line information systems and perhaps some interactive program development. But any further on-line requirements would require an upgrade to a medium-sized computer.

As an example, the computer system configured in Figure 6-8 would be considered on the high end of the small computer systems classification. This system supports a 20 million dollar light manufacturing firm with all of the standard computer-based information systems, including an on-line order entry system. Half of the applications use a data base management system which is a subset of one used by larger computer systems. The other computer system components illustrated in Figure 6-8 are discussed in detail in Chapter 7. A small computer system is illustrated in Figure 6-9.

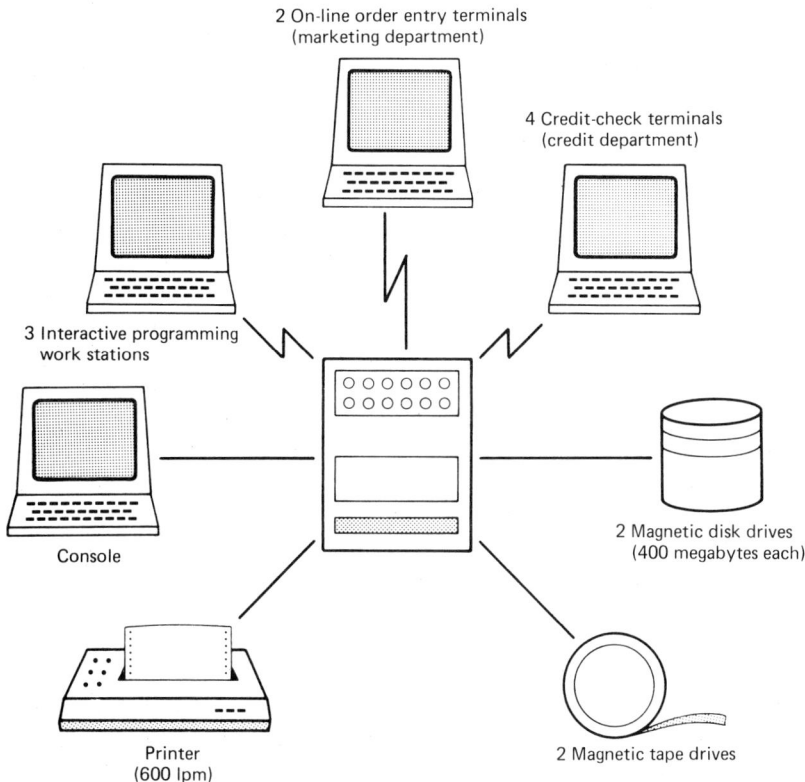

FIGURE 6-8 A small computer system (high-end). The host is two steps up from the entry level.

FIGURE 6-9 A small computer system. (*Courtesy of IBM.*)

Large Computer Systems

Any one (or more) of the top three to five computers in a major manufacturer's line of computers would be used to form the nucleus of a large computer system. It should be noted that several vendors only manufacture large-scale computers. The speed of a large computer enables more and faster peripherals to be attached and the most sophisticated software to be executed.

A large computer system is usually a network of computers. A large host computer is connected to several small computer systems that are used to off-load certain processing functions (data communications interface, and data retrieval and manipulation) from the host.

At this level of sophistication there are no typical large computer systems because these systems are tailored to meet the demands of a large corporation. Figure 6-10 illustrates the configuration of a computer system that would be considered on the low end of what would be considered a large computer system. The magnitude of a very large computer system is seen in Figure 6-11.

Medium-Sized Computer Systems

Small and large computer systems are much more readily indentifiable than medium-sized computer systems. Medium-sized systems are those which do not seem to fit in either the small or the large computer

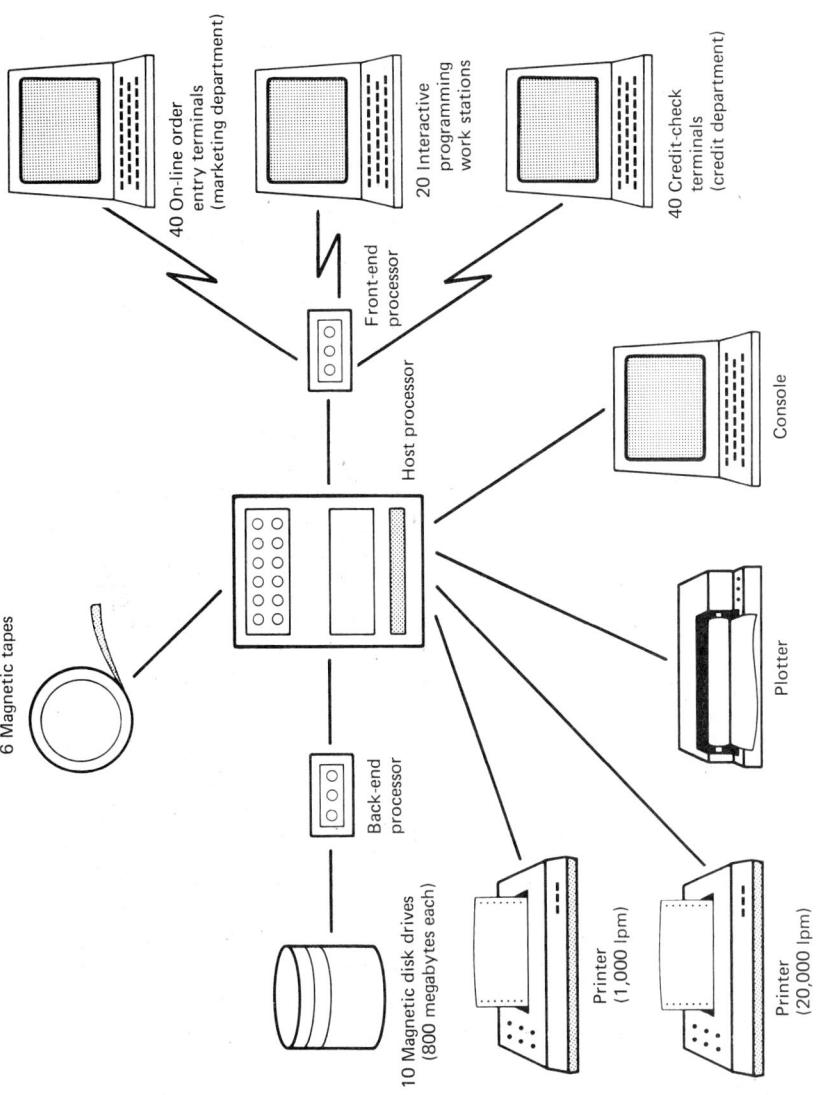

FIGURE 6-10 A large computer system (low-end).

111

FIGURE 6-11 A large computer system. (*Courtesy of IBM.*)

system classification. Figure 6–12 is an example of the medium-sized system category.

INTEGRATED COMPUTER NETWORKS

Through the mid-1970s, a company could get more "bang for the buck" by purchasing large computer systems. This is not necessarily true today. Companies are linking small, medium, and large computers to form integrated computer networks. In this way computers can be decentral-

FIGURE 6-12 A medium-sized computer system. (*Courtesy of IBM.*)

ized and moved closer to the people that use them. The concept of integrated computer networks is often referred to as **distributed data processing (DDP)**. DDP is also an organizational concept and is discussed in Chapter 3.

Most distributed data processing systems will have a host computer that maintains the corporate-wide data base and services those departments that do not have their own computer system. **Distributed computer systems**, usually located in the functional areas, are entirely self-contained and have all the necessary software and hardware to operate as stand-alone computer systems. Approaches to the distribution of computer systems are presented in Chapter 10.

SPECIAL-PURPOSE COMPUTERS

Up to this point the discussion has centered on those computer systems with the flexibility to do a variety of tasks: computer assisted education, payroll, climate control, and so on. These are called **general-purpose computers**. A **special-purpose computer** is architecturally the same as a general-purpose computer except that it is "dedicated" to a specific application.

Special-purpose computers would generally fall in the small computer classification. They are installed in aircraft to aid in navigation and general flight control. They are used for materials handling in warehouses to select and move containers without human intervention.

Most special-purpose computer systems are used for process control. However, they are also found in information systems/data processing applications. For example, a stand-alone word processing system is simply a small computer system that is dedicated to the word processing application.

An important point to be made is that a special-purpose computer is just another computer system. What makes it unique is its dedication to one application and the special input/output interfaces required for that application. The following sections describe several applications for special-purpose computers.

Computer-Aided Design

Computer-aided design (CAD) has revolutionized the way in which engineers design a product. A CAD system consists of a computer, a graphics terminal, and a plotter. An engineer can design a part at the terminal and produce the blueprint automatically on a plotter. By working in two or three dimensions, an engineer can manipulate the design to the desired specifications. Some CAD systems provide the added dimension of color graphics.

Robotics

Special-purpose computers are used to control industrial **robots**. This integration of computers and industrial robots is called **robotics**. The most common industrial robot is a single mechanical arm that is controlled by a computer. The arm, called a *manipulator*, is capable of performing those motions of a human arm. The manipulator is fitted with a "hand" that is designed for each specific task, such as painting, welding, moving parts, and so on. An industrial robot is best at repetitive tasks, moving heavy loads, and working in hazardous areas.

A computer program is written to control the robot just as a program is written to print payroll checks. The robot performs the movements depicted by the program being executed by the robot's computer. The program includes such commands as when to reach, where to reach, when to grasp, and so on.

Computer-Aided Manufacturing

Computer-aided manufacturing (CAM) is a term that was coined to highlight the use of computers in the manufacturing process. There are literally thousands of uses for special-purpose computers in the manufacturing environment. Robots and computer-aided design are typical CAM applications. The movements of **numerically controlled (NC) machine tools** are also programmed and controlled by a computer. The machine tool could be a lathe, a drill, a milling machine, or almost any tool used in the manufacture of parts.

Other CAM applications for special-purpose computer systems include materials handling and assembly line control.

Integrated CAD/CAM

The integration of the computer and manufacturing is called **integrated CAD/CAM**. In integrated CAD/CAM the computer is used at every stage of the manufacturing process. The various computer systems are connected and feed data to one another to maintain continued operation. The computer is part of the manufacturing process from the time the part is conceived until it is shipped. An engineer uses a CAD system to design the part and produce an "electronic data base" of design specifications. The specifications are input to another computer system that generates programs to control the robots and numerically controlled machine tools.

Integrated CAD/CAM actually goes one step further than the finished part. The special-purpose process control computers can be linked to the company's general-purpose information systems computers. The process control computers provide input to order processing, inventory management, shop floor scheduling, and general accounting.

GENERAL CAPABILITIES AND LIMITATIONS
OF THE COMPUTER

Before making a decision to computerize a particular function, a user manager consciously or unconsciously compares the existing manual system to the capabilities and limitations of a computer-based system. The following discussion is presented as a guide for comparison.

Capabilities

Speed. Even small computer operations (execution of an instruction) are measured in milliseconds (thousandths of a second). Larger computer operations are measured in microseconds, nanoseconds, and picoseconds (one millionth, one billionth, and one trillionth of a second, respectively). The computer's speed in the handling of repetitive tasks and the manipulation of alphanumeric data is unquestioned.

Accuracy. An IS professional may work for 10 years before experiencing a system error (update wrong record, incorrect addition, and so on) that is directly attributable to the computer system. Although the IS professional may examine the cause of hundreds of errors, only in the most isolated instances can these errors be attributed to other than procedural or program logic error (both human errors). Hardware errors are usually detected by the computer system and brought to the attention of the operator immediately. If a production information system is in any way affected by a hardware error (failure), the malfunction is corrected before any output is distributed to the user.

Reliability. Although computers do not take sick days and coffee breaks, they do need preventive maintenance (P.M.). Periodic preventive maintenance (perhaps one hour per week) comprises the major portion of a computer system's downtime. Anything below 99% uptime is usually unacceptable. Unfortunately, downtime sometimes occurs at the most inconvenient times. A company may minimize the effect of downtime and increase reliability by decentralizing. In a decentralized environment, if one computer goes down, the others are still operational. In a centralized environment, even short periods of downtime can have significant effects on corporate operation.

Memory capacity. Computer systems have total and instant recall of data and an almost unlimited capacity to store it. On-line storage of data (data directly accessible to the computer) is limited, but off-line storage (e.g., magnetic tape reels) is, for all practical purposes, unlimited.

Limitations

Inflexibility. There are many aspects of a computer-based information system that lend credence to the charge that computers are inflexible. In a manual system, the boss can simply direct a couple of administrative assistants to drop their routine Thursday morning tasks in favor of a higher-priority job. A scheduled production run on a computer can also be rescheduled, but usually at a high cost to available person-power and computer resources. As another example, the boss might ask the assistant to underline the names of all salespersons under quota on the weekly sales reports. This simple task could be accomplished in minutes in a manual environment. Such a request for a computer-based information system would require approval, reprogramming, and testing. Computers have no innate intelligence and accomplish no task unless specifically directed to do so.

Complexity. The complexity limitation is overrated. Computers and information systems are not complex at the user manager/executive level. The user manager reading and understanding the contents of this book will acquire the knowledge necessary to eliminate "complexity" as a limitation.

Cost. The cost limitation is also overrated. Computer systems are implemented because they, in some way, contribute to corporate profit. The front-end investment is usually the primary obstacle, even though the payback period may be as little as one year and seldom more than four. With computer power becoming less expensive each year, computers remain one of the best investments a corporation can make. However, this investment should never be made unless the expenditure can be offset by an equal or greater contribution to profit.

SCOPE OF THE COMPUTER INDUSTRY

Relative to the other more established industries, the computer industry is a mere babe in arms. Since its humble beginnings in 1951, thousands of companies have been formed either to manufacture computers or computer components, or to provide some type of material or services support. User managers and especially corporate officers should be aware of the scope of the industry and the variety and type of companies that comprise the industry. Even the small company will have regular dealings with at least half of the computer-related businesses listed below. Therefore, corporate management should know the difference between PCMs and OEMs.

The scope of the computer industry is described below in 14 separate business classifications. A particular corporation, depending upon the equipment, materials, and services offered, may fit into several of these business classifications. For example, Control Data Corporation markets computers and software and provides consulting and education services.

Computer systems manufacturers. These companies manufacture computers. Most manufacture not only the computer (also called the central processing unit, CPU, processor, and main frame), but also some or all of the peripheral equipment necessary for configuring a computer system. Most of these manufacturers market and service the hardware they sell, but several major manufacturers market their products through a middleman. Companies in this classification range in size from the hobbyist, who assembles and sells three computers a year, to IBM.

Leasing companies. Most computers are available for purchase or lease. The monthly rental of a computer system is roughly based on what the monthly payments would be if the computer were purchased over a period of four years. Leasing companies purchase computers primarily from the manufacturers. They then lease these computers at a monthly rental that is less than that of the manufacturer. The leasing company profits by keeping computers under contract and in commission for five or more years. To make this arrangement profitable for all concerned, both client and leasing company must accept some risk. Since lease agreements are usually long term, the client must accept the risk of the computer becoming economically obsolete. The leasing company accepts a similar risk. If the manufacturer announces a line of computers with twice the power at half the cost before the initial investment is recouped, the leasing company must substantially reduce the monthly rentals on those machines not under contract and hope to minimize their losses. In the trade, leasing companies are referred to as the "third party."

Peripheral manufacturers (plug compatible). Plug-compatible manufacturers (PCMs) manufacture peripheral devices that can be attached directly to another manufacturer's computer. A PCM might manufacture disk drives and tape drives that operate and sometimes look like those marketed by the computer manufacturer. These devices are called "plug compatible." A PCM disk drive can replace a disk drive made by the computer manufacturer (usually IBM) by simply unplugging one and plugging in another. As a rule, plug-compatible equipment is less expensive than that of the computer manufacturer.

Supplies and accessories companies. There are vast arrays of supplies and accessories needed to support computers and information processing. Consumable supplies include stock and preprinted paper, punched cards, magnetic tapes, and so on. Accessories may include special folders for storing computer printouts, racks built specifically to hold magnetic tapes and disks, and special tables for interactive terminals. Companies in the supplies and accessory classification use retail outlets, field marketing representatives, and mail order to distribute their products.

Software houses. The product of a software house is the software and accompanying documentation for a particular computer-based system (financial accounting system, job scheduling system, and so on). These **proprietary software packages** are the property of the software house and are marketed to industry, government, and education. A client obtains a license agreement to use a particular product. The license agreement can be both purchased and leased. The systems developed by software houses are somewhat generic in that the end product must be applicable to a number of environments.

Information systems service bureaus. Information systems servide bureaus (usually called "service bureaus") provide almost any kind of information processing services. These services include, but are not limited to, developing information systems, providing computer time, data reduction, and general system documentation.

Methods and procedures companies. These companies develop and market methods, techniques, and procedures that are applicable to the IS environment. These are usually marketed in the form of camera-ready manuals. Some are accompanied by supporting software. Product examples include system development methodologies, project management and control systems, and IS career development programs.

Original equipment manufacturers (OEM). The OEM is the supplier, not the manufacturer, of small computer systems. They purchase the equipment from the manufacturer and market it to the general public, usually after adding some value to the system in the form of software. OEMs cater to those computer manufacturers that do not have a marketing or distribution network.

Turnkey companies. A turnkey company installs a complete "turnkey system," both hardware and software, with minimum personnel involvement from the purchasing company. Rather than purchase the hardware and software separately and install an information system themselves, a company may contract with a turnkey company to handle everything. The deliverable is a working system or group of systems.

Computer retail outlets. Retail outlets for new and used computers, and computer-related equipment are a recent phenomenon. They were originally opened for the personal computer market but have expanded their scope of services to include small computer systems. Retail outlets service the equipment they sell and offer consulting, education, and software services as well.

Data communications networks. The vehicle through which data are transferred between remote points is provided by data communications carriers. Although data are transmitted via satellite, lasers, microwave, and other means, the primary mode of data transmission is still the telephone network. A particular company can lease a communications link from New York City to Chicago that is capable of transmitting a certain amount of data per unit time (baud rate). Once leased, this line is dedicated to the leasee. A single company will have difficulty utilizing more than 15% of the leased line's capacity. Some **value-added networks** (VANs) have emerged to exploit this under-utilization. VANs lease lines from common carriers and, in turn, provide data communications capabilities at a lower cost. They do this by allowing two or more companies to share the same communication channel and thereby use the line more efficiently.

Facilities management companies. Facilities management companies offer an alternative to those companies that would like to have an internal information systems organization but do not want the responsibility of managing it. Facilities management services come in a variety of formats. Their services are often sought after corporate management becomes disillusioned and/or dissatisfied with their existing IS management and operation. A contract is signed whereby the facilities management company would offer any one or a combination of the following services: IS management team only, professional personnel (programmers and analysts), operations personnel, software packages, and/or hardware. These companies tend to specialize in a few specific fields such as health care, education, banking, and so on.

Time-sharing services. These companies sell computer time. The name is derived from the fact that clients "share" time and software on a central computer owned and operated by the time-sharing company. The typical client will "log on" (or make a connection) to the time-sharing service computer from a remote terminal. The client might use available software packages, disk space, and computer time and is charged for each according to use. Time-sharing services are used by those companies having a need for some computer usage but not enough to justify a computer; by those companies needing specialized software packages; and by those companies needing supplemental computer capacity.

Word processing companies. Word processing (WP) companies should not actually be a separate business classification since WP is simply another application of computers. Nevertheless, a group of companies dedicated to office automation, and specifically WP, have emerged and should be recognized. These companies manufacture and sell WP computers and associated equipment, develop WP software, and provide office automation consulting. In an attempt to disassociate themselves from computer systems manufacturers, software houses, and consulting firms, WP companies tend to play down the fact that they use computers. These companies would more appropriately be classified as computer-systems manufacturers, software houses, and consulting companies.

Consulting companies. Consultants contract with companies to provide advice relating to information services. Consulting companies have a broader range of quality of service than do the other business classifications. There are relatively few pure IS consulting companies. Most complement their consulting with contract systems design and programming services or provide other non-IS related services (e.g., auditing, management consulting). See Chapter 3 for details on the role of IS consultants.

Education. There is a constant need for IS professionals and users to update their education. This need has spawned a number of companies that provide IS education services. These services are packaged in the form of public seminars, in-house seminars, and multimedia self-paced courses. The number of companies in this field has grown so rapidly that several companies have been formed which do nothing but keep track of IS educational activity and offerings.

Publishers of information services materials. Most major publishers publish books in the computer/information processing area, but this classification refers to those companies whose products are directed exclusively to IS professionals. These companies are of two types. The first publishes journals, periodicals, and/or newspapers, and the second publishes reports and studies that are periodically updated with the technology.

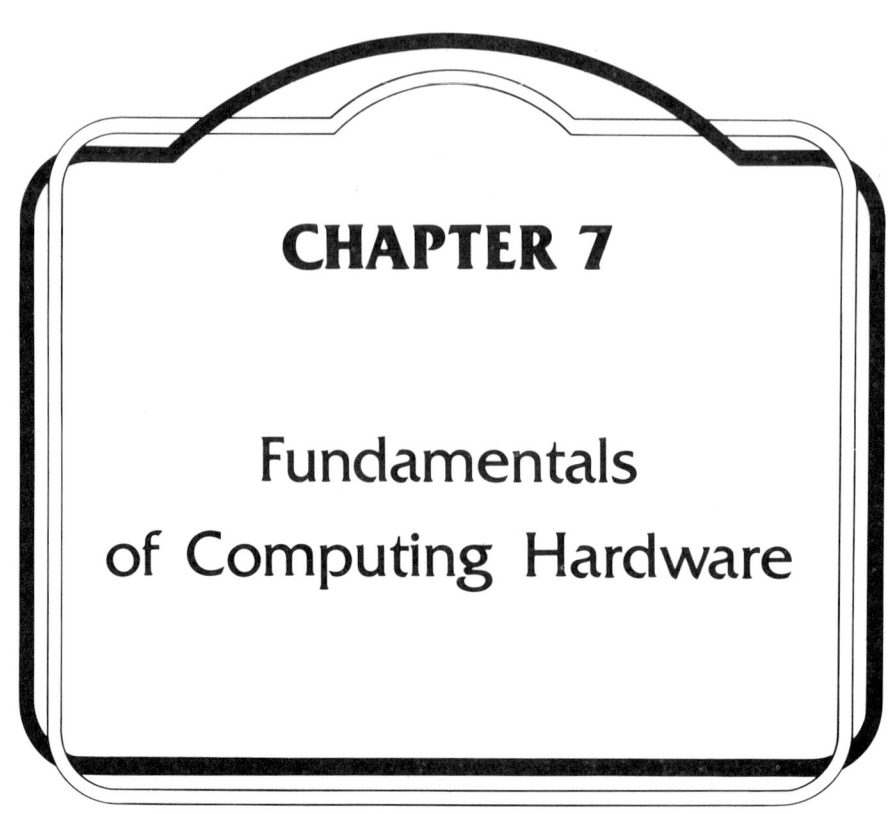

CHAPTER 7

Fundamentals
of Computing Hardware

This chapter is devoted to discussing the fundamentals of computing hardware, considerations of computer systems configuration, and the hardware evaluation and selection process. Hardware refers to the equipment in a computer system. For the purpose of discussion, hardware is classified in the following categories: the computer, data reduction and collection devices, input/output devices, data storage devices, and data communications devices.

BASIC COMPONENTS
OF A COMPUTER SYSTEM

Figure 7-1 illustrates the basic components of a computer system: input, processing, output, and data storage (primary and secondary). Machine-readable data are "input" from a peripheral device to primary storage (usually considered part of the computer). "Output" is data transmitted from primary storage to a peripheral device. Peripheral devices can be input only (e.g., card reader), output only (e.g., line printer), or both (e.g.,

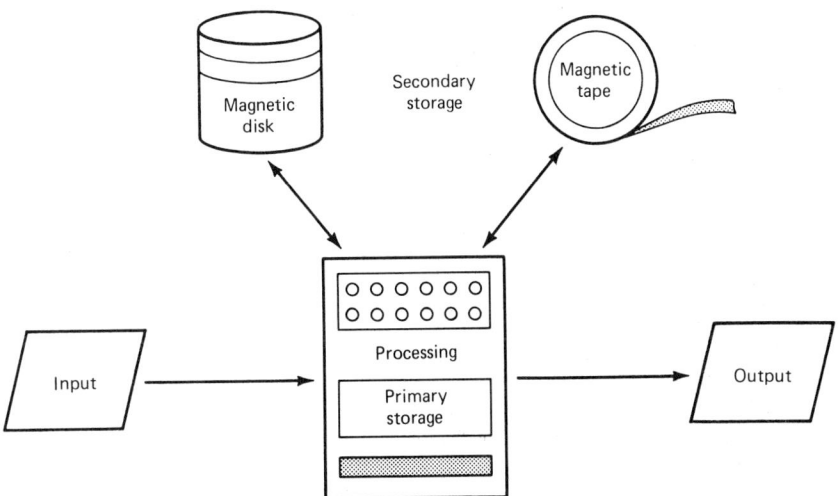

FIGURE 7-1 The basic components of a computer system.

magnetic disk drives). Input data are said to be "read" and output data is said to be "written." Permanent data files are stored on secondary storage media (magnetic disks, magnetic tapes) and must be mounted on the appropriate drives to be processed.

A record (such as Juanita Barthel's payroll record) must be read from the secondary storage device to primary storage before the record can be processed. The computer makes programmed changes to the record and/or prepares the record for output to other peripheral devices. If any changes are made to the record, the record is written back to the permanent file on the secondary storage device in its altered state. *All input and output (I/O) must be read to or written from primary storage in order to be processed.*

Conceptually, a computer system is no more complicated than the above discussion. The technical aspects of how these devices achieve this interaction can be extremely complex, but the complex aspects are not of concern to the users. The user, however, should have a basic awareness of hardware capabilities, limitations, and functions in order to give informed input to the system analysis and design process. The following hardware discussion is presented with this objective in mind.

THE COMPUTER

There may be one or several computers in a given computer system. The primary computer that controls the activities of subordinate computers is called the **central processing unit (CPU)**, the **host**, or the **mainframe** computer.

The CPU executes only one instruction at a time, even though it appears to be handling many tasks simultaneously. At any given time, several tasks will compete for CPU time. One will be given priority and the others will have to wait. The CPU rotates between competing tasks so quickly that there is a seemingly simultaneous execution of all tasks; however, this continuous rotation between task requirements takes its toll on computer efficiency. In order to improve efficiency, other **processors** (another term for computers) are strategically placed in the computer system to off-load certain administrative tasks (such as checking all data to ensure that it was accurately transmitted). Figure 7-2 illustrates how some of the more common subordinate processors fit into a computer system configuration. Each of these processors and their functions are discussed in the following paragraphs.

Front-end processors relieve host computers of communications-related duties. For example, before the host computer receives any remote data, the front-end processor translates the coded data to a format recognized by the host and checks for transmission errors. The front-end processor also establishes the data link between the remote terminal and the host computer and maintains **traffic** statistics. Traffic refers to the amount of data being transmitted over a communications link.

The **back-end processor** handles all administrative chores associated with retrieval and manipulation of data stored on secondary storage devices. For example, the CPU directs the back-end processor to retrieve a particular employee's record. The back-end processor accomplishes all tasks necessary to retrieve the record and transmit it to the CPU for processing.

The **down-line processor** is an extension of the front-end processor. Its name is derived from its physical location. It is located "down-line" at, or near, a remote site. The down-line processor formats and prepares the input from several remote stations, then transmits it to the front-end processor. The down-line processor also receives and distributes output. This type of configuration is used to achieve a more efficient transmission line utilization.

The **distributed processor** is an extension of the CPU or host. Distributed processors are the nuclei of small computer systems dedicated to information systems production processing and are "distributed" to the functional areas. They may also have subordinate processors like the front-end processor.

The **parallel processor** is itself a host and serves to augment the processing capability of the other host and to provide backup capability. The parallel and host processor share the same peripherals and subordinate computers.

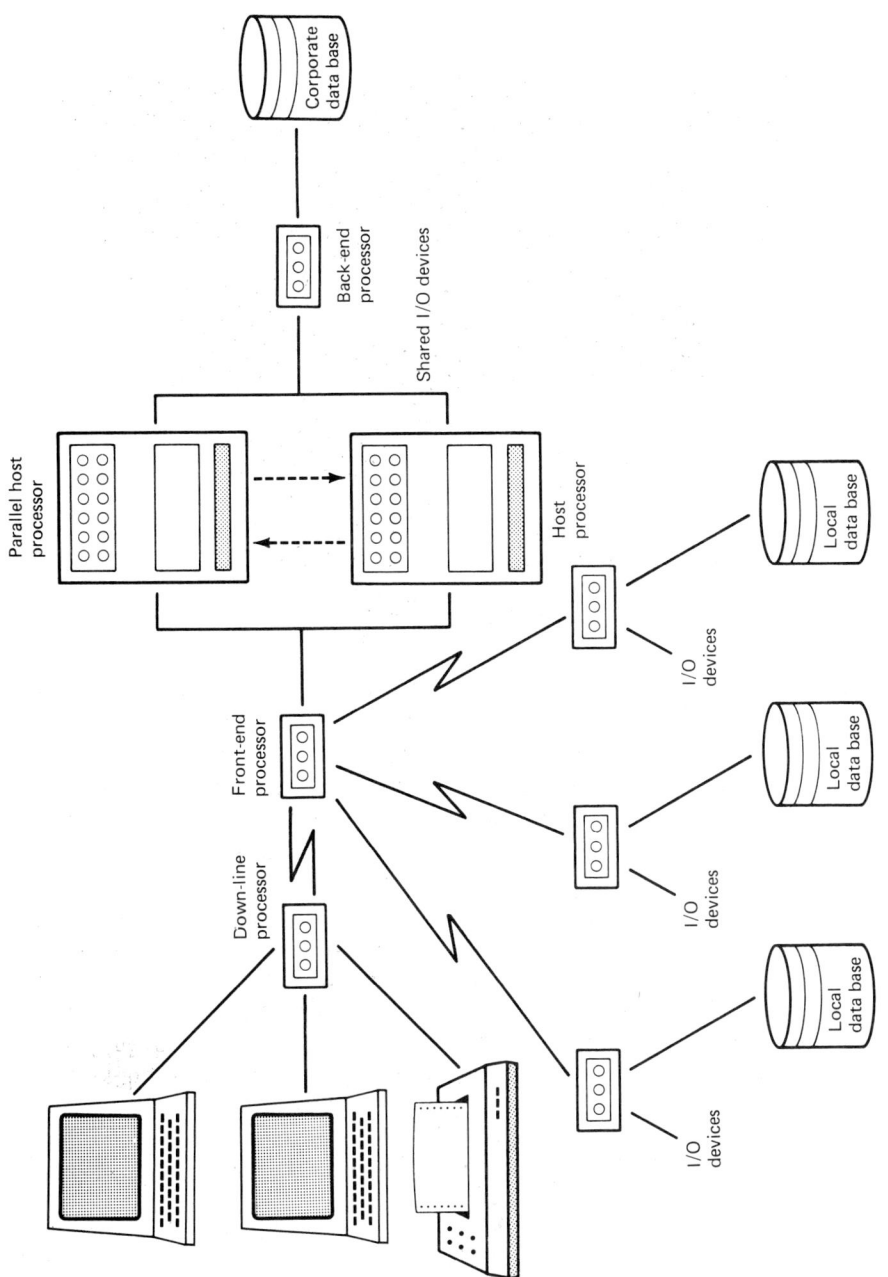

FIGURE 7-2 Host and subordinate processors.

125

A computer system can be configured with none or all of the subordinate computers shown in Figure 7-2. Circumstances dictate which, if any, of the processors should be included.

Parameters Used to Describe Processors

A technical description describing the features and options for any given computer is complex and of little value to a user manager (and most IS professionals). But a general description is helpful for putting a computer's capacity into perspective. In general, a computer (or processor) is described in terms of its *speed* and the *size* of its primary storage.

Speed. Unfortunately, there is no standard measure of computer speed (used interchangeably with power and capacity). If speed is the performance criteria upon which you are basing a decision for a new automobile, one vendor can state with reasonable assurance that a particular automobile can attain a speed of 100 miles per hour. Another vendor can claim that his automobile has a top end of 130 miles per hour. These vendor performance ratings are easily verifiable. This is not the case with computers.

KOPS (thousands of operations per second) or **MIPS** (millions of instructions per second) are commonly accepted but flawed measurements of computer capacity. They are accepted by default—so far no one has come up with anything better.

The KOPS rating is derived by testing the speed at which a given computer can execute a typical mix of jobs. The MIPS rating is derived by simply measuring the number of instructions executed per second under optimum circumstances. The MIPS measurement favors computers that are oriented to scientific work. The KOPS measurement favors those oriented to information systems.

In the single processor batch environment of the 1960s, KOPS and MIPS were a reasonably valid means of comparison. Today, complicated data communications-based computer systems with numerous subordinate processors provide an almost infinite number of configuration possibilities. This effectively eliminates any possibility of valid computer-to-computer comparisons. For this reason, user managers and executives, especially those involved in hardware selection, should put MIPS and KOPS in perspective and use them only as a gross measure of computer capacity. A decision to select one computer over another should never be based on KOPS or MIPS.

Memory Size. The other parameter used to describe computers is the size of primary storage (also called **core, main memory,** and memory). Memory size affects the computer in that a lack of memory may not permit a computer to operate at capacity performance. Memory is also a very ambiguous describer of computers. First of all, memory is not technically part of the computer. Nevertheless, speed and memory size are always stated together when describing computers. Memory size is stated in terms of the number of "bytes" or "words." For purposes of illustration, the byte is roughly equivalent to a character (e.g., "A," "1") and a word is made up of from 1 to 10 characters depending upon the type of computer. Since different computers use different methods to store characters, and since bytes and words vary in size, memory size must be qualified each time it is stated (e.g., 512,000 60-bit words, 10 characters/word).

Memory is stated in terms of "K" (a convenient designation for 1024 bytes or characters of storage). A computer might have 256K bytes of main memory and another computer might have 30K words of main memory. If the latter could store 10 bytes to the word, the computer is said to have 300K bytes of main memory. Ironically, it is still possible for the 256K computer to have more memory than the 300K computer; therefore, the bytes would have to be qualified. There are no marginal returns for the user manager knowing this extra level of qualification. The byte-level comparison, though not perfectly accurate, is close enough for most evaluation purposes.

Sections of the Processor

The user manager can live a long and healthy life without a thorough or even a fundamental understanding of computer architecture (internal components and their functions). However, a basic understanding of the terminology and concepts of computer architecture helps to remove the mystique surrounding the computer. Armed with this understanding, a user manager is more comfortable when interacting with IS personnel. Although computer architecture and its nomenclature vary considerably between vendors, the basic components are the control section, the arithmetic and logic section, the main memory, and the input/ouput section.

Control Section. The control section reads and interprets program instructions (e.g., add 5.236 to the contents of main memory location 420 and store the sum in the same location) and directs the appropriate component to perform the operation. **Synchronous** computers proceed with the execution of the next and subsequent instructions at a predetermined rate. **Asynchronous** computers proceed to the next instruction only after the current instruction has been executed. Synchronous computers are the higher-speed computers.

Arithmetic and Logic Section. The arithmetic and logic section performs all arithmetic calculations and logic operations. The numbers of alphanumeric data to be operated on are moved to an **accumulator**. It is in the accumulator that the computation or comparison is made. These operations are done in binary form, the numbering system of computers, and are ultimately translated to decimal form upon output. Examples of arithmetic operations include the computation of social security tax, day-end inventory, and so on. Examples of logic operations include determining whether Smith alphabetically precedes Smyth, or whether the inventory level has fallen below the reorder point.

Main Memory. Even though main memory or primary storage can be treated as a separate hardware unit, for all practical purposes it is considered a computer component. All programs and data must reside in main memory before programs can be executed or data can be manipulated. It was previously mentioned, but it should be reemphasized, that all I/O must be read to or written from main memory in order to be processed. A program instruction or a piece of data is stored in a specific main memory location. Each location has an **address** by which the instruction or data can be found, accessed, and processed. Main memory technology is illustrated in Figures 7-3 and 7-4.

Input/Output Section. The input/output section controls the flow of data in and out of main memory. Data channels, or paths for data transmission, are connected to the I/O section. The input/output section is sometimes considered an extension of the control section.

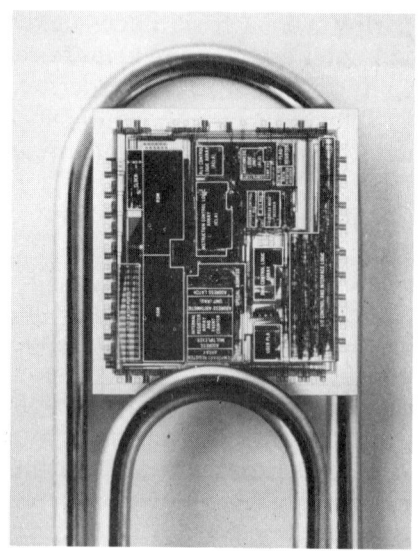

FIGURE 7-3 This microprocessor chip contains all of the different sections of the computer including main memory (labeled RAM and ROM). (*Courtesy of Bell Telephone Laboratories.*)

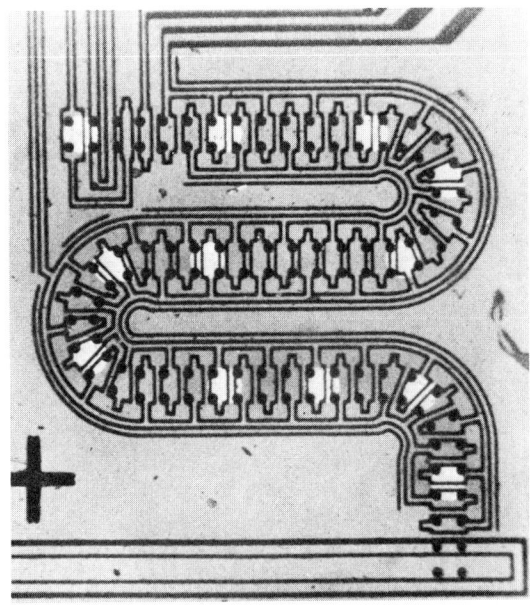

FIGURE 7-4 This bubble memory circuit is the state of the art in primary storage. (*Courtesy of Bell Telephone Laboratories.*)

Computer Operation

Figure 7-5 illustrates the fundamental operation of a computer by showing the interaction between the computer components. The example illustrates how a number (value = 2) can be added to an existing total (value = 10) in main memory location *eight* and outputted. The steps are as follows:

STEP 1. A number is entered on the keyboard of a video display unit (in this case, value = 2) and stored in main memory location *one.*

STEP 2. The 2 in location *one* is moved to the *accumulator* (value = 5, from a previous operation). The 2 remains in storage location *one* and the 5 in the *accumulator* is destroyed. The value of the *accumulator* becomes 2.

STEP 3. The total in location *eight* (value = 10) is added to the contents of the *accumulator* (value = 2). The addition of 10 to the contents of the *accumulator* (value = 2) changes the contents of the *accumulator* to 12.

STEP 4. The contents of the *accumulator* (value = 12) is moved to main memory location *eight* for output. The 12 cannot be outputted directly from the *accumulator.*

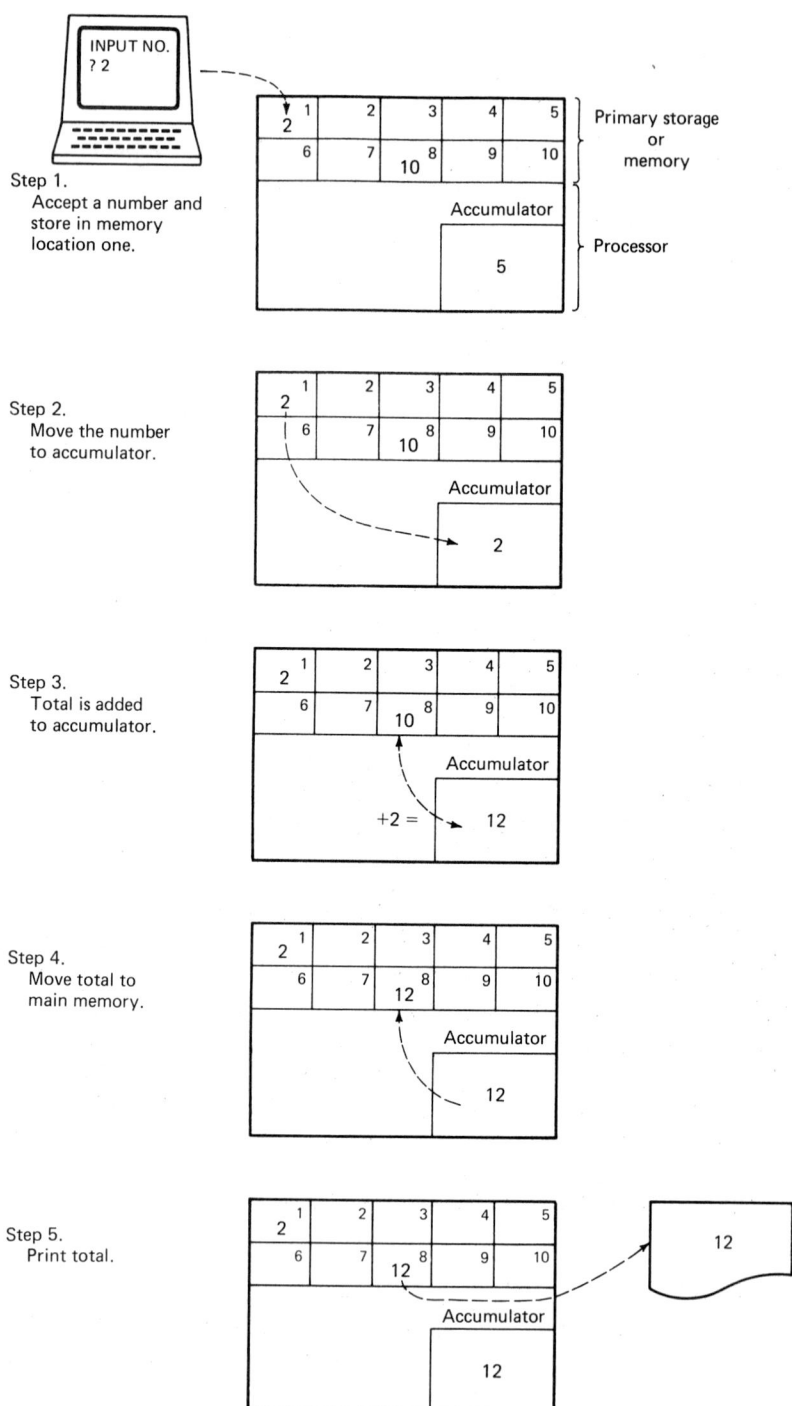

FIGURE 7-5 Computer operation.

STEP 5. The contents of main memory location *eight* (value = 12) is outputted to the *printer*.

More complex arithmetic and I/O tasks are simply repeats of these basic steps. Logic operations are similar, with values being compared between main memory and the accumulator.

DATA ENTRY AND COLLECTION DEVICES

Data entry devices are used (1) to transcribe source data to a **machine-readable format**; or (2) to input source data that is already machine readable. Until recently the traditional pattern of data entry required users to complete source documents manually and DP keypunch operators to key data from source documents into punched cards (machine-readable format). The data then had to be re-keyed for verification. These punched cards were then entered into the computer system. This process, illustrated in Figure 7-6, requires three transcription steps and results in a cumbersome deck of cards.

Current data entry devices and methods can eliminate one, two, and in some cases, all three of these transcription steps. For example, rather than have an order clerk manually record order information on

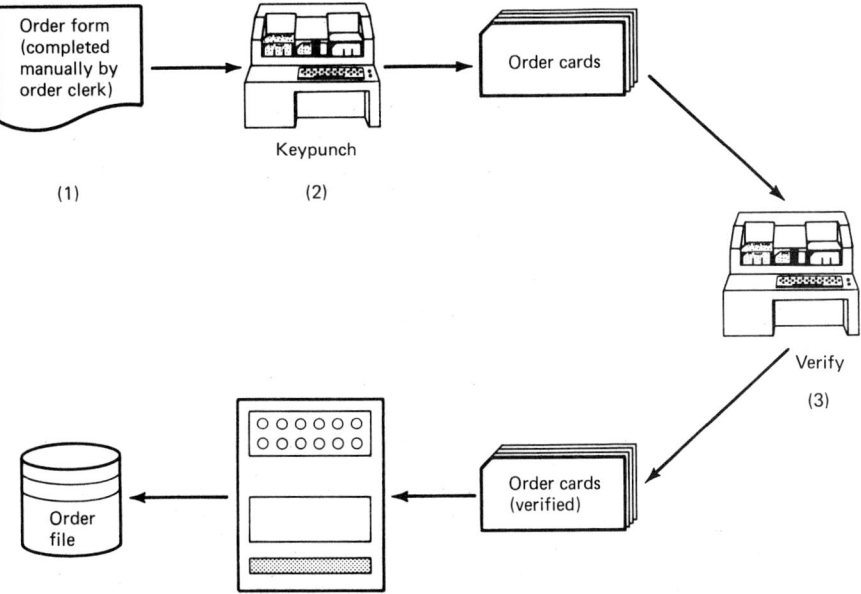

FIGURE 7-6 The traditional data entry pattern. Numbers indicate transcription steps.

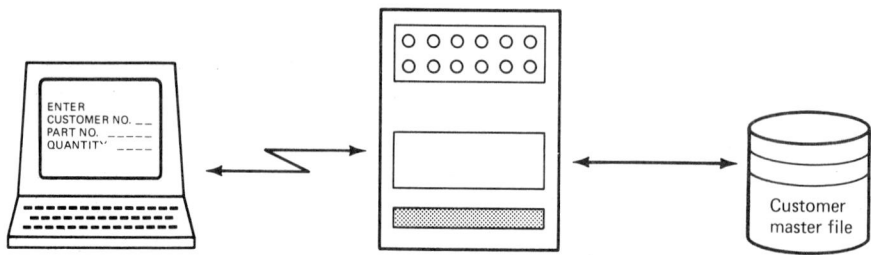

FIGURE 7-7 On-line data entry.

an order form, the clerk would enter appropriate data directly into the system via an on-line terminal. Input is verified by operator sight checks and machine "reasonableness" checks (limit checks, range checks, consistency checks, and so on). This vastly simplified and more accurate (fewer opportunities for error) approach to data entry is illustrated in Figure 7-7.

The trend in data entry is to minimize the number of transcriptions by entering data as close to the source (usually the functional area) as possible. Until recently, data entry has been synonomous with key-strokes, whether on a cash register or a card punch. The keystroke will always be the basic mode of data entry, but recent innovations are eliminating the need for key-driven data entry in certain applications. For example, the bar codes on grocery products at supermarket check-out counters have eliminated much of the key entry tasks (see Figures 7-8 and 7-9). Data entry is an area with an enormous potential for

FIGURE 7-8 The UPC bar code is now preprinted on most grocery items. (*Courtesy of IBM.*)

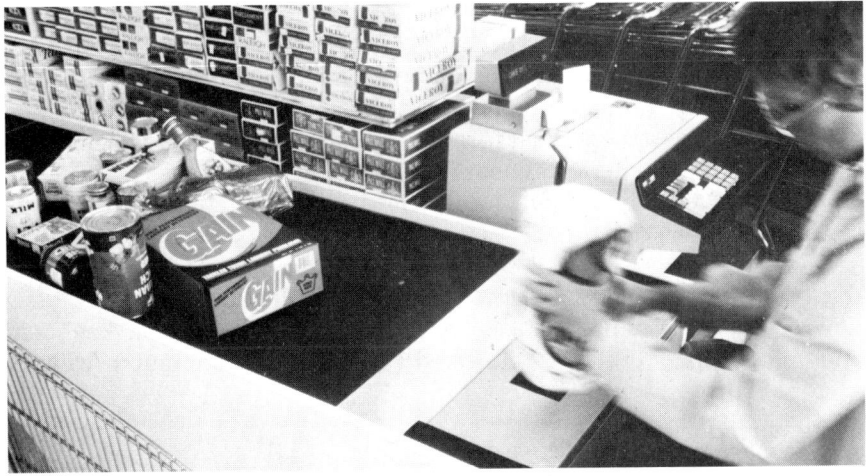

FIGURE 7-9 A supermarket checkout system. (*Courtesy of IBM.*)

increases in productivity. Most companies have not tapped the potential of existing data entry technology. The following is an overview of this technology.

Key-Driven Devices

Key-driven devices will usually have a standard alphanumeric keyboard with an optional numeric keyboard (10-key pad) for high-speed numeric entry (see Figure 7-10). Some keyboards will also have special-

FIGURE 7-10 An alphanumeric terminal keyboard with a 10-key pad. Page and cursor movement keys are on the right. The top two rows are special function keys. (*Courtesy of Hewlett-Packard Co.*)

function keys which can be used to instruct the computer to perform a specific operation that may otherwise require a number of keystrokes. For example, a word processing keyboard might have a special-function key that allows the operator to scan through the pages of text quickly. Some keyboards are designed for a specific application and will not have a standard alphanumeric keyboard.

Key-driven data entry devices can be on-line (connected directly to the computer) or off-line.

Off-line. The most common mode of off-line data entry is cluster key-to-disk processing. Data entry stations, consisting of a keyboard and video display unit, are "clustered" about a small computer (called a

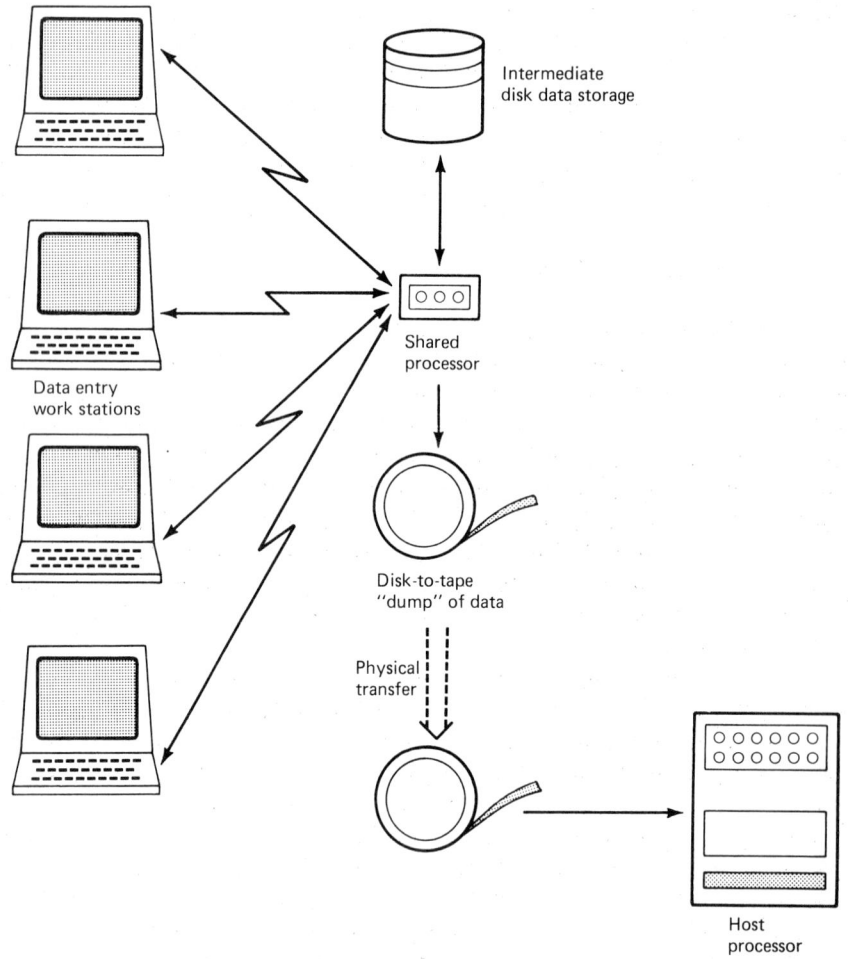

FIGURE 7-11 Off-line data entry.

shared processor) dedicated to the data entry function. The computer is programmed to provide the operators with appropriate display screens and prompts to facilitate the data entry function for a given application. For example, the display on the operator's screen may be the image of the source document.

Figure 7–11 illustrates the process by which data are entered using an off-line key-to-disk data entry cluster, and Figure 7–12 shows this form of data entry in progress. Operators key in data that are stored intermediately on a magnetic disk, thus the "key-to-disk" nomenclature. Source documents are batched for each operator, and they transcribe the source data to disk. At appropriate intervals, the contents of the disk are "dumped" (transferred) to a magnetic tape (a standard nine-track tape that is compatible with host computer tape drives). Data are transferred to the host for processing by physically removing the magnetic tape on the shared processor and loading it to a host computer tape drive. Typically, the magnetic disk used for intermediate storage is not compatible with the disk used by the host.

Stand-alone data entry work stations accommodate only one operator. These units are controlled by a microprocessor and store data on a diskette (floppy disk) or a magnetic cassette tape. The diskette is a thin five- or eight-inch, flexible, circular disk that is stored permanently in an equally flexible square jacket (like a phonograph record). The magnetic tape cassettes are similar to those used with portable tape recorders. The contents of the diskettes and cassette tapes are transferred to a standard host compatible nine-track tape for processing. These stand-

FIGURE 7–12 A small office computer used for key-to-disk data entry and limited on-line inquiry. Data can be transferred to a larger central computer for processing. (*Courtesy of Wang Laboratories, Inc.*)

alone units do not offer the flexibility or operator convenience of the clustered configuration. With the flexibility and ease of operation offered by on-line and clustered data entry, stand-alone units are becoming part of the history of computers.

Point-of-sale (POS) terminals that are not connected to the host computer would also fall into the off-line key-driven data entry classification. Daily sales, inventory, and other data are recorded on magnetic tape or disk at a central collection site and batched to the host processor, usually at the end of the business day.

On-line. In an on-line data entry environment (see Figure 7-13), the host computer provides interactive support to remote data entry operations. Each work station consists of keyboard input and a video display unit. Operators in an on-line data entry environment are usually organizationally attached to the functional area. The primary advantage of on-line data entry is that records are immediately updated as the transaction occurs, versus being periodically batched in an off-line environment. For example, it is conceivable that in an off-line environment two salespeople might check the most recent stock status report and find the availability of 400 widgets, then promise immediate delivery of 400 widgets each. In an on-line environment, the inventory file would reflect all transactions up to each salesperson's inquiry, thereby precluding the possibility of an erroneous delivery promise.

FIGURE 7-13 Remote work stations used for on-line data entry and inquiry. (*Courtesy of IBM.*)

In the above example, as soon as the first sale was made, the inventory status would be changed to reflect the sale. The next salesperson would find no widgets in stock.

Point-of-sale terminals can also be on-line. The most important aspect of an on-line POS system is not the recording of the transaction, but the ability to check customer credit status and limits.

Optical Character Recognition

Optical character recognition (OCR) provides a way to encode certain data in machine-readable format, thereby precluding the need to key that data in manually. For example, in a bank check/deposit system, the individual account number and bank number are encoded on all checks and deposit slips; therefore, only the date and amount are entered manually. Optical character recognition is also used for original source data collection. As an example, in credit card purchases, the individual account number, retail store number, and amount are recorded on the transaction slip such that the date can be read visually and by machine. Figure 7–14 shows a document to be read by optical character recognition.

Until recently OCR devices required that data be encoded in special stylized type fonts. Advances in OCR technology enable these devices to read almost any printed matter, including most common typewriter styles. Special OCR devices can even read hand printing that is recorded on a standard form and written according to special rules. OCR devices are classified as page readers (regular typewritten pages), document readers (capable of reading documents of varying sizes), continuous form readers (e.g., cash register tapes), and hand-held wand readers (brushed over the printed matter to be read—see Figure 7–15).

OCR devices are most appropriate when data can be encoded (printed) by the computer on a **turnaround document** and when visual recognition is important. A utility bill is a perfect example of this application. The utility bill is a turnaround document that can be read visually by the customer. When the document and payment are returned, no data entry is required unless the bill is not paid or the amount of payment is other than the billed amount. All data pertinent to the reconciliation process are machine readable by OCR.

Optical mark readers (OMR) scan preprinted forms, like those used for standardized testing, and sense marks which, when placed in a particular location, indicate a particular character. OMR is somewhat dated but still applicable in an environment where data entry training is impractical. OCR devices can read hand-printed letters with a high level of accuracy, but individuals must be trained to make these machine-readable letters.

Included in optical character recognition technology is **bar coding.** Bar codes represent alphanumeric data by the width and combination of vertical lines (see Figure 7-8). The Universal Product Code (UPC) originally used for supermarket items is gaining momentum and is now

FIGURE 7-14 An invoice for electricity service containing a statement and a turnaround document. The account number, date, and amount due are printed on the machine readable turnaround document (top portion). When payment is received, the amount is entered in machine readable handprint only if the amount received is different from the amount due. The bill is then reconciled via an OCR reader that recognizes both OCR type fonts and hand printed characters.

FIGURE 7-15 This portable terminal permits off-line data entry at the source via keyboard and optical wand scanning. Collected data can be transmitted to a computer for processing from any telephone. (*Courtesy of MSI Data Corporation, copyright 1982.*)

being placed on other consumer goods. The advantage of bar codes over characters is that the position or orientation of the item being read is not as critical. In a supermarket the data can still be recorded even if a bottle of catsup is merely rolled over the slot scanner.

Magnetic Strips

Magnetic strips are used on a variety of cards and badges to facilitate data entry. Magnetic strips placed on the back of plastic cards are encoded with such information as an account number and a privacy code for use in an automatic teller machine (ATM). Magnetic strips contain much more data per unit space than printed characters or bar codes. Also, magnetic strips are appropriate when the data are confidential (as with the above mentioned privacy code). Employee cards and security badges are being issued with magnetic strips. The data encoded on these cards and badges contain authorization for access to physically secured areas (such as a computer center).

Voice Data Entry

Voice data entry is a viable method of inputting limited amounts of data. Even though voice input is well within the technology and relatively inexpensive, it has not been widely accepted. Current voice data input is limited to numbers and a few words. Even with this limitation, there are a number of applications where voice data entry is appropriate.

Although in the experimental stage, researchers have developed data banks of several thousand words that can be used to transcribe complete sentences with a high degree of accuracy. It is only a matter of time before user managers can state their information requirements in simple English, thus eliminating the need for time-consuming keystrokes.

Portable Data Entry

Portable data entry devices are hand held and usually off-line. One hand-held terminal combines a limited keyboard with a hand-held wand. (See Figure 7-15.) A stock clerk in a department store has an application for such a device. The clerk uses the wand to identify the product and enters the number on the keyboard to order. The data are captured on a magnetic cassette tape and later transferred to the computer for processing.

A recent innovation is a pressure-sensitive writing pad that recognizes hand-printed alphanumeric characters.

OUTPUT DEVICES

Technically speaking, all peripheral devices including data entry, data storage, and communication devices can be classified as output devices. This discussion, however, is limited to those devices that produce a hard copy (e.g., printouts) or soft copy (e.g., screen display, video display units) output. These devices are the means by which the computer communicates with the end user. Included in this category are printers, micrographics, video display units (VDUs), audio response units, and plotters.

Printers

Printers prepare hard-copy printed output. A printer is classified as a **serial printer** (or **character printer**), **line printer**, or **page printer**. Print speeds vary from up to 1,000 lines per minute (lpm), 3,000 lpm, and 21,000 lpm, respectively.

Printers are further categorized as **impact** or **nonimpact**. An impact printer uses some type of hammer or hammers to "impact" the ribbon and the paper, much like a typewriter. Nonimpact printers are required for print speeds in excess of 3,000 lpm. Nonimpact printers use chemicals, lasers, and heat to form the images on the paper.

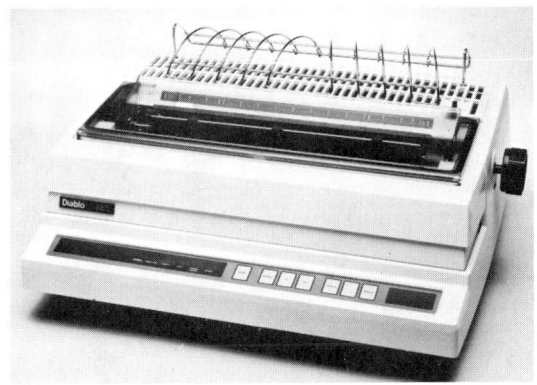

FIGURE 7-16 A serial printer. (*Courtesy of Diablo Systems Incorporated, XEROX.*)

Serial printers. Serial or character printers are used both as remote terminals (teleprinters—see Figure 7-16) and as the primary printer for small, low-volume computer systems. Impact serial printers use **dot-matrix** and **daisy-wheel** technology. Nonimpact serial printers employ **ink-jet** and **thermal** technology. Regardless of the technology, the images are formed *one character at a time* as the print head moves across the paper.

Dot-matrix. The dot-matrix, or simply matrix, printer configures printed dots to form the images. Several columns of small print hammers are contained in a rectangular "print head." The hammers are activated independently to form a dot character image as illustrated in Figure 7-17. The characters in Figure 7-17 are formed within a 7 × 5 dot matrix. The number of dots within the matrix varies from one printer to the next.

The quality of the printed output is directly proportional to the number of dots in the matrix. Some high-quality dot-matrix printers (33 × 18 matrix) form characters that appear solid and can be used for business letters as well as routine data processing output. These printers are called **dual-mode** because of their dual-function capabilities.

Dot-matrix printers are more flexible than printers of fully formed characters (daisy-wheel). Depending on the model, dot-matrix printers can print a variety of sizes and types of characters (including optical character recognition characters),

FIGURE 7-17 A dot-matrix printer output illustrating how printed dots are used to form characters.

print in colors, print graphics, and print bar codes. This is done without physically changing the type mechanism.

Daisy-wheel. The daisy-wheel printer has a high-quality output and is used exclusively for word processing applications or in a combination word processing/data processing mode. An interchangeable daisy-wheel (like the one shown in Figure 7-18) containing a character set of fully formed characters is spun to the desired character. A print hammer strikes the embossed character on the print wheel to form the image. The print quality is at least equal to that of the best electric typewriters.

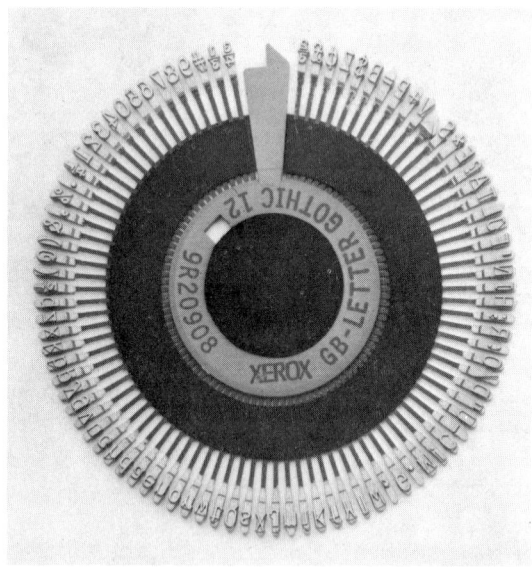

FIGURE 7-18 An interchangeable daisy-wheel. (*Courtesy of Diablo Systems Incorporated, XEROX.*)

A typical application of the daisy-wheel printer is to produce a business letter that has been entered and edited on a word processing computer. Although daisy-wheel printers have the highest-quality text output, they are the slowest of the serial printers, with a maximum print speed of 60 characters per second.

Ink jet. Ink-jet printers squirt "dots" of ink on the paper to form images in a manner similar to that of the dot-matrix printer. Some ink-jet printers are capable of multicolor output.

Thermal. The thermal printer is an inexpensive alternative to the other serial printers. Heat elements are activated to produce dot-matrix images on heat-sensitive paper. The major disadvantage of this type of printer is the requirement for the more expensive heat-sensitive paper. The advantages include compactness, limited noise, and purchase price.

Line printers. Line printers are impact printers that print *a line at a time* (see Figure 7–19). The two most popular types of line printers are the band line printer and the matrix line printer.

FIGURE 7–19 A line impact printer. (*Courtesy of IBM.*)

Band. Band line printers have a print hammer for each character position (usually 132) in the line of print. Several similar character sets of fully formed characters are embossed on a horizontal band that is continuously moving in front of the print hammers. The paper is momentarily stopped and, as the desired character passes over a given column, the hammer is activated and the image is formed on the paper. Band printers are capable of printing on continuous feed paper, plain cut sheet ($8\frac{1}{2}''$ × $11''$ and $8\frac{1}{2}''$ × $14''$), mailing labels, and cards and documents of varying sizes.

Matrix. Matrix line printers print a single line of *dots* at a time. The needle-like hammers are lined up across the width of the paper. Like serial matrix printers, the characters are formed in rectangular dot configurations. Matrix printers are much more flexible than band printers and can perform the same type of print operations as serial matrix printers (see above). However, they cannot achieve the print speeds of the band printers. Interestingly, the fastest serial matrix printers (1,000 lpm) have higher output speeds than the fastest line matrix printers (700 lpm).

Page printers. Page printers are nonimpact and use electrophotographic printing technology to achieve high-speed hard-copy output by printing *a page at a time* (see Figure 7-20). Operating at peak capacity during one 8-hour shift, a page printer can produce almost a quarter of a million pages of output. This enormous output capability is normally directed to persons outside the company. Large banks use page printers to produce statements for checking and savings accounts; insurance companies use them to produce policies; and utilities use them to produce utility bills.

Page printer technology provides the capability to superimpose preprinted forms on regular, continuous feed, plain stock paper. This eliminates the need to purchase expensive preprinted forms. Unlike the impact printer, the page printer cannot make multiple copies by using multiple-ply paper. However, at 21,000 lines per minute, it does not take long to reprint the entire job. Also, the carbon paper does not have to be **decollated** (separated) from the multipart paper used to produce multiple copies on line printers. Page printers have the capability to print graphs and charts and offer considerable flexibility in the choice of size and style of print.

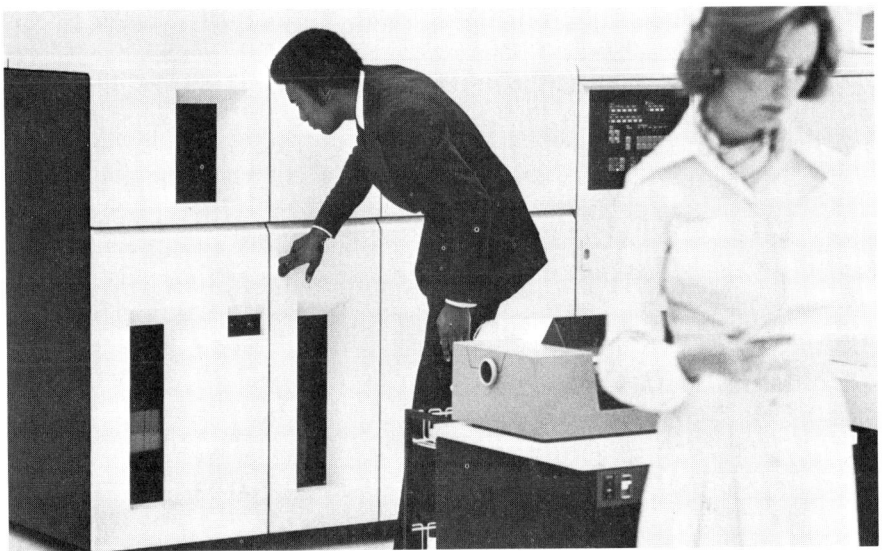

FIGURE 7-20 A high speed page printer. (*Courtesy of IBM.*)

Printer Summary. Hundreds of printers are produced by dozens of manufacturers. There is a printer manufactured to meet the hard copy output requirements of almost any company. Almost any combination of features can be obtained. A company can specify the speed, quality of output, flexibility requirements, and even noise level. Printers sell for as little as a good pair of shoes or as much as a small office building.

The trend in computer centers is to produce less printed output, especially internally. Most hard-copy outputs have been used for reference and inquiry, not for permanent records. The soft copy is a superior and less expensive alternative to hard-copy printed output. The rapid increase in the number of on-line terminals has all but eliminated the need for printed output to be distributed within the company.

Computer Output
Microfilm/Microfiche (COM)

COM devices prepare microfilm and microfiche for off-line microform readers. First, images (output) to be miniaturized by COM devices are prepared (as if to be printed) on the host computer and placed on a magnetic tape. The magnetic tape is then loaded on an off-line COM device and the images are miniaturized for microform readers. In the miniaturization process, the images are displayed on a very small, high-resolution video display unit. A camera exposes a small segment of the microfilm for each display, thereby creating multiple images in a grid pattern. The microfilm is then developed and cut into $4'' \times 6''$ sheets of microfiche. This process, illustrated in Figure 7-21, is substantially faster than preparing a hard-copy output.

COM is applicable in IS environments where files must be updated daily (usually at night) and made available for reference. For example, many banks use COM to provide tellers with account status information. Each day, microfiche containing the status of accounts is distributed

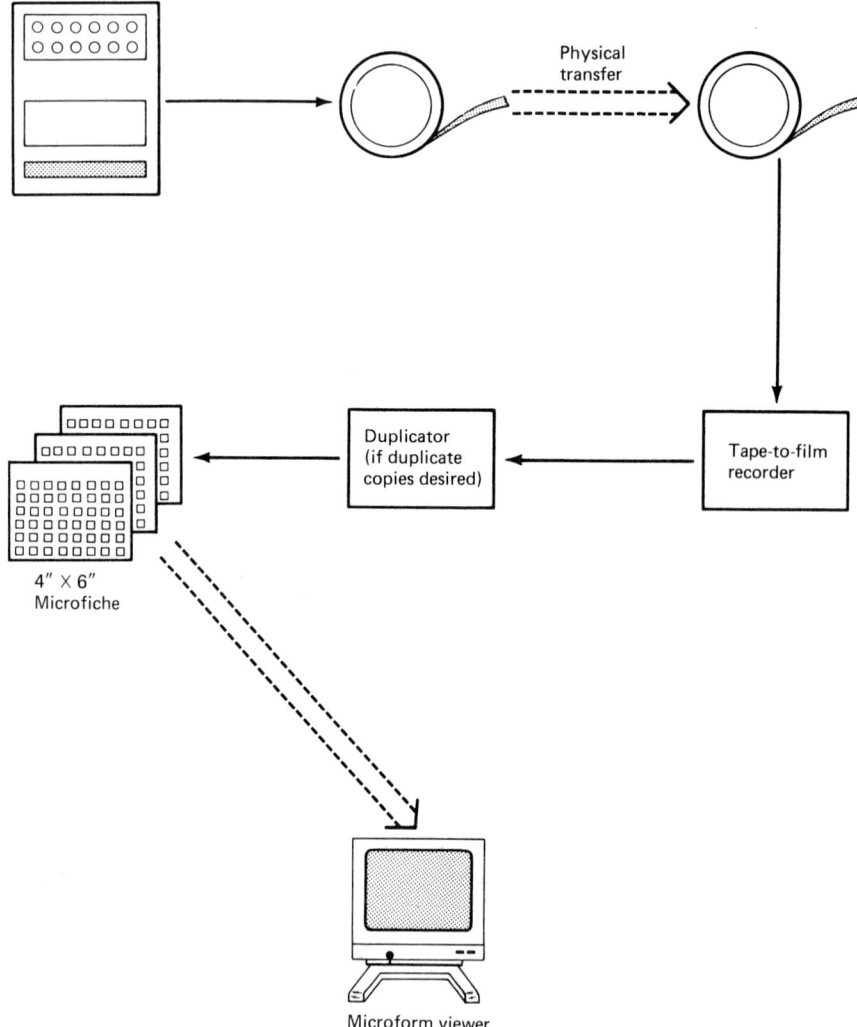

FIGURE 7-21 The computer output microfilm/microfiche (COM) process.

to the appropriate locations. COM is an alternative to on-line systems when up-to-the-minute information is not critical. COM is also used extensively in lieu of hard-copy archival storage.

Computer-assisted retrieval (CAR) uses the processing capability of the computer to assist in the selection of the appropriate microfiche. In CAR, the operator of the microform reader communicates a request to the computer and a mechanical apparatus feeds the appropriate microfiche to the reader.

Terminals

A terminal is an end point in a computer network and can be any device from a teleprinter to a computer system. However, most references to a terminal allude to a device that provides an operator the capability to interact with the computer. The input mechanism is usually a keyboard. The output mechanism is either a character printer or a video (or visual) display unit (VDU). Video or visual display terminal (VDT) and cathode-ray tube (CRT) are alternative names for VDU. In trade vernacular, the VDU is also affectionately called the "tube," short for cathode-ray tube. Some of these terminals are intelligent. An **intelligent terminal** has an embedded microprocessor that performs some functions that facilitate operator interaction which would otherwise be handled by the host computer. Some intelligent terminals can be programmed by the operator to accommodate a specific function, while others have "hard-wired" programs that cannot be altered. Most commercial terminals have some degree of intelligence.

Video Display Units. Video display units (VDUs), like that shown in Figure 7-22, contain a cathode-ray tube "screen" that provides alphanumeric (A/N) and/or graphic displays. Although the size of the screen varies, most alphanumeric screens can display 24 lines, 80 characters each. Alphanumeric VDUs have limited graphics capability.

Graphics terminals can display, with a high resolution, graphs, charts, line drawings, and A/N characters. The screens of graphics terminals, especially those used for engineering design, are much larger than those of A/N terminals, as can be seen from Figure 7-23. Those graphics terminals used in design provide a pressure-sensitive pad that allows the operator to interact with the system. The operator can issue commands and create images on the screen.

Color graphics terminals add a new dimension to visual output by using colors to highlight various aspects of the output. For example, in a Gantt chart the planned duration of a particular activity can be shown in one color and that portion of the activity completed can be shown in another color. Color graphics can be used to present A/N information

FIGURE 7-22 A video display unit with keyboard and light pen. (*Courtesy of IBM.*)

FIGURE 7-23 A graphics terminal with keyboard and pressure-sensitive function pad. (*Courtesy of Applicon Incorporated.*)

more efficiently. Instead of a sales manager having visually and arithmetically to compare a salesperson's performance against quotas and against other salespeople, a simple histogram can be used to illustrate graphically individual performances and performance relative to others. Color graphics terminals are an economically viable alternative to standard black and white A/N VDUs. Within a short time, the difference in price will not be a consideration, especially when one considers the overwhelming benefits of color graphics capabilities.

Most VDUs have a keyboard that allows the operator to communicate with the computer, thus completing the interactive cycle. Some VDUs are also equipped with a hand-held light-sensitive pen that can be used to interact with the computer. An engineer can use the pen to create an image on the screen. A functional area user manager can use the pen to select the desired function from the menu of possible computer functions, thereby eliminating the need for key entry.

A wide variety of VDUs are used regularly by clerks and company presidents for a variety of applications, from data entry to strategic planning.

Teleprinters. Teleprinters are character printers with keyboard input and are used as terminals when hard-copy output is desired. Computer interaction is more cumbersome with teleprinters than with VDUs. For example, when the operator makes an input error on a VDU the characters in error are deleted from the screen. Errors made on a teleprinter are permanent. Corrections inevitably result in the input being difficult to read. It is possible, but extremely difficult, to use teleprinters for text input in word processing applications. A remote facility having several VDUs will often have one teleprinter for those instances where the operator needs a hard copy of the output.

Portable Terminals. Portable terminals have a built-in **MODEM** (acoustical coupler) that enables the operator to use any telephone for a communications link to the host computer. Almost every feature and combination of input and output is available on portable terminals. Input is usually via keyboard and output is usually printed, displayed on a small screen, or voice response. Portable terminals are used at home by programmers to take advantage of computer availability on the second and third shifts. Salespeople use portable terminals to make an inquiry or to log a sale while in a customer's office. Executives use these terminals to make the corporate information resources available to them wherever they travel.

Terminal Summary. Terminals are used by secretaries for word processing, by programmers for interactive program development, by clerks for recording transactions, by management for making decisions, by engineers for computer-aided design, by computer operators to communicate with the computer (via the console), and by shop foremen for line scheduling. These are just a few of hundreds of uses for terminals. Whether it is the stock boy in the supermarket or the company president, the computer will play an active role in the daily duties of most workers. Their vehicle for communication with the computers is the terminal.

Audio Response Unit

There are two types of audio response units: One uses a recording of a human voice and the other uses a speech synthesizer. The first type is used extensively by the telephone company and banks. This type of unit selects output from up to 200 user-recorded words or phrases, just as the printer would select characters.

The speech synthesizer converts raw data and even hard-copy printed matter to electronically produced speech. Existing technology limits speech synthesizers to environments where there is no alternative. For example, an OCR device can scan a book and use a speech synthesizer to transpose printed matter into spoken words for blind persons. As the quality of the output improves, speech synthesizers will surely replace audio response units that use recorded human voices.

FIGURE 7-24 A drum plotter. (*Courtesy of CalComp, a Sanders Graphics Company.*)

Plotter

A plotter is a device that converts data to hard-copy graphs, charts, and line drawings. There are basically two types of plotters, the drum and the flatbed (see Figures 7-24 and 7-25). The pen(s) and the drum move concurrently to produce the image on the drum-style plotter. Only the pen(s) moves on the flatbed plotter. The mechanics of this vary considerably from one plotter to the next. In either case a pen, or a variety of pens, that include different colors and pen styles, are moved about the paper to complete the image. Although more expensive, the flatbed plotter offers better line quality and speed.

If precision is not a prerequisite, an electrostatic plotter/printer (see Figure 7-26) can be used to copy a graphic image. These are used primarily for plot previewing.

DATA STORAGE DEVICES

Over the years, manufacturers have made available a variety of devices for permanent storage of data and programs. Paper tape, punched cards, the data cell, and others are now obsolete. Although other devices exist, the overwhelming majority of both off-line and on-line storage of data are on magnetic tape, magnetic disk, and mass storage

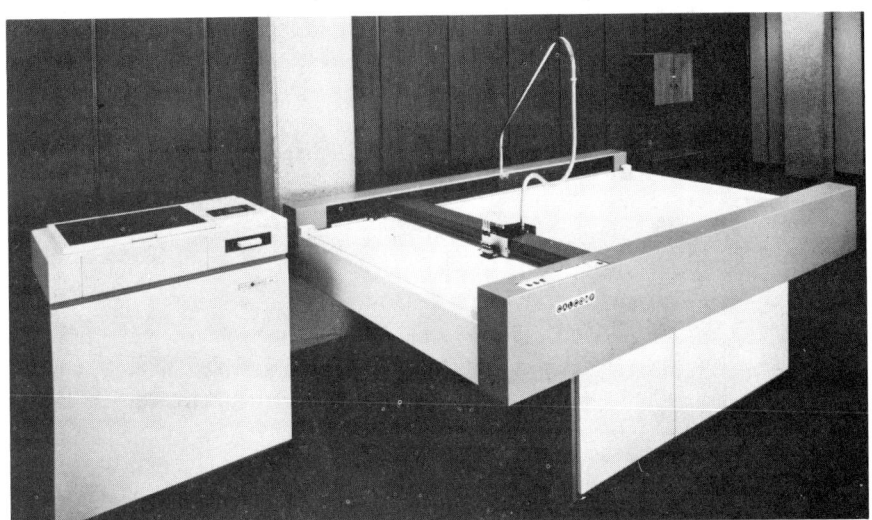

FIGURE 7-25 A flat-bed plotter. (*Courtesy of CalComp, a Sanders Graphics Company.*)

FIGURE 7-26 An electrostatic plotter. (*Courtesy of CalComp, a Sanders Graphics Company.*)

devices. These permanent data storage devices are called *secondary storage* (as opposed to *primary storage*). Secondary storage is also called auxiliary storage. The basic options, terminology, and operation of these secondary storage media and devices are discussed below.

Magnetic Tape Drives

The unit on which a reel of magnetic tape is mounted and processed is known as the tape drive. Because magnetic tape is processed from beginning to end, data are said to be stored sequentially. Magnetic tapes come in two basic forms: reel and cassette. Tape cassettes (Figure 7-27) are used primarily for intermediate, low-volume storage (e.g., off-line POS data collection). Reels (Figure 7-28) contain a thin mylar tape that is ½-inch wide and 600, 1,200, or 2,400 feet in length.

The basic principles of tape data storage are illustrated in Figure 7-29. The surface of the tape can be electronically magnetized to represent two states. The state is represented by a **bit** and shown by a 1 or a 0 in Figure 7-29. These bits are grouped and configured to represent a particular character (or **byte**). That is, a particular combination of 1's and 0's (called an **encoding** system; see Chapter 8), represents the characters of "ACE" and "ACME" as illustrated in Figure 7-29. Because

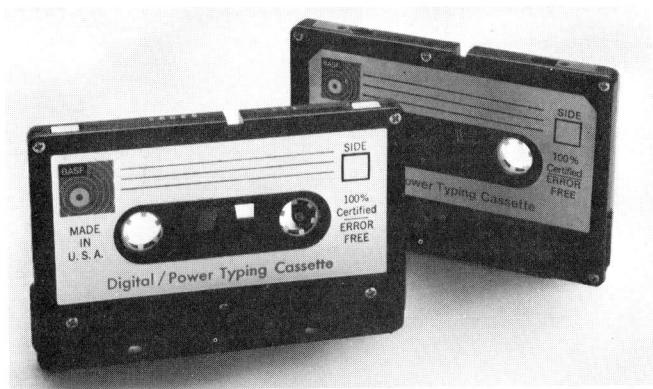

FIGURE 7-27 Digital data cassettes. (*Courtesy of BASF Systems Corporation.*)

these character configurations are adjacent to each other, this is called **parallel** data representation. Magnetic tapes have nine **tracks**. The top row of bits in the figure are stored in the first track.

Records are usually grouped together in blocks of two or more and separated by **interblock gaps (IBG)**. The blocking of records facilitates the reading and writing processing. Each time the computer is instructed to "read" from a magnetic tape, all data between IBGs is transmitted to main memory. When the computer is instructed to "write" to a tape, the data are transmitted from memory to the tape drive. Then, the data and an IBG are written on the tape.

Records are **blocked** to enable the computer to read or write more records at a given time. In Figure 7-29, the customer records are said to be "blocked two." Because data are transmitted to main memory, which

FIGURE 7-28 2400 foot magnetic tape reels. (*Courtesy of BASF Systems Corporation.*)

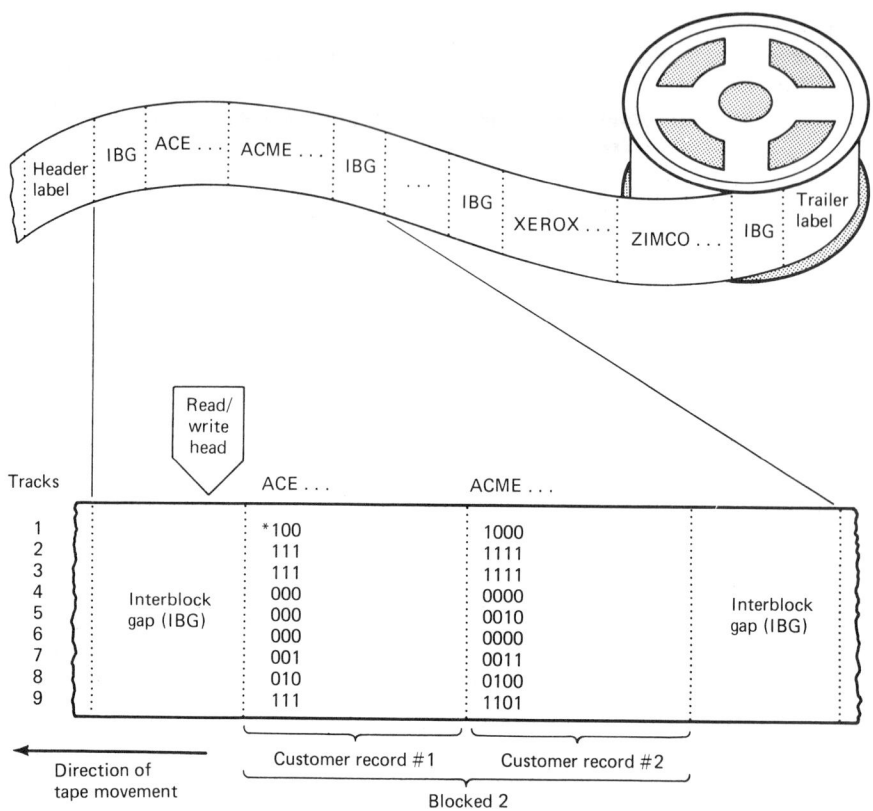

*Parity bit added to
maintain even parity.

FIGURE 7-29 Cross-section of magnetic tape containing a customer master file.

has limited storage capacity, there is a practical limit to the number of records that can be blocked. The IBGs are not only a signal to stop the reading process, but they also provide some margin of error for the rapid start/stop operation of the tape drive.

The tape passes under a **read/write head** and the data are either read and transmitted to main memory or transmitted from main memory and written to the tape. On any given run, a tape will either be input or output, but not both.

A tape drive is rated by the density at which data can be stored and the rate at which this data can be transmitted to the computer. Tape density is measured in **bytes per inch (BPI)** or the number of characters that can be stored per linear inch of tape. The **transmission rate** is the number of characters that can be transmitted to main memory per second and is computed by taking the tape speed (inches per second) over the read/write head, times the tape density (BPI). For example, a tape drive with a tape speed of 75 inches per second and a tape density of 1,600 BPI is capable of transmitting data at a rate of 120,000 characters per second. A standard 1,600-BPI, 2,400-foot magnetic tape has the capacity to store over 40 million characters of data.

Tape processing (called sequential processing) is discussed in detail in Chapter 8.

Magnetic Disk Drives

Disk drives are the devices that read and write data to magnetic disks. The variety of magnetic disks are shown in Figure 7–32. In order of increasing storage capacity, they are the five-inch **diskette** (also called a **floppy** or **flexible** disk), the eight-inch diskette, the disk **cartridge** (comes in a variety of sizes and shapes), and the **disk pack**. Because data can be accessed "directly," these devices are commonly referred to as **direct access storage devices** or **DASDs**. Since disk drives (specifically those using disk packs) are far and away the most common DASDs, a reference to a DASD is a reference to a disk drive.

Data are stored **serially** in concentric circles called **tracks**, as illustrated in Figure 7–33. The disk packs are continuously spinning, making all data available on each revolution. A disk pack may consist of several disks with data recorded on each side (disk face surface). Disk drives have read/write heads for each disk face surface (see Figure 7–34).

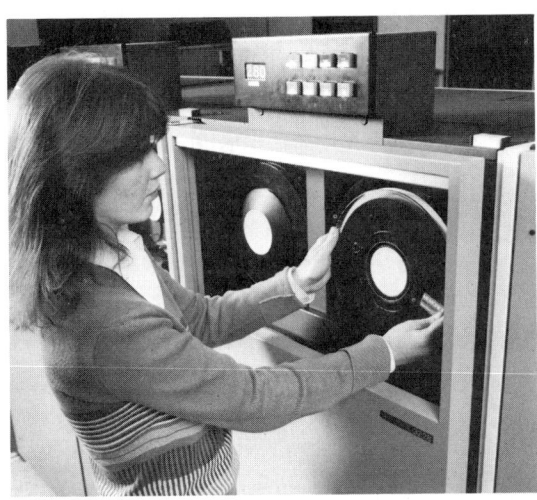

FIGURE 7-30 Mounting a magnetic tape reel on a tape drive. (*Courtesy of Memorex Corporation.*)

FIGURE 7-31 Cutaway of a magnetic tape drive. (*Courtesy of Storage Technology Corporation.*)

These heads are mounted on a movable **access arm** that moves to the appropriate **cylinder** in order to access or write a record. The cylinder is a collective reference to all tracks of the same number. For example, each disk face surface will have a track 2 and the disk pack will have a cylinder 2.

In Figure 7-33 the access arm is positioned over track 000 in position to read the "ACE" customer record. If instructed to read the "ACME" record on track 002, the access arm would be positioned over track 002 until the "ACME" record passed under the read/write head. Each access or write results in a **disk seek**. A typical disk seek (e.g., access a customer record) is measured in milliseconds (thousandths of a second). This is relatively slow when compared to the processing speed of a computer.

(A)

(B)

(C)

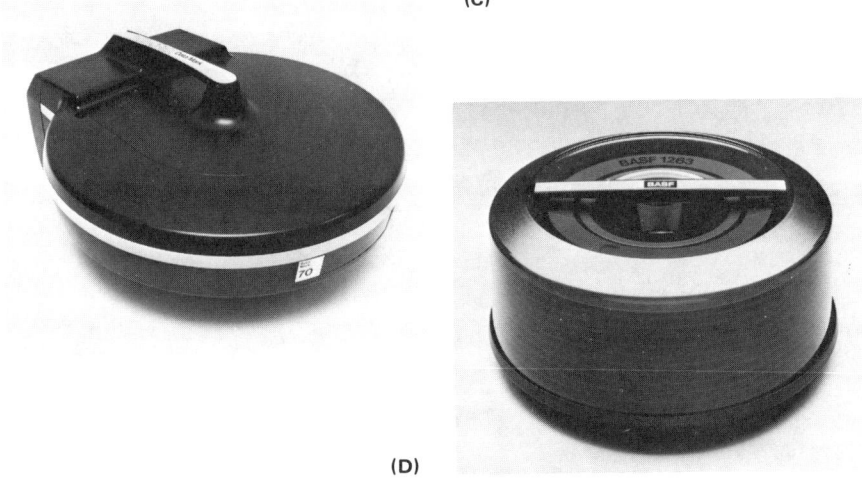

(D)

FIGURE 7–32 A. 5 1/4'' and 8'' diskettes. B. Disk cartridges. C. Data module disk cartridge with read/write mechanism sealed in enclosure. D. Interchangeable disk pack. (*Courtesy of Memorex and BASF Systems Corporations.*)

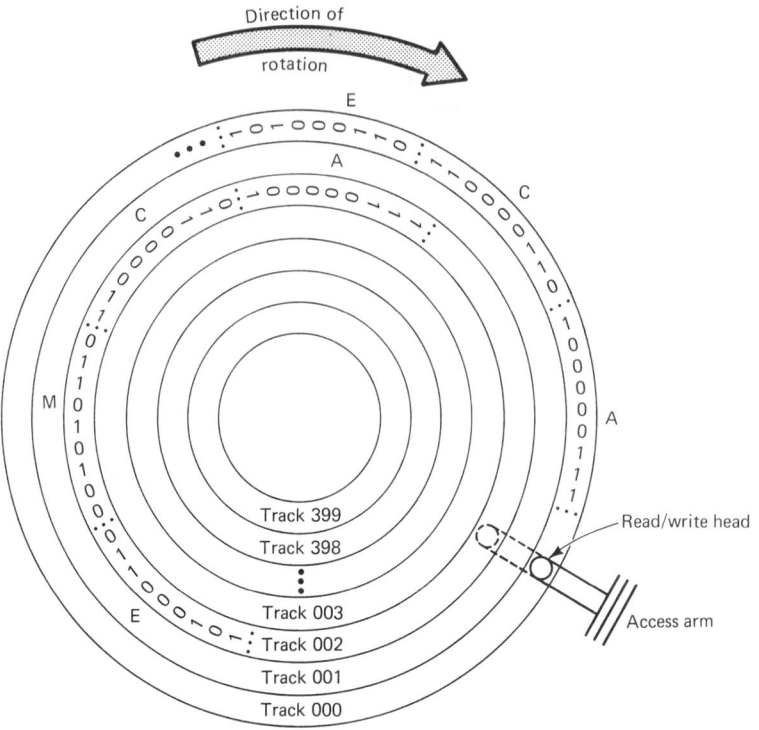

FIGURE 7-33 Top view of a magnetic disk.

FIGURE 7-34 Cutaway of a fixed magnetic disk that is normally in a sealed environment. (*Courtesy of Memorex Corporation.*)

The vast majority of disk drives accommodate interchangeable disk packs, thereby allowing operations personnel to load one master file (e.g., personnel file) for processing, then exchange disk packs and load another master file (e.g., inventory file). See Figure 7-35. Some disk drives have fixed disks and read/write heads for all tracks. These disk drives eliminate the time required for the access arm to move to the appropriate track. The trade-off between fixed and interchangeable disks is speed of access and flexibility.

Smaller "hard" disks (versus "floppies") are contained in a cartridge. These interchangeable cartridges contain from one to seven disks. Diskettes mentioned earlier in the data entry section are used with very small computers and for situations that require low-volume direct access.

The storage capacity of disks ranges from approximately 500,000 characters for diskettes to 800 million characters for the standard interchangeable disk pack. Disk processing (called random or direct processing) is discussed in detail in Chapter 8.

Mass Storage Devices

The mechanics of mass storage devices vary between vendors, but the objective is the same. These devices are used when direct access is required for very large amounts of data. Because these devices are very mechanical and can be overworked, the number of "seeks" per month

FIGURE 7-35 Magnetic disk drives. (*Courtesy of Memorex Corporation.*)

FIGURE 7-36 Cartridges used for data storage in a mass storage device. (*Courtesy of IBM.*)

must be limited. If the application can accommodate these limitations, mass storage devices are an inexpensive alternative to magnetic disks. Mass storage devices are also called DASDs. Figure 7-36 shows a mass storage device in cartridge form; Figure 7-37 illustrates the honeycomb storage of the cartridges.

FIGURE 7-37 Inside view of a mass storage device. Cartridges are mechanically retrieved from their honeycomb-like storage bins and loaded to the read/write station for data manipulation. (*Courtesy of IBM.*)

DATA COMMUNICATIONS DEVICES

Data communications hardware consists of the devices and the channels that facilitate remote data communication. To the user, these devices are conceptually transparent, but visibly very real. MODEMs and cluster controllers are devices that prepare data for transmission over communications channels. These data are received by a transmission control unit or a front-end processor and are prepared for transmission to the host processor. The communication links or channels are also considered part of the data communications hardware. Chapter 10 is dedicated to these devices, the communication links, and data communications in general.

COMPUTER SYSTEMS
CONFIGURATION CONSIDERATIONS

A computer system is configured by selecting the computer(s) and peripherals to best fit the requirements of the corporation. With the variety of computers, peripheral devices, and data communications alternatives, the number of possible configurations is endless. It is unlikely that any two medium or large computer systems would be configured in the same way. Even two computer systems that appear physically equivalent would probably have different features on the CPU and peripherals. For example, the capacity of one main memory might be 4 megabytes (4 million characters) and another might be 6 megabytes. Some very small computer systems are sold with a standard configuration and no optional features.

A company should not purchase unnecessary hardware capacity or configure a system that falls short of meeting operational requirements. Before configuring a computer system, the following considerations should be discussed as they relate to existing and future operations.

Processing requirements. This consideration deals with requirements for computing capacity and is one of the most difficult to assess. Sometimes the only data point is that existing hardware is insufficient. An estimate of processing requirements is made by carefully examining existing and potential applications, historical utilization statistics, and by using the experience of IS professionals.

Storage capacity. This consideration refers to the amount of secondary (auxiliary) storage required for the corporate data base and all software.

Types of data access. Data can be accessed on-line and/or off-line, or sequentially or directly (randomly).

Main memory capacity. Since all programs and data must be resident in main memory before a program can be executed and the data can be processed, main memory requirements must be estimated. Main memory is critical for on-line systems because an insufficient memory will result in a reduced response time.

Output requirements. The type, volume, and application of output must be considered. For example, after estimating the hard-copy output requirements and the applications, the appropriate combination of character, line, and page printers would be specified.

Input requirements. Again, type, volume, and application of input must be considered. For example, the number of keystrokes per day would be important in determining the number of on-line data entry terminals.

Usage. This consideration refers to the percent utilization of the computer system. Some companies do all processing during the day shift, a strategy which requires enough computing capacity to be able to do this. Another company with the same capacity requirements might buy a smaller computer system and operate it 24 hours a day.

Future needs. Corporate officers must look at where they are now and where they want to be, and must assess whether a particular computer system has the potential to grow with the organization (upward compatibility).

Facilities. Depending on the computer, certain environmental, security, electrical, and space requirements must be considered.

Backup computer availability. Part of any contingency plan would be the designation of a backup computer site. A reciprocal agreement is usually made with another company.

Software support availability. The availability of compatible proprietary software is a major consideration, whether it is systems software, (e.g., data base management systems) or applications software (e.g., financial accounting systems).

Number and location of on-line users. Since some computers have theoretical and practical limits as to how many on-line terminals can be serviced, the estimated number of on-line users is a critical input to CPU selection. The location of on-line users affects the selection of the data communications support hardware.

The above considerations are mentioned briefly because it is not at all uncommon for a user manager to be a member of a hardware evaluation and selection committee, especially when the functional area department is paying the bill. In these cases, the user manager should be aware of the general areas considered for computer system configuration. Much of the input to the configuration process is supplied by the user (e.g., output requirements, input requirements, number of on-line users).

HARDWARE ACQUISITION

Acquisition Policy

Many corporations have an implied or real policy regarding the acquisition of computing hardware. The existence of a hardware acquisition policy eliminates the need for corporate and IS managers to debate the merits of the various acquisition alternatives for each major hardware acquisition. Such a policy not only saves personnel time, but adds an ongoing consistency to the process of building and maintaining the company's hardware base. Since many users regularly purchase computing hardware, they are affected by this policy and should have an input to its formation.

A serious problem now facing almost every medium-sized and large corporation is uncontrolled decentralization of computers and information processing. The advent of the inexpensive, full-capability small computer has prompted many user managers to establish their own small computer centers. Decentralization becomes uncontrolled when users evaluate and select their hardware in isolation of IS standards and policies. To insure corporate-wide compatibility and the availability of professional expertise, user managers should check prevailing corporate policy before acquiring hardware. A small amount of time spent now will avoid the hassle of interfacing incompatible computer hardware in the future.

A special case of uncontrolled decentralization is the proliferation of word processing computers. Autonomous word processing systems can be simple, short-term solutions to one phase of a very complex corporate information processing problem. Installation of stand-alone, incompatible word processing systems has a tendency further to embed inefficient and redundant office systems, thereby impeding efforts to integrate corporate systems. The user manager considering the purchase of a word processing system should check corporate compatibility standards with IS personnel. For example, there should be a method of transferring data from the host to the word processing system and vice versa.

The following acquisition policies are simplified examples of the variety of policy options adopted by corporations.

- Always purchase.
- Always lease (to include lease/purchase agreements).
- Lease from a third-party vendor.
- Do not mix vendors for a particular computer systems configuration.
- Always acquire hardware from a particular vendor.
- Automatically order new equipment upon announcement (a policy reserved for very large companies).

There are overwhelming advantages to having an established corporate policy for computing hardware acquisitions. For example, the question of buy versus lease will inevitably surface and be debated for virtually every major hardware acquisition. These decision-making efforts could better be channeled to selection of the appropriate device and away from the mechanism for payment. For example, a general policy statement on whether to buy or lease and/or under what circumstances to buy or lease would result in a savings of time for IS and user management.

At a minimum, the question of buying versus leasing should be resolved. Cash flow within the company is typically the determining factor. The purchase option requires a large initial outflow but results in a substantial cash inflow from investment tax credits and accelerated depreciation. Still, the net cash outflow at the onset is substantially more than the lease alternative. The fundamental trade-off of the buy-versus-lease question is whether or not to risk premature economic obsolescence. The secondary trade-off is whether or not to forfeit the flexibility afforded by a short-term lease. These trade-offs point out the basic shortcoming of each option. The corporation electing to lease equipment is usually afforded a number of lease options by the vendor. Some vendors offer both short- and long-term leases and a lease with an option to purchase.

Note: *The long-term lease (six or more years) may be a viable option for the corporation with a short-term cash flow problem. Long-term leases result in a significant reduction in monthly charges. However, today's rapidly changing technology almost guarantees more computing power for the dollar next year. Only under rare circumstances are long-term leases a wise economic move.*

The question of buy versus lease is not always resolved by selecting the least expensive option. Long-term flexibility, immediate cash flow, and other considerations have a direct bearing on the decision to buy or lease.

Pitfalls in the Selection of Computing Hardware

There are certain pitfalls that should be avoided in hardware selection. Wholesale mixing of vendors can create serious maintenance and operational problems. This is not to say that mixing of vendors should not be considered, but simply that mixing of vendors should be approached with caution. Do not believe everything you are told by the vendor or by a user of the vendor's equipment. For the most part, vendors are honest and wish to provide the necessary information for an informed decision. However, the complexity of computers provides a vehicle to distort truths and to make unrealistic comparisons. All vendors exploit these loopholes. Some users are reluctant to speak the truth about a vendor's equipment and/or their support because it reflects directly on them. A user's recommendation of a particular vendor's system should be valued but tempered by the fact that egos play a part in all recommendations. Another pitfall is the signing of a long-term contract (six or more years). These contracts are seldom economically justified over the term of the contract.

Hardware Evaluation and Selection[8]

Hardware costs can consume as much as 50% of the IS budget and from 0.3% to 3% of the total corporate budget. However, a rule of thumb places hardware costs at 20% to 25% of the IS budget. These figures highlight the significance of having a hardware evaluation and selection methodology that will consistently result in acquisition of

---

[8] This methodology is presented in more detail in another book by L. Long, *Data Processing Documentation and Procedures Manual* (Reston, VA: Reston Publishing Company, 1979), pp. 205–28.

the most appropriate computing hardware. This section presents a proven method for hardware evaluation and selection.

Hardware Selection Committee. The hardware selection and evaluation process should not be accomplished by an individual. There are too many variables that require a subjective evaluation. A collective evaluation will yield a more reasonable set of alternatives. For this reason, a hardware selection committee made up of IS personnel and, in some cases, interested (and technically informed) users. A committee should have a cross section of hardware, systems software, applications software, operations, and functional area expertise.

An individual or group of persons within IS and some user departments should be charged with maintaining an ongoing expertise and knowledge of the computing hardware marketplace, even during times of little or no acquisition. Hardware acquisition is ongoing, even in small corporations; therefore, a continuity of knowledge needs to be maintained from one year to the next.

Communication with the Vendor. If done correctly, the vendor should receive at most three documents requesting input into the hardware evaluation and selection process: the request for information (RFI), the request for proposal (RFP), and the follow-up decision statement after the selection is made. These are the only formal communications with the vendor. The RFI is optional.

Request for Information. The request for information (RFI) is helpful when the corporation is not well informed of the scope and availability of computing hardware. The RFI has a side benefit that is not apparent when initially sent to the vendors. The RFI can be used to identify interested vendors. Those that do not respond or respond in a lukewarm manner can be immediately scratched as potential vendors. The RFI is not meant to be a request for proposal (RFP) and this should be stated in the RFI. The RFI is simply a letter sent to appropriate vendors to canvass the marketplace and determine which suppliers have viable alternatives and/or are willing to compete for the business. The RFI should include a general description of the existing computing environment, the changes in operations and/or technology that prompted the RFI, some historical perspective, the present computer system configuration (if any), and a brief statement of any problems, constraints, or limitations.

Request for Proposal. The request for proposal (RFP) is comprised of information and directions for the vendor, standardized forms, and requests for certain data and information. It is the formal request to a vendor for a proposal. It is recommended that the RFPs be distributed in a joint meeting of IS personnel, users (if part of a selection committee), and competing vendors. During this meeting, the RFP can be explained in detail and vendors can ask questions necessary to clarify parts of the RFP. The joint meeting eliminates the possibility of unknowingly giving an unfair advantage to a vendor.

Unless standardized forms are utilized for responses to RFPs, the hardware evaluation and selection committee will find it difficult to compare various alternatives proposed by vendors. It is to the vendor's advantage to put the requesting company in a situation where they are "comparing apples to oranges." Cost is not always the bottom line. The use of standardized forms (see Figures 7-38 through 7-41) provides a common denominator for evaluation of the RFPs.

The text of the RFP should include:

- A general description of the past and present computing environment.
- A time-phased definition of the objectives for the proposed hardware acquisition and/or upgrade.
- A description of alternative approaches being considered.
- Guidelines for the RFP responses (scope, format, and deadline).
- Details of cost presentation (purchase only, lease, lease-purchase, discount rate, depreciation schedules, tax rate, horizon, and so on).
- References (companies who can support vendor claims).
- Award procedure.
- Award criteria.
- Proposed implementation schedule.
- New systems requirements.
- Contact persons within the corporation (the vendor should be restricted as to who can be contacted).

Included after the above introductory material in the RFP are:

- Hardware/software vendor questionnaire
- System characteristics
- Cost summary
- Benchmark results
- User surveys

Report Title:	System Characteristics	Date	Vendor

Feature	Included in bid	Available		Comments
		Date	Cost	

FIGURE 7-38 System Characteristics form.

Report Title:	Benchmark Results	Date	Vendor

Job name	Circumstances	CPU time (seconds)	Elapsed time (minutes)	Response time (seconds)		Comments

Page ___ / ___

FIGURE 7-39 Cost Summary form.

168

| Report Title: | Cost Summary | | | | | | | | | | | Date | | Vendor | | |

Item	Initial purc./Rent		Year 2		Year 3		Year 4		Year 5		Total	
	Desc.	Cost	Desc.	Cost	Desc.	Cost	Desc.	Cost	Desc.	Cost	Desc.	Cost
Total net cost, with:												

Page ___ / ___

FIGURE 7-40 Benchmark Results form.

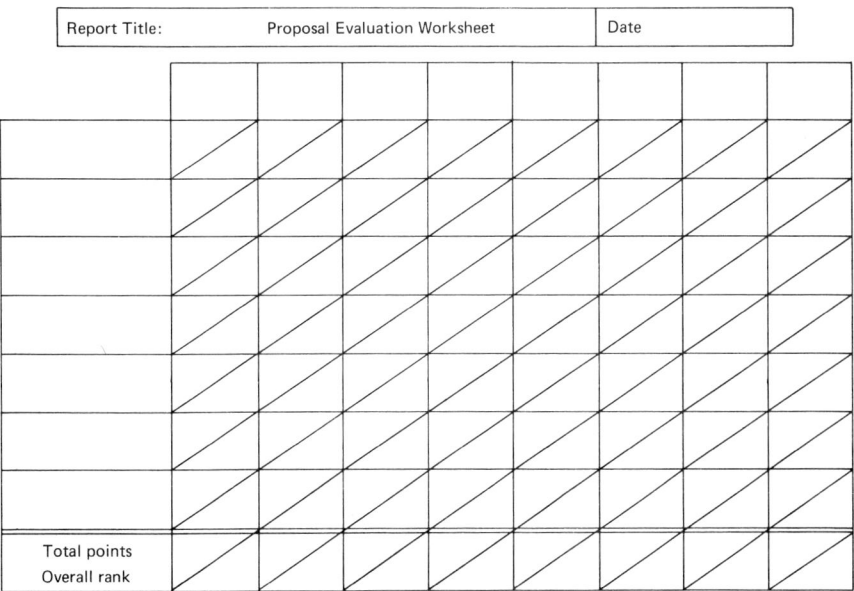

FIGURE 7-41 Proposal Evaluation worksheet.

These sections of the RFP are discussed briefly below.

The Hardware/Software Vendor questionnaire poses specific questions to the vendor for which the company expects a response. This questionnaire should be comprehensive. A vendor wanting the business of a particular corporation will be more than happy to answer these questions. The questions could be on systems software, applications software, communications capabilities, hardware interfaces, environment and power specifications, access controls, reliability, and other areas.

The System Characteristics form, Figure 7-38, allows the organization an opportunity to list features that are of particular interest to them. It is not a specification sheet. It is intended to display cost, availability, and any comments regarding these specifically listed features. The vendor's responses can be more easily compared when each addresses specific characteristics.

The Cost Summary in Figure 7-39 provides a vehicle by which costs can be presented in a standard format for ease of comparison among vendors. The cost can be presented over time if future systems upgrades are proposed. If discounted cost figures are requested, the discount rate should be identified so that all vendors use the same rate.

The Benchmark Results form, Figure 7-40, ensures a standardized presentation of benchmark results. A form of this type is intended for only the most basic types of information; however, it does allow the selection committee a method of easy comparison of benchmark results between vendors.

Evaluation of Responses. The evaluation is accomplished by the hardware selection committee. The Proposal Evaluation Worksheet shown in Figure 7-41 is used to display graphically both individual and cumulative evaluations for each proposal. In this matrix form, each criterion is given a relative point value for evaluating each proposal (100 total points possible). The vendors and/or vendor alternatives are listed on the top of each column. Each criterion, with its associated relative point value, is placed in the respective boxes for each row. Suggested award criteria are total cost, availability of software, system flexibility, system reliability, compatibility with existing activities, backup, and an overall evaluation.

Each evaluator rates each proposal against each criterion. The worksheets are gathered from the committee members and the results are tabulated and displayed on a cumulative worksheet. Each proposal can be ranked relative to each criterion and overall. These rankings and relative point values provide valuable insight to the selection process.

Machine Room Tour

After reading this chapter, ask an IS manager for a tour of the machine room. Ask the guide to explain briefly and illustrate the operation of each device. A tour will help the reader gain and retain an understanding of the operation and use of the various hardware devices.

CHAPTER 8

Data Management

Data management encompasses the storage, retrieval, and manipulation of data. To interact effectively with IS personnel during systems development and ongoing operation, user managers should have a solid working knowledge of the concepts, approaches, and terminology in this chapter.

DATA AND INFORMATION

A computer system does not store information, it stores data. Data are the raw material from which information is derived and are stored for periodic access on secondary (auxiliary) storage devices (tape and disk). Information is data which has been assimilated, accumulated, and massaged into a meaningful format. To highlight the difference between data and information, consider the following example. A department head asks all employees to write their age on a separate sheet of paper. Each sheet of paper contains a piece of raw data that has very little meaning. However, from this data the manager can extract information. He could determine how many employees are over 50, the average age, the age of the youngest person, and so on. The often-used phrase, "information processing," is a misnomer. *Data* are processed to produce *information*.

HIERARCHY OF DATA ORGANIZATION

Information systems have a hierarchy of data organization whereby each succeeding level is a result of combining elements of the preceding level until an integrated data base is achieved. This hierarchy is illustrated in Figure 8-1. The first level, bits, is transparent to the user, but the other five levels are logical extensions of user input and requirements. Data are the foundation of any information system, and an end user's knowledge of data organization and approaches to processing is requisite to a quality computer-based information system. The following section discusses each level of the hierarchy and relates each level to the next.

Bits

The **bit** is the basic unit of primary or auxiliary storage. The computer is electronic and can therefore realize only two states. Physically these states are achieved in a variety of ways (current direction, on-off, magnetic arrangement of ferrous oxide coating on tapes and disks). Since each bit can only represent two states, bits must be combined to form alphanumeric characters. Alphanumeric characters are stored temporarily in main memory (primary storage) and permanently on auxiliary storage via **bit configurations**. These are internal representations of alphanumeric characters (e.g., 11000001 represents an "A" and 11110001 represents a "1," using the **EBCDIC** encoding system).

Alphanumeric characters are **encoded** to a bit configuration upon input and **decoded** upon output. There is no industry standard encoding system. The most popular encoding systems are the six-bit Binary Coded Decimal (BCD), the seven-bit ASCII-7 code, and the eight-bit Extended Binary Coded Decimal Interchange Code (EBCDIC—pronounced 'ĕb-sē-dĭk).

The six-bit code can represent up to 64 characters (2 to the sixth power). Seven-bit codes can represent 128 characters and eight-bit codes 256 characters. The question might arise as to why one would use eight bits when six will do. The 64 possible combinations of a six-bit code can

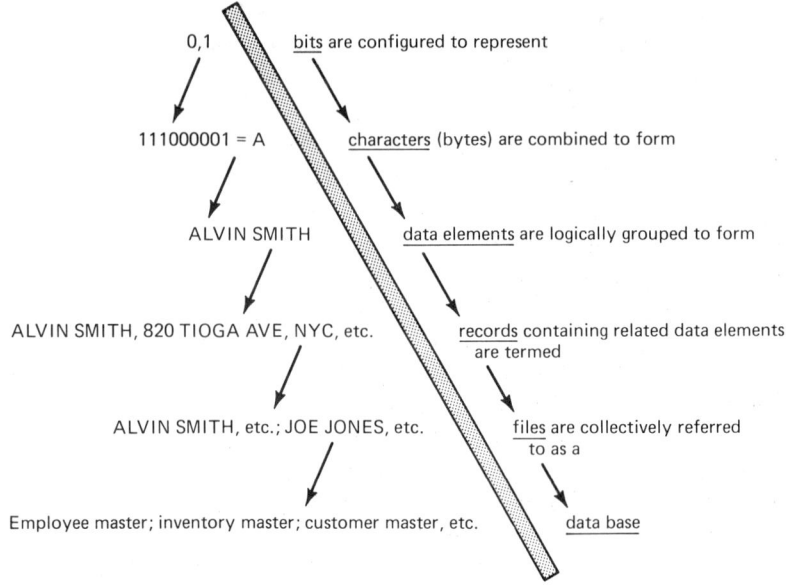

FIGURE 8-1 Hierarchy of data organization.

be used to represent the alphabet, the numbers, and a couple of dozen special characters. If upper- and lowercase alpha characters are desirable, a seven-bit code with 128 possible configurations would be required.

It is difficult to conceive of a need for more than 128 possible bit configurations. The eight-bit encoding system (EBCDIC) was introduced to take advantage of the fact that only four bits with 16 possible combinations (2 to the fourth power) are required to represent numeric data. Therefore, an eight-bit code can actually be used to represent *two* decimal digits. Since much of the stored data is strictly numeric, data can be stored more efficiently by "packing" two digits into eight bits. The combination of eight EBCDIC bits is called a **byte**. Six BCD bits make up a byte. In BCD and ASCII-7, a byte is synonymous with a character. In EBCDIC, numeric data can be packed into one byte, therefore EBCDIC bytes are not one-to-one with characters. However, byte and character are often used interchangeably in reference to storage capacity. A disk pack may have an 800 **megabyte** capacity (800 million bytes of permanent storage). Main memory may have 8 megabytes (8 million bytes of high-speed temporary storage for processing). Smaller storage devices are measured in **kilobytes** (thousands of bytes). Megabytes and kilobytes are generally shortened to "M" and "K," respectively.

Logically, an EBCDIC byte is eight bits, but physically there are actually nine bits. Since these bytes are transferred between the computer, peripheral devices, and remote terminals at high rates of speed, the hardware uses a built-in checking procedure to ensure that the transmission was completed accurately. The extra **parity bit** is part of the checking procedure used to detect if a bit has been "dropped" during transmission. A computer will use either even or odd parity; that is, every byte will contain an even or odd number of "on" bits. If a computer uses even parity and an EBCDIC "A" (with an odd number of bits—11000001) is written to magnetic tape (see Figure 7-29), then a parity bit is added before transmission to maintain an even parity (i.e., **1**11000001—parity bit is in bold). The number of "on" bits is counted before the character is written to the tape. If the count is odd, a parity error occurs and the operator is alerted.

Characters (bytes)

As a character is entered through a keyboard, optical character recognition (OCR), or other device, it is immediately translated to a bit configuration of a specific encoding system. A single computer system may use several encoding systems. For example, some use ASCII for data communications and EBCDIC for data storage.

Data Elements

Data elements are best described by example. Social security number, first name, stock number, street address, and marital status are all data elements. The data element is the lowest-level logical unit in the data hierarchy. Bits and bytes must be combined to form a logical unit. A date is not necessarily one data element, but three data elements: day, month, and year. The same is true for address. The data elements in an address are street address, city, state, and zip code. Logically, date and address could be treated as one data element, but output of such a data element would be cumbersome. For example, since the street address is normally placed on a separate line on output, the address data elements should be separated. Also, name and address files are often sorted by zip code, thereby necessitating that zip code be handled as a logical entity (data element).

Depending on the context of use, data elements are also referred to as **fields** (fields of record). *Data element* is the generic reference, where **data item** is the actual entry or "occurrence." For example, social security number is a data element, and 445487279 and 440214158 are the data items.

Data elements are often coded on input to save keystrokes during the data entry process and to save storage space. For example, the "sex" data element on the employee master file is usually coded. Instead of entering "male" or "female," the data entry operator simply enters

"M" or "F." Upon output, the "M" or "F" is translated to "male" and "female," respectively.

Data elements can be designed such that a coded data item, like account number, can have special meaning and provide information to the user. For example, a six-position account number for a university might be coded as follows:

Position	A/N	Code	Description
1	Alpha	G	General
		E	Educational
		R	Research
2–3	Alpha	BI	Biology
		CE	Civil Engineering
		CH	Chemical Engineering
		EE	Electrical Engineering
		FA	Fine Arts
		ZY	Zoology
4–6	Numeric	N/A	Unique numerical project identifier

As an example, RBI001 would designate the account number for research project number 1 in the biology department.

Records

Related data elements are logically grouped to form a **record**. Figure 8-2 lists several of the data elements that might be contained in an employee record and the data items for an occurrence of an employee record. The record is the lowest-level logical unit that can be accessed from the data base. For example, if the personnel manager needs to know the marital status of Alvin E. Smith, his entire record would be accessed from auxiliary storage and transmitted to memory for processing.

Data elements	Data items
Employee/social security number	445447279
Last name	SMITH
First name	ALVIN
Middle initial	E
Department (coded)	ACT
Sex (coded)	M
Marital status (coded)	S
Salary (per week)	800.00
.	.
.	.
.	.

FIGURE 8-2 An employee record.

Files

A **file** is a collection of logically related records. The employee master file contains a record for each employee. An inventory file contains a record for each inventory item. The accounts receivable file contains a record for each customer. Occasionally the term "file" is used to refer to a named area on a secondary storage device that may contain program code, text material, data, or even output reports.

Data Base

The **data base** is all corporate data that serves as a resource for computer-based information systems. The corporate data base is sometimes segmented into applications areas. One application area, the finance and accounting data base, might contain six separate files. It should be noted the the "file" method of data organization is inherently redundant; that is, data elements must be repeated in several files for processing purposes. In a university, for example, the placement office, residence operations, financial aid office, and the registrar are all likely to maintain student files. Certain data such as student name, campus address, and so on are duplicated in each file. While investigating the feasibility of developing an integrated student information system, analysts at a large southwestern university uncovered 75 separate computer-based files that maintained student name and campus address. Sophisticated data base management software provides improvements over the traditional file system and allows users to minimize the redundancy of stored data. Data base management systems are discussed in detail later in this chapter.

DATA MANIPULATION AND RETRIEVAL —TRADITIONAL FILE PROCESSING

Data are stored according to the hierarchy of data organization, but there are several options for processing data. Traditional **flat files** can be processed either sequentially or randomly. These traditional modes of processing are discussed in this section. An integrated data base uses data base management systems software to organize and process data. This approach is discussed in the next section.

Traditional file processing involves the sorting, merging, and processing of flat files. A flat file consists of logically related records that are processed by a **key data element** (e.g., customer number, stock number). For example, an order file (containing transactions) is processed "against" the customer master file to produce the shipping orders and invoices.

Sequential Processing

Sequential files, used for **sequential processing,** contain records that are ordered according to a key data element. The key (sometimes called a control field) in an employee record might be social security number or employee name. In the first instance, the employee records would be ordered and processed numerically by social security number. In the second case, the records would be ordered and processed alphabetically by last name. A sequential file is processed from start to finish. A particular record cannot be updated without processing the entire file.

Although DASDs, like magnetic disks, can be used for sequential processing, the primary media for sequential files is magnetic tape. Using magnetic disks for sequential processing negates the advantage of magnetic disks: random processing.

Sequential processing of an inventory file update is illustrated in Figure 8-3 and 8-4. Figure 8-3 contains the contents of an *inventory master file* sorted by stock number (the key) and a *transaction file*, also sorted by stock number. Both files must be sorted and arranged in ascending sequence by stock number prior to processing.

Figure 8-4 shows both the master and transaction files as input and the *new inventory master file* as output. Since the technology does not permit records to be "rewritten" on the master file, a new master

Inventory master file (sorted by part number)

	Part no.	Price	No. used to date	No. in stock
One record →	2	.25	40	200
	4	1.40	100 [120] *	1,00 [80]
	8	.80	500	450
	.	.	.	.
	.	.	.	.
	.	.	.	.
	20	4.60	60 [72]	14 [2]
	21	2.20	50	18

Transaction file (sorted by part number)

Part no.	No. used today
4	20
20	12

*[ ] s reflect updated values

FIGURE 8-3 Inventory master and transaction files.

file tape is created to reflect the updates to the master file. The processing steps are illustrated in Figure 8-4 and explained below.

Prior to processing. If the two input tapes are not sorted by stock number, this is done and they are mounted on the tape drives. Typically the master file would be sorted, but the transaction file would need to be sorted prior to the update run. A blank tape is mounted on another tape drive. This tape will ultimately contain the updated master file. The arrows under the stock numbers indicate which records are positioned before the read/write heads on the respective tape drives. These will be read next. Each file has an end-of-file marker (EOF).

STEP 1. The first record (4) on the transaction file is "loaded" to main memory. Then, the first record on the master file (2) is loaded to main memory. A comparison is made of the two keys. Because there is not a match (4 ≠ [is not equal to] 2), the first record on the master file is written without being changed to the new master file tape.

STEP 2. The next record (4) on the master file is read and loaded to main memory. After a positive comparison (4 = 4), the record of stock number 4 is updated (see Figure 8-3) to reflect the use of 20 items and then written to the new master file. Those records that are updated are graphically identified in Figure 8-4 by being enclosed in boxes.

STEP 3. The next record from the transaction file (20) and the next record from the master file (8) are read and loaded to main memory. A comparison is made. Since the match is negative (20 ≠ 8), the record for stock number 8 is written without change to the new master file.

STEP 4. Records from the master file are individually read, loaded, and the stock number compared to that of the transaction record (20). With each negative comparison, the record is written, without change, to the new master file. The read-and-compare process continues until a match is made (20 = 20). Record 20 is updated and written to the new master.

STEP 5. A read is issued to the transaction file and an **end-of-file (EOF) marker** is found. This end-of-file marker indicates that there are no further transactions. All records on the master file following the record for stock number 20 are written to the new master file and an end-of-file marker is recorded on the new master. All tapes are then automatically rewound and removed from the tape drives for off-line storage and processing at a later time.

Advantages of Sequential Processing. Sequential processing has several distinct advantages. It is conceptually simple. Computer-based systems are often extensions of sequential manual systems. Sequential processing uses magnetic tape which is the least expensive of all storage media. The cost per byte of storage is only a fraction that of disks.

Sequential processing is very efficient for **high-activity** files. High-

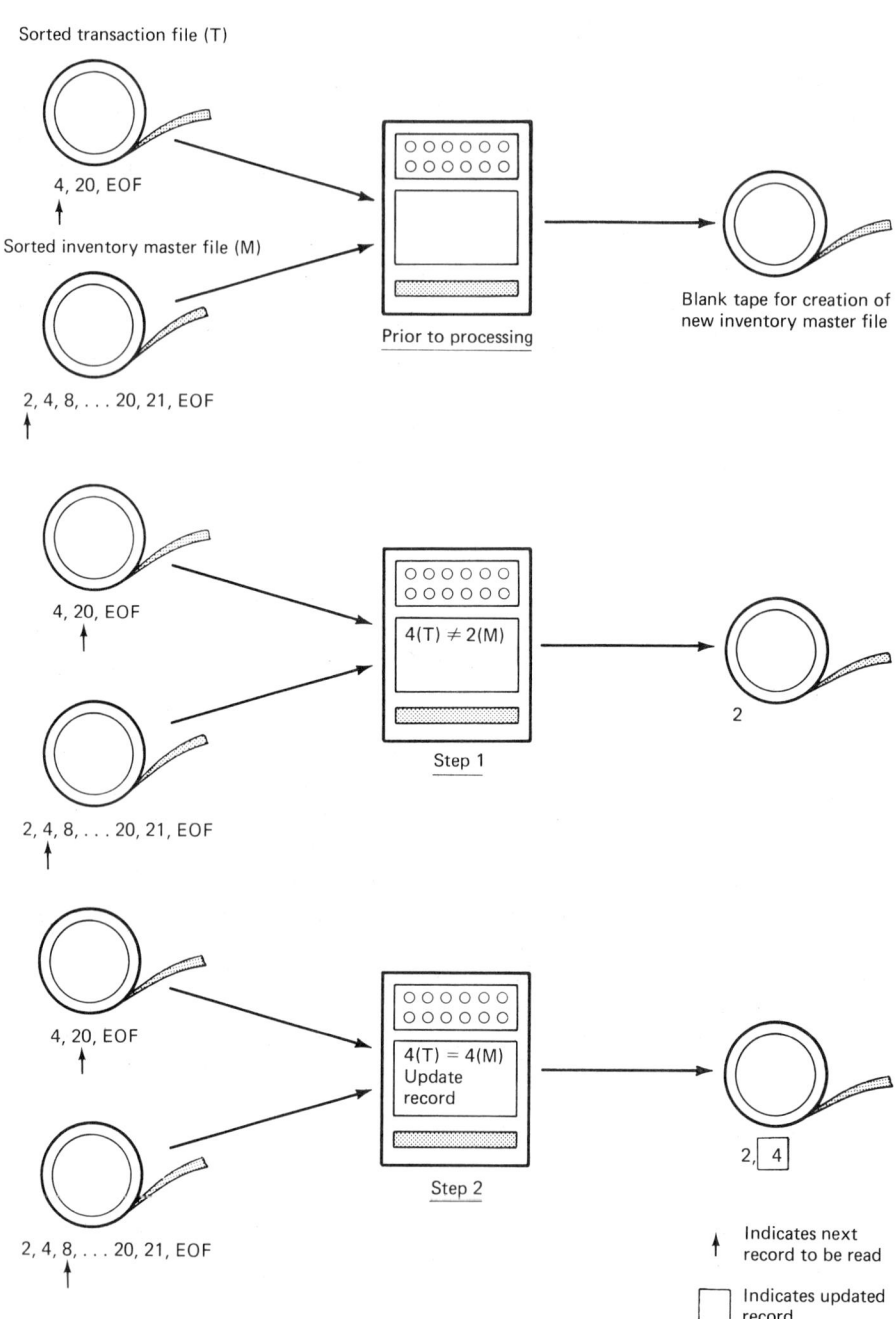

Sorted transaction file (T)

4, 20, EOF

Sorted inventory master file (M)

Prior to processing

2, 4, 8, . . . 20, 21, EOF

Blank tape for creation of
new inventory master file

4, 20, EOF

$4(T) \neq 2(M)$

Step 1

2, 4, 8, . . . 20, 21, EOF

2

4, 20, EOF

$4(T) = 4(M)$
Update
record

Step 2

2, 4, 8, . . . 20, 21, EOF

2, 4

↑ Indicates next
record to be read

☐ Indicates updated
record

FIGURE 8–4 Update of an inventory master file using sequential processing and magnetic tapes.

180

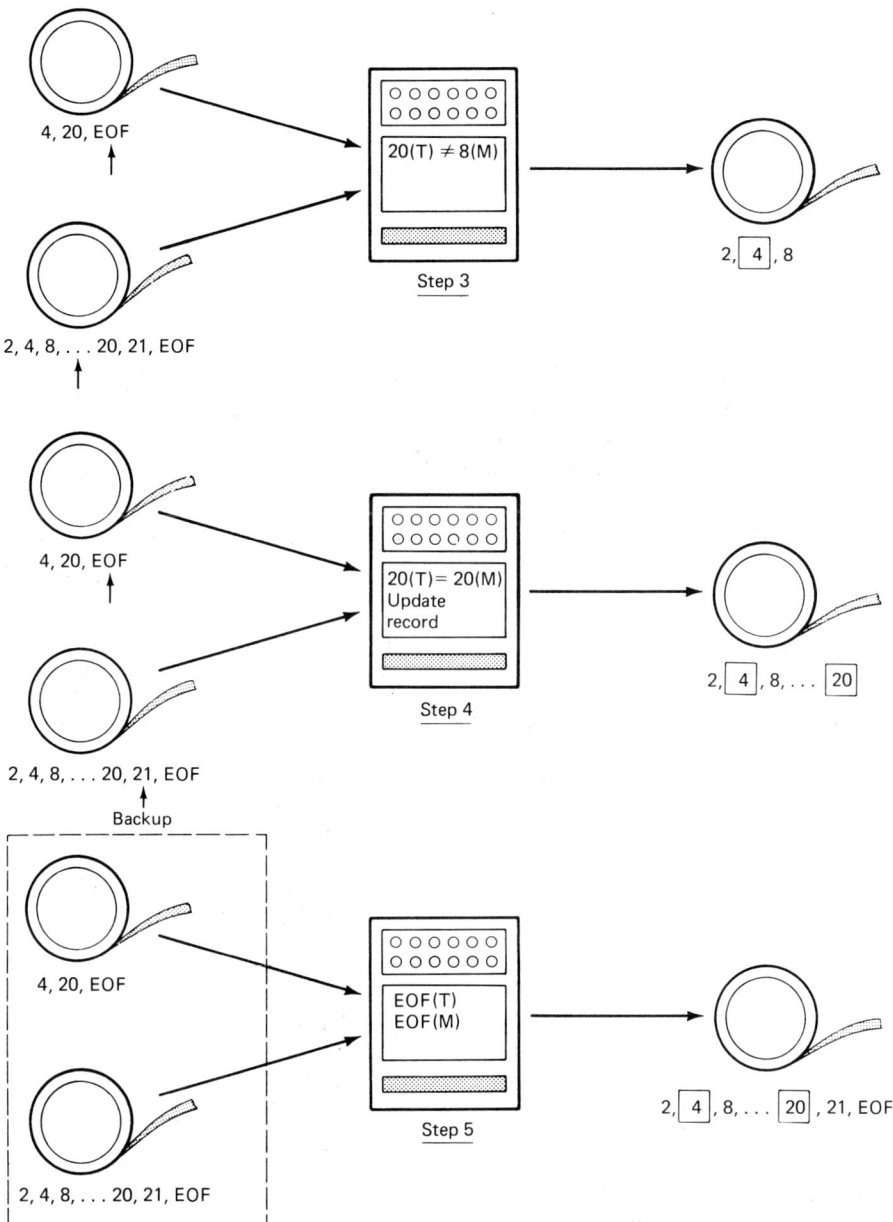

FIGURE 8-4 Continued.

activity files have a high percentage of the records updated or accessed each time the file is processed. Unlike disk files, which require considerable mechanical movement to access a record, records in high-activity sequential files are always close to or under the tape read/write head.

Backup is always a key consideration in maintaining the corporate data base. If the accounts receivable master file is accidentally or purposefully destroyed, some companies would have a difficult time surviving without appropriate backup. The backup is built into sequential processing. After the new master file is created, the old master file and the transaction file provide the backup. If the new master is destroyed, the transaction file could simply be run against the old master file to recreate the new master file. The backup is illustrated by the dashed line in Step 5 of Figure 8–4.

Backup files are handled and maintained by *generation*, with the up-to-date master file being the first generation. The second generation is noted by the dashed line in Step 5 of Figure 8–4. Most computer centers maintain a third generation (from the last update run) as a backup to the backup. This is called the **grandfather-father-son method**, with the son being the up-to-date master file.

Disadvantages of Sequential Processing. For many years sequential processing was the only alternative, and data centers simply accepted certain built-in disadvantages. The entire file must be processed, even when only one record is accessed or processed. Any transactions run against a sequential master file must be sorted by the appropriate key field. Sorting is time consuming and requires additional computer runs. Finally, sequential processing is by nature a batch process; therefore, a file never reflects an up-to-the-minute status.

Random or Direct Access Processing

A **direct access** or **random file** is a collection of records that can be processed randomly (in any order). This is called **random processing**. Only the value of the record's key field is needed for the record to be accessed or updated. The storage media most often used for random processing are magnetic disks. It is possible to access records on a direct access file by more than one key. For example, a salesperson inquiring about the availability of a particular product could inquire by product number and, if the number is not known, by product name. The file, however, must be created with the intent of having **multiple keys**.

Indexed Sequential Access Method. The procedures and mechanics of how a particular record is accessed directly are for the most part

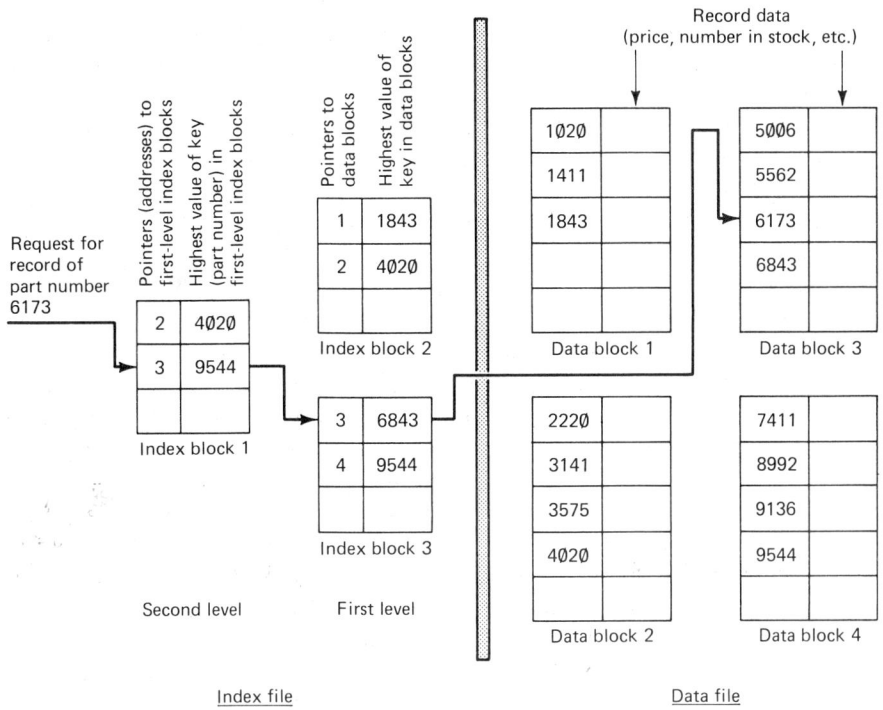

FIGURE 8-5 Record access using ISAM.

transparent to programmers and, certainly, to user managers. However, some familiarity will enable you to understand the capabilities and limitations of direct access methods. This is important during the design of an information system. The most popular method of direct access is the **indexed sequential access method (ISAM)**. The following explanation is a brief overview of ISAM (pronounced 'i-sam).

The disk access arm, and therefore the read/write head, is usually not positioned over the track containing the desired record (see Chapter 7 for a review of disk operation). In ISAM, the access of any given record is, in effect, a series of sequential searches through several levels of indices. These indices minimize the search time for locating the record to be processed. Figure 8-5 illustrates how indices are used to locate a particular record using ISAM.

When an ISAM file is created, several data records are grouped together or *blocked* and an *index file* is created. The index file is also blocked, but in a hierarchical manner. The number of levels of index blocks varies with the size of the file. Each index block contains "index records." Extra index records are included in each block to leave space for records to be added in the future.

Each index record contains a value of a key and a "**pointer**" to the next level of index block or directly to a data block (first level). The pointer is a *physical address* depicting the disk location (i.e., disk pack, disk face surface, track, and record number) of the first index record in an index block or the first data record in a data block. To simplify the example in Figure 8-5, the actual disk addresses are omitted and replaced with the numbers of the index and data blocks.

The key value in each index record is the *highest value key* contained in the next level index block or the data block. The first record in index block 1 contains a pointer to index block 2; therefore, the highest key value in index block 2 (4020) is included in the first record of index block 1.

Step through the following example using Figure 8-5 as a point of reference and you should have a basic understanding of how an ISAM file works. The search always begins with the highest-level index block (second level in the example) and progresses through each successive level in the index file to the data file. Each index block is searched sequentially beginning with the first index record in order to determine which block to search at the next level.

ISAM is most easily understood by example. Suppose you would like to retrieve the record for part number 6173. The search would begin with the first record of index block 1. Since 6173 is greater than the highest key value in index block 2 (4020), the search would proceed to the next index record in index block 1. Since 6173 is less than 9544, the search is directed to index block 3 (in the next [first] level of index blocks).

The records of index block 3 are searched sequentially until the search is directed to the next index level *or*, in the example, a data block. Since 6173 is less than 6843, there is no need to search any more records in index block 3. In the example, the search is directed to *data* block 3. The data block is searched sequentially until the record for part number 6173 is located. The third record of data block 3 contains the record for part number 6173. The record is read and transmitted to main memory for processing.

On the surface ISAM files may seem cumbersome. In practice, however, the search process for each record is completed in a few milliseconds. It should be emphasized again that the search and retrieval process is transparent to the programmers and user managers. The programmer has only to issue a "read" for part number 6173. The computer and ISAM software do the rest.

Direct Access Using Hashing Algorithms. Another method of accessing records randomly uses a **hashing algorithm** to calculate arithmetically a disk address for each record. The advantage of "hashings" over

ISAM is that there is usually only one disk seek required. The address of a record is derived from the key field. For example, to obtain the record of part number 6173, the key value (6173) is processed through an algorithm. There are a wide variety of hashing algorithms.

The limited number of disk seeks permit hashing methods to retrieve records more quickly than ISAM. ISAM, however, permits records to be accessed sequentially as well as randomly. These are the basic trade-offs between the two random access methods.

Principles of Random Processing. Figure 8-6 illustrates the principles of random processing. The *unsorted* inventory master and transaction files of Figure 8-3 are used. The following processing activities occur.

Prior to processing. The unsorted transaction tape and the inventory master disk pack are loaded on their respective drives. The transaction tape may be a log of transactions that were entered throughout the day. The master file is an ISAM file.

STEP 1. The first transaction record (20) is read into main memory. The computer issues a read for the record of stock number 20 on the inventory master file. The record is transmitted to main memory. The record is updated and written back to the same location on the master file. The updated record is simply written over the old record.

STEP 2. The second record from the transaction file (4) is read into main memory and the master file is updated in the same manner as Step 1.

STEP 3. An attempt is made to read another record from the transaction file and the end-of-file marker is found indicating there are no more updates. The transaction tape is rewound and both files are removed for off-line storage.

Unlike sequential processing where the backup is built-in, random processing requires a special run to provide backup to the inventory master file. This is usually done at regular and frequent intervals by "dumping" the master file from disk to tape as illustrated in Figure 8-7. If the inventory file is destroyed, the inventory master file would be recreated by dumping the backup file (on tape) to disk (the reverse of Figure 8-7).

Advantages of Random Processing. The advantages of random processing have persuaded the majority of computer users to adopt this mode of processing. Processing can be performed with unsequenced data. Several adjacent files can be processed concurrently (e.g., accounts receivable, customer master, general accounting files). An updated record can be written to the same physical location. There are times when sequential processing of a ISAM file is desirable—when an alphabetized

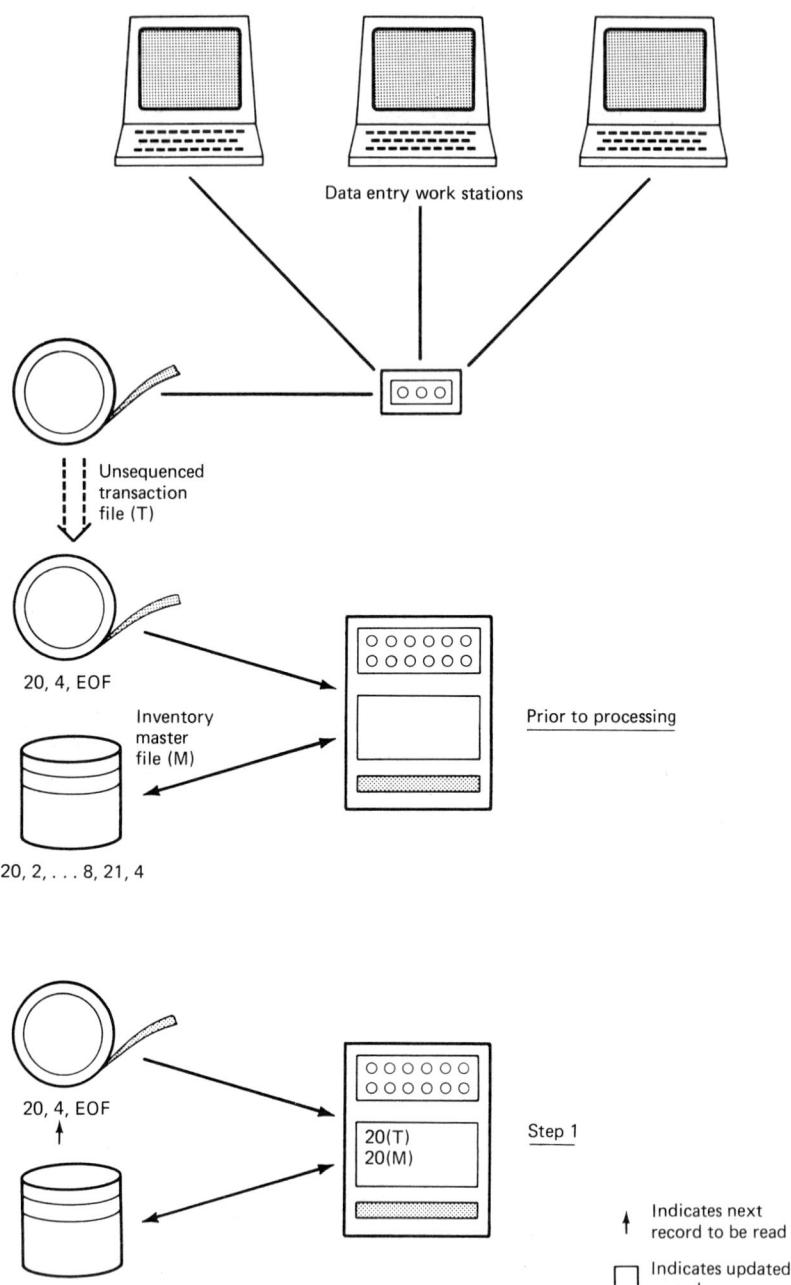

Data entry work stations

Unsequenced transaction file (T)

20, 4, EOF

Inventory master file (M)

20, 2, . . . 8, 21, 4

Prior to processing

20, 4, EOF

20, 2, . . . 8, 21, 4

20(T)
20(M)

Step 1

↑ Indicates next record to be read

☐ Indicates updated record

FIGURE 8-6 Update of an inventory master file using random processing and magnetic disks.

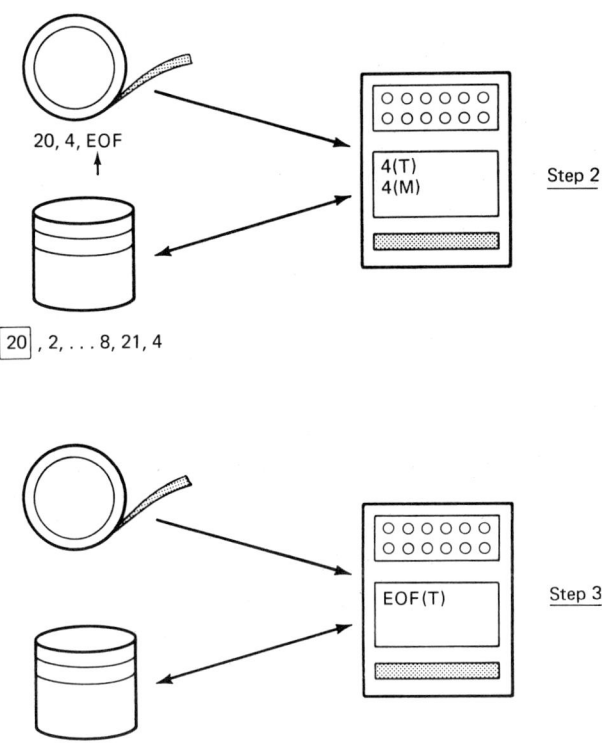

FIGURE 8-6 Continued.

directory of company employees is compiled, for example. For these cases, ISAM files can be processed sequentially.

Disadvantages of Random Processing. The primary disadvantages of random processing are the high cost of the data storage media and the special provisions required for backup.

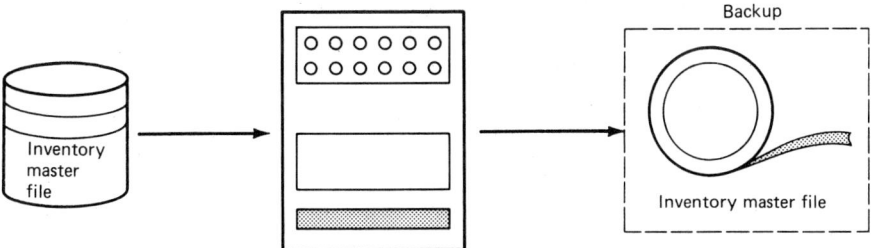

FIGURE 8-7 Backup procedure for random processing.

CLASSIFICATION OF FILES

Most references are either to the "master" or the "transaction" files. Other file classifications include table, backup, archival, and output. These files are described below.

Master files. The master file is the permanent source of data for a particular application area. The master file contains records that are accessed regularly to provide information and updated to reflect the current situation. Typical master files are the inventory master, employee master, accounts receivable master, and so on.

Transaction files. The transaction file contains records of data activity (transactions) for an information system. These transactions are batched to make up the transaction file. For example, the data from the weekly pay sheets are transcribed and batched on a transaction file and run against the payroll master file to print the payroll checks and the payroll register.

Table files. Table files are tables. Rather than build a table into the programming software, a separate table file is established to facilitate the updating process. For example, the rate schedule of a utility company or the tax rates for the Internal Revenue Service are stored on a table file.

Backup files. The backup file is a duplicate of an existing production file. Backup files can be used to recreate production files in case they are destroyed.

Archival files. Archival files are not used for current processing but are maintained for historical reference. The IRS, for example, might want to examine the history of an individual over the last 15 years. In effect, archival files are a snapshot of corporate operation at any given point in time.

Output files. An output file contains the digital image of information that is to be printed on a printer, displayed on a screen, or plotted. Output files are created when an output device is not available. The output is "spooled" (stored on an auxiliary storage device) until the output device is available.

DATA MANIPULATION AND RETRIEVAL—
INTEGRATED DATA BASE
MANAGEMENT SYSTEMS

Up to this point the discussion has centered on traditional file processing, where files are processed as autonomous logical entities and usually associated with a particular functional area. In order to integrate the traditional files of functionally adjacent departments, files must be prepared by sorting records and merging files. This can be time consuming and, in some cases, impractical.

A file is usually designed to meet the specific requirements of a particular functional area department. If a department desires to use part of the data maintained on a file designed for use by another department, they must extract and reformat the data for their usage. Rather than accommodate another department's functional requirements, most departments invariably elect to create and maintain a similar (but different) file that better suits their purposes. The net result is an excessive number of files, each filled with redundancies. A previous example alluded to a university that maintained over 75 separate computer-based files containing student records. Each of these files had to be updated each time a student married or changed addresses.

Data redundancy is costly and can be minimized by designing an integrated corporate data base to serve the corporation as a whole and not any specific department. The integrated data base is made possible by **data base management systems (DBMS)** software.

DBMS technology was introduced in the early 1970s but did not gain widespread acceptance until the late 1970s. Early DBMS "packages" were inefficient and required substantially more hardware capacity than traditional file processing. Now hardware requirements have been reduced to the point that DBMS software is even available on small computer systems. The delay in acceptance and implementation can be attributed primarily to lack of expertise of IS professionals and the unwillingness of user managers to cooperate and compromise in establishing a corporate data base. There is now a widespread knowledge of the design and operation of DBMS software and a recognition on the part of user managers that information should be treated as a corporate resource.

Benefits of a Data Base Environment

Economic Benefits. A DBMS provides the potential to minimize data redundancy through advanced data structure techniques. Even with the aid of a DBMS, some redundancy must be built in to the corporate data base in order to enhance processing. This **controlled data redundancy** is miniscule when compared to that of a traditional file environment. By minimizing data redundancy, data collection and update procedures are simplified. In the previous example, student address would be updated in only one place: the data base.

The data base environment also benefits IS technical personnel. An integrated corporate data base opens new doors for the systems analyst. Analysts are able to provide information that would not be possible with traditional files. The programming task is not nearly as complex with a DBMS since data are more readily available. Moreover, the data are "independent" of the programs. This means that user managers can add, change, or delete data elements from the data base and not affect existing applications programs. In the past, it was not at all uncommon for such a request to necessitate the modification and testing of dozens, and sometimes hundreds, of programs. There are other significant technical advantages to data base management systems that are beyond the scope of this book.

Information Benefits. An integrated corporate data base provides a structure that addresses information requirements in an orderly fashion. The data base is, in reality, the only vehicle by which to take full advantage of the corporate information resource. The data base/DBMS combination renders enormous flexibility in report generation and, therefore, in the decision-making process.

DBMS software is especially valuable in the support of on-line systems. The corporate data base is not only accessible, but would typically reflect the current status. Timeliness is critical to many inquiries. For example, a plant manager forced to shut down a work station due to equipment malfunction may inquire about the status of other work stations and use this information to reroute work in progress.

Approaches

The processing constraints of traditional files are overcome by data base management system software. To do this, data base management systems rely on sophisticated **data structures**, or the manner in which the data elements and records are related to each other. The data structures vary considerably between data base management systems. There are three basic approaches to the development of data base management systems software.

1. The Committee on Data Systems Languages (CODASYL)[9] devel-

---

[9] CODASYL is an industry-funded organization in which volunteers from different organizations cooperate to develop and recommend standards for data base management systems, programming languages, and other computer-related activities.

oped and issued guidelines based on the **network** or **plex data structure.**

2. IBM's Information Management System (IMS) uses a **hierarchical data structure.**

3. Some recent designs have been based on the **relational data base model.**

The fundamental concepts and terminology are considerably different for each of these approaches. Therefore, to minimize confusion and enhance understanding, only the CODASYL or network approach is used in the following illustrations and discussions.

Data Base Design

The following example is presented to illustrate both the principles of data base management systems and an approach to data base design. Consider the following scenario.

A library maintains a file that contains the following data elements on each record:

- ◆ Title
- ◆ Author(s)
- ◆ Publisher
- ◆ Publisher's address
- ◆ Classification
- ◆ Publication year

The head librarian wants more flexibility in obtaining decision-making information. The librarian's requests could not be met with the existing file. After conferring with IS personnel, they decided to implement a CODASYL-based data base management system.

An examination of the existing file highlights certain data redundancies. Each book or title has a separate record. Therefore, the *name* of an author who has written several books is repeated for each book written. A given publisher may have hundreds and even thousands of books in the library, but in the present data organization, the *publisher* and *publisher's address* are repeated for each title they publish.

One approach to data base design is to use the *subject–attribute matrix* as an aid to identifying data base records and the relationships between these records.[10] The following steps describe this approach to data base design.

---

[10] Kerry Nemovicher, "The EIDOS System: A Computer-Aided Methodology for Database Design," dissertation, Lehigh University, 1981.

	ATTRIBUTES	Author	Publisher	Publication year	Title	Classification	Address	
SUBJECTS								
Title	M	1	1		1			
Author		M		M				
Publisher	M			M		1		

1 One-to-one relationship
M One-to-many relationship

FIGURE 8-8 Subject-attribute matrix.

STEP 1. The logical *subjects* are listed on the left-hand side of the subject–attribute matrix of Figure 8-8. In this example the subjects are title, author, and publisher. All possible *attributes* are listed along the top of the matrix. Attributes are simply data elements that provide information about any of the subjects.

STEP 2. The relationship between a subject and an attribute is either *one-to-one, one-to-many,* or no relationship exists. For example, a particular title will have only one publisher. Therefore, there is a one-to-one relationship between title and publisher. A title, however, can have several authors. Therefore, there is a one-to-many relationship between title and author. These relationships are noted in Figure 8-8 with a "1" (one-to-one), "M" (one-to-many), or no entry (no relationship).

STEP 3. The **data base record** is similar to the record of a traditional file in that it is a collection of related data elements and is read from or written to the data base. The data base record is also called a **segment.** In this step, the subject–attribute matrix is used to identify the records. This is done by listing those attributes for each subject for which there is a one-to-one relationship. Generally, there is one record for each subject. The "title" record includes the publisher, publication year, and classification. Other records are shown graphically in Figure 8-9.

The attributes with one-to-many relationships are not included in the record in order to minimize data redundancy. These relationships will be retained, but through

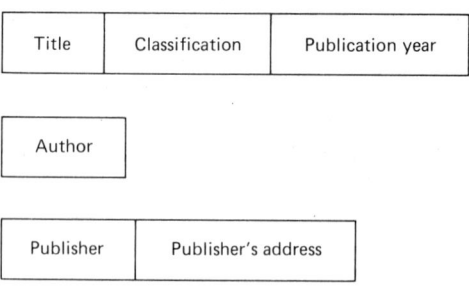

FIGURE 8-9 Data base records.

Title	Classification	Publication year	Author 1	Author 2	Author 3	Author 4

FIGURE 8-10 The traditional file alternative to the "Title" record of Figure 8-9.

the use of data structures. In traditional file organization, the "author" data element would have been included in a "title" record as shown in Figure 8-10.

STEP 4. The next step in the data base design process is to establish the relationships between the records. The one-to-many relationships noted in the subject-attribute matrix are illustrated graphically in Figure 8-11. The one-to-many relationship between the publisher and title records is noted by a line connecting the two records. The line has one arrow towards the publisher record. The two arrows towards the title record represent the possibility of more than one title per publisher. This publisher-title combination is called a set. Other sets are title-author, author-publisher, author-title, and publisher-author. Many-to-many (two arrows on each end) relationships can cause confusion in processing and are not permitted.

STEP 5. The next step is to eliminate redundant attributes and sets. In this example there are no attribute redundancies. There are, however, redundant sets. Keep in mind that the objective is to enter the data base on author, title, or publisher and then retrieve data from other records by using links established by the sets. Any set that is redundant to this objective is eliminated. In this example it is easy to see that the author-publisher sets or the author-title sets are redundant. A decision is made to eliminate the author-publisher sets since author and title would be matched more often than author-publisher. The resulting schema is shown in Figure 8-12. The schema is a graphic representation of the logical structure of the data base.

The head librarian can now make such inquiries as:

♦ List all titles written by a particular author.
♦ List those titles published in 1981 by Prentice-Hall (alphabetically by title).

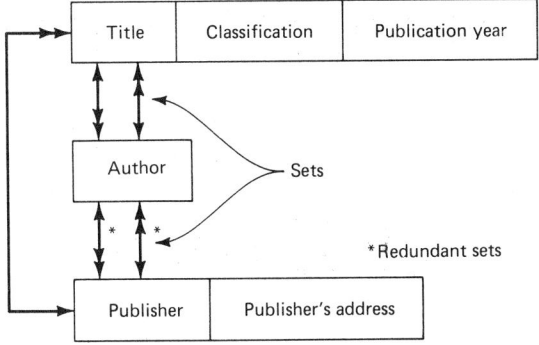

FIGURE 8-11 Relationships between data base records.

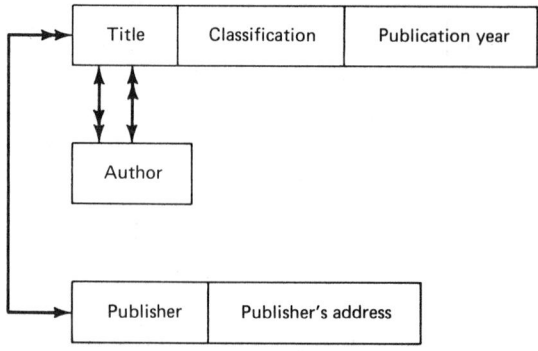

FIGURE 8-12 A completed network schema.

♦ List those authors who have published with at least three different publishers since 1978.

The data base, as designed, makes these and other similar inquiries relatively easy to obtain. Similar inquiries to the library's existing file would require not only the complete processing of the file, but perhaps several passes and some preparatory sorting and merging.

If the head librarian decides after a year that another record or attribute is needed, the data base administrator (DBA) can recreate the

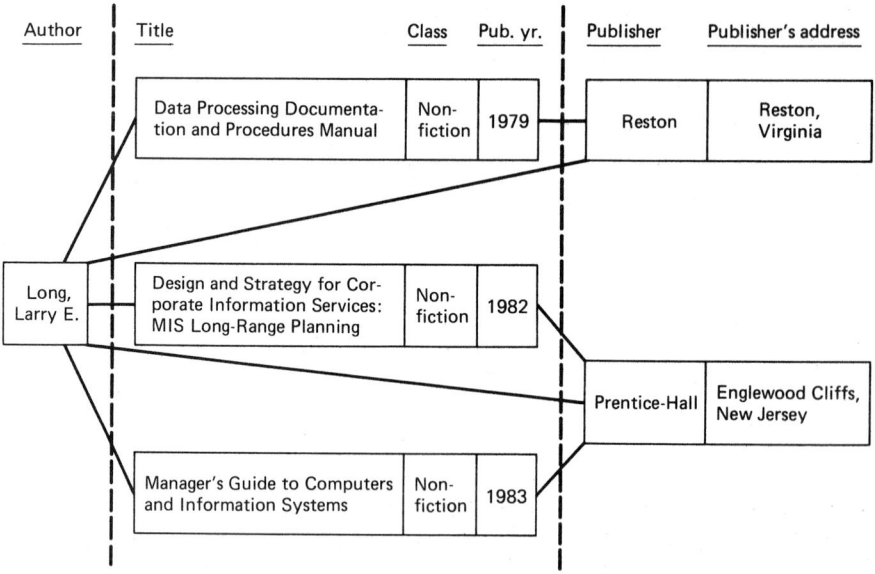

FIGURE 8-13 An occurrence of the data base structure.

data base, adding attributes and even sets without affecting existing programs.

Figure 8-12 represents the schema. Figure 8-13 is called an **occurrence** of the data base structure. The schema and the occurrence are analogous to the data element and the data item. One is the definition and the other is the actual value or contents.

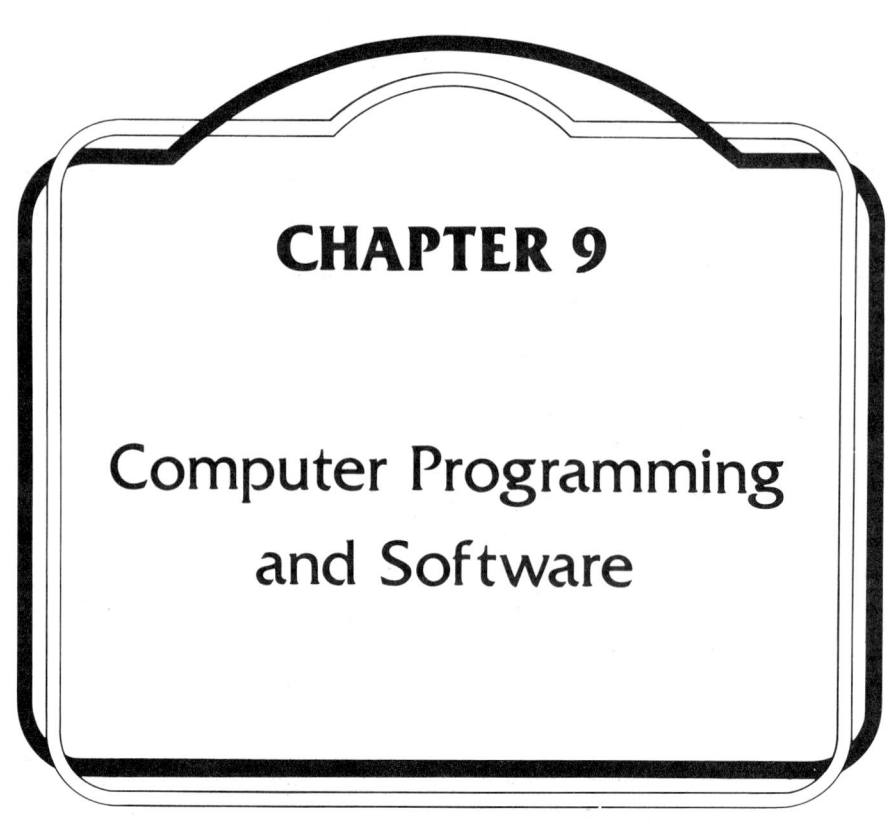

CHAPTER 9

Computer Programming and Software

A computer does nothing until programmed to do so. The **program** is a series of instructions to the computer that are compiled through the act of programming. The end result of programming is **software**.

Until the mid-1970s programming was strictly a function of IS professionals. A combination of the user becoming more knowledgeable and the availability of high-level programming languages has mainstreamed the user into the area of software development. A user manager may find it easier to do the programming from his office for many requests rather than to submit a service request for someone else to do it.

The hierarchy of programming languages and appropriate language examples are presented in this chapter. The fundamentals of programming are also introduced to provide an overview of programming to the reader who has no programming experience.

The second part of this chapter presents software in general and systems software in specific. Applications software is contrasted to systems software. Approaches to developing applications software are presented in detail in Part III.

HIERARCHY OF PROGRAMMING LANGUAGES

The hierarchy of programming languages is illustrated in Figure 9–1. Languages are categorized as either low-level or high-level. The "level" refers to the level of the sophistication of the programmer/computer interaction. For example, in **query languages** the programmer (often a user manager) need only relate to the computer "what to do," not necessarily "how to do it." In **high-level languages** the programmer must provide instructions detailing "what to do" and "how to do it," but software aids help to simplify the programmer's task. **Low-level languages** require the programmer to detail every machine-level opera-

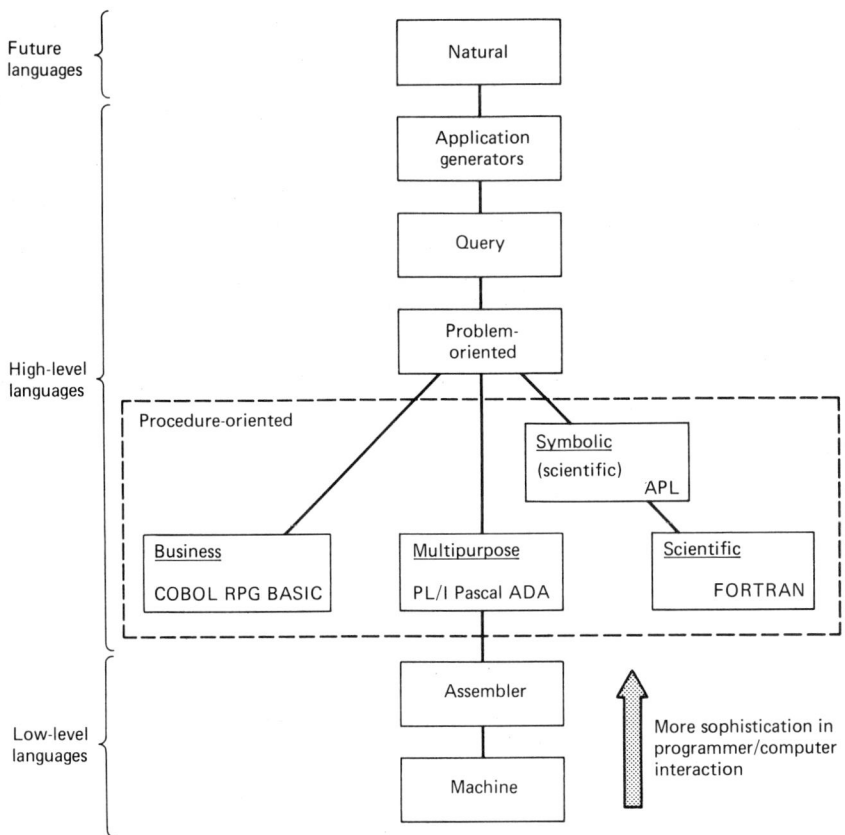

FIGURE 9–1 Hierarchy of programming languages.

tion to be executed by the computer. In high-level programming languages, the programmer does not have to keep track of the data storage locations in main memory; this is done automatically. In low-level languages, the programmer must incorporate logic into the program to monitor the physical location of data in main memory.

LOW-LEVEL LANGUAGES

Although people talk of programming in COBOL, PASCAL, and FORTRAN, there is only one language that can be executed on any given computer. That is called a **machine language**. All other languages are "compiled" (translated to machine language) and ultimately executed in the language of that particular machine.

Machine language programs are cumbersome because instructions (**operation codes** or **op codes**) and the locations on which the data are to be operated (**operands**) are presented in binary, a series of ones and zeros. A symbolic language, sometimes called **assembler language** or assembler-level language, has an instruction set that is essentially one-to-one with the machine language. The advantage of assembler languages is that mnemonics rather than ones and zeros are used for instructions. For example, rather than a string of ones and zeros, an "add" instruction would simply be "A."

Machine and assembler-level languages were used frequently for applications program development and exclusively for system software development prior to 1970. IS people believed that resultant programs used the computer more efficiently. Since then, the use of high-level languages has surpassed low-level languages in both human and computer efficiency. For this reason, most of the actual programming is done in high-level languages.

HIGH-LEVEL LANGUAGES

Procedure-Oriented Language

A procedure-oriented language (POL) is extremely flexible and can be used to depict almost any scientific or business procedure. Instructions are **coded** (or written) sequentially and processed according to user specifications. For example, payroll systems are coded using POLs. The execution of each instruction is sequential unless triggered by the logic of the program to do otherwise. In a production payroll system, a particular sequence of program instructions is executed depending upon whether the employee being processed is salaried or hourly. The program flow sequence is repeated for each employee. There are three major classifications of POLs: scientific, business, and multipurpose. Each is discussed below.

Scientific. Scientific languages are algebraic/formula-type languages and are designed specifically for meeting typical scientific processing requirements—matrix manipulation, precision calculations, and so on. The first and still the most popular scientific language is FORTRAN (Formula Translator). Although FORTRAN has been used by default as a business language (the computer did not support any other language), FORTRAN has limited business processing capabilities.

A Programming Language (APL) has caught on quickly with a number of users, primarily engineers. APL is unique in that an interactive keyboard with special symbols is used to code the program.

Business. Again, the most popular business language was the first, COBOL (Common Business Oriented Language). It is a powerful but extremely wordy language. The premise for the development of COBOL was that it should be a language whose instructions approximate the English language. Some programmers find it cumbersome to use. However, COBOL has tremendous momentum and acceptance and, therefore, is continually being improved. It will remain a popular business language for some number of years, but the relative percentage of use is declining. COBOL is most appropriate in any environment that has recurring processing cycles (for example, the printing of payroll checks) and a considerable amount of data manipulation.

The American National Standards Institute (ANSI) has established standards for COBOL and other languages. The purpose of these standards is to make programs written for one computer "portable" to another computer (i.e., one of another manufacturer). Unfortunately, the ANSI standards are only casually followed; consequently, COBOL programs are only partially portable.

Perhaps the next most popular business language is Report Program Generator (RPG). RPG was originally designed for use on IBM's entry-level computers by small businesses operating in a batch environment. RPG differs somewhat from other POLs in that the programmer must also specify certain processing requirements by selecting the desired programming option (e.g., when to print subtotals, record selection, and so on).

The original intent of the developers of BASIC is explicit in the name—Beginners All-Purpose Symbolic Instructional Code. It was initially used as a tool to teach programming, but it became so popular that the capabilities of the "beginners" language were substantially enhanced. BASIC is now the primary language used for applications programming on small computer systems. It is also used extensively on larger systems, but not for production systems. Some might classify BASIC as a multipurpose POL since it is also commonly used for light scientific work.

Multipurpose. Multipurpose languages are equally effective for both business and scientific applications. By far the most visible of these multipurpose languages is Programming Language/I (**PL/I**). PL/I was made available in 1965 by IBM, but, as any language, it required several years of field testing to work out the bugs. Many companies, primarily IBM users, have adopted PL/I as the only POL that they use. When initially introduced, PL/I was hailed as the answer to many of the shortcomings of existing programming languages. However, PL/I has still not experienced the widespread acceptance that was originally anticipated. The slow acceptance of PL/I is due, not to lack of quality or capability, but to the substantial investment that companies had in COBOL and FORTRAN and their enormous momentum.

The language experiencing the most rapid rate of growth is **PASCAL**, named after the 17th century mathematician, Blaise Pascal. PASCAL is considered the state of the art in POLs. Although only 1% or 2% of the commercial production programs are written in PASCAL, its power, flexibility, and self-documenting structure are factors that cannot be overlooked for long. Perhaps the factor that will contribute most to its acceptance and continued growth is that most college and university computer science curriculums are advocating PASCAL as the POL of the future. This exposure has created interest and expertise that is being carried to the business world upon graduation.

A recent introduction is ADA, a multipurpose language developed by the United States Department of Defense. Although only a relative few people know and understand the usage of ADA, its developers are optimistic about widespread acceptance, not only in the military, but in the private sector as well.

Problem-Oriented Languages

The instruction set of a problem-oriented language is designed specifically for a particular application and to solve a particular set of problems. Problem-oriented languages do not require the detail of procedure-oriented languages. For example, there are several problem-oriented languages that are designed for statistical analysis. The user of such a language concentrates more on input and desired output than on the mathematics. The mathematics is embedded in the language.

Problem-oriented languages have been designed for and are used in scores of applications. These applications do discrete and continuous simulation (e.g., GPSS, SIMSCRIPT, GASP-IV), program machine tools (e.g., APT), aid engineers in the analysis of stress points in buildings and bridges (e.g., COGO), assist in statistical analysis (e.g., SAS), and aid office workers in word processing (e.g., Scribe).

A procedure-oriented language has the flexibility to do statistics, word processing, and any other application addressed by a problem-oriented language. A problem-oriented language, though, is limited to the application for which it was designed.

Query Languages

Users and user managers are apt to use query languages more than other high-level languages. Depending upon the environment, however, a user might find a particular problem-oriented language helpful. Query languages are the personification of the trend to user involvement. A user manager, with a few hours of training and practice, can effectively use a query language. The manager can extract information or a report from an information system in a fraction of the time that it would take to relate specifications to a system analyst or programmer. The user need only specify what to do. The query language software automatically specifies how to do it.

Query languages use high-level English-like commands to retrieve and format data for management inquiries and reporting. An inquiry can be made interactively (in direct communication with the computer) via a query language. The output is immediately displayed upon execution of the program and/or a hard copy of the output is produced. Features of query languages include English-like commands, limited mathematical manipulation of data, automatic report formatting, sequencing (sorting), and record selection by criteria.

The following example illustrates a query language and how it would be used. A personnel manager visualized the report shown in Figure 9-2. To achieve this report, the manager used a query language called EASYTRIEVE (a software product marketed by Pansophic Systems, Inc.) to program the request. The program is illustrated in Figure 9-3.

Statement 1 of Figure 9-3 specifies that the payroll data are stored on a file called "FILEA." Although only one file is used in this example, requests requiring the use of several files or a data base are no more difficult. Line 2 describes the data elements within the file that are required to produce the report of Figure 9-2. The user would need a prior knowledge of the **record layout**. The record layout designates the relative position of each data element within the record, its type, and whether it is alphabetic or alphanumeric. The first entry, department, begins at the 98th position of the record and is three numeric characters in length ("N" for numeric and "A" for alpha-

```
8/29/84          PAYROLL FOR DEPARTMENTS 911,914          PAGE    1


                 EMPLOYEE     EMPLOYEE                NET        GROSS
   DEPARTMENT      NAME        NUMBER    SEX          PAY         PAY

        911       ARNOLD       01963      1         356.87      445.50
        911       LARSON       11357      2         215.47      283.92
        911       POWELL       11710      1         167.96      243.20
        911       POST         00445      1         206.60      292.00
        911       KRUSE        03571      2         182.09      242.40
        911       SMOTH        01730      1         202.43      315.20
        911       GREEN        12829      1         238.04      365.60
        911       ISAAC        12641      1         219.91      313.60
        911       STRIDE       03890      1         272.53      386.40
        911       REYNOLDS     05805      2         134.03      174.15
        911       YOUNG        04589      1         229.69      313.60
        911       HAFER        09764      2          96.64      121.95
   DEPARTMENT TOTAL                               2,522.26    3,497.52

        914       MANHART      11602      1         250.89      344.80
        914       VETTER       01895      1         189.06      279.36
        914       GRECO        07231      1         685.23    1,004.00
        914       CROCI        08262      1         215.95      376.00
        914       RYAN         10961      1         291.70      399.20
   DEPARTMENT TOTAL                               1,632.83    2,403.36

   FINAL TOTALS                                   4,155.09    5,900.88


   17    RECORDS TOTALED
```

FIGURE 9-2 A payroll report. (*Courtesy of Pansophic Systems, Inc.*)

numeric). The name field begins at position 17 and is 20 alphanumeric characters in length. The statement is terminated by a series of nines.

Record selection criteria are specified by an "IF" statement as shown in statement number three. The manager is interested only in those employees from departments 911 and 914. Other "IF" statements could be used for more record selection.

```
1. FILE FILEA
2. DEPARTMENT 98 3 N NAME 17 20 A EMPL# 9 5 N
   SEX 127 1 A NET 90 4 P2 GROSS 94 4 P2 9999
3. IF DEPARTMENT = 911,914
4. SORT DEPARTMENT
5. CONTROL DEPARTMENT
6. T1PAYROLL FOR DEPARTMENTS 911,914
7. LIST DETAIL DEPARTMENT NAME 'EMPLOYEE,NAME' EMPL# 'EMPLOYEE,NUMBER'
   MORE SEX NET 'NET,PAY' GROSS 'GROSS,PAY'
```

FIGURE 9-3 EASYTRIEVE program to produce the report of Figure 9-2. (*Courtesy of Pansophic Systems, Inc.*)

Statement 4 specifies that output should be sorted by department; that is, 911 employees listed before 914 employees. Employee names could have been sorted alphabetically within department by including another "sort" statement.

Statement 5 designates those points in the output where a total should be accumulated and printed. In this case, totals are required for each department.

Statements 6 and 7 allow the personnel manager to title the report and label the columns. Statement 6 is a first level title. Statement 7 specifies that abbreviated program labels be replaced by more explicit column headings ("EMPLOYEE NAME" is substituted for "NAME"). These statements can be omitted for "quick and dirty" reports. The COBOL equivalent of the personnel manager's request would require over 150 lines of code.

Query languages can be used interactively to request such information as: Which employees have more than 20 sick days since January 1? Are there any deluxe single hospital rooms to be vacated by the end of the day? What is a particular student's grade average in all math courses taken? List departments that have exceeded budget alphabetically by the department head's name; and so on. Minor inquiries to large files and data bases are made easy by query languages. For example, to a secretary not knowing the gender of Pat Brown, querying the data base will be faster than making embarrassing phone calls.

Application Generators

The concept of an **application generator** is still not well defined, but the objective of those now available and in various stages of development is the same: a language capable of specifying all programming tasks for the development of an information system without the need for procedure-level instructions. Some application generators have approached this objective through an interactive dialogue with the programmer. The file creation and maintenance, data entry, management reports, and other system requirements are "programmed" by selecting preprogrammed functions from a "menu" of available functions.

Application generators are currently in the infant stage of development. Existing application generators do not have the flexibility of procedure-oriented languages and cannot be used to develop sophisticated information systems. However, when used for the purposes intended, programmer productivity can be increased by as much as 100%. As they mature, application generators will play an ever-increasing role in information systems development.

LANGUAGES OF THE FUTURE

The next step in programming language sophistication is the **natural language**. The premise behind a natural language is that the programmer will need little or no programming training. The programmer will simply write, or perhaps verbalize, specifications without regard to programming instructions or syntax (rules for creating program instructions).

Researchers are currently working to develop natural languages. Initially, natural languages will have certain syntax restrictions. Although it is difficult to comprehend, it is inevitable that the language of the future will be an unrestricted dialogue between an individual and a computer.

PROGRAMMING FUNDAMENTALS

The following section is presented to provide the user manager with an overview of the principles of procedure-oriented programming languages. The vast majority of production programs are written in POLs like COBOL and BASIC. Although the typical user manager will not have an occasion to actually engage in this type of coding, he or she will frequently interact with those who do. A knowledge of the fundamentals of programming will make that interaction more efficient and provide insight into the concepts of query languages.

In POLs, a sequence of instructions (also called **statements**) are executed one after another unless control of execution is transferred to another portion of the program by a "test-on-condition" instruction. For example, a payroll program handles salaried employees differently than hourly employees. Gross wages are computed for hourly employees and retrieved from the data base for salaried employees. A unique sequence of instructions would be required for each operation (hourly and salaried). Once gross wages are determined, the processing steps and, therefore, the program instructions, are the same for both (e.g., payroll deductions, social security computation, printing of checks, and so on). In Figure 9–4 key statements were selected from a BASIC payroll program to illustrate the "sequence" and "test-on-condition" aspect of programming. The instructions are self-explanatory. An actual program written to compute and print payroll checks would require several hundred lines of code (LOC) or instructions.

Each POL has an instruction set that has at least one instruction in each of the following general instruction classifications:

> **Computation.** Computation instructions allow the programmer to add, multiply, subtract, divide, and take a number to a particular power (see Statement 120, Figure 9–4).

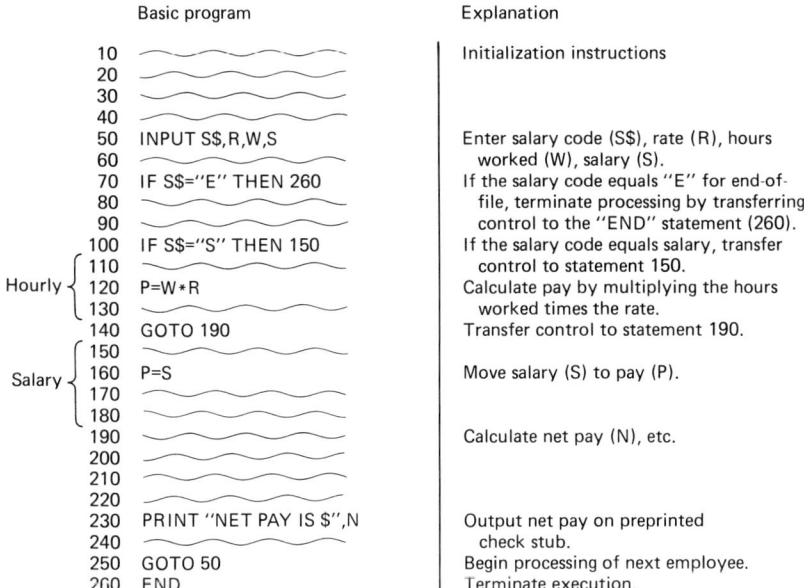

Basic program

Explanation

```
 10 ~~~~~~~~~~~~~~        Initialization instructions
 20 ~~~~~~~~~~~~~
 30 ~~~~~~~~~~~
 40 ~~~~~~~~~~
 50 INPUT S$,R,W,S        Enter salary code (S$), rate (R), hours
 60 ~~~~~~~~~~~              worked (W), salary (S).
 70 IF S$="E" THEN 260    If the salary code equals "E" for end-of-
 80 ~~~~~~~~~~              file, terminate processing by transferring
 90 ~~~~~~~~~~~             control to the "END" statement (260).
100 IF S$="S" THEN 150    If the salary code equals salary, transfer
110 ~~~~~~~~~~              control to statement 150.
120 P=W*R                 Calculate pay by multiplying the hours
130 ~~~~~~~~~               worked times the rate.
140 GOTO 190              Transfer control to statement 190.
150 ~~~~~~~~~~
160 P=S                   Move salary (S) to pay (P).
170 ~~~~~~~~~~
180 ~~~~~~~~~
190 ~~~~~~~~~             Calculate net pay (N), etc.
200 ~~~~~~~~~~
210 ~~~~~~~~~~
220 ~~~~~~~~~~~
230 PRINT "NET PAY IS $",N   Output net pay on preprinted
240 ~~~~~~~~~~                check stub.
250 GOTO 50              Begin processing of next employee.
260 END                  Terminate execution.
```

Hourly { 110, 120, 130

Salary { 150, 160, 170, 180

FIGURE 9-4 Key statements in a BASIC payroll program.

Data transfer. Data can be transferred internally from one main memory storage location to another. Assignment statements also come under this classification. These statements allow a programmer to associate a literal "NET PAY IS," or numeric value with a particular named main memory location (called a **variable**). In the example of Figure 9-4, "S$" references the contents of the main memory location used to store the salary code. The hourly rate is stored in a main memory location referenced by "R." Statement 160 is an assignment statement and assigns the value of "S" to "P."

Control (decision and/or branch). These are the only instructions that can alter the sequence of program execution. There are unconditional and conditional instructions which prompt a decision and/or a "branch" to another part of the program. In the example of Figure 9-4, a conditional instruction at statement 100 transfers control to statement 150 if the employee being processed is salaried (S$ = "S"), otherwise the next sequential instruction is executed (statement 110— hourly sequence). Statement 70 is also a conditional branch instruction that is used in conjunction with an unconditional branch instruction (statement 250) to cause the program to "loop" until all employees are processed. Although the syntax varies between languages, conditional branch instructions are generally referred to as "If" statements and unconditional instructions as "Go To" statements. The "End" statement (number 260) terminates program execution.

Input/output. I/O statements direct the computer to "read from" or "write to" a peripheral device. For example, the programmer can read a record from a magnetic disk file or write a line on the printer. In Figure 9-4, statement 50 allows input (from keyboard) and statement 230 permits output (to printer).

Format. A record is simply a string of characters when read from disk to primary storage. The format statements assemble these character strings for processing. Format statements are also used to edit output to make it easier to read. Monthly salaries might be stored as 333333 on a disk file; however, on output, a decimal point and dollar sign are added. The output, $3333.33, is said to be edited.

SOFTWARE

The term *software* refers collectively to the programs used to direct the operational activity of the computer. There are two general categories of software: applications and systems. **Applications software** is designed and written to perform user-oriented applications, such as accounts receivable and payroll. **Systems software** is more generalized and is usually applications-independent. It supports the basic computer functions as well as *all* applications areas (not a specific application). Because applications software is discussed in detail in Part III of this book, the following discussion will center on systems software.

Systems Software

Systems software can be logically divided into several major categories. The following discussion provides an overview of each.

Compiler. The compiler translates the instructions of a high-level language, like COBOL, to instructions that the computer can interpret. Remember: Each computer executes all programs, whether written in BASIC, FORTRAN, or COBOL, in the language of that machine. High-level programming languages are simply a convenience and are not executable in their "source" format.

The **source program** consists of statements written by a programmer and compiled by a compiler. This process is illustrated in Figure 9-5. A programmer develops a COBOL program interactively. The programmer requests that the program be executed and the COBOL compiler is "called" from auxiliary storage and loaded to main memory. The compiler then translates the source program to an **object program**. The object program is in machine language and is usually stored on auxiliary storage for recall at a later date and/or executed immediately. The compilation process can be time consuming, especially for large programs. During regularly scheduled production runs, the object program is simply "called" (retrieved from disk storage) and executed. No compilation is necessary. If any changes are made to the source program, then it must be recompiled to create an up-to-date object program.

Interpreters. An interpreter ultimately performs the same function as a compiler, but in a different manner. An interpreter translates and executes each source program statement

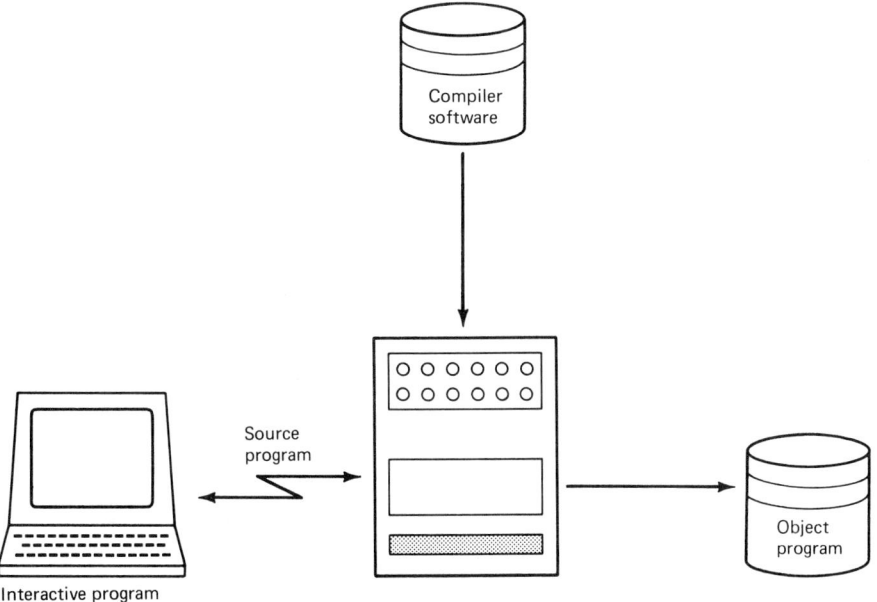

FIGURE 9-5 The compile process.

before translating and executing the next statement. The advantage of interpreters is that an error in statement syntax is immediately brought to the attention of a programmer, and corrections can be made during program development. The disadvantage is that interpreters do not use computing resources as efficiently as the compiler.

Simulators and emulators. This category of system software allows one computer to operate as if it were another. Simulators and emulators are particularly helpful when converting to a noncompatible computer. Programs written originally for the old computer can be executed on the new computer until existing programs can be converted to the format of the new computer. Technically, an emulator is a hardware/software combination and a simulator is strictly software.

Utility programs. Utility programs are often-used service routines. These programs provide functions such as file backup (dumping the employee master file from magnetic disk to magnetic tape), testing aids (taking a "snapshot" of main memory at the point of a program error), and application aids (sorting of the employee master file by social security number within department).

Operating system. The operating system, also called an executive, a monitor, and a supervisor, controls the execution of all applications and systems software programs. The operating system may provide scheduling of tasks, input/output control, machine utilization accounting (e.g., number of seeks per disk drive, etc.), allocation of main memory, data management, and other related services. The objectives of an operating system are to:

1. Minimize **turnaround time** (elapsed time between submittal of a job and receipt of output);
2. Maximize **throughput** (amount of processing per unit time); and
3. Optimize the use of main memory and peripheral devices.

A related concept is **virtual machine.** Virtual machine software is embedded in the operating system and allows programs that require two or more different operating systems to be executed concurrently on the same computer. Virtual machine capability is helpful when converting from one operating system to another.

Communications software. The operating system of some computers controls the flow of **traffic** (data) to and from remote locations, but this function is usually handled by a communications software specifically designed for this purpose. Communications software is executed on both the front-end processor and the host computer.

Data base management systems. DBMS software was discussed in detail in Chapter 8. Most data base management systems have a family of programs used to support the data management function.

Performance measurement. Performance measurement software is used to monitor, analyze, and report on the performance of the overall computer system and the computer system components.

Software-Related Concepts

All but the smallest computers have **multiprogramming** capabilities. Multiprogramming is the seemingly simultaneous execution of more than one program at any given time. The computer gives each program a small "slice" of time in rotation. The speed at which programs are executed makes processing appear as if each program has a dedicated computer.

Since all data and programs to be processed must be resident in main memory, main memory is a critical factor in determining the throughput of the computer system. Once main memory is saturated, no more programs can be executed until a portion of main memory is freed. **Virtual memory** is a systems software addition to the operating system that allows the CPU to increase throughput by expanding main memory through software.

The principle behind virtual memory is quite simple. Remember, a program is executed sequentially, one statement after the next. By putting programs in "pages" (segments), only that portion of the program (page) being executed is resident in main memory. The rest of the program is stored on a DASD. When another page of the program is needed, it is "rolled" (moved) into main memory. The advantage of virtual memory is that main memory is effectively enlarged, giving programmers more flexibility. The disadvantage is the cost in program efficiency. A program that has many branches to many pages will execute slowly because of the time required to roll pages from disk storage devices to main memory.

CHAPTER 10

Data Communications

Data communications is the collection and/or distribution of data from and/or to a remote facility. Even though **telecommunications** has a broader meaning, it is often used interchangeably with *data communications*. Another term that is commonly associated with data communications is **teleprocessing** or **TP**. *Teleprocessing* is a more encompassing term than *data communications* and implies the use of data communications for data processing. **On-line systems** and **communications-based systems** are alternative phrases used to describe information systems that use data communications.

IMPACT OF COMMUNICATIONS-
BASED SYSTEMS

As discussed in Chapter 3, the trend in information services is toward decentralization and distributed data processing (DDP). Decentralized IS operation does not necessarily imply data communications, but most are communications-based. All DDP systems are by definition communications-based. DDP and IS decentralization are, for all practical purposes, interchangeable. The corporation following the trend away from centralized batch systems should be aware that communications-based technology and systems will have a significant impact on organizational structure, personnel, management, budget, and quality assurance and control.

Impact on Organizational Structure

In a centralized environment the information services function is physically and organizationally removed from the functional areas. The fundamental objective of DDP is to realize a more direct involvement in IS on the part of the user community. Computing hardware and IS personnel become the responsibility of the end user. To accommodate these personnel, special groups and departments must be integrated into the current organizational structure. This integration usually necessitates a major revision of the corporate and department organizational structures.

Impact on Personnel

Remote facilities can range in size from one or two terminals for management inquiries to a medium-sized computer system supporting a number of data entry/inquiry terminals. The impact on user personnel will come in the form of training and possibly as a change of careers. An administrative assistant might be retrained to make ad hoc management inquiries via a query language. Other user personnel might enter the information services career paths as programmers, analysts, operators, and so on.

Those user departments/divisions receiving hardware for a DDP installation will probably inherit a full compliment of IS professionals—programmers, analysts, operators. These personnel become part of the functional area organization.

Impact on Management

The user manager's scope of responsibility will be expanded in a DDP environment. Responsibilities have traditionally included personnel management and a thorough knowledge of the functional area. In DDP, the user manager must acquire some knowledge of IS-related skills (e.g., systems analysis, programming, hardware operation, IS planning, and so on) to manage personnel who are primarily involved in IS-related activities.

Impact on Budget

The user manager will probably have to add several major line items to the departmental budget (increased payroll for IS personnel, purchase and maintenance of computing hardware, computer-related supplies, and so on).

Impact on Quality Assurance and Control

In a centralized IS environment, user managers are heavily dependent upon information services for quality assurance and control. In DDP, the functional areas are responsible for the integrity of input, quality of information systems, accuracy of output, control of distribution, and in general, all those aspects of data processing that were taken for granted in a centralized environment.

TELEPROCESSING APPLICATIONS

The number of teleprocessing applications is limited only by the imagination. Most corporations will take advantage of the existence of a communications network to implement several diverse applications. The following general TP application categories are presented to highlight the application potential of a communications network.

> **Electronic mail.** Electronic mail is usually associated with office automation. In the electronic mail application, the computer is a vehicle by which to route messages to persons within and, in some cases, external to the corporation. Persons throughout the organization are assigned an electronic mail box in which messages are received and stored. A typical application might involve a national sales manager and regional managers. The national sales manager can respond immediately to the competition's price reduction by informing regional sales managers of a commensurate price reduction via electronic mail. The message would originate on a terminal at the national office and would be routed to the electronic mail boxes of the regional managers. The regional managers are informed of the message by an electronic "flag." The manager can request that the message be displayed on the VDU and, if desired, that a hard copy be printed.

Inquiry/response. In inquiry/response, the operator, possibly a user manager, makes some type of inquiry and the computer (via an information system) responds. For example, the director of personnel might inquire about the training record of a particular employee. A sales person in a department store might inquire about a customer's credit limit.

Word processing. In word processing, the operator uses software for text processing. Although much of the current word processing is done with stand-alone units, many companies use the more powerful host processor software to take advantage of the availability of the corporate data base. For example, a secretary needing to send the same letter to all customers can integrate word processing and the corporate data base and merge the preformatted letter with the name and address from the customer master file.

Data entry. Data can be entered directly into the system from remote locations via a communications network. For example, tellers in branch banks record each transaction as it occurs.

Data collection. In a number of instances, communications networks are used to collect data. One of the best examples is the point-of-sale (POS) terminals in a department store chain. Throughout the business day every sales transaction is automatically logged on a computer-based file. The data are collected and batched for processing.

Process control. Data communications is also used to control processes. For example, sensors in streets throughout a city continuously monitor the direction and volume of traffic and optimize the flow of traffic by controlling traffic signals.

Remote computing. Communications networks provide end users with the opportunity to use the computer for computational purposes. In one large corporate research center, over 400 engineers and scientists use 150 remote terminals.

Interactive programming. Applications and systems programmers and users take advantage of remote and immediate access to computers to write their programs. Program development is made easier with on-line debugging aids and immediate diagnostics.

Diagnostic evaluation. Customer engineers (CEs), the title used for those who work on computing hardware (repair and preventive maintenance), routinely use diagnostic software in a remote facility to isolate the source of a software or machine error.

JUSTIFICATION FOR
TELEPROCESSING SYSTEMS

The actual justification for a TP system would depend on the specific application; but, a few key points to consider will provide some short-term direction to the evaluation process. Perhaps the primary reason a user manager elects to "go on-line" is fast response. A user can make an inquiry and get a response immediately. The user can also enter data, send messages, and so on, without the typical one-day turnaround of a batch system.

The data base in an on-line environment reflects the current status. For example, when salespeople in Oklahoma City and Tulsa are selling products from a warehouse in Wichita, they cannot both promise one-day delivery on the only "gerifarckle" in the Southwest. Once a salesperson logs the order on the central system, the item is flagged and sold.

To varying degrees, teleprocessing provides for centralized files and decentralized operation. Rather than pass data to the IS department, the entire operation of the system is supported by functional area personnel.

Not only do on-line systems result in increased capabilities and flexibilities, but operational expenses are reduced. In batch environments, much of the user work is duplicated by IS personnel. For example, the user enters an order manually on an order form. These same data are then transcribed by data entry personnel in information services. This not only involves an unnecessary transcription step, but increases the probability of error. An on-line system also provides the opportunity for user managers to make their own ad hoc inquiries, thereby saving the expense and hassle of retaining the services of in-house programmers and analysts.

BASIC PATTERNS
OF DATA COMMUNICATIONS
HARDWARE CONFIGURATIONS

A network of computers can be configured in the following basic patterns: point-to-point, star, hierarchical or tree, ring, and mesh or network.

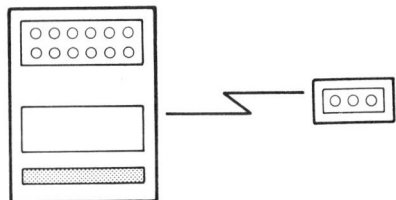

FIGURE 10-1 Point-to-point configuration.

Point-to-Point Configuration

The **point-to-point** configuration involves the communication of two remote computers. Figure 10-1 illustrates a typical point-to-point configuration.

Star Configuration

The **star** configuration is illustrated in Figure 10-2. A large centralized computer, called the host, is connected to a number of smaller computer systems. The smaller computer systems can communicate with each other via the host and usually share the host's corporate-level data base.

Hierarchical Configuration

The **hierarchical** or **tree** configuration is shown in Figure 10-3. The hierarchical configuration links computers at one level to those at the next. Communications between computers at a given level are routed to a higher-level computer, then back down the chain. A hierarchical configuration can mirror the corporate organizational structure. For example, a headquarters computer can be linked to regional computers which can be linked to district computers. A third-level computer is not necessarily smaller than a second-level computer. A district office in the heavily populated Northeast might have a heavier processing load than the entire Southwest region.

Ring Configuration

The **ring** configuration is illustrated in Figure 10-4. It is most appropriate where communications between adjacent computers is desirable and processing inconvenience is an acceptable alternative to leasing extra lines to link all computers. Computer 1 in Figure 10-4 communicates with computer 3 through computer 2. If for some reason computer 2 is down, communication would be routed through 5 and 4.

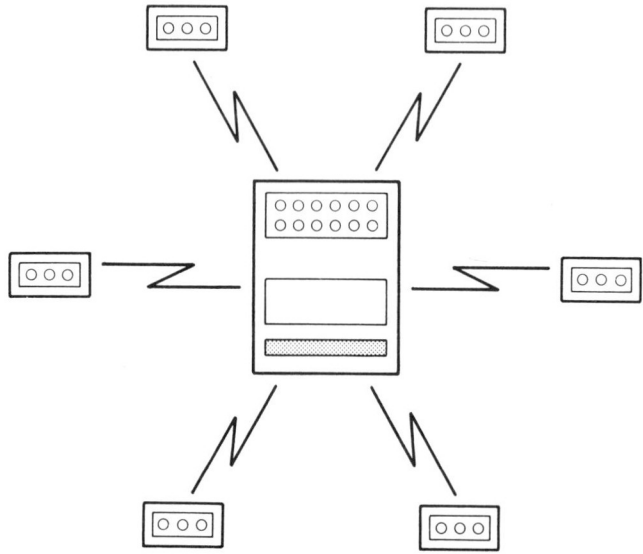

FIGURE 10-2 Star configuration.

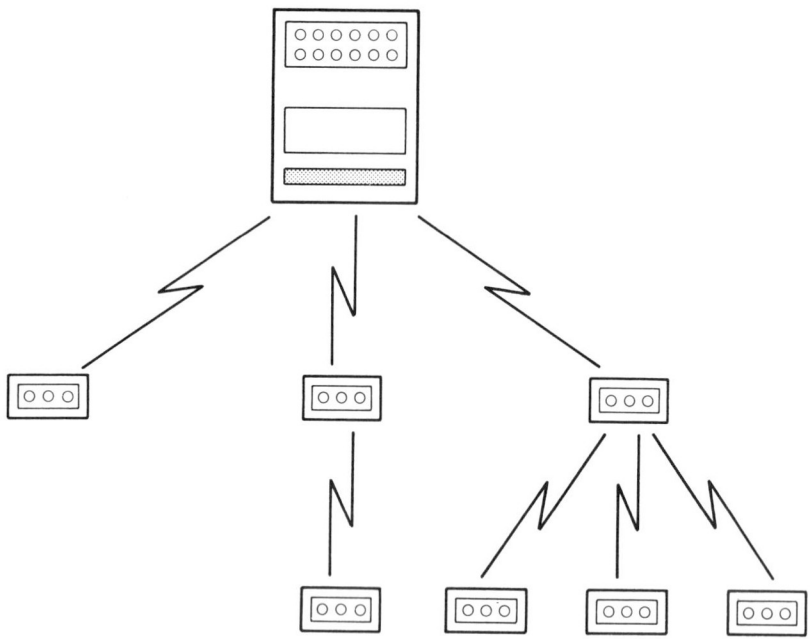

FIGURE 10-3 Hierarchical configuration.

216

Network or Mesh Configuration

The **network** (or **mesh**) configuration, illustrated in Figure 10–5, provides data links as required. If computers 4 and 3 have only isolated requirements for communicating with computer 5, then links need not be established at all nodes. Any computer system in a communications network is referred to as a **node**.

Hybrid Configuration

A pure form of any of the above configurations is seldom found in practice. Most communications networks are configured as hybrids. A hybrid configuration is deemed a ring, star, and so on, depending on its most dominant configuration characteristic. A distributed data processing system would use the configuration most appropriate for its corporate circumstances.

DATA COMMUNICATIONS HARDWARE

Figure 10–6 can be used to illustrate the basic hardware components used in data communications. The terminal in a communications network can be anything from an interactive low-volume VDU to a medium-sized computer system. Each terminal is assigned an "address."

The **MODEM** (<u>mo</u>dulator-<u>dem</u>odulator) is a device that is used to convert computer-compatible electrical signals to signals suitable for transmission facilities (e.g., analog signals for telephone lines). These "modulated" signals are then "demodulated" by another MODEM to computer-compatible electrical signals for processing. The modulation-demodulation process is not required for transmission facilities capable of carrying computer-compatible data (digital data). A MODEM is always required when the operator uses the telephone to "dial up" the computer. This type of MODEM is called an **acoustical coupler**.

The **concentrator** or **multiplexor** is a "down-line" (remote from host processor) device used to collect data from a number of low-speed devices like VDUs, then transmit "concentrated" data over a single higher-speed line. The concentrator, also called a **cluster controller**, is an economic necessity when there are several low-speed terminals in one remote location. The cost of one high-speed line is considerably less than the cost of having a dedicated low-speed line for each terminal. A concentrator accepts data (or messages) from several keyboards operated at human speeds, then formats and sends the data at high

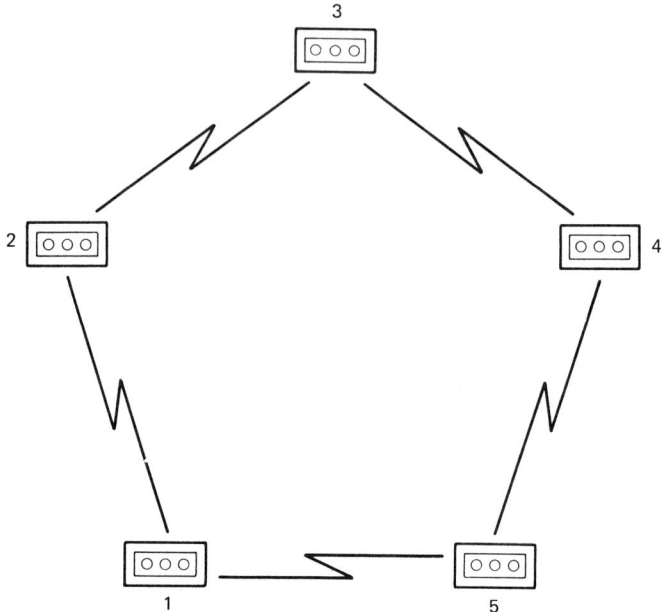

FIGURE 10-4 Ring configuration.

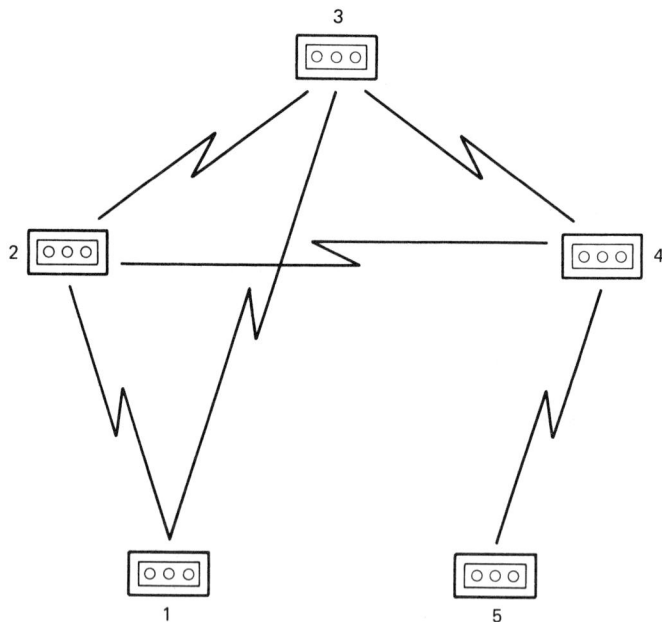

FIGURE 10-5 Network or mesh configuration.

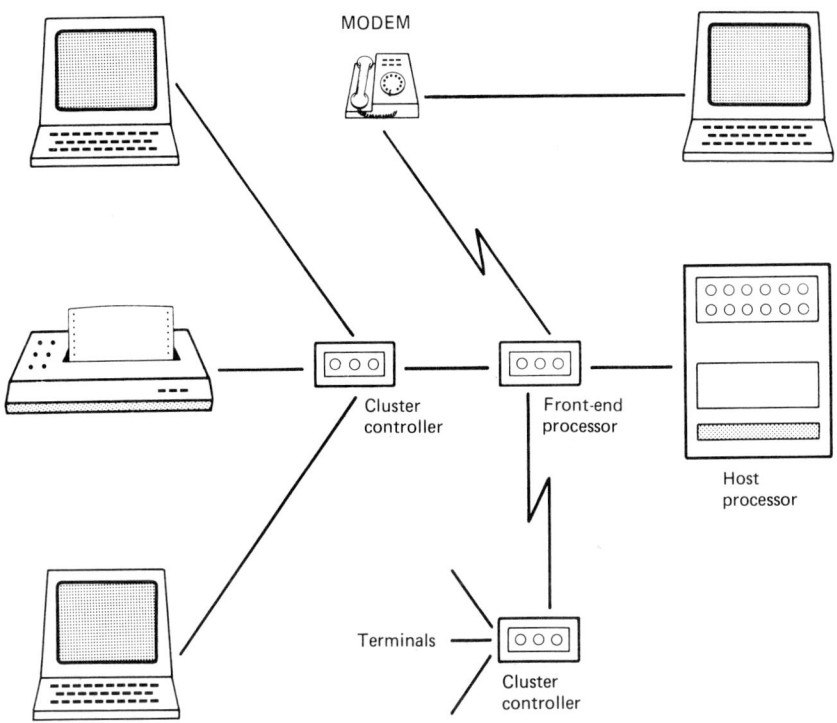

FIGURE 10-6 Hardware components in data communications.

speed to a **front-end processor**. The front-end processor reassembles the individual "messages," then transmits them to the host computer for processing. The process is reversed for messages sent from the host computer.

The front-end processor, also called a **transmission control unit**, is a computer that relieves the host computer of a number of processing tasks associated with data communications. The front-end processor handles such tasks as parity checking, code translation, some preprocessing and editing, establishing the appropriate link between computer and terminal, and routing messages to and from main memory.

THE COMMUNICATION CHANNEL

The data link between remote devices is referred to as a **communications channel**, a **line**, or a **link**. A channel provides a vehicle by which to transmit data between two or more points. The channel may consist of one or a combination of the following transmission facilities:

♦ Telephone lines
♦ Telegraph lines
♦ Satellites
♦ Lasers
♦ Coaxial cable
♦ Microwave
♦ Optical fiber

Data are stored and transmitted in bits (0, 1 signals). A channel's speed is rated by the number of bits that can be transmitted per second. This is called the **baud rate**. *Bits per second* and *baud rate* are not exactly the same, but in practice they are used interchangeably.

Channels are split into three general categories according to baud rate: subvoice grade, voice grade, and wideband or broad band.

Subvoice grade. Subvoice grade lines are one step below telephone lines. Such lines were commonly used when hardware technology limited output to seven characters per second, but today there is little or no demand for subvoice grade lines.

Voice grade. These are regular telephone lines that range in speed from 600 to 9,600 baud. A regular telephone line can be "conditioned" to transmit data up to 9,600 baud and with greater accuracy. This added capability is accompanied by a commensurate cost to the user. To put voice grade line speed into perspective, a 1,200 baud line can handle approximately 120 characters of data per second. Voice grade lines are used primarily for high-speed links between computers and cluster controllers, but can also be used for low-speed, computer-to-computer communication.

Wide band. Wide-band or **broad-band** channels have a capacity of over one million baud and are used primarily for computer-to-computer communication.

Types of Channels

It is impractical, not to mention illegal, for a corporation to string a coaxial cable between Philadelphia and New York City. It is also impractical to build microwave relay stations or send up satellites. For these reasons, most corporations turn to common carriers like AT&T and Western Union to provide channels for their data communication networks.

A corporation can lease a permanent or semi-permanent connection between transmitting devices (**leased line**). A permanent line is a dedicated line, 24 hours a day. A semi-permanent connection gives the corporation the right to use the line during certain hours of the day. When a corporation leases a line, the charge is based on baud rate capacity, distance (per air mile), and whether it is permanent or semi-permanent.

A **dial-up**, or **public**, or **switched line** is billed strictly on a time-and-distance charge, as if making a long-distance telephone call.

A **private line** is installed, owned, and maintained by the user. A private line is part of a **local network**, sometimes called a "local net." A local network is limited to a building or perhaps a series of buildings on the grounds of the corporation. A fully dedicated leased line is sometimes referred to as a private line.

An alternative to common carriers are **value-added networks** (VANs). VANs are "specialized" common carriers which may or may not use the facilities of common carriers but which, in each case, "add value" to the network. The value added over and above the standard services of the common carriers may include electronic mail and allowing noncompatible computers to communicate with each other. A VAN not only offers added services but does so at a reduced rate. To illustrate how, consider the following scenario. The ABC corporation leases a dedicated New York-Philadelphia 9,600 baud line from a common carrier. ABC is likely to use only 15% of the capacity of the line. A VAN could lease the same line from the same common carrier and use the line to capacity by combining the data transmission of several corporations requiring New York-Philadelphia hookups. The VAN uses computers on each end of the line to collect the data and to redistribute the data to appropriate destinations. In effect, four or five corporations share the same line and its cost with no loss in performance.

Line Direction

Lines that transmit data in only one direction are called **simplex**. Those that transmit data in both directions, but not at the same time, are called **half-duplex**. A line that transmits data in both directions at the same time is called a **full-duplex** line (see Figure 10–7). Since information systems are interactive and usually require bi-directional transmission, lines are either half-duplex or full-duplex. "Line" is in reality a misnomer because a full-duplex line is simply two half-duplex lines.

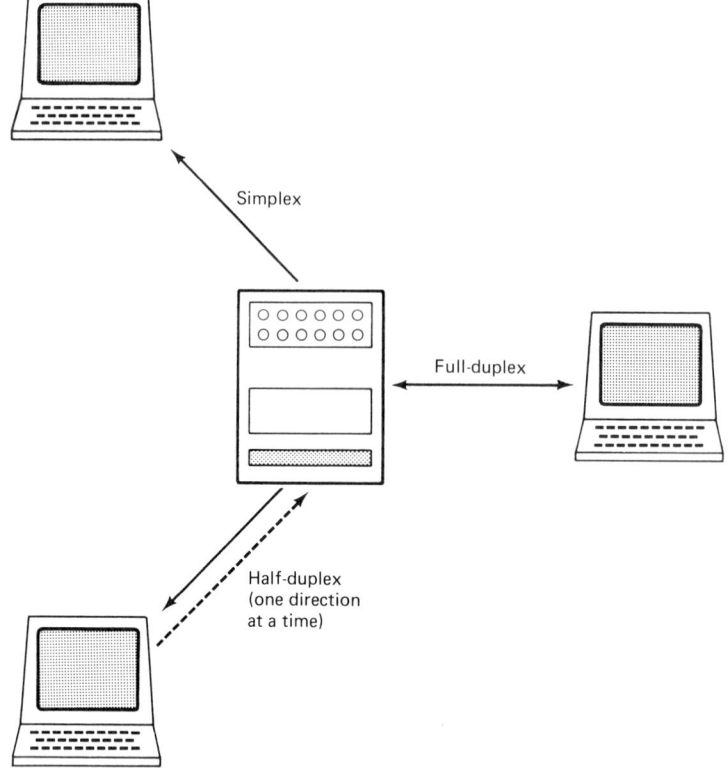

FIGURE 10-7 Line direction in a communications network.

Line Arrangement

Suppose a utility company is headquartered in St. Louis and operates branch offices in the cities noted in Figure 10-8. Corporate officers would like to establish a data communications network linking all remote offices with the headquarters in St. Louis. The first task in determining line arrangement is to analyze the workload at each location such that the workload can be distributed evenly among the lines. To do this, the analysis must determine:

- Average daily and hourly message volume
- Peak daily and hourly message volume
- Type of messages sent
- From where and to where sent

The objective in line arrangement for a communications network is to minimize circuit miles (number of air miles), make connection with all remote points, and avoid line overloads. Lines should also be arranged such that alternative routing is possible.

Figures 10-8 and 10-9 illustrate two solutions to line arrangement for the utility company. In Figure 10-8 terminals are connected via a 4,800 baud line, with a cluster controller at Mexico to control I/O from all cities on the Mexico-Galesburg and Mexico-Rolla channels. When more than one terminal is connected to a single communications channel (e.g., Mexico-Galesburg), the channel is called a **multipoint** or **multidrop** line. The cluster controller, or the computer, continually polls terminals on the line for messages.

In Figure 10-8, both 1,200 and 9,600 baud lines are used with cluster controllers at Burlington, Jacksonville, and Mexico. These are only two of a myriad of possible line arrangements. The best way to determine which arrangement is best is to use the data derived from

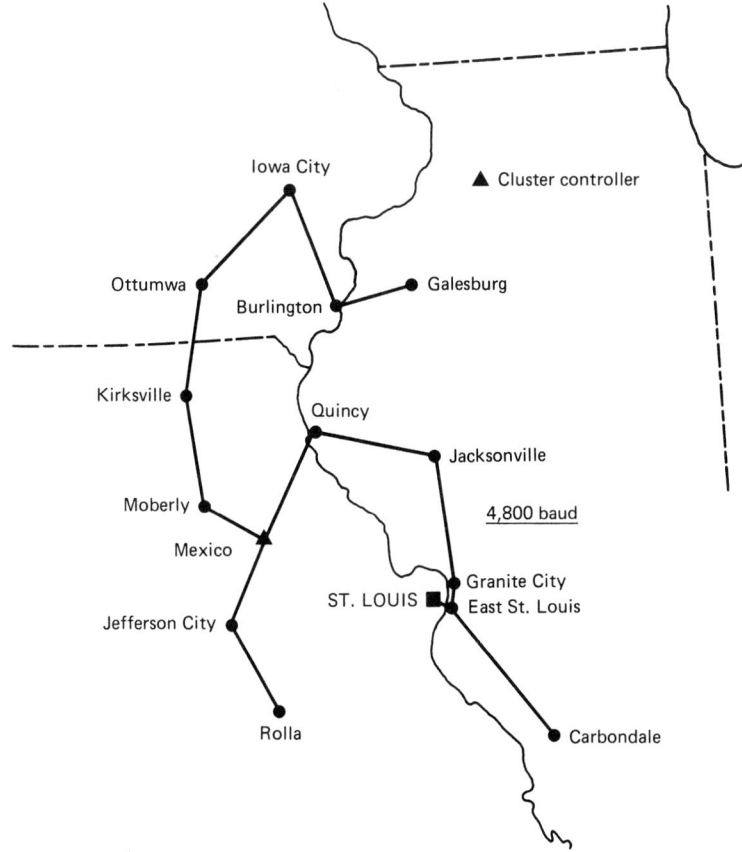

FIGURE 10-8 A line arrangement alternative.

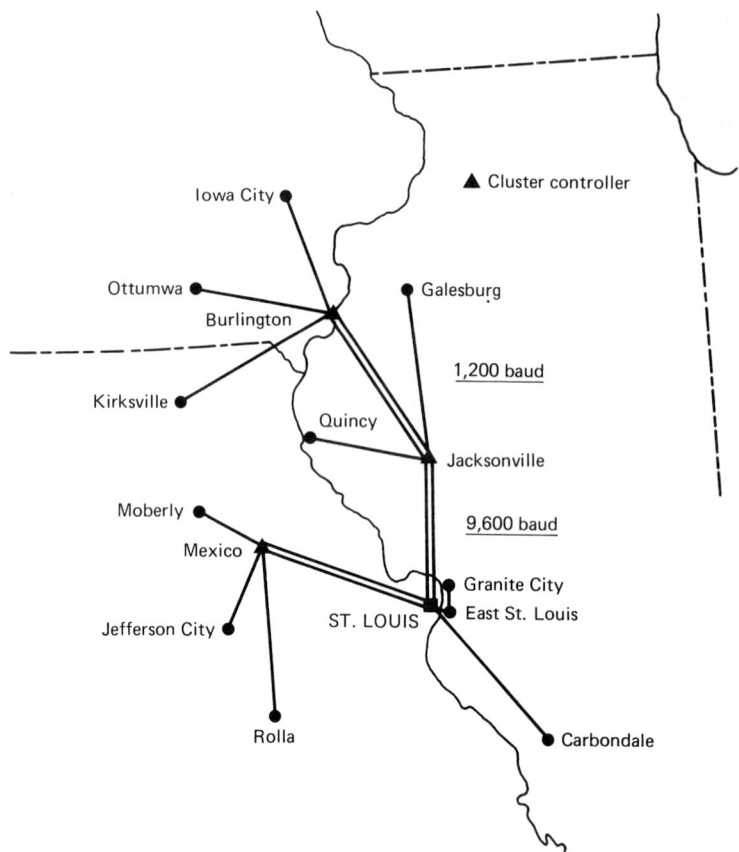

FIGURE 10-9 A line arrangement alternative.

the workload analysis and simulate the operation of each alternative network. The results of a simulation can prove or disprove the feasibility of the network and render important data on response time, queue length at peak volume, and so on. See the definitions of response time and queue length below.

MAKING THE CONNECTION
FOR DATA TRANSMISSION

In a computer network each terminal and computer system is assigned an address. A **message** containing data is coded in a series of bits called a **bit stream**. A message is sent from one address to one or more other addresses within the network (see Figure 10-10). The content of a mes-

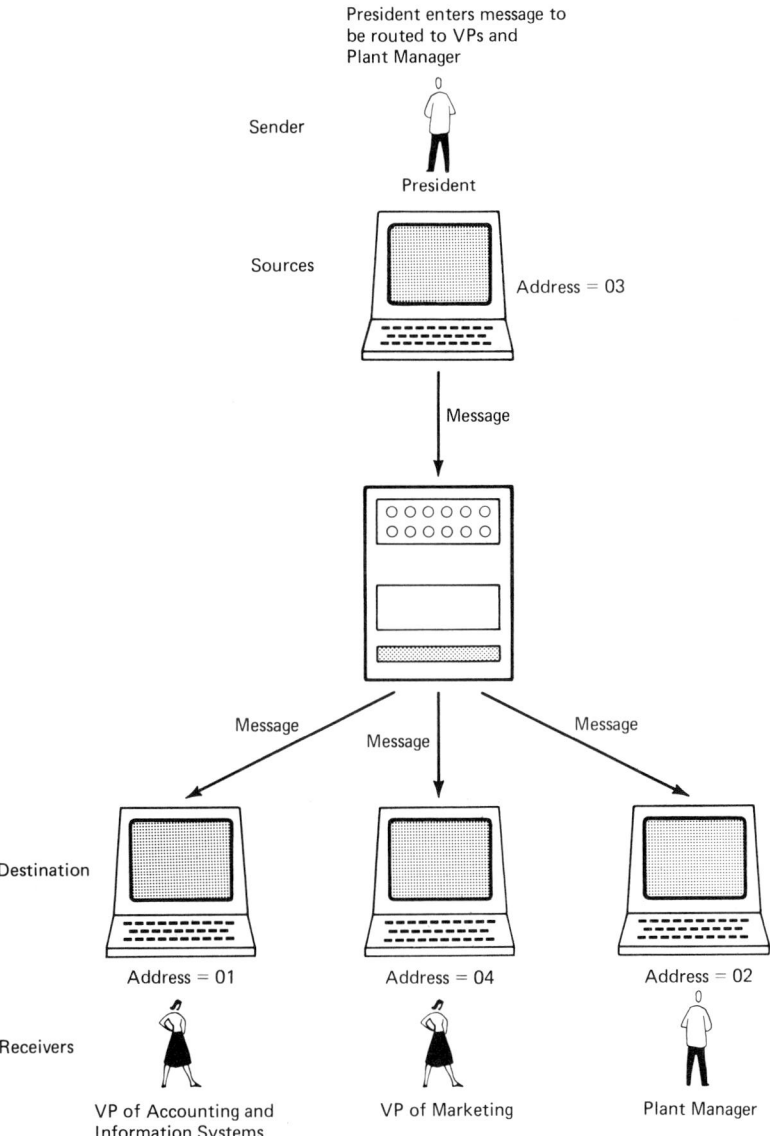

President enters message to
be routed to VPs and
Plant Manager

Sender

President

Sources

Address = 03

Message

Message

Message

Message

Destination

Address = 01

Address = 04

Address = 02

Receivers

VP of Accounting and
Information Systems

VP of Marketing

Plant Manager

FIGURE 10-10 Message routing.

sage could be anything from a program instruction to an "electronic" memo from the president of a company to all vice-presidents.

The person originating a message is the **sender**. The terminal or computer sending the message is the **source**. A **receiver** is the individual or department receiving the message. The terminal or computer receiving the message is the **destination**.

DATA COMMUNICATIONS
TERMS AND CONCEPTS

Certain communications-related terms and concepts are commonly used in casual conversation and should be part of the user manager's vocabulary. Those relating to *remote data transmission* are discussed first, followed by those dealing with *system interaction.*

Remote Data Transmission

Traffic. Traffic refers to the number of inquiries, data elements entered, messages sent, and so on. In short, traffic is the volume of data flow. Traffic, in a data communications sense, is analogous to automobiles (bits) and highways (channels). Communications traffic is also given a general quantitative value such as "light" or "heavy."

Port. A computer has a limited number of entry points, called *ports*, through which data can be sent and received. The number of ports is a constraint on the number of remote channels that can be connected to a computer.

Polling. Polling is a method of line control that permits several remote terminals to communicate with the computer over the same communications channel. In order to service the terminals, the computer "polls" or continuously sends messages in rotation to each terminal to determine if a message is ready to be sent. If a particular terminal has a message to be sent and the line is available, the computer accepts the message and polls the next terminal. The polling process is transparent to the user.

Protocol. The term protocol refers to established rules governing the physical, electrical, and data interface in a communications network. Only those rules for transferring data and control information over a communication link are of concern to the end user. These protocols are classified as **asynchronous** and **synchronous**. In asynchronous transmission, data are transmitted at irregular intervals on an as-needed basis, and are most appropriate for low-speed I/O devices. In synchronous transmission, the receiving and sending nodes operate in synchronization to enable high-speed data transmission. There is no commonly accepted communications protocol at this time; therefore, devices using incompatible protocols require a front-end processor to convert the message to a compatible protocol. Common protocols are IBM's bi-synch and synchronous data link control (SDLC), and X.25, a recognized standard adopted by the International Standards Organization for international data communications.

System Interaction

End user. The individual providing terminal input or using terminal output is called the end user.

User friendly. A system is said to be user friendly when someone with relatively little experience can interact successfully with an on-line system. User-friendly systems simplify user interaction by using words and phrases that can be easily understood. Such systems have "help" commands which allow end users to request more detailed instructions if they need them or if a problem occurs.

Time sharing. An end user in any on-line system shares computer time with persons on other terminals. This is called time sharing.

Response time. Response time is defined as the time elapsed from when a message is sent to when a response is received. A message could be the update of a name and address file, and a response could be a visual display of the updated record. The response time will vary considerably depending upon the complexity of the inquiry, the number of terminals contending for processing time, the speed of the host computer, and the channel speed. Response time is an important consideration when designing an on-line information system. Although response time in almost any information system can be made almost immediate, the cost may be prohibitive. Therefore, user and IS managers must determine what is an acceptable response time for a particular application. Typically, anything over three seconds is unacceptable, except during peak work loads.

Queue length. The number of persons waiting to be served by an operator at a remote terminal (e.g., airline ticket agent) is referred to as the queue length. The queue length also describes the number of messages that have been sent but must be "queued" before processing.

Transaction log. The transaction log is a record of all on-line transactions, usually over a period of one day. When an address is updated on an employee master file, the transaction is also logged on secondary storage, usually on a magnetic tape. The transaction log is backup to the day's processing if for some reason the employee master file is destroyed before day's end.

Connect time. Connect time is the elapsed time between the time the end user "logs on" or establishes a link between the terminal and the computer, and the time the user "logs off" or the link is terminated.

Part **III**

MANAGEMENT INFORMATION SYSTEMS

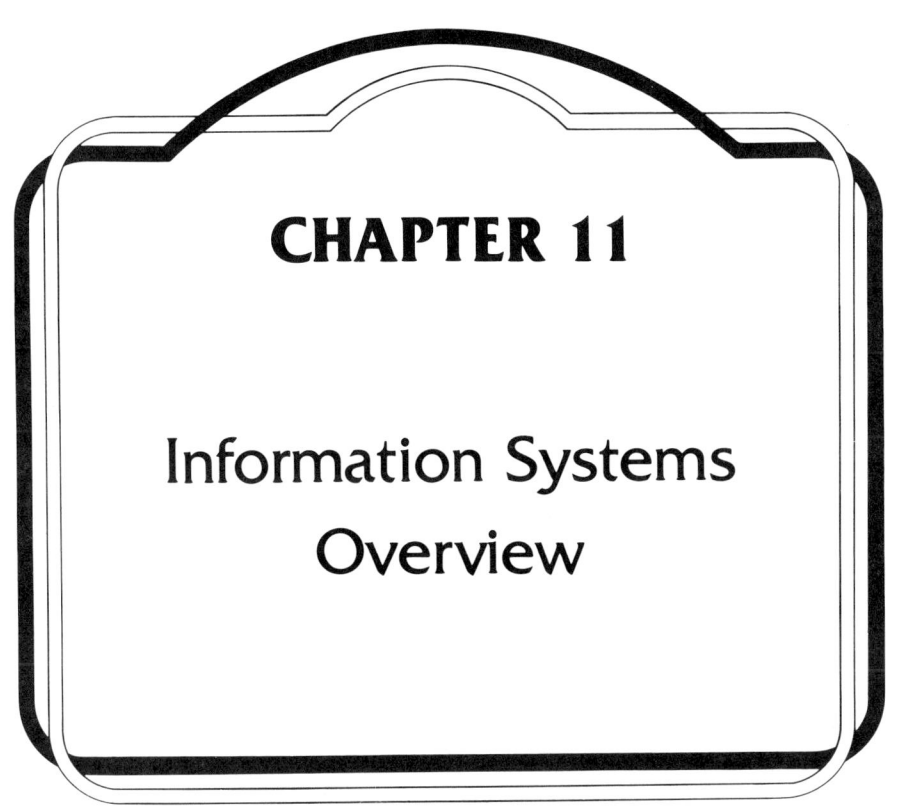

CHAPTER 11

Information Systems
Overview

In the early 1970s, *management information system* or MIS (defined and discussed in Chapter 1) had a broader meaning than it does today. It is now used interchangeably with *information systems*. In the context of this book, an information system provides data processing and management information capabilities. The purpose of this chapter is to present and describe general information principles and considerations.

The reader should be aware that data processing systems do not provide true management information capabilities. The term information system is inappropriately applied to many data processing systems.

TYPES OF INFORMATION SYSTEMS

An information system can be manual or computer-based, autonomous or integrated, and batch or on-line. The typical information system would be a combination, but, of course, not both autonomous and integrated.

231

An *autonomous system* is designed for and supports a specific application area, like personnel. The autonomous system has its own files that are invariably sprinkled with redundancy.

Integrated information systems are integrated through the data they use. Systems utilizing a shared data base are said to be integrated. For example, the payroll system requires data that are normally found in the human resources and accounting systems.

The vast majority of computer-based information systems were developed from a manual system base. Until recently, a lack of design expertise and/or IS user communication resulted in manual systems being "computerized." That is, the work flow of the computer-based system simply mirrored that of the manual system. These systems are usually autonomous and use the computer as a data processor. They are seldom designed with the ultimate intent of integration.

Information systems can also be classified as batch, on-line, or a combination. Transactions and data are batched for processing or report generation. As an example, banks encode the amount on the checks, then batch, sort, and process all checks at the end of the day. In order to preclude the possibility of an airline ticket agent in Dallas and another in Atlanta selling the last seat on a Los Angeles to San Francisco flight, airline reservations systems must be on-line to reflect the current status of the data base. Most on-line information systems also have batch processing requirements.

Even with the advent of information resource management (IRM) and the widespread recognition of the potential of computer-based information systems, the vast majority of systems are still autonomous batch systems. Most of these systems have outlived their usefulness and are being redesigned into integrated, on-line systems. By definition, integration requires intense cooperation between functional area managers and corporate officers. IS professionals can serve as advisors, but functional area conflicts and differences regarding integrated information systems should be resolved by the user community. The resolution of these differences to achieve a truly integrated environment is the IS challenge to user managers (see Information System Policy Committee in Chapter 4).

INFORMATION SYSTEMS
BY INDUSTRY GROUP

The potential for a data processing or information system can be found in every functional area in every industry group. Those functions or application areas that are routinely computerized are listed below by industry group. Most of these systems can be integrated to some extent with functionally adjacent systems (e.g., payroll, accounting, and personnel). The list is included to illustrate possible application areas and is not meant to be exhaustive.

General
(applicable to most industry
and government groups)

♦ Payroll
♦ Accounts receivable
♦ Accounts payable
♦ General ledger
♦ Inventory management and control
♦ Human resource development
♦ Budgeting
♦ Financial analysis
♦ Purchasing
♦ Word processing

Manufacturing

♦ Order entry and processing
♦ Dispatch and distribution
♦ Production scheduling
♦ Manufacturing resource planning (MRP), formerly materials requirements planning
♦ Market analysis
♦ Computer-aided design (CAD)
♦ Computer-aided manufacturing (CAM)
♦ Project management and control
♦ Standard costing

Health Care

♦ Patient billing
♦ Room census
♦ Pharmacy (including drug interaction)
♦ Nurse station scheduling
♦ Diagnosis
♦ Admissions
♦ Patient history

Retail

♦ Point of sale (POS)

Universities and Colleges

♦ Admissions
♦ Registration and class scheduling
♦ Computer-aided instruction (CAI)
♦ Alumni development
♦ Placement services
♦ Residence operations
♦ Financial aid

Banks

♦ Deposit
♦ Loan
♦ Electronic funds transfer
♦ Lease
♦ Trust
♦ Investment

Publishers

♦ Circulation
♦ Page formatting
♦ Typesetting

Transportation

♦ Reservations
♦ Fleet maintenance
♦ Rate analysis

Insurance

♦ Policy administration
♦ Claims processing
♦ Commission and agency reporting

♦ Actuarial accounting
♦ Rating and writing (automobile, home)

Local Government

♦ Utility billing
♦ Tax collection
♦ Police and fire dispatch
♦ Urban planning
♦ License and permit administration

State Government

♦ Welfare
♦ Employment security
♦ Highway patrol

Federal Government

♦ Social security administration
♦ Internal revenue service
♦ Grant administration
♦ National crime data base

LEVELS OF INFORMATION

An information system is designed to process data at the clerical level and provide information for managerial decision making at all levels of management. A corporation is divided into four levels of activity: *strategic*, *tactical*, *operational*, and *clerical*. When interacting with the design team, the user manager should be keenly aware that information should be tailored to the level at which it is directed.

The quality of an information system is directly proportional to the use of its output. A system that provides the same 20-page summary at the clerical and strategic levels is defeating the purpose of an information system. The secretary never uses the report because there is no need to know and it was never requested anyway; the president never uses the report because it would take too long to extract the few bits of information that are important. This scenario is more common than one might expect. The user manager is responsible for relating very specific information needs to the design team. A breakdown in communication will result in too much, too little, or even bad information. The key to effective information systems is to "filter" information at various levels of activities.

Clerical-level personnel are concerned primarily with the transaction-handling portion of an information system. Clerical is used in the generic sense to refer to persons involved in repetitive tasks. In an accounts receivable system, a data entry operator charged with reconciling receipts is interested in the total number of receipts processed as a control figure to match against a physical count.

Personnel at the *operational level* have well-defined tasks that might span a day, a week, or as much as three months; these tasks are essentially short-term. Their information requirements are performance reports and reports required for immediate operational feedback. In the accounts receivable example, the credit manager might want a report of all customers 60 days in arrears.

At the *tactical level*, managers concentrate on achieving a series of goals required to meet the objectives set at the strategic level. The information requirements are usually periodic, but on occasion, managers require "what if" reports. Tactical-level managers are primarily concerned with operations and budget from year to year. In the accounts receivable example, a controller might benefit from a monthly report showing total receipts and write-offs.

Managers at the *strategic level* are objective-minded. Their information system requirements are often one-time reports, "what if" reports, and trend analyses. In the accounts receivable example, the president might request a plot of receipts and write-offs over time with supporting statistical analysis.

The quality of an information system is dependent upon getting the right information to the right people at the right time.

SOCIAL IMPACT

The assessment of the social impact of the various corporate information systems is the responsibility of IS and functional area managers. All proposed and existing information systems should be reviewed to identify those systems with the potential for having an adverse social impact. Existing systems should be reviewed periodically.

The social impact can be *internal* and/or *external*. The severity of the impact ranges from employees' short-term displeasure with new procedures to the long-term effect of employees losing their colleagues through computerization. These examples illustrate possible adverse internal social impacts of information systems. If it is known that the implementation and, in some cases, the mere consideration of computerization of a particular application system will have an adverse social impact, the user manager should cooperate with IS and corporate management to minimize the impact and its reverberations at the social level.

External social impact refers to those persons (customers, clients, service, creditors, and others) who have dealings with the company. A change in a procedure might have a significant impact on the corporate image and, therefore, the profitability of the company. For example, a large, multistate public utility company elected to eliminate the local offices in 12 small towns that they serviced. The residents were then asked to mail payments to a central location. The company did not assess the impact of this change in policy. Residents became irate at not having the opportunity to hand carry their payment to the local office or even to mail their payment to the local office. The net result was that the utility company had to reopen the local offices and completely overhaul the newly installed billing system.

LEGAL IMPLICATIONS
OF INFORMATION SYSTEMS

An information system should be developed within the bounds of any applicable law. At present, many legal questions about computers and information systems are being debated for the first time. There exists a paucity of data by which to evaluate these questions. Actuarial data are almost nonexistent and, therefore, insurance against computer crime and negligence is not only expensive, but of questionable worth.

At present, laws governing the information systems industry are few, and those that do exist are subject to interpretation. The Privacy Act of 1974, the Foreign Corrupt Practices Act of 1977, and various state laws on privacy are only the skeleton of what will be adopted in the near future.

Computer-based information systems place the company in many situations in which, if something went wrong, the company would be liable and subject to suit. For example, a man who was essentially communicating with a computer was continually sent dunning notices for not making payments on an automobile. He had not only made all installment payments, but had completed payment in full. The company's records and procedures were in error, but the company forcibly repossessed the automobile without thoroughly checking their procedures and the legal implications. The man had to sue the company for the return of his bought-and-paid-for automobile. The court ordered the company to pay him a substantial penalty fee.

For years, functional area and IS personnel have taken legality of operational systems for granted. The enormous complexity of modern information systems provides ample opportunity for negligence to occur. Functional area managers should be appraised of those aspects of proposed or existing information systems which are vulnerable to either premeditated illegal IS activities or negligence.

Privacy

The proliferation of federal and state laws encourages corporate management to adopt policies that accommodate all laws. This is particularly true for corporations with interstate communications networks. By adopting the privacy principles embodied in HR 1984, management can be reasonably assured that production systems will conform to any applicable state or federal laws on privacy. The following 10 principles regarding the privacy of personal data and information can serve as system development guidelines to meet present and future legislation on privacy.

1. Permit any person to inspect his or her own file and have copies made at reasonable cost.
2. Permit any person to supplement the information in his or her file.
3. Permit the removal of erroneous or irrelevant information and notify previously notified agencies, organizations, and persons that the material has been removed.
4. Prohibit the disclosure of information in the file to individuals in agencies (organizations) other than those who need to examine the file in connection with the performance of their duties.
5. Require the maintenance of a record of all persons inspecting such files and their identity and purpose.
6. Ensure that the information be maintained completely and competently with adequate security safeguards.
7. Require that, when information is collected, the individual be told whether the request is mandatory or voluntary and what penalty or loss of benefit will result from noncompliance.
8. Require that the person involved in handling personal information act under a code of fair information practices, know the security procedures, and be subject to penalties for any breaches.
9. Permit anyone wishing to stop receiving mail because his or her name is on a mailing list to have that right.
10. Prohibit agencies or organizations from requiring individuals to give their social security number for any purpose not re-

lated to their social security account or not mandated by federal statute.

Fraud and Negligence

There are two causes of illegal IS activities. The first is negligence, which is usually the result of poor control of I/O. Negligence results when someone dealing with the company is inconvenienced. The aforementioned case of the repossessed automobile is an example of negligence. The other category is a premeditated or conscious effort to defraud the system. An example of this would be the well-publicized Equity Funding case of insurance fraud, 1975.

Virtually any computer-based system, especially one that deals with money and materials, is vulnerable to fraud and has the potential to place the corporation in a compromising position through negligence. For the most part, acts of fraud and negligence are prosecuted under laws that are not designed for handling computer or information systems-related crimes. Although the potential for either act is everpresent, the best assurance against such acts is a good system design and an active program of periodic internal audits. A corporate IS audit group is a good vehicle for detecting potential loopholes and periodically documenting the validity of the system. The Foreign Corrupt Practices Act has encouraged corporations to establish an IS audit group. The act requires corporations to maintain tighter internal controls on accounting procedures. To comply, the IS auditing group should evaluate system and internal accounting controls, document system evaluations, correct disclosed weaknesses, and monitor systems and internal accounting controls to ensure ongoing compliance.

Corporations not having an internal IS audit group that complies with the Foreign Corrupt Practices Act are compromising their position of defense in the case of negligence suits. If such a group does not exist, user managers should suggest its formation (see Chapter 13 for guidelines).

TECHNOLOGY TRANSFER

Need

At the most recent apex of technology, one would think that the computer/information processing area is highly automated and somewhat people-independent. Such is not the case. It is ironic that although many IS tasks are computer assisted, information services is very labor intensive. To complicate matters, a limited work force contributes to the high cost of this white-collar labor. However, limited information services resources has not slowed the demand for more and better information systems. To intensify the situation, it sometimes seems to IS managers that all requests are high priority and are needed today!

With a few exceptions, virtually every computer center suffers from a shortage of human resources and an intense demand for these resources. One answer to this dilemma is technology transfer. **Technology transfer** is a buzz word that implies the application of existing technology to a current problem or situation. It took corporations (and vendors) almost 20 years to recognize the potential of IS technology transfer. The solution may or may not be technology transfer, but, as a matter of policy, its potential should be investigated. Some companies build in a requirement to investigate the potential for technology transfer during the feasibility study phase of the systems development process.

Sources

Technology transfer can take the form of procedures, software, documentation, pitfalls, alternative approaches, and so on. The following are sources of technology transfer.

- Software vendors
- Hardware vendors
- Other similar companies
- Consultants
- Computer/information processing-related books
- Journals and periodicals
- Conferences
- Professional seminars

A software vendor can offer fully documented information systems. Hardware vendors can help customers with similar problems to make contact. A similar company can identify possible pitfalls to implementation of a particular system. Consultants can use their experience and expertise to fill technical voids. Books, journals, and professional meetings are a continuing source of state-of-the-art technology.

Proprietary Software

Although technology transfer includes everything from data base management systems to planning techniques, **proprietary software** (also called **packaged systems**) is usually synonomous with technology transfer. Proprietary software is developed by a software vendor with the intent of marketing the end product. The end product consists of the programs (software), associated documentation, and often related education and consultation.

Proprietary software can be categorized in five major areas. These categories are hardware-related, systems software, data management, system design, and applications software. The category of primary interest to user managers is applications software (i.e., accounts receivable, patient billing, payroll). The user manager is normally the ultimate authority for acceptance or rejection of the applications software.

Catalogs are available that list and describe the thousands of proprietary applications software packages. User managers interested in the possibility of this type of technology transfer should work closely with IS personnel to identify potential vendors.

A serious problem confronting software vendors is "piracy" of proprietary software. Most licensing agreements preclude the licensee from copying proprietary software and accompanying documentation for use by another company. It is so easy to do and on the surface, this breach of contract appears harmless, but it is unlawful. An unknowing comptroller asked that a proprietary system be copied for the convenience of a contract programming group doing work on his company's computer system. This error in judgment proved expensive for the corporation when the vendor went to court for restitution.

Make versus Buy. The decision to purchase a proprietary software package or to develop an information system in-house follows the classic lines of reasoning for make-versus-buy decisions. However, several other points should be considered. There is an optimum mix of proprietary and in-house developed software for any given corporation. As a rule of thumb, analyst/programmer efforts should be channeled to the development of systems whose characteristics are unique to that particular corporation. Those systems that are relatively standard may be considered candidates for proprietary software implementation. Large corporations, by virtue of their size and inflexibility to accommodate packaged system specifications, are less apt to choose proprietary software, even of very standard systems.

The corporation that does not take advantage of the potential of proprietary software is not utilizing corporate information service's resources effectively. On the other hand, there are detrimental ramifications for those corporations that use packaged systems across the board. These corporations forfeit the opportunity to develop valuable in-house expertise. Not having the expertise limits their flexibility to respond to ad hoc requests and to develop specialized information systems as the need arises.

User Acceptance of a Packaged System. When systems are developed by in-house personnel, certain traditional procedures remain intact. Invariably, proprietary software packages, designed to accomplish the same function, use different procedures. Strategies for implementing a packaged system are either to change internal procedures or to modify the package. Change is always hard to accept. Throughout the 1970s most corporations elected to modify the packages. Over half of the systems were modified by the licensee, and a third of the systems were modified by the vendor. Ten to twenty percent were installed without modification, usually in very small computer centers.

A lesson learned from the 1970s is that it is not uncommon for a modified packaged system to be more expensive than if the same system were developed in-house from scratch. The wise functional area manager will make every effort to implement packaged systems with few or no changes to the software. It is the user manager's responsibility to examine the documentation of the packaged system and either accept or reject each aspect of the system prior to implementation. Too often management waits until the system is up and running before they become familiar with system operation. This is too late. An up-front evaluation is critical to the ultimate success of a packaged information system.

Not-Invented-Here Syndrome. Both user and IS personnel have delicate egos. The ego of a user manager who has developed procedures that have been successful for 20 years is somewhat damaged when he or she finds it necessary to modify these procedures to accommodate a software package. On the other hand, IS professionals consider it a slap in the face when corporate management discards an existing system and denies them the opportunity to develop a new and better system in-house. The result is the *not-invented-here syndrome.* It is human nature for programmers and analysts to believe that they can develop a better information system than some software vendor on the other side of the country. Even when user and IS personnel agree that the rational decision is to implement a packaged system, the not-invented-here syndrome is still a factor. In-house programmers and analysts are relegated to modifying someone else's creation. It is simply more fun to create than modify. For this reason, programmers and analysts are somewhat reluctant to cooperate.

The following is one of thousands of examples of how the not-invented-here syndrome affects system success. The president, provost, and registrar or a large university made an abrupt decision to purchase a packaged student information system for $80,000. The university's system and programming staff was eagerly awaiting the opportunity and the approval for in-house development of such a system. The staff was told, not consulted, about the decision. After almost three years and $300,000, the project was aborted. A consultant later attributed this failure to the not-invented-here syndrome. This scenario is repeated all too often.

The not-invented-here syndrome is mentioned to highlight the importance of total involvement during the decision process. Although analysts and programmers are the responsibility of IS managers, user managers should be keenly aware that decisions they make regarding package software can affect their attitudes and even their careers. For this reason, user managers should make special efforts to solicit input from line analysts and programmers as well as IS managers. When the decision is supported by line personnel, the implementation process is simplified.

Warnings. "No packaged software system is a panacea." Just because an inventory control system is operational and people are happy with it at the ABC Corporation does not mean that the package will yield the same results at the XYZ Corporation. Each package should be evaluated with caution and implemented with extreme care. The system may be beneficial, but don't expect it to solve all of the problems.

"Don't be first." It's unfortunate, but many software vendors routinely field test their software at the expense of their clients. That is, these packages are not fully tested and are debugged after they have been implemented in a few accounts.

"Don't sign the contract before the package is on the market," even if a company is using it successfully. In some cases a vendor will try to sell a system before it is ready (limited documentation, software incomplete, and so on).

"Don't assume that the package will require only minor modifications" without an in-depth look at the package documentation and a complete system demonstration. All functional area managers affected by the proposed packaged system should carefully examine every facet of the system, then bring to the attention of IS management those facets of the system that must be modified.

"Do not proceed without complete or almost complete user acceptance." Invariably, packaged software requires some compromises on the part of all users involved. The user who has not approved the system prior to signing the contract will be reluctant to make the necessary compromises. This may ultimately delay implementation and, in some cases, cause project failure.

"The purchase price may represent as little as 25% of the fully installed cost of the packaged system." Too often modifications are deemed minor and not considered in the economic analysis. These modifications can and will be expensive, and in almost every case are a major cost of systems implementation.

"The conversion and implementation phase is no easier with proprietary software." The implementation of a system, whether developed in-house or purchased, is a formidable task, and managers should anticipate similar problems.

Evaluation and Selection of Proprietary Software. The hardware evaluation and selection methodology discussed in Chapter 7 is equally applicable to the evaluation and selection of proprietary software.

ROLES AND RESPONSIBILITIES

The quality of an information system and the potential profitability of a corporation are very much dependent on a clear definition of user/ information services roles and responsibilities. If there is any confusion during the system life cycle about who should do what and when, then management should insist that these roles and responsibilities be articulated in the form of a development methodology and corporate policy (see Chapter 12 and Chapter 4 respectively).

The following roles and responsibilities are appropriate in most organizations. However, minor variations should be made to accommodate existing circumstances.

User Roles and Responsibilities

Information Systems Policy Committee (ISPC). The high-level IS steering committee is normally composed of user executives. The charge of this committee is, therefore, a user responsibility. An example charge is presented in Chapter 4. The ISPC approves major requests for IS services, sets priorities, resolves interdepartmental differences, and establishes corporate-wide IS policy.

Receptivity to Change. Computerization, by its very nature, is change. People, by nature, resist change. It is not uncommon for an entire functional area department to resist the implementation of an information system, even when departmental personnel are assured and believe that the end product will make their jobs more productive and personally gratifying. It is the responsibility of user managers to create the proper environment for acceptance of the inevitable changes that accompany the implementation of a computer-based information system. Perhaps one of the best ways to encourage acceptance is demonstration. It is time well spent to demonstrate a successful information system (within or external to the corporation). Personnel should be encouraged to interact with those who have just experienced the "trauma" of computerization.

Systems Service Request. The responsibility of compiling and submitting a request for services from the IS department resides with the end user.

Support of Information Services Projects. If not a member of the project team, the user manager should nevertheless stay abreast of project activities. After all, the resultant product will have a major affect on the department's procedures, operation, and success. The user manager is asked to "sign off" at each major milestone. Some managers simply go through the motions and take for granted that the project is progressing and the system will be exactly what is wanted. The sign-off procedure is a user responsibility and is critical to the success of the project.

The signature indicates satisfaction and concurrence with not only the basic system design, but with the detailed specifications. User managers and their staff should meet with appropriate project team personnel to make sure that they understand and concur with every aspect of the proposed system. The importance of the sign-off at the end of Phase II can not be overemphasized because the system specifications are then "frozen." Changes made during Phase II require only a small fraction of the personpower of the same changes made after system implementation. For example, a change in file design may require one person less a day than during Phase II. After implementation the same change may require several persons for months. The user must identify design deficiencies early and not sign off until the system is thoroughly understood and the department is satisfied. Specific user responsibilities during the system development process are discussed in detail in Chapter 12 and illustrated in Figure 12-2.

Education. User managers and user personnel are responsible for providing functional area training for information services personnel (e.g., inventory models, AICPA accounting principles, and so on). This training can be administered individually or in group sessions depending on the size of the project team. It is also helpful if the user manager can suggest alternate sources of information (books, journals, formal classes).

The user may also require some computer/information systems related training. The administration of this training is the responsibility of the information services department. The user's responsibility is participation. These training programs cover such topics as how to use a specific piece of computing hardware, operational aspects of a computer-based system, and general computer-related training, to mention a few.

Data Entry. Depending on the extent of the distribution of traditional IS functions, the user community could be charged with almost any facet of information services, from data entry to programming. At a minimum, the user departments are responsible for input to the system. In on-line systems this entails the transcription of source data to machine-readable format via video display units. In batch systems, the user is responsible for the completion of accurate and legible source documents. These documents are batched and routed to information services for data entry. A serious problem in the batch transcription process is that many source document characters are illegible. This results in frequent calls and visits to user departments or, worse, an error in the data base. User managers should be aware that legibility is as important as accuracy and should encourage clerical personnel to be cognizant of the importance of being both accurate and neat.

Funding for Information Services Rendered. Depending on corporate policy, the user departments may be responsible for funding all, some, or none of the services rendered by the IS department. Those corporations that have adopted a chargeback system typically bill users for internal consulting, analyst and programming services, hardware utilization, on-line storage utilization, and materials.

Periodic Evaluation of Information Systems. An information system is "owned" by (the property of) the user departments, not the information services department. It is therefore the user manager's responsibility periodically to initiate formal reviews of their information systems. These reviews create a proactive attitude towards system enhancements. The process is described in Chapter 4.

Information Services Roles and Responsibilities

Staying Abreast of Technology. With the state of the art of technology changing almost daily, no corporation can afford to neglect opportunities for cost-effective increases in capabilities. In order to take advantage of available technology, IS personnel must make a concerted effort to stay abreast of the technology. Any technological innovations that have the potential to increase productivity or improve effectiveness should be brought to the attention of IS and user management.

Serving as a Catalyst. IS personnel should be catalysts in the identification of opportunities for new information systems and enhancements to existing information systems. Any opportunity to improve data processing or the management decision-making process should be brought to the attention of the appropriate functional area managers.

Providing a Source for Advice. IS personnel are a source of advice and consultation for the user community. The IS department should provide a mechanism by which users can request advice on computers/information processing (i.e., user liaison).

Assisting Users in a System Development Process. The system development process is a 50/50 proposition whereby functional area expertise is combined with technical expertise and the result is a computer-based information system. Prior to 1980, the prevailing attitude of both user and IS personnel was that system development was the responsibility of information services. Today, the information system is owned by the user and is therefore the responsibility of the user. The IS responsibility is to "assist" users with their information systems project.

Providing Operational Capability for Information Systems. The information services department is responsible for the hardware-based portion of the production system. This, of course, does not apply to DDP environments. It includes machine room, control, output distribution, and data entry (in batch environments only).

There is sometimes confusion regarding data base responsibilities. The corporate data base is stored on mass storage devices controlled and operated by IS personnel. The data base administrator is responsible for the physical and logical maintenance of the data base. However, any changes to the data base are prompted by user input; therefore, the accuracy of the data base is the responsibility of the user, not the data base administrator.

Maintaining Information System Documentation. For any given information system, the documentation package includes system and programming documentation, "run instructions" for computer operators, data base documentation (which may support one or more information systems), and the user manual. Any enhancements to a system must be reflected in the aforementioned documents. These documents are distributed and maintained by IS personnel.

Providing an Environment for Corporate Integration. The common denominator in a corporation is not money. It is data. Data comprise the vehicle by which to integrate functionally adjacent corporate entities.

Every corporation, educational institution, and government agency is wrought with redundancies in data and procedures. It is the responsibility of information services to provide the technological capacity (hardware and technical expertise) to minimize or eliminate these redundancies.

Providing User Education Programs. Education of the user in the area of computers and information processing is widely recognized as a significant contributor to an organization's success. User managers and executives are taking advantage of professional seminars, university-sponsored classes, user-oriented books, and in-house seminars. In-house user management seminars are the responsibility of information services. There is such a demand for computer/information processing awareness and knowledge that it is easy to cost-justify user education, even in small corporations.

The following programs could be offered formally to larger groups and informally to small groups or individuals, depending on the requirements for user education.

User management seminar. This seminar is appropriate for managers at the operational, tactical, and strategic levels. The content would be similar to that of this book.

User analyst seminar. Many functional area managers are hiring analysts to interface with information services personnel. Although some of these analysts have excellent IS backgrounds, most do not. They would benefit from a seminar concentrating on the system development methodology.

Information system orientation. The purpose of this program is to provide an overview of a particular computer-based information system. The program is primarily based on the contents of the user manual.

General information services orientation. This program is directed to secretaries, administrative assistants, and clerical personnel. The purpose of this session is to explain the information services organization and its role within the corporation. The objective is to encourage involvement for those persons who are directly affected by a computer-based information system.

Special-function seminars. As technology advances and new capabilities are made available, the best way to make users aware of these capabilities is through special-function seminars. Seminars might be presented on the concepts of distributed data processing, new equipment, how to use query languages, word processing, process control, data base management systems, new concepts in design, and so on.

Maintaining a Balance between Being Responsive and Being Responsible. Limited resources are available for development and maintenance of information systems. Therefore, information services must maintain a balance between being responsive and being responsible. For example, an information services manager cannot channel previously committed resources from one project in an attempt to be responsive to another user. The IS manager cannot disregard the responsibility to keep the approved project on schedule. This is an almost daily conflict that IS managers must resolve.

Standards and Procedures. The information services department is responsible for development and maintenance of standards and procedures relating to computers and information processing. Any given computer center will have hundreds of standards and procedures ranging from programming conventions, to standard procedures for systems development, to standardized interfaces for word processing equipment.

Strategic Information Services Planning. The strategic IS planning function is the responsibility of the high-level IS steering committee, if one exists. However, IS personnel serve as functionaries to develop the plan for approval by the steering committee. Strategic IS planning is discussed in detail in Part IV.

Vendor Interactions. As a matter of corporate policy, both hardware and software vendors should be directed, at least initially, to a central location. Since IS managers routinely interact with a variety of vendors, IS is the logical point for the initial vendor interaction. This approach minimizes the possibility of an inexperienced user being sold a bill-of-goods by an unscrupulous vendor. (Overall, the integrity of vendors is high). Another reason for this approach is standardization. For example, the purchase of stand-alone word processing computers is very popular, but if each user department purchased one independently of the other departments, the obvious benefits of hardware compatibility would be negated.

Word Processing. The rationale for assigning word processing responsibility to information services closely parallels the rationale for assigning IS responsibility for vendor interactions. The user manager making a one-time decision on a word processing approach and word processing equipment would be using his or her time inefficiently. To make an informal decision, the user would have to become familiar with the vast array of word processing alternatives. IS is responsible primarily for technical support and advice, and not necessarily for specific word processing applications. Word processing hardware is normally distributed to the user area.

Hardware Acquisition. Any acquisition of computing hardware should be centralized. It is only logical that IS be assigned this responsibility. Again, the primary reason for the centralization of this activity is to maintain hardware and, possibly, software compatibility.

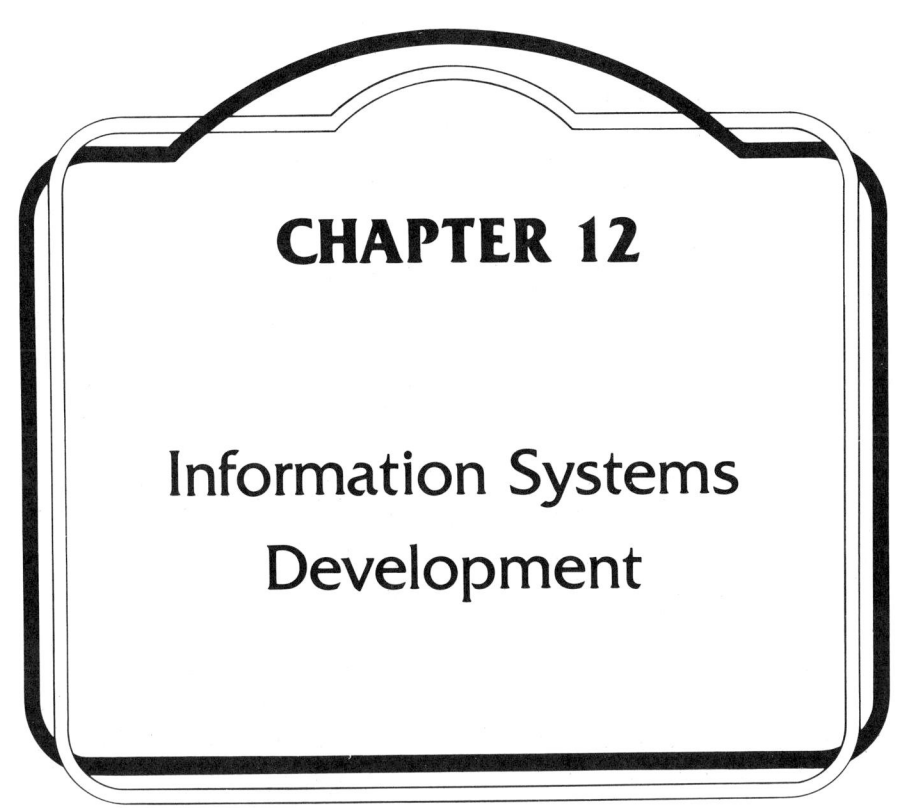

CHAPTER 12

Information Systems Development

The process for developing a computer-based information system, whether it be an on-line airline reservation system or an inventory control system, is essentially the same. The process consists of certain basic activities that are learned by every IS professional. But because individuals tend to interpret the process differently, most corporations have adopted a standardized **systems development methodology**. These methodologies, like software, can be purchased commercially or developed in-house.

Systems development methodologies identify activities to be performed, the relationship and sequence of these activities, and key evaluation and decision milestones. The submittal of the feasibility study and the completion of the functional specifications are two of many milestones in a typical methodology.

BENEFITS OF A SYSTEM
DEVELOPMENT METHODOLOGY

Documentation

Documentation has long been a problem in information systems development and maintenance. A methodology encourages project team members to produce documentation as a byproduct of the design; therefore, documentation is up to date and complete upon system implementation. A change control mechanism is built into the methodology to ensure up-to-date documentation at all times. Computer centers without methodologies tend to rely on the individual's taking the initiative to update system and program documentation within their realm of responsibility. This mode of operation has failed and resulted in unnecessary waste of resources. When an individual leaves a legacy of undocumented systems and programs, valuable personnel time must be expended to sort out what was done.

Project Management

Since development tasks (activities) are identified and sequenced, the input necessary for the implementation of a project management system is made available. Project planning and control in the IS environment is almost impossible without a standardized systems development methodology.

Monetary Savings

Methodologies have the potential to yield significant dollar and personpower savings. Perhaps the greatest savings is realized by eliminating the three-steps-forward, two-steps-backward approach to system development. A methodology provides direction and ensures that important aspects of systems development are not overlooked. For example, a good methodology will require that cost, schedule, procedural, software, operating, and equipment constraints be identified before proceeding with systems design. Appropriate user and IS managers sign off on these written constraints. Without such guidelines, project teams often proceed in one direction (three-steps-forward), only to find out that much of the work has to be redone (two-steps-backward) because of a design constraint violation.

The probability of developing a quality system that meets user requirements is much higher when the project team follows the guidelines of a well-written system development methodology. Figure 12-1 highlights the economic importance of doing it right the first time.

Sometimes user and IS managers look only at the development cost, but systems costs should be evaluated over the entire system life cycle (including years in production). Figure 12-1 illustrates that although a system developed using a methodology will demand a greater up-front commitment of resources, the resultant design should be superior, and, therefore, minimize requirements for system changes. These changes are made easier by good documentation. On the other hand, a system designed according to individual preference and without the aid of a system development methodology will inevitably result in a system of marginal quality and a considerably higher cost of maintenance. It is not unusual for the entire project team of a poorly designed system to be assigned to full-time maintenance of the same system.

SYSTEM DEVELOPMENT RESPONSIBILITY MATRIX

The system development responsibility matrix of Figure 12-2 denotes when and to what extent individuals, groups, and departments are involved in the systems development process. The involvement of these entities is noted for each activity as:

- ◆ A—Approval
- ◆ C—Consultation
- ◆ P—Participating responsibility
- ◆ R—Primary responsibility

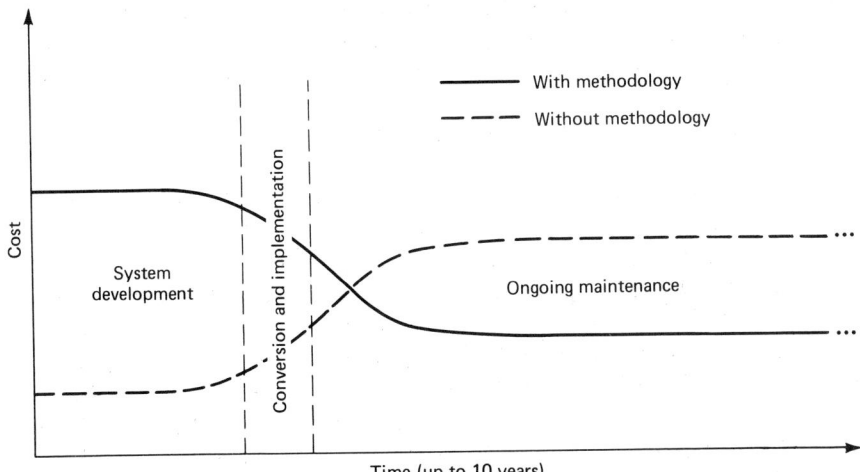

FIGURE 12-1 System cost over the life of the system.

		Entities							
Key A = Approval C = Consultation P = Participating responsibility R = Primary responsibility ◇ = Milestones		Feasibility study team	Project team	Information services management	Unassigned programmers and analysts	Functional area managers	Unassigned functional area personnel	Information systems policy committee	Information systems audit group
Phase I System initiation and feasibility study									
Activity: No.	*Description*								
1	Submit service request				C	R	P		
2	Evaluate service request (*minor only)			A*				A	
3	Appoint feasibility study team			R		P			P
4	Identify constraints	R		P		P			
◇A 5	Document present system	R				C	C		
6	Investigate technology transfer	R		P		P			
7	Complete preliminary design of proposed system	R				C	C		
8	Define scope of project	R		C		C			
9	Prepare benefit/cost analysis	R		P		C			
◇B 10	Make decision on feasibility study	C		C		C		A	
Phase II Systems analysis and design									
11	Appoint project team			R		P			P
12	Estimate and make personnel commitments	R	P			P		C	P
13	Train personnel	R					P		
14	Establish detailed schedule	R	C			C			
15	Interview user personnel	R				C	C		
16	Specify data base requirements	R			P				C
17	Establish controls and backup procedures	R							P
18	Complete detailed design	R				C			C
◇C 19	Conduct user/information services walkthrough	P	R			A			A
20	Select hardware (*major acquisitions)	P	R					A*	

FIGURE 12-2 System development responsibility matrix.

		Entities							
Key A = Approval C = Consultation P = Participating responsibility R = Primary responsibility ◇ = Milestones		Feasibility study team	Project team	Information services management	Unassigned programmers and analysts	Functional area managers	Unassigned functional area personnel	Information systems policy committee	Information systems audit group
Phase II Systems analysis and design (cont'd.)									
Activity: No.	*Description*								
21	Prepare layouts		R			C	C		
22	Describe data entry specifications		R						
◇ 23	Prepare program descriptions		R						
Phase III Programming									
24	Appoint chief programmer		P	R					
25	Prioritize and assign programs		R						
26	Schedule program preparation		R						
◇ 27	Write, test, and document programs		R						
Phase IV Conversion and implementation									
28	Complete conversion plan		R			P			P
◇ 29	Conduct system acceptance test		R			P	P		P
30	Develop user manual		R						
31	Present user-training program(s)		R			P	P		
◇ 32	Create and convert files/data bases		R				P		
◇ 33	Complete parallel operation		R/A	P/A		P/A			
Phase V Post-implementation evaluation									
34	Update cost		R						
35	Conduct post-implementation review		R			C	C	C	
◇ 36	Prepare system review schedule			P		R			

FIGURE 12-2 Continued.

255

Along the left-hand side are the major activities listed by each of the five phases of the methodology. The responsibility matrix is the basis for the discussion of the systems development process. The activities are presented in the order in which they are accomplished. For ease of cross reference, the activities are numbered both on the matrix and in the discussion.

The diamonds to the left of certain activities on the responsibility matrix are placed arbitrarily to designate major milestones in the development process. The milestone occurs at the completion of these activities. The milestones can be used for scheduling and as predesignated points for evaluation of project progress. A company would normally use the same milestones for each development project. More milestones are needed for unstructured projects that have a greater risk of failure.

The entities listed across the top of Figure 12–2 are described below.

Feasibility study team. The team consists of user and IS personnel assigned to accomplish the feasibility study (Phase I activities).

Project team. The team consists of user and IS personnel assigned to develop and implement a computer-based information system or a major enhancement to an existing system.

Information services management. This refers to the IS management team and not necessarily to a specific person. In a small organization, involvement would probably be limited to the director of IS. In a larger organization, the manager best suited to the particular task would be involved.

Unassigned programmers and analysts. This encompasses all IS professionals who are not assigned to the feasibility study team or the project team in question.

Functional area managers. All functional area (user) managers who affect or are affected by the proposed development project are included in this responsibility entity.

Unassigned functional area personnel. This encompasses all functional area personnel, except the manager, who affect or are affected by the proposed development project and are not assigned to the feasibility study team or the project team.

Information systems policy committee. The Information Systems Policy Committee (ISPC) is the high-level steering committee for all corporate information services. The ISPC membership and charge are discussed in detail in Chapter 4.

Information systems audit group. One of the functions of the IS audit group is to ensure that proper controls are built into a computer-based information system during the development process. The information services audit function is introduced (organizationally) in Chapter 3 and explained (functionally) in Chapter 14.

THE SYSTEM DEVELOPMENT PROCESS

System development methodologies vary in scope, complexity, sophistication, and approach. One methodology has 3 phases, another 15 phases, but each depicts essentially the same activities to be accomplished. The most important point to be made in this chapter is that the best development methodologies are those that continually involve the user. In the past, the user manager, in cooperation with an IS development team, completed the general functional specifications. The system was then developed by IS personnel. Systems development is now a 50/50 proposition; therefore, user managers should be very familiar with the system development process in general, and their own corporate methodology in particular.

The system development process will be described in five phases. These phases are:

- ◆ Phase   I—System Initiation and Feasibility Study
- ◆ Phase II—System Analysis and Design
- ◆ Phase III—Programming
- ◆ Phase IV—Conversion and Implementation
- ◆ Phase V—Post-Implementation Evaluation

Phase I—System Initiation and Feasibility Study is completed prior to the commitment of resources for the development of a proposed system. Much of the work and documentation compiled in Phase I is input to Phase II. During Phase II—Systems Analysis and Design, systems analysts and users work together to compile detailed functional and system specifications. These specifications are submitted to programmers, and Phase III—Programming, is initiated. Once the software has been developed, the data files are created, the existing system is converted, and the new system is implemented during Phase IV—Conversion and Implementation. Phase V—Post-Implementation Evaluation begins the production stage of the system life cycle and signals the requirement for the often overlooked post-implementation evaluation.

This section contains a step-by-step description of the system development process. For specific details, interactions, approaches, forms, and so on, the user manager should contact the manager of information services, discuss the current corporate methodology, and review the company's internal manual describing the methodology.

Phase I—System Initiation and Feasibility Study

There is less agreement on the activities of Phase I than on the other four phases. The approach presented here includes an appeal procedure for rejected service requests and incorporates investigation of the potential of technology transfer into the process. The end product of Phase I is in two parts. The first part is the actual **feasibility study**, which contains a description of the proposed system (or enhancement) and the benefit/cost analysis. The second part, a **general system design**, is necessary for meaningful assessments of costs and benefits. The general system design is direct input for Phase II—Systems Analysis and Design.

The premise behind incorporating some general system design into the feasibility study is that too many feasibility studies are based on a concept rather than a design. When too little time is spent on describing system objectives, cost estimates and even benefits are erroneous. Feasibility studies that are conducted around a concept are doomed to cost overruns and user dissatisfaction. The time spent on a general systems design is time well spent, even if the feasibility study is rejected. The documentation compiled will inevitably prove valuable in other projects.

The following numbered activities correspond to the system development responsibility matrix, Figure 12-2.

1. Submit service request

The service request procedure was presented in detail in Chapter 4 to illustrate a formalized IS procedure. Figure 4-1 illustrates a procedure that includes an appeals process for rejected requests. The service requested is ultimately for the user and, therefore, should be initiated by the user. User managers are encouraged to request assistance from IS personnel, but it should be reemphasized that functional area managers are responsible for completing appropriate documentation for both large and small requests for service.

2. Evaluate service request

See Chapter 4 and especially Figure 4-1 for a description of a bi-level procedure for evaluating service requests. As noted on the responsibility matrix, IS management can only approve minor projects (minor being defined by corporate policy).

3. Appoint feasibility study team

IS and user management collaborate to assign the proper mix of personnel to a feasibility study team. The team should be comprised of at least one systems analyst and at least one user representative. The size of the team depends on the scope and time frame of the feasibility study.

The user representative should be intimately familiar with all current functional area operations. The user manager, the executive assistant, or functional area analyst are logical choices. Analysts with a computer-information processing background are becoming popular in the user areas.

One person should be appointed as the **feasibility study team leader,** even on two-person teams. Until about 1980, most feasibility study teams and project teams were headed by a senior systems analyst or a project leader, both of whom were permanently assigned to the IS department. To further encourage user involvement by placing the ultimate responsibility with the end user, more and more companies are adopting the policy that a user should be the project team leader. Those companies experiencing success with such a policy have appointed users with excellent management skills and some computer/information processing knowledge. In any case, the leader must make a total commitment to the team effort. When a user is required to continue routine functional area duties while serving as leader, the project is usually doomed to failure. Several companies have adopted a policy that automatically assigns the manager of the functional area most affected by the system to be the feasibility study team leader and the project team leader (Phases II–V). The manager is subsequently released from operational duties and devotes his or her full time to managing the study or project. The difficulty in such arrangements has been in mainstreaming the user manager back into the functional area after absences of from two months to three years.

4. Identify contraints

At the onset of the systems development process, the feasibility study team works closely with the IS and user managers to identify the equipment, costs, schedule, procedural, software, and operating constraints that may limit the definition and design of the proposed system.

5. Document present system

The rationale for documenting the present system is that the team cannot accomplish an effective preliminary design of a proposed system if they do not fully comprehend the existing system. Most manual systems evolved and were not designed, per se. In these cases, documentation must be developed from scratch. When the proposed system is an upgrading of an existing computer-based system, the feasibility study team need only ensure that existing documentation is complete and up-to-date.

Any documentation completed on the existing system will provide valuable input to the design process (if the system is approved for development). It can also provide basic documentation and probably insight to the existing system if the proposed system is rejected. The four-part present system documentation consists of (1) system reports and documents, (2) system data files, (3) system data elements, and (4) a chart illustrating the present system data, information, and work flow.

The first three documentation items, the reports, files, and data elements, are classified as:

- *Presently used and will be retained* in their present format in the proposed system;
- *Presently used but will be revised* for use in the proposed system; or
- *Presently used but will be deleted* and no longer maintained in the proposed system.

For example, all existing reports and standardized documents would be listed and given a status as defined above. The reports would also be identified relative to cycle (e.g., daily, weekly) and distribution.

All data files in the existing system would be identified with respect to storage medium (3 X 5 card, magnetic tape, manila folder, magnetic disk, and so on) and storage scheme. For example, a name and address file might be stored on 3 X 5 cards and maintained alphabetically by name. The number of files maintained in a manual system is always surprising, even to the functional area manager. To complete the existing file documentation, an example and brief description of one record from each file is attached to the list of files.

System data elements (e.g., social security number, customer name, part number, and so on) are listed without respect to file association. Invariably, these data elements are duplicated on several files. Besides the status indicators, each data element is described if the title is not self-explanatory. Other information about the data element includes update requirements (e.g., daily, weekly, monthly, as required [AR], and so on), source (agency, document, system, person, and so on), and responsibility (name of department and/or title of person responsible for update). Figure 12–3 illustrates a typical form that might be used to document the present system's data elements.

The operational procedures of the present system are documented by reducing the system to the basic component parts of input, processing, and output, then by graphically depicting the logical relationships between these parts. There are a variety of graphical techniques available to do this. Perhaps the most popular, though not necessarily the best, is flowcharting. Other more "structured" techniques include IBM's Hierarchical plus Input-Processing-Output (HIPO), bubble charts, data flow diagrams, Nassi-Shneiderman charts, Warnier diagrams, and decision tables. Examples of flowcharts, HIPO charts, Warnier diagrams, and decision tables are illustrated in Phase II, activity 18. A graphic description of present operational procedures provides an overview of the system's data, information, and work flow, with an emphasis on the elements within the system that control the flow. The charts should delineate

Report Title	System Data Elements					Date	
System Title Medical Information System						ID MIS	

No.	Title	Description	Present	To be revised	To be deleted	Update requirement	Source	Responsibility
1	Name-1st	Patients	X			--	Ad form	Admissions
2	Name-MI	"	X			--	"	"
3	Name-last	"	X			AR	"	"
4	No. children	"			X	AR	"	"
5	Sex	M or F		X		--	"	"
6	Marital status			X		AR	"	"

AR-As required

FIGURE 12-3 Present system documentation: system data elements.

manual and computer processes and place all processes in the proper sequence. These charts are organized and presented in a manner that best displays the operational procedures. They can be by subsystem activated by random events, by function, by minor and major cycles, by subsystems, hierarchical, or a combination. Very few systems are strictly sequential; therefore, a modular approach is applicable in most cases.

6. Investigate technology transfer

In an attempt to make better use of existing technology, many corporations are building an investigation of the potential for technology transfer into their systems development methodologies. A corporate policy encouraging the investigation of the possibility and/or feasibility of technology transfer will inevitably yield significant savings in human resources. This is particularly true in the case of programmers and systems analysts. Judicious transfer of technology will allow these personnel to concentrate their efforts on industry-specific application areas for which there is no existing software.

An investigation of the potential for technology transfer begins by canvassing those companies known to have already implemented systems of similar size and operation to the one proposed. The feasibility study team should also research commercial software catalogs for applicable proprietary software. If technology transfer is deemed feasible, the feasibility study team describes how the technology can be used and the extent of modifications required to accommodate the existing environment.

If investigation of the potential for technology transfer is standard procedure, the requesting company should adopt a policy of cooperating with other companies that make similar inquiries to them.

7. Complete preliminary design of proposed system

The feasibility study team interviews functional area personnel to obtain general system requirements, then translates these requirements into a preliminary system design. The design process is iterative, with user managers and the feasibility study team in continuous communication about ideas, approaches, and so on.

The preliminary design of the proposed system is documented by a word picture and a graphic illustration. The word picture describes, in nontechnical terms, the fundamental operation of the proposed system and would typically parallel the graphic illustration. The word picture would also enumerate those procedures, approaches, and/or methods of the proposed system that are expected to deviate considerably from the present mode of operation. Also, the word picture would describe the relationships between the proposed system and both manual and automated systems with which the proposed system must be compatible.

The graphic illustration reduces the proposed system procedures to their component parts and emphasizes their logical relationship. Appropriate techniques are discussed in detail in Phase II, activity 18.

8. Define scope of project

The feasibility study team cooperates with IS and user management to assess the degree of complexity depicted in the preliminary design. Estimates of human resource requirements (user, IS, and other) are made for each subsequent phase of the development project. Training and computer-time requirements are also noted.

9. Prepare benefit/cost analysis

Once the preliminary design has been completed and the project has been "scoped," the benefit/cost analysis can be initiated. Unfortunately, both user and IS managers tend to hurry to this stage of feasibility study. In so doing, critical steps are omitted and consequently, benefits and cost estimates are erroneous. An accurate reflection of benefits and cost cannot be based on a concept. Some kind of a design is imperative.

Another mistake that is embedded in the mechanics of the corporate decision-making process is the inevitable translation of intangible benefits to dollar savings. The complex integrated systems of today make significant contributions to corporate profit, but they do so over the long run and in subtle, less visible ways. The evaluation of the merit and worth of IS projects is a subjective process that requires a knowledge of the tangible cost and benefits. In addition, decision makers must have a thorough understanding of both positive and negative intangible benefits. The use of the dollar as a common denominator for all benefits and costs is an oversimplification of the evaluation task. The introduction of earnings figures for such intangible benefits as "better customer relations" or "increased prestige" serves only to compound the error in the "bottom line." Too often the bottom line is blindly accepted as gospel, when, in fact, half of the estimates are at best, mush, and at worst, ridiculous. When intangibles are reduced to dollars, bad estimates are substituted for the decision maker's better judgment.

The best way to evaluate a proposed information system is to weigh the positive and negative intangible benefits against the net worth of the system (savings minus cost). A comprehensive explanation of intangible benefits—for example, increased service, fewer errors on invoices, faster turnaround—should accompany a summary report of costs and savings.

Figure 12-4 illustrates how one-time and recurring costs can be presented in a minimum of cost categories. These costs can be presented by budget center and for the corporation as a whole. The cost categories are labor, materials and equipment, travel, and miscellaneous. For each category, one-time cost estimates (development) are noted in the first column and recurring cost estimates (production) are noted over the horizon of the system life cycle. The net worth of the project to the company can be computed by subtracting costs from estimated savings and discounting the cash flows according to corporate policy.

   10. Make decision on feasibility study

The feasibility study is completed and all but the technical supplement is submitted to the ISPC for action. The technical supplement contains background information required for the preparation of the feasibility study. The technical supplement also contains the general system design and the framework from which to initiate Phase II—System Analysis and Design. Of primary interest to the ISPC are the initial service request, scope, word picture, and benefit/cost analysis.

The ISPC acts on the feasibility study as described in Chapter 4. The ISPC can:

   1. Reject the proposal.
   2. Approve the proposal and assign a top priority to its development and implementation.
   3. Approve the system with less than top priority and place the request in a queue of approved systems at the appropriate priority position. (Periodically the queue is reviewed and, as resources become available, the committee gives the go-ahead to the highest-priority project(s)).

Phase II—Systems Analysis and Design

Very few feasibility studies are approved for immediate implementation. The elapsed time between approval and project initiation may be as much as two or more years. Once the project is given the go-ahead, Phase II—Systems Analysis and Design is initiated. In Phase II, the format and content of all I/O are described, the file/data base specifications are prepared, the hardware is selected, and the detailed systems design is completed. The final activity in Phase II is the preparation of

Budget Center		Project Title and Number								

Cost item		One-time cost	Yearly recurring costs							
		Year	Year 1	Year 2	Year 3	Year 4	Year 5	Year 6	Year 7	Year 8
Labor											
Mat. and Eq.	Materials										
	Equipment										
Travel	Per diem										
	Transportation										
Miscellaneous											
Total costs											

FIGURE 12-4 Cost summary.

265

program descriptions which identify and contain the specifications for the various program modules. It is important to note that no programs are written in Phase I or II. A common mistake, often costly in terms of system quality and level of ongoing maintenance, is to press Phase II to a premature completion in order to begin Phase III—Programming. A poorly designed system will invariably extend the project by doubling, or even tripling, the amount of programming required.

11. Appoint project team

Like the feasibility study team, the project team should include one or more systems analysts and one or more user representatives from each functional area within the scope of the proposed system. When possible, an IS auditor is appointed to the team, not as a functionary, but more as an advisor on security and controls. Since programmers are not active participants until the end of Phase II, programmer appointments can be deferred until that time. Members of the feasibility study team do not necessarily become members of the project team. Original members are often committed to other projects during the interim between the end of Phase I and the beginning of Phase II. It is advisable, however, to appoint members of the original feasibility study team when possible. The project team leader can be either IS or user.

Some companies have permanent project teams that are organized by functional area. For example, a project team may be dedicated to maintenance and new systems development in the human resource development area, another in accounting and finance, and so on. The alternative is to work from a pool of IS and user professionals and appoint the team on a project basis. The trade-offs are apparent. The functionally organized project teams inevitably suffer from inefficient use of resources by being understaffed during peak activity periods and overstaffed during periods of reduced activity. This type of team organization, however, provides a greater opportunity for individuals to develop functional area expertise. Perhaps the best approach to IS project team organization is to organize by functional area, but to maintain the flexibility to move members between teams to achieve workload leveling.

Depending on the complexity and scope of the project, each project team has a different optimum number of members. The team leader's management ability is a significant variable. Where some managers can effectively manage 20 or more people, others have difficulty with 3. The team size and relative progress of the project are always areas of interest to user and IS, as well as to corporate management. A misconception held by many corporate managers is that if you double the number of people on the project team, you can finish the project in half of the time. This is simply not the case. A straightforward pro-

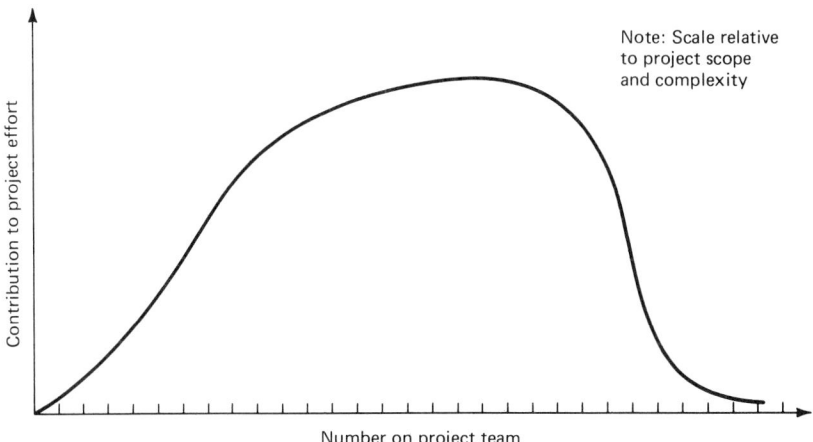

Note: Scale relative to project scope and complexity

Contribution to project effort

Number on project team

FIGURE 12-5 Project team size.

ject that is neatly packaged into readily identifiable modules might be implemented in half the time with twice the personpower. However, most projects range from complex to extremely complex and require close coordination between all members of the team.

Figure 12-5 illustrates what happens when the size of a project team is increased. Up to a certain number, each additional person assigned to the project team enhances the contribution to project progress. After that, each additional member actually reduces the per person contribution to the project effort. There is a point at which the marginal returns for the addition of more persons actually become negative and their membership becomes counterproductive to the project objectives. In a desperate attempt to meet a project deadline, management sometimes demands that all resources be diverted to the critical project. Figure 12-5 graphically illustrates what happens when a project team has too many members. Close coordination becomes impossible. When the head does not know what the tail is doing, project progress comes to a standstill, even though every member is busily engaged in some type of project-related-activity.

There is an optimum size for a given project team. All managers and corporate officers involved should be well aware of this maxim: *It is better to delay system implementation than to throw good money after bad by increasing the size of the project team past its limits.*

12. Estimate and make personnel commitments

The success of a project is highly dependent on the extent and timeliness of cooperation by user and corporate managers, other functional area personnel, and, to some extent, IS personnel (e.g., data base administrator, user liaison, and so on). A written and signed commitment of personnel is necessary, or even the most critical projects will be delayed because someone (or some department) will forget or not honor an earlier verbal commitment. The members of the project team and others involved directly in the system development process (with interviewing, data gathering, and so on) should be listed with their relative time commitment for each phase (see Figure 12-6). Person-power requirements are derived from the results of the feasibility study.

A project that proceeds without a written commitment of personnel is doomed to unnecessary delays and possibly failure. This document puts the importance of the development project into proper perspective. Many of those persons involved in the project are not on the project team. Since most of these people perceive their routine activities to be more important than any external project involvement, a written commitment is imperative. Unfortunately, the project commitment is sometimes an overload to their regular work assignments. In these

Report title: Estimated Personnel Requirements			Date: Nov 12, 8X		
System title: Market Analysis System			ID: MARS		

Department/Division	Functional title	% Time		
		Phase II	Phase III	Phase IV
Management Info. Div.	Systems Coordinator	60	30	80
" " "	System Analyst-Senior	100	10	80
" " "	" " "	100	10	80
" " "	" " "	60	0	0
" " "	Programmer-Senior	0	80	20
" " "	Programmer	0	100	100
Marketing Div.	Director	10	20	30
" "	Assistant Director	10	20	30
" "	Clerk	10	10	40
" "	"	10	10	40

FIGURE 12-6 Estimated personnel requirements.

cases managers must be directly involved, encouraging timely and active participation.

Figure 12-7 is included to give the reader a feel for the relative requirements for personnel commitments by phase. The bottom portion of Figure 12-7 depicts what percentage of the total project effort is devoted to each of the five phases of system development. A range of "percent effort" is presented for each phase. Corporate policy and the development methodology will effect the relative percentages. For example, a methodology that emphasizes the design phase (III) will certainly have more clearly defined program specifications, thereby

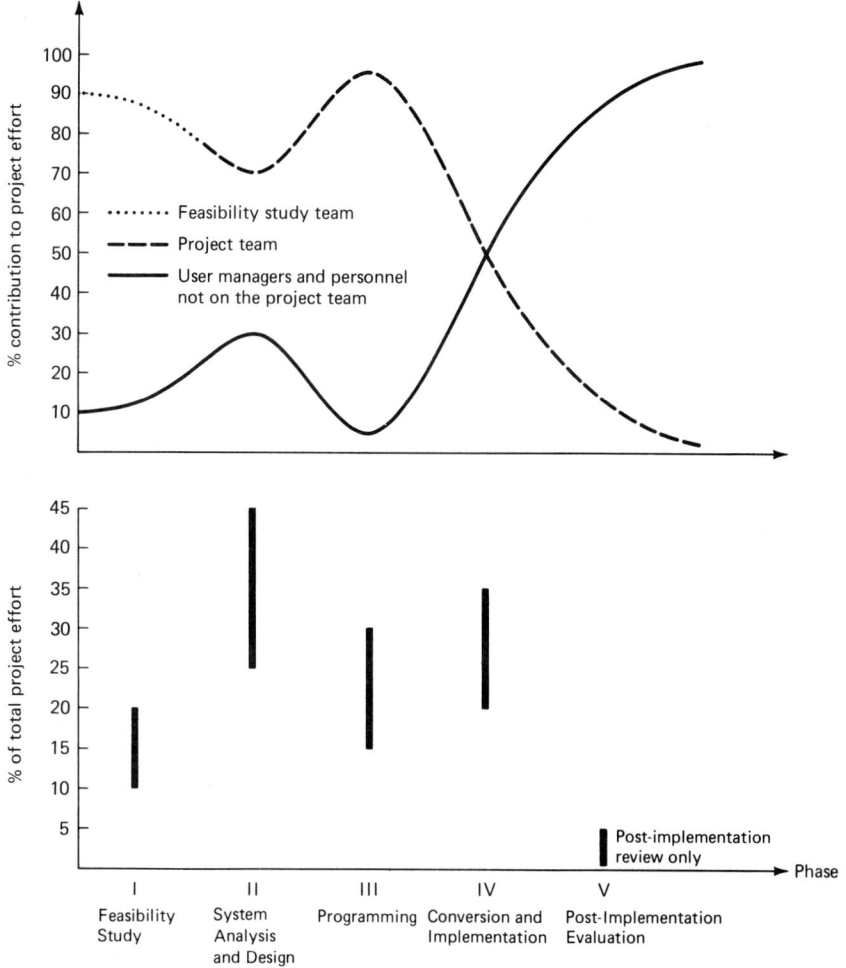

FIGURE 12-7 Relative project effort.

reducing the time required for the programming effort. As a rule (but only up to a point) the effort devoted to Phase II—System Analysis and Design is inversely proportional to the effort devoted to Phase III—Programming. In a well-designed system, Phase II will comprise a greater percentage of the project effort than Phase III.

The top portion of Figure 12-7 illustrates the relative percent contribution to the project effort by the project team (user and IS personnel) and by users who are not members of the project team. Note that during Phase II, 30% of the effort is contributed by users who are not on the project team. During Phase II—System Analysis and Design, the project team must be in continuous communication with users at every level. During programming, users are only peripherally involved. During Phase IV—Implementation and Conversion, the user is involved in training, testing, data conversion, and parallel operation. In Phase IV, project team and user work side by side until the system is implemented. In Phase V, the system is turned over to the user.

13. Train personnel

Users involved in data base design and IS personnel involved in production scheduling will probably require some training to achieve effective communication during the systems development process. As a rule of thumb, IS personnel are responsible for training in the information systems areas, and user personnel are responsible for training in the functional areas.

The product of this activity is a list of names and titles of individuals who will require some type of training. Each line item would be accompanied by a brief description of the type of training, where and by whom the training will be conducted, and the time frame. Some training will be required immediately and other training, like data entry, will be deferred until close to implementation.

14. Establish detailed schedule

With a standardized approach to systems development, management can establish milestones (see Figure 12-2, activities 5, 10, 19, 23, 27, 29, 32, 33, and 36), then use historical statistics and experience to estimate the completion dates of the intermediate and final activities. The project team leader must work closely with IS and functional area management to ensure the availability of personnel at critical points in the development process.

The systems development process is essentially linear (one activity follows another) and is not difficult to monitor with the proper guidelines (a methodology) and reasonable estimates. Figure 12-8 illustrates

+ Activities for completion of milestones

Phase	Milestone	Activities	Estimated starting date	Actual starting date	Days ahead/behind	Estimated completion date	Actual completion date	Days ahead/behind
I	A		Sept. 1, 198W	Sept. 1, 198W	OS	Oct. 1, 198W	Oct. 15, 198W	12B
	B		Oct. 1, 198W	Oct. 20, 198W	14B	Nov. 1, 198W	Dec. 1, 198W	22B
*II	C	14 15 16 17 18 19	Sept. 15, 198X	Sept. 1, 198X	13A	Dec. 25, 198X	Dec. 20, 198X	3A
	D	(20) 21 22 23 / (13)	Jan. 5, 198Y	Jan. 5, 198Y	OS	Feb. 15, 198Y		
III	E	24 25 26 27	March 1, 198Y			June 30, 198Y		
	F	28 29	July 1, 198Y			July 15, 198Y		
IV	G	30 31 32	July 25, 198Y			Sept. 10, 198Y		
	H	33	Oct. 1, 198Y			Oct. 31, 198Y		
V	I	34 35 36	Nov. 1, 198Y			Feb. 1, 198Z		

/ = Activity begun X = Activity completed O = No action required

+ Corresponds to methodology in Figure 12-2.

A = Number of working days ahead
B = Number of working days behind
OS = On schedule

*Phase II–V estimates are not entered until the feasibility study is approved for implementation.

FIGURE 12-8 Information system project schedule.

a typical information system project schedule. One of three marks is superimposed over the activity numbers to indicate the status of that activity. The number is circled if circumstances dictate that the activity is unnecessary. After work commences on a particular activity, a diagonal line is drawn through the number of the appropriate activity (e.g., $\cancel{3}$). The diagonal is made into an "X" once the activity is completed (e.g., **X**). A Gantt chart is also used to give a graphic overview of project progress.

Prior to beginning a set of milestone activities, a more detailed schedule is prepared. These intermediate activities are scheduled individually. Those activities requiring more than an elapsed time of two weeks are scheduled in two-week increments. Figure 12–9 illustrates a detailed information system project schedule for the activities of milestone E.

The following procedure can be used to make estimates of cost, personnel, and appropriate time requirements. This iterative approach results in a group consensus and is particularly appropriate for IS projects. It is assumed that those participating in the estimation process have a knowledge of the problem or task and the ability to provide meaningful rationale to support their opinions. The participants in the information system project scheduling process might include the project team leader, affected user managers, and other experienced IS personnel who may not be associated with the project. The following steps describe an approach to making reasonable estimates:

A. The project team leader presents the task (e.g., establish milestone dates for project scheduling) and appropriate background information.

B. Each participant submits a written estimate (cost, personnel requirements, or time).

C. The project team leader plots, on a linear scale, the estimate of each member of the group.

D. The upper and lower quartiles and the median are calculated and marked on the scale.

E. Those participants whose estimates fall in the lower and upper quartiles are asked to explain their rationale for their low or high estimates.

F. The project team leader coordinates an open discussion based on the plotted estimates.

G. Steps B through F are repeated until the returns for increasing the accuracy of the estimates do not merit another iteration. The dispersion of the estimates should be reduced with each iteration.

H. The estimate is the median or the mean (as appropriate). The dispersion of the estimates is an indication of the risk involved. The greater the dispersion (spread), the greater the risk.

Milestone E—detailed						
Activities	Estimated starting date	Actual starting date	Days ahead/ behind	Estimated completion date	Actual completion date	Days ahead/ behind
24 Appoint chief programmer	March 1, 198Y			*March 3, 198Y		
25 Prioritize and assign programs	March 5, 198Y			March 12, 198Y		
26 Schedule program preparation	March 15, 198Y			March 25, 198Y		
27a Write, test, and document programs	April 1, 198Y			April 11, 198Y		
27b "	April 15, 198Y			April 30, 198Y		
27c "	May 1, 198Y			May 14, 198Y		
27d "	May 15, 198Y			May 31, 198Y		
27e "	June 1, 198Y			June 14, 198Y		
27f "	June 15, 198Y			June 30, 198Y		

*Based on actual starting date for Milestone D activities.

A = Number of working days ahead.
B = Number of working days behind.
OS = On schedule.

FIGURE 12-9 Detailed information system project schedule: Milestone E activities.

15. Interview user personnel

The user interview process commences with this activity. Project team members periodically meet with appropriate users to resolve issues and determine system requirements. The user interview and feedback process is ongoing throughout the system development process.

The basic inputs to the detailed system design are: (A) the preliminary design (from the feasibility study), (B) an evaluation of the existing system and its components (also from the feasibility study), and (C) the input, processing, and output requirements (provided by the user).

A. The project team, in cooperation with appropriate user personnel, examines the I/O needs and frequencies depicted in the preliminary design of the feasibility study. Each I/O is evaluated relative to its need and worth. Many outputs are "nice to have" but are simply not worth the effort required to produce them. I/O is also assessed relative to cycle and time frame. Cyclic inputs and outputs are optimized by evaluating the frequency-versus-worth trade-off. For example, if a weekly status report would suffice, there is no need to produce a daily status report. In on-line systems, response time requirements are examined to determine if they are too stringent and can be relaxed with little effect on operational efficiency or whether the reponse time requirements are insufficient.

B. The present system documentation provides valuable input into the design. Existing reports, forms, source documents, and others, can be physically traced to the ultimate user to determine if the document is relevant and timely and, if so, what can be done to improve it. The project team is responsible for all changes made to existing system inputs and outputs. Duplication should be eliminated when possible by incorporating similar inputs and/or outputs and eliminating superfluous information.

C. An immediate result of preliminary interviews is a general description of all outputs of the proposed system (reports, displays, or transactions). Each output is described relative to cycle, primary user, output media, content, and distribution.

16. Specify data base requirements

The data base is designed to support the processing and, specifically, the output of the system. The first step in data base design is to identify all data elements required for the system. Available data elements are included in the present system documentation. Invariably, the format of many of the existing data elements is changed. Other data elements needed to support the functional requirements of the system are identified.

The project team develops and documents what is referred to as a **data dictionary**. In a data dictionary, data are listed without regard to data base or file organization and with certain basic information being maintained for each data element. In the data dictionary example of Figure 12-10, each data element is assigned an arbitrary number for cross-reference, a title, a description (if necessary), whether or not it is coded, a programming label, the number of storage positions (characters), format and storage (applies primarily to programmers), and responsibility. The user must identify the person or department responsible, the number of positions, and whether the data element is coded. The data dictionary form of Figure 12-10 can also be used to cross-reference each data element with all source documents, reports, files, and data bases in which it occurs. Each coded data element is documented in the manner described in Chapter 8.

After all data elements have been identified, the project team, in cooperation with the data base administrator, designs the record layouts and files. Or, in a data base environment, they design the data base schema. See Chapter 8 for a discussion of file organization and data base design. The output of this activity is the data dictionary and a detailed technical description of the files and/or data base schema.

17. Establish controls and backup procedures

Controls are built into the design to ensure the accuracy, reliability, and integrity of the information system. The project team describes all physical and administrative controls to be embedded in the system design. A wide range of techniques are used on input, during processing, and on output to control the system. Input is **verified** before processing. During processing, techniques such as **reasonableness checks** and **check digits** are used to minimize or eliminate gross errors in computation or transaction. **Record counts** and **site checks** are representative of the many techniques that are used to ensure the accuracy of the output.

To avoid catastrophe during a system failure, **backup** and **check-**

REPORT TITLE Data Dictionary	DATE
SYSTEM TITLE	ID

SOURCE DOCUMENTS (S), REPORT (R), FILE (F), or DATA BASE (D)

No.	TITLE / LABEL	NO. POS.	PICTURE/FORMAT	DESCRIPTION	STORAGE	RESPONSIBILITY	CODED	Payroll Ck (R)	Payroll register (R)		Payroll master (F)	Accounting (F)		Time sheets (S)
1	Social Security No. / SSN	9	99999	employee	P	Personnel	NO	X	X		X			X
2	Last name / LNAME	13	X(13)	employee	E	Personnel	NO	X	X		X			X
3	First name / FNAME	10	X(10)	employee	E	Personnel	NO	X	X		X			
4	Middle initial / MI	1	X	employee	E	Personnel	NO	X	X		X			
5	Department / DEPT	3	XXX	employee affiliation	E	Personnel	YES		X		X	X		X
6	Sex / SEX	1	X	M or F	E	Personnel	YES				X			
7	Salary / SAL	6	9999	monthly	P	Personnel	NO	X	X		X			

(actual size is 11″ × 16″)

FIGURE 12-10 A data dictionary.

point/restart procedures are defined. These procedures describe the extra processes included in the system to cope with system failures. In the case of system failure, backup files and/or backup transaction logs are used to recreate processing from the last "checkpoint." The system is "restarted" at the last checkpoint and normal operation is resumed. Periodically during the chronology of system processing, operations establishes a checkpoint such that any processing to that point in time is saved and cannot be destroyed.

18. Complete detailed design

The detailed system design is the result of analysis of I/O, processing, control, and backup requirements. The preliminary system design or general system design (see activity 7) depicted the relationship between major processing activities. The detailed design is expanded to include all processing activities and associated I/O. This is the cornerstone activity of the system development process. It is here that the functional specifications are integrated with technical and procedural innovations to achieve a system. The detailed system design is the culmination of all previous work. Moreover, the detailed design is the blueprint for all subsequent project activity.

A number of techniques used for graphically illustrating the system design are mentioned but not discussed in activity 5. Three techniques—flowcharting, HIPO, and Warnier diagrams—are briefly discussed here. The most popular technique used graphically to depict work flow and the overall system design is the flowchart. Flowcharts illustrate work and data flow via specialized symbols which, when interconnected by **flow lines**, portray the logic of the system. A subset of system flowcharting symbols is shown in Figure 12–11. A portion of an operational payroll system is depicted by flowcharts in Figure 12–12.

Flowcharts have definite drawbacks. A flowchart, unlike the other two techniques discussed in this section, does not encourage analysts to use the **top-down approach** or modular approach to system design. As a result, systems designed using flowcharting techniques can be more difficult to design, comprehend, and maintain. The popularity of the flowchart is derived from the enthusiasm for being the first.

Hierarchy plus Input-Processing-Output, or HIPO, is a method of illustrating all input, processing, and output in successive levels of detail in a hierarchical manner. Figure 12–13 illustrates a HIPO Volume Table of Contents (VTOC) for a payroll system. The VTOC is one of several standard forms used in HIPO design. The system is broken into a hierarchy of logical modules and depicted in the VTOC. These are subsequently broken into finer levels of input-processing-output detail using Overview Diagrams and Detail Charts. There are usually a number

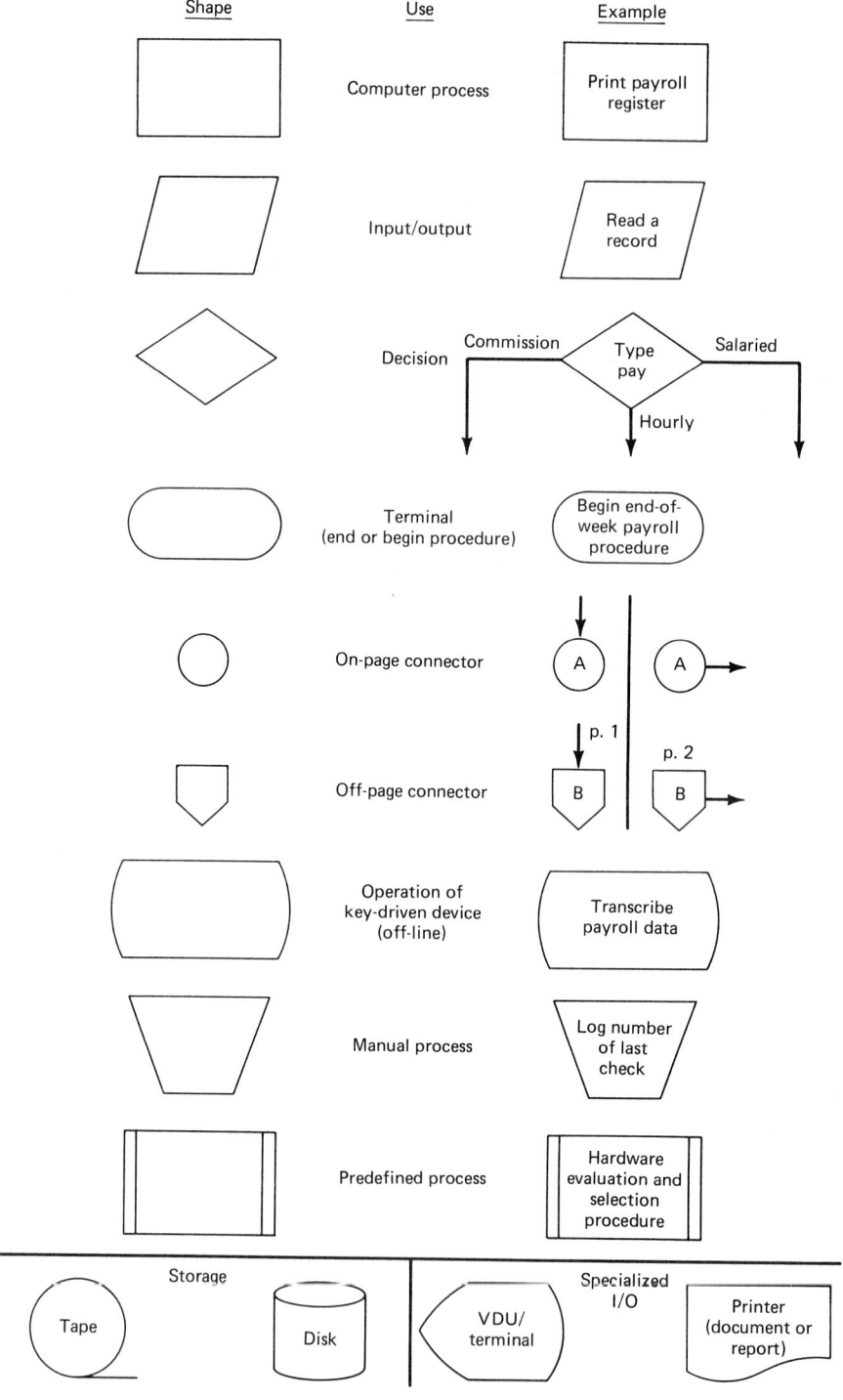

Shape	Use	Example

Computer process — Print payroll register

Input/output — Read a record

Decision — Type pay (Commission, Hourly, Salaried)

Terminal (end or begin procedure) — Begin end-of-week payroll procedure

On-page connector — A | A

Off-page connector — B (p. 1) | B (p. 2)

Operation of key-driven device (off-line) — Transcribe payroll data

Manual process — Log number of last check

Predefined process — Hardware evaluation and selection procedure

Storage — Tape, Disk

Specialized I/O — VDU/terminal, Printer (document or report)

FIGURE 12-11 Subset of system flowcharting symbols.

of VTOCs that carry the hierarchy of design into successive levels of detail. For example, module 1.2.1, hourly report processing (Figure 12–13), would be the highest-level module on another VTOC. The advantages gained by HIPO's structured approach are offset by the cumbersome volume of paperwork required to document the system.

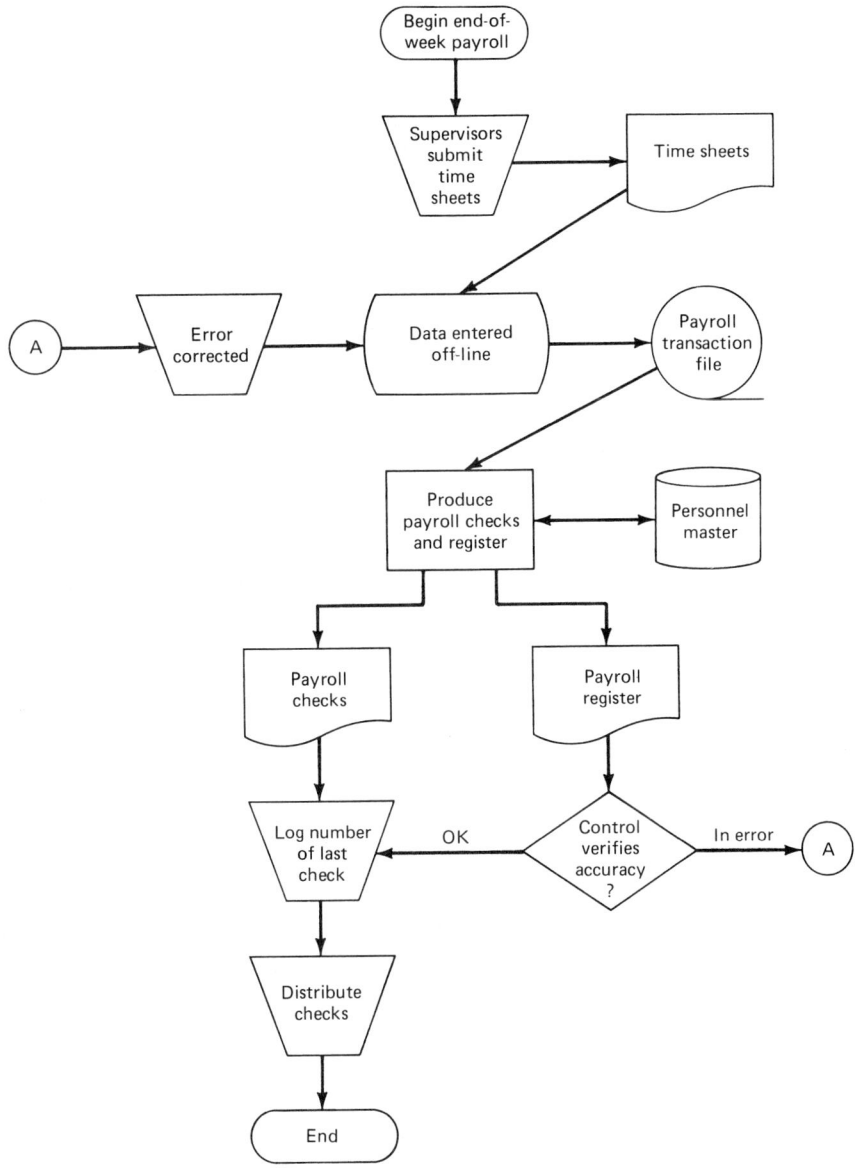

FIGURE 12-12 Simplified payroll system flowchart.

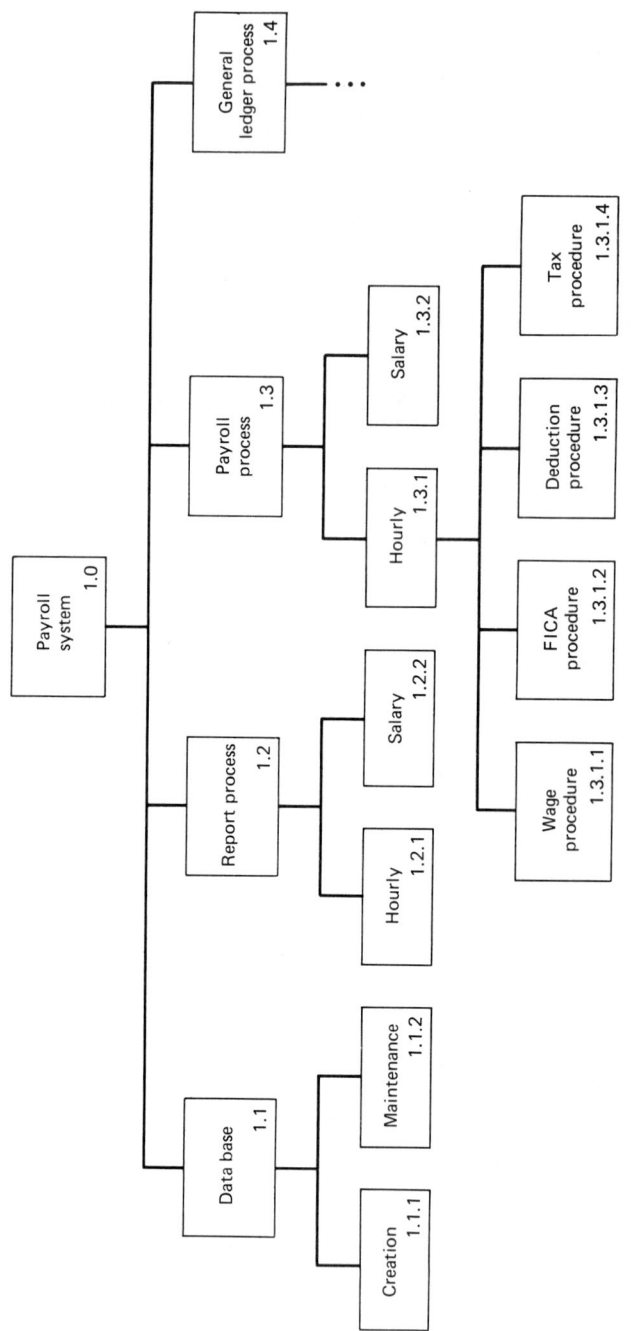

FIGURE 12-13 HIPO: volume table of contents.

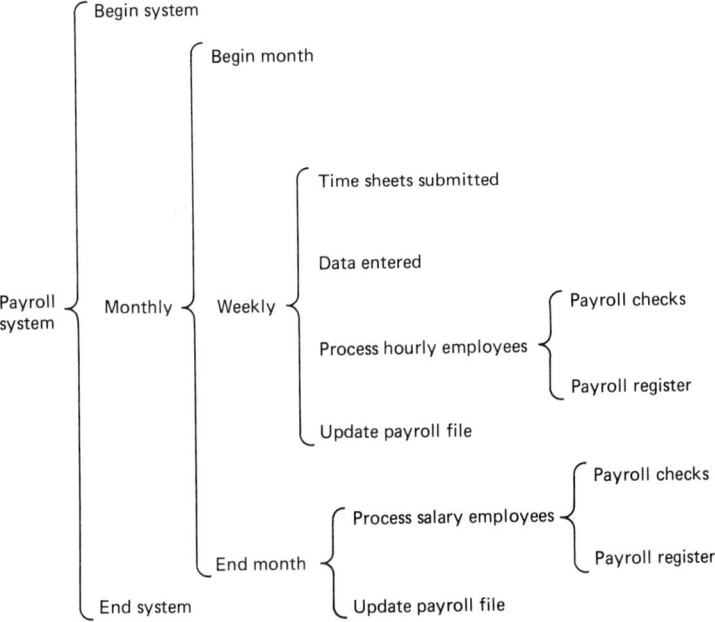

FIGURE 12-14 A Warnier diagram.

Warnier diagrams, illustrated in Figure 12-14, can be used to design the overall system, data structure, report contents, and data element codes. The premise behind the Warnier diagram is that the system should be designed around the data structure. The greatest advantage of Warnier diagrams is their applicability to a variety of circumstances.

The decision table illustrated in Figure 12-15 is a vehicle that can be used to illustrate graphically what course or courses of action should be taken for all possible circumstances. The example in Figure 12-15 is an extended-entry decision table and one of many types of decision tables. A decision table has a condition stub (upper-left quadrant), action stub (lower-left quadrant), condition entry (upper-right quadrant), and action entry (lower-right quadrant). The decision table is not an effective vehicle for illustrating data and work flow and is best used to supplement another design technique. The major advantage of decision tables is that consideration must be given to every alternative, option, condition, variable, and so on. Unlike flowcharts, HIPO charts, and other design procedures, the level of detail is not a matter of analyst discretion.

The analytical tools discussed above are alternatives to lengthy word narratives that are usually confusing and subject to interpretation. However, well-written narratives can and should be used in support of graphic design techniques.

Pay type	Salary		Hourly		Commission	
Time frame	End of week	End of month	End of week	End of month	End of week	End of month
Print paychecks		X	X		X	X
Print payroll register		X	X	X		X

FIGURE 12-15 A decision table.

There is no one best analytical and design technique. The best is a combination of techniques that fit the circumstances of a particular company. In any case, a modularized top-down approach is a modern day imperative. In top-down design, the basic system objectives are established by top-level management, then successive levels of detail are added to the design based on input gathered at each level of the corporation. Most systems are too complex to be conceptualized as a whole; therefore, systems are divided into more intelligible modules. The premise behind modularization is "divide and conquer," and it works.

19. Conduct user/information services walkthrough

A **structured walkthrough** is a peer evaluation procedure that is effective in minimizing the possibility of something being overlooked or done incorrectly. It also provides an opportunity for peer personnel to evaluate what has been suggested (i.e., system design) and, perhaps, to make constructive recommendations. The purpose of a walkthrough is to provide valuable feedback to the project team, not to pass judgment on system quality.

The structured walkthrough is initiated at the discretion of the project leader and is typically done after system design and other critical points in the system development process (e.g., test plan, program descriptions, and so on).

The people involved in a structured walkthrough are members of the project team, a coordinator, participants (identified below), a secretary, and perhaps a neutral manager. One or all of the project team members act as *presenters* and explain that portion of the system which they authored. The *coordinator* is in charge of the walkthrough and coordinates the interaction between presenters and participants. The *participants* are selected on the basis of their knowledge of and interest in the topic being presented. They should have no direct involvement with the project. The *secretary* keeps a written record of significant points. A *neutral manager* is often invited to attend the first walkthrough. This person's presence encourages everyone involved with the walkthrough to attend to the matter at hand (sometimes a problem with walkthroughs).

The procedures of a structured walkthrough are simple. The material (i.e., system design) to be reviewed is distributed to the participants several days in advance. The coordinator is charged with the responsibility of contacting and communicating with all persons involved in the walkthrough. During the actual walkthrough, the presenter(s) explains the system design and accompanying documentation. This is done by "walking through" the system step by step, perhaps with the aid of one of the design tools. Participants make suggestions which are discussed and documented by the secretary. A walkthrough would normally last no longer than 1½ hours. A walkthrough session can actually become counterproductive if this time limit is exceeded. If necessary, more sessions are scheduled to complete the walkthrough.

The project team evaluates all recommendations and incorporates those that have merit into the system design. A walkthrough is valuable for obtaining meaningful feedback prior to system implementation.

20. Select hardware

If extra hardware is required to support the system being developed, appropriate hardware must be selected and ordered. The hardware acquisition process is usually the responsibility of information services management. A hardware evaluation and selection procedure is detailed in Chapter 7.

21. Prepare layouts

Up to this point in the development process the outputs have been identified and described relative to content, but the programmer needs to know the specific format of the output (how it should appear on the output device). This detailed output specification is called a **layout**. Screen (VDU) layouts are produced by the project team. The layout specifies such items as title, headings, output formats, and, in the case of screen layouts, input formats.

Some hard-copy reports and documents require preprinted forms. The project team, in cooperation with a commercial forms representative, designs and orders the preprinted forms (e.g., payroll check and stub).

The project team is also responsible for the design and content of all manually produced reports and documents that originate within the scope of the system. Any changes, additions, or deletions are coordinated with the affected user manager.

22. Describe data entry specifications

The data entry specifications detail what and how data are to be entered into the system.

23. Prepare program descriptions

At this point in the systems development process, the existing system has been thoroughly analyzed, and its strengths have been incorporated into the design of the proposed system. The proposed system and its supporting data base have been designed, and detailed specifications have been prepared for all I/O. The project team is now ready to identify and define all programs required for completing the software necessary to make the proposed information system operational. The graphic representations of the system (flowcharts, HIPO charts, and others) are the primary input to identifying required programs.

The project team compiles the following documentation for each program.

♦ Type of programming language (e.g., COBOL, BASIC, FORTRAN)
♦ A narrative description of the program describing the tasks to be performed
♦ Description and layout for each output to be produced by the program
♦ Frequency of processing (e.g., daily, weekly, on-line, etc.)
♦ Limitations and restrictions (e.g., sequence of input data, volume restrictions, response time, maximums, minimums, etc.)
♦ Detailed specifications (e.g., sorting, editing criteria, specific computations and logical manipulations, tables, etc.)

Phase III—Programming

The project team is now ready to begin communication with the computer. The communication or computer interface takes the form of instructions which are imbedded in computer programs. The computer programs comprise the software necessary to make the system operational. All software required to support the information system is developed during Phase III—Programming.

User involvement (see Figure 12-7) is concentrated on the front- (Phase II) and back-ends (Phases IV and V) of the system development process. If Phase II is done correctly and the user/project team interaction is effective, the user will have little or no involvement during the programming phase. Most of the involvement will revolve around points of clarification in the system design and, perhaps, some preliminary planning for Phase IV—Conversion and Implementation.

Unfortunately, some user managers are intensely involved during programming. This is an indication that Phase II was poorly executed and probably incomplete when programming was initiated. This happens all too often, especially in crisis-oriented environments where intense demands are placed on the project team to produce a finished product. Since the ultimate product of the system development process is software, programming is sometimes initiated prematurely. This mode of system development will inevitably result in an inferior system that does not satisfy the user's requirements and a system that is expensive to maintain. The cost over the life of such a system may be two or three times that of a quality system. The cost of not doing it right the first time is discussed and illustrated earlier in this chapter.

24. Appoint lead programmer

The project leader is usually a systems analyst or a user and is not directly involved in the programming function. The individual managing the programming function should be an active participant; therefore, for programming efforts requiring two or more persons, a lead programmer is appointed by IS management. However, the project team leader still has overall project responsibility.

The lead programmer, sometimes called the **chief programmer**, may spend as little as 10% of his or her time in production programming (with five or more subordinate programmers), or as much as 80% of his or her time in production programming (with only one other programmer to supervise). The chief programmer team organization is described in Chapter 3.

25. Prioritize and assign programs

An information system may require hundreds of programs to complete the software package. These programs are not necessarily written in the order in which they will ultimately be executed. Many variables must be considered when setting up the schedule for program development. The chief programmer considers the following when prioritizing the programs.

- The need for creation and maintenance of test files
- Program dependencies (where one program is dependent on the output of all or part of another)
- The length and complexity of the program

Programs are assigned according to a programmer's level of expertise, availability, and familiarity with the system. Because programmers are often assigned to other project teams and a wide range of expertise and experience are represented, matching programmers with programs is no easy task.

26. Schedule program preparation

The Program Progress Chart (Figure 12-16) can be used by the chief programmer to schedule and monitor the activities of subordinates and the status of any given program. Since there is a basic pattern for program development, a technique similar to that used to monitor project progress (Figures 12-8 and 12-9) can be used to monitor the progress towards completion of a particular program. The **Gantt Chart** of Figure 12-17 is a graphic representation of the Program Progress Chart (Figure 12-16) and is a common management tool seen on the bulletin boards of almost all chief programmers and project team leaders.

27. Write, test, and document programs

A programmer will work on two to five programs at any given time. The general procedures for the development of any given program are essentially the same.

- Prepare general program logic diagram
- Prepare detailed program logic diagram
- Code program (write program statements)
- Test and debug program
- Document program

Phase IV—Conversion and Implementation

The objective of Phase IV—Conversion and Implementation is to integrate the work of Phases I, II, and III, and to implement the information system into the functional area(s). The project team and affected user departments are heavily involved throughout Phase IV (see Figure 12-7).

Even though the individual components (programs) of the system have been tested in Phase III, there is no guarantee that when integrated, the system will work; therefore, integrated systems testing is accomplished in Phase IV. During Phase IV the project team trains users in the operation of the information system, converts existing files, and

REPORT TITLE **PROGRAM PROGRESS CHART** DATE

SYSTEM TITLE Materials Requirements ID MR

Program Title	Label	Programmer	Percentage of Time	General logic	Detailed logic	Code program	Test and debug	Documentation	Estimated Start Date	Actual Start Date	Ahead/Behind	Estimated Completion Date	Actual Completion Date	Ahead/Behind
Daily update	007 MR	Lois James	50	X	X	X	X	X	Sept. 15	Sept. 20	5B	Oct. 30	Nov. 30	21B
Supervisor	006 MR	Phil Morrison	100	X	X	X	X	X	Sept. 15	Sept. 15	OT	Nov. 15	Nov. 1	10A
Schedules	008 MR	John Speer	80			/			Oct. 1			Jan. 1		
Inventory status	042 MR	Mary Lou Cummings	40	X	X				Oct. 15	Oct. 20	4B	Nov. 1		
Materials list	102 MR	Lois James	20	X	X				Nov. 3	Nov. 15	10B	Jan. 15		
Audit--daily	001 MR	Jim Jones	100						Dec. 1			Mar. 1		
Audit--weekly	002 MR	John Speer	20						Dec. 10			Jan. 15		

FIGURE 12-16 Program progress chart.

287

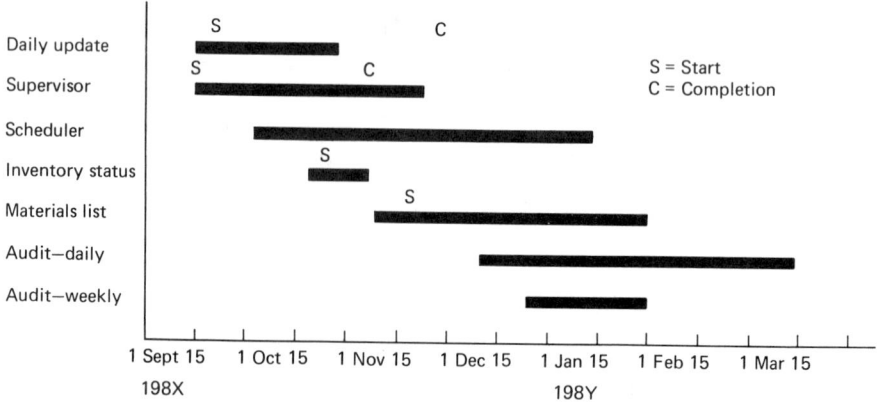

FIGURE 12-17 A Gantt chart for program schedule (see Figure 12-16).

creates the data base. The system is turned over to the functional area(s) after parallel operation.

28. Complete conversion plan

The system conversion process is, in itself, a system and should be treated as such for the best results. The project team, in cooperation with the user manager and IS audit group, collaborates to develop a conversion plan. The conversion plan includes the details for system acceptance testing, files/data base conversion, user training, and parallel operation (if necessary). The conversion plan details user and IS duties and responsibilities and the time frame over which they are to be executed.

29. Conduct system acceptance test

Although the individual program modules have been tested, they have not been integrated and tested as a system. An information system may have a hundred or more programs and a dozen files that must be tested as a unit to ensure harmony of operation and the satisfaction of the user. The integrated test validates all systems and applications software, input/output, files/data base, and procedures. User personnel are active participants during testing.

It is probable that errors will be found, that aspects of the system were overlooked, and that procedural shortcomings will surface. Invariably, a part of the acceptance testing procedure is to make minor modifications in design and programming. If the system is developed correctly, any such modifications will be to fine-tune the system. Any major modifications should be delayed until after the system is implemented and in production for at least a year. This delay avoids committing valuable resources to responding to what is usually a knee-jerk reaction to change. Presumably the project team leader and affected user managers will have signed off on every facet of the information system, making the need for major modifications unlikely. A requirement for a major modification at this time is a clear-cut indication that someone neglected their project responsibilities.

The actual integrated system test is accomplished in two parts. First, test data are used to verify each subsystem. Once all subsystems function properly, the entire system is tested with "live" data. Test data are created to test specific circumstances, whereas live data are actual data, usually from past processing.

When testing on-line systems, in which response time is critical, several live testing sessions are included to test the capacity of the system. The system may be operationally perfect, but an undersized computer or an inefficient program may result in an unacceptable response time.

30. Develop user manual

The project team develops a **user manual** and conducts user training sessions concurrent with system acceptance testing. Every information system should have a user manual that provides instructions and explanations for the operation of the system. The user manual and associated training are critical to the ultimate success of the system. Just having a user manual is not sufficient. The manual must be a quality document that provides quick and easy reference to the operation of every facet of the system. At a minimum, the user manual would include:

- Objectives of the system
- Description of the system
- Work flow and general operating procedures
- Instructions for completing and understanding input/output
- Data collection and update procedures
- Controls
- Other (e.g., glossary of unique terms, description and use of hardware, performance criteria, and so on)

The contents of the user manual are derived from the system documentation; however, this material must be written and compiled in a format that can be understood and which will not be misinterpreted by its intended user.

31. Present user training programs

The user manual is of little value without associated training. Members of the project team conduct a series of training programs to acquaint users with the system. The general content of a user training program includes:

- Purpose and objective of system
- Differences between the existing system and the new system
- Overview of system operation
- How to use the user manual
- Duties and responsibilities of IS and user personnel (relative to the system)

A large department store chain implemented an on-line point-of-sale (POS) system and distributed user manuals to each POS terminal location. With no formal training, the salespersons were left to their own resources to decipher the user manual (over 100 pages) and utilize the system. The salespersons' inability to handle other than basic transactions disenchanted customers and they took their business elsewhere. The department store chain almost folded before they recognized that the problem was not marketing, quality of products, or location. The problem was a lack of user training.

32. Create and convert files/data bases

Very seldom is a system implemented that needs no revision to existing files/data bases. Certain files and data bases must be created and others converted to the appropriate format. The user department is responsible for assimilating and preparing the data for transcription to machine readable form. The user department may also be responsible for the transcription/data entry function. Data preparation can be time consuming if the data are not readily available or are stored manually (e.g., 3 × 5 cards).

The user, with guidance from the project team, is responsible for the integrity of newly created and converted files. The validation process is a combination of visual site checking and computer checking. Random sampling can be used effectively on extremely large files/data bases.

Time phasing is critical during the creation/conversion process. Once a file/data base is created, it must be continuously updated thereafter. The best strategy is to organize the creation/conversion process such that it is completed just prior to the initiation of parallel operation (or, when parallel operation is not required, system implementation).

33. Complete parallel operation

Parallel operation refers to the simultaneous operation of the existing system and the new information systems. Parallel operation is common practice, especially if system failure significantly affects corporate operations. User and IS resources are spread thin during parallel operations because both systems must be maintained. Parallel operation is made more difficult because those involved are still on the initial stage of the learning curve.

Parallel operation is usually scheduled for one major system cycle, usually one month. The project team leader, affected user manager, and appropriate IS managers continually monitor the progress of parallel operation. Some organizations have accepted a policy to complete at least one major cycle under parallel operations. Others terminate maintenance of the existing system as soon as management deems the new system fully operational.

If a major system failure occurs during parallel operation, parallel operation is discontinued and appropriate revisions are made. Timeliness is important because the files and data bases must be maintained.

As companies improve their system testing procedures, IS and user personnel gain confidence in their ability to implement a working system. Some companies forego parallel operation. There is greater risk associated with this strategy, but efforts can be concentrated on implementing the new system successfully. In some cases, time and limited resources preclude parallel operations and management's only alternative is to implement the new system and hope that system testing was thorough.

Phase V—Post-Implementation Evaluation

Phase V—Post-Implementation Evaluation is neglected more often than not. With other pressing information system projects demanding resources, the system is accepted, good or bad, with little or no post-implementation evaluation. Post-implementation evaluation and periodic system evaluations should be part of the system development process. Any information system will require some "fine-tuning" just after implementation. To do this the system must be evaluated as it is used in production. Even the best planned pre-implementation test will not surface certain problems that will inevitably be discovered once the system is put into operation. The rewards for commissioning and accomplishing evaluation activities come in the form of higher-quality systems and increased user satisfaction.

34. Update cost

The project team leader updates the project costs to reflect the final system development cost for Phases II, III, and IV. Costs are also compiled to reflect the ongoing cost for system operation.

Accurate and consistent cost data may not be available until at least one month after implementation.

35. Conduct post-implementation system evaluation

The **post-implementation system evaluation**, a critical examination of the system, is conducted by selected members of the project team and affected user departments. During the first several months of system operation, resistance to change, anxieties, the learning curve, and unanticipated problems render an immediate post-implementation evaluation inappropriate. The evaluation would usually take place between three and six months after the termination of Phase IV.

The post-implementation system evaluation is conducted to determine:

Actual versus anticipated performance. Certain criteria should have been built into the system design (e.g., response time at peak work load). Actual performance is compared to anticipated performance.

Extent to which system accomplished objectives. The system is evaluated with respect to those objectives set forth in the feasibility study. For example, is the system providing more timely information for the comptroller to make better decisions?

Unexpected benefits or burdens. Almost any computer-based system will result in unexpected benefits and burdens. These benefits or burdens provide direct input into the evaluation of the overall effectiveness of the information system.

A candid discussion of mistakes. It is rare that a system is implemented without several mistakes being made during the development process. A candid and detailed discussion of mistakes made by the project team, user managers, user personnel, other IS personnel, or the ISPC should be documented. These mistakes are not enumerated to indict an individual or group, but to highlight why they were made and what can be done to eliminate them in future projects.

The results of the post-implementation evaluation are presented to IS and user management for action.

36. Prepare system review schedule

Too many data processing and information systems remain intact without any concerted effort being made to substantially upgrade them. In these systems the enhancements are no more than routine maintenance and are a result of user reaction. The reactive approach to system improvement is far less effective than the proactive approach guaranteed by **periodic system reviews.**

For whatever reason, periodic reviews are overlooked unless they are prompted by a formally documented review schedule. The Periodic System Review Schedule of Figure 4–3 is completed shortly after the post-implementation review. The elapsed time between reviews is based on system complexity and volatility. A standardized procedure for periodic system reviews is presented in Chapter 4 and the content is discussed in Chapter 13.

The periodic system reviews are the responsibility of the functional area managers. Recommendations resulting from the reviews will ultimately be reflected in a service request submitted by the user manager.

AXIOMS FOR INFORMATION SYSTEMS DEVELOPMENT

The following axioms, if taken to heart by both IS and user personnel, will result in better information systems and an overall smoother corporate operation.

Don't Defer Automation Indefinitely

There is a point at which it becomes economically advisable for a transaction-based manual system to be automated (see Figure 12–18). In manual systems, the solution to increased volume is to hire more persons, thus making the cost of processing the five-hundredth transaction the same as the first transaction. Although the initial outlay

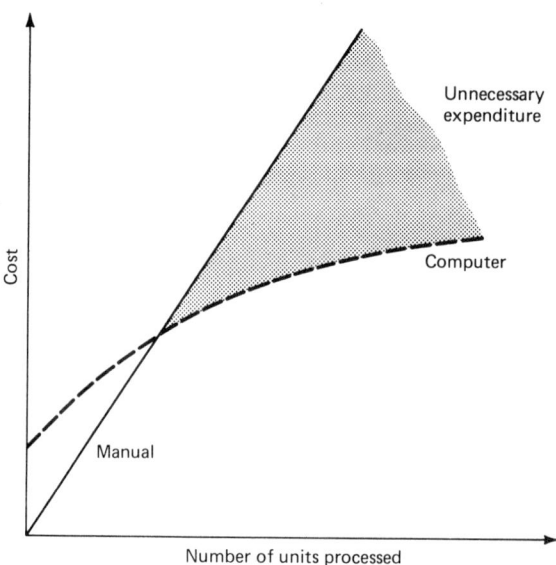

FIGURE 12-18 Break-even point for conversion from a manual to a computer-based system.

for automating a system is substantial in terms of time and dollars, the cost per transaction processed decreases as volume increases. Figure 12-18 is based solely on transaction processing and does not reflect the intangible or informational benefits derived from a computer-based system.

Divide and Conquer

Address system development by dividing the system into modules that are small enough to be intellectually manageable. Lack of communication is one of the most serious deterrents to quality information systems. Once systems are modularized, interactions can be effectively concentrated on a single segment of the system. The result is an efficient transfer of information between user and IS personnel.

Don't Begin
Detailed Specifications
Prematurely

The project team should not advance from one level of generalization to the next until the current level is understood by all concerned. Depending on the complexity of an information system, there may be as many as eight levels of generalization. The project team should resist the temptation to address "bits and bytes" during the early stages of system development. Unfortunately, it is not uncommon for members of the project team to begin programming long before Phase II is complete. Skipping levels of generalization will invariably result in unnecessary rework.

Include Performance Criteria in the System Design

The quality and/or performance of the system should be measurable. The criteria for success should be identified prior to development, and the capability to evaluate the system relative to these criteria should be built into the system design. This allows user managers to evaluate if the system is meeting objectives and to pinpoint operational deficiencies.

Emphasize Consistency of Quality Throughout the System Development Process

Quality should be continuous and consistent throughout the system development process. The only way this can be achieved is through good project management. Of the 36 activities depicted in Figure 12–2, one cannot be slighted in favor of another. The resultant system is no better than the quality of the output of the lowest-quality activity. For example, a neglect of the system acceptance test in favor of an intense effort during parallel operation violates the consistency of effort rule; therefore, the quality of the system is reduced. As another example, a decision to omit the investigation of technology transfer and concentrate efforts on in-house development will inevitably result in more work and lower quality in the long run.

Adopt a System Development Methodology

A system development methodology that provides guidelines for system development is a must. The merits of a methodology are discussed earlier in this chapter.

Document during Development

Documentation can be used to structure the development process. Some project teams neglect documentation until after implementation. Project teams adopting this strategy find themselves covering the same territory more than once. For example, a user manager is interviewed by the project team and no notes are taken. Studies have shown that without written documentation, only a small percentage of what transpired at a meeting can be recreated after several weeks' elapsed time.

Abort Obviously Ineffective Projects

As the saying goes, "don't throw good money after bad money." Projects should be cancelled once it becomes apparent that the output of a particular project will not live up to the user's expectation or is no longer consistent with corporate objectives. Too many poorly conceived systems are carried to completion when they should have been aborted.

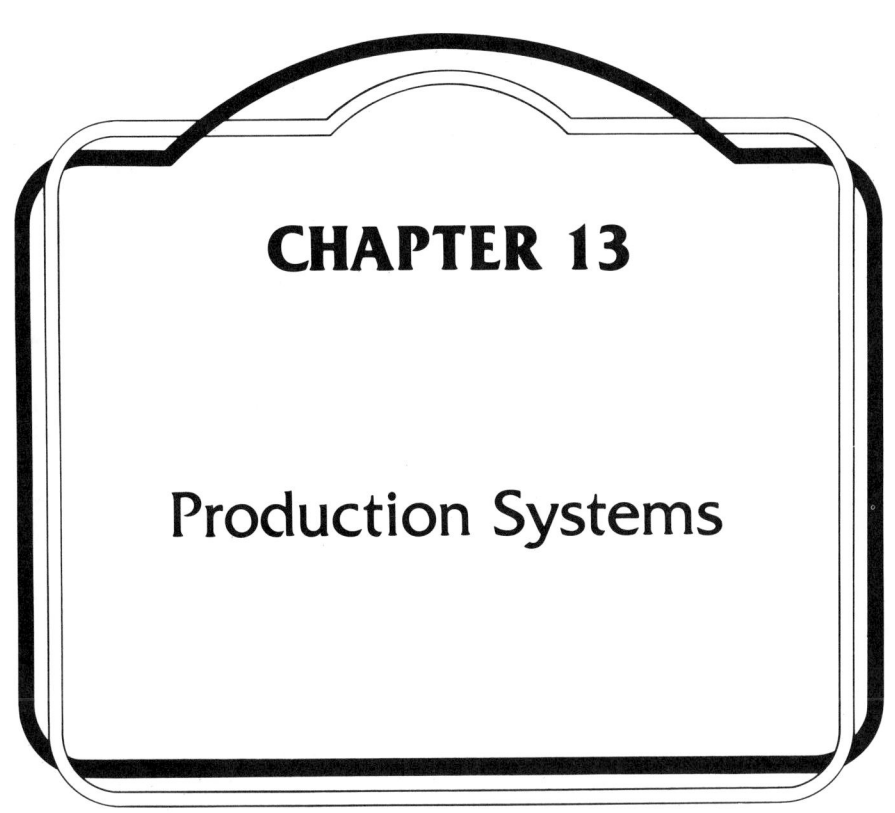

CHAPTER 13

Production Systems

Production is the third stage of the information system life cycle (birth, development, production, and death—see Figure 2-1). A system is in the production stage from the time it is first deemed operational until the time the system is replaced. Once a system becomes operational, the user department is responsible for virtually all systems interaction. Information services, in a centralized environment, is responsible for technical support, processing, and distribution of hard-copy output.

The production-related topics of data reduction, operations, and I/O distribution and control are discussed in this chapter. Also discussed are periodic system reviews, information systems auditing, risk analysis, and cost allocation.

PRODUCTION—INPUT, PROCESSING, OUTPUT

Input—Data Reduction

Data Reduction. Data reduction, synonymous with data entry, is the process by which data are entered into the system. Data that are not in machine-readable format must be transcribed before becoming part of a computer-based file. For example, a supervisor enters the number of hours worked on a time sheet. A warehouse clerk manually records the movement of inventory items. These data are then transcribed to machine readable format, usually via a key-driven device (see Chapter 7 for discussions of other data entry alternatives). In some systems, the data are already in a machine-readable format, thereby eliminating the need for key entry. For example, a salesperson in a department store might use a hand-held wand to enter price and inventory data directly from an article's price tag.

Verification. Whether data are entered on-line by user personnel or batched for transcription by information services, the user is responsible for the integrity of the data being entered into the system. Data verification is accomplished in several ways. During the keypunch era, verification was accomplished by keying all data directly into the same card from the source document twice. Re-keying data is still used, but to a lesser extent, for key-to-disk data entry. The premise behind the method is that it is highly unlikely that an operator will key in the same wrong character twice. Although cumbersome and time consuming, this method results in very few data entry errors. The integrity of the data is usually jeopardized during completion of the original source document. Since most of these source documents are compiled manually, legibility becomes an important factor. Most keying errors are a result of the data entry operator misinterpreting a handwritten character.

Verification in on-line data entry is accomplished by operator sight checks and by software checks. In an on-line order entry system, salespeople enter orders directly into the system instead of manually completing an order form. Sight verification is used in on-line systems in the same manner that it is used to produce the source document in batch-oriented systems. The operator simply reads input data on the VDU screen to verify that what was entered is correct. Logic can be designed into the software to check the limits, reasonableness, and proper match of certain data elements. For example, if a company's maximum order to date is 25 items and an order is entered for 2,500 items, the entry is flagged for validation. As another example, the software can verify data elements that are currently on the corporate data base. Each time an operator enters the number of an active customer, the item is flagged if the number is not on the data base.

Productivity. The user manager should be aware that data entry is a task of vigilance and that operators require incentives to maintain productivity and accuracy. Efforts should be made to give data entry operators a sense of importance. This can be accomplished by periodically involving them in discussion sessions which emphasize the importance of the data entry task to the overall system. These sessions also provide a forum for operator feedback into the operational effectiveness of the system. Allow operators to establish their own performance criteria using the nominal group technology technique described in Chapter 16. The spirit of competition can be enhanced if bonuses and merit increases are based on performance.

Processing—Operations

Unless processing is distributed to the functional areas (i.e., DDP), the operations function is usually under the auspices of corporate information services. The purpose of the operations functions is to operate computing hardware in support of production information systems. These systems are selected (proprietary software) and/or developed by sister IS functions (programming and systems) in cooperation with user departments. The manager of operations takes givens like hardware and information systems, and schedules production to meet assigned deadlines.

Managers should be cognizant of other demands placed on a computer center. These demands may not affect a particular manager's realm of responsibility, but they are equally important to corporate operations. In a typical computer center, not only are dozens of information systems scheduled for production, but other items as well. For instance, numerous one-time and/or ad hoc jobs, programs for development and testing, systems for quality assurance testing, data and files for conversion, preventive maintenance, parallel operations, general maintenance, and hardware upgrades must also be scheduled. In case of system failure, priority is given to those systems most critical to overall corporate operation. Others are worked into the schedule as time permits.

Output—Distribution and Control

Most information systems have some hard-copy output requirements. In centralized environments the control and distribution of
these documents is the responsibility of information services. The IS
department usually has a control group that uses a variety of techniques
(control totals, consistency checks, and so on) to verify the accuracy
of system output. The control group also maintains receipt and distribution logs for each output. User signatures are often required before
sensitive documents can be released.

PERIODIC SYSTEM REVIEWS

A schedule for periodic system reviews was established as part of the
Phase V—Post-Implementation Evaluation of the system development
process. Periodic system reviews are scheduled no less than three months
nor more than one year apart. Both IS personnel and users are active
participants in system reviews. Depending on the size of the system, a
comprehensive review could take from one person-week to several person-
months. The review team is charged with examining:

- System efficiency
- System effectiveness
- Turnaround time
- Response time
- Relevance of information
- Distribution and control of I/O
- I/O formats and content
- File, records, and data base organization
- Update and backup procedures
- Currency of system documentation

Deficiencies and suggestions for improvement are documented and
submitted to appropriate functional area managers.

A standardized procedure for setting up periodic system reviews
is presented in Chapter 4.

INFORMATION SYSTEMS AUDIT

Every corporation should have an internal information systems auditing
group (or auditor) that reports to a high-level neutral office. The infor-

mation systems audit staff functions to ensure the integrity of production information systems. There are three types of information system audits. These are system development audits, operational audits, and applications audits.

System Development Audits

In systems development audits the information systems audit staff serves as advisors to or members of the development project team. Their presence guarantees that appropriate audit controls are embedded in the original system design. The system development activities in which the information systems audit group is involved are noted in Figure 12–2.

Operational Audits

Operational audits are periodically conducted on the operations section of information services to ensure that proper controls exist and are being followed. Separation of duties, rotation of operators, and mandatory vacations are examples of such controls and procedures. Adherence to the separation-of-duties principle precludes the possibility of the same person providing the input, doing the processing, and validating the output. By rotating operators regularly, system controls will ultimately detect any attempt by an operator to defraud the system. A corporation is vulnerable when one operator has sole responsibility for running a particular information system. For the same reason, many companies have a mandatory vacation policy requiring programmers and operators to take their vacations in blocks of no less than two weeks. Auditors use these and a number of other techniques to minimize the possibility and opportunity for abuse of a computer system.

Applications Audits

The objective of periodic applications audits is to validate the integrity of computer-based systems. This is contrasted to a periodic system review where present and future needs as well as system effectiveness are the key considerations. In an applications audit, information systems auditors validate that a production system is working according to design specifications. To do this, auditors may trace a summary report back to the original transactions and vice versa. They intentionally try to block or foul the system in order to check internal controls. Special audit software is used to aid in the information systems audit process. For example, audit programs provide the auditor with file sampling capabilities. The auditor uses these programs to check records for quality, completeness, accuracy, and efficiency.

SECURITY

Threats to Security of Information Systems

Any system, whether it be manual or computer-based, has points of vulnerability. Security is assessed and addressed at both the information systems level and at the computer center level (including remote facilities, if applicable). It is encumbent upon user and IS management to reduce the risk of a security violation by identifying points of vulnerability, and then taking the necessary precautions to provide an acceptable level of security.

Management should make a special effort to address the threats to computer center and information systems security posed by computer criminals. White-collar crime is real and exists undetected in some of the most unlikely places. It is a sophisticated crime with sophisticated criminals and is more widespread than estimates would lead us to believe. Most corporate crimes are never detected. Any statistics on computer crime reflect only those crimes that are reported. System development, operations, and applications audits can be used to minimize the threat.

Computer Center Security

Computer centers are vulnerable in the following areas:

Hardware. If the hardware fails, the system fails. Certain failures cannot be avoided, but preventive maintenance and implementing physical security precautions to prevent access by unauthorized personnel will minimize this threat.

Software. Software can be modified to the detriment of the corporation. Close control of software and software documentation will minimize the possibility of any unauthorized software changes being made. But, IS managers must be cognizant of the potential of software modification by the in-house staff. Bank programmers have been known to modify programs to overlook withdrawals from their accounts or make small deposits from other accounts to their accounts. Other enterprising programmers in other industries have been equally imaginative and equally criminal.

Files/data bases. The corporate data base is the raw material for information resource management. In some cases these files/data bases are the life-blood of the corporation. For example, how many corporations could afford to lose their accounts receivable files? Most organizations have incorporated backup procedures that ensure that if the active corporate data base is destroyed, it can be reactivated. Some files have value and can be sold. For example, a list of contributors to a political campaign was considered valuable, was stolen, and later was sold.

Data communications. The mere existence of a data communications network poses a threat to the security of the information system. A knowledgeable criminal can tap into the system from a remote location and use the system for personal gains. In a well-designed system this is not an easy task, but the potential exists. Criminals have taken advantage of many communications-based systems.

Personnel. User and IS managers alike are paying more attention to who they hire to work on sensitive information systems. Someone who is grossly incompetent can do just as much damage as one who is inherently dishonest.

Information System Security

Information system security is classified as physical or logical. Physical security refers to hardware, facilities, magnetic tapes, and other things that can be accessed, stolen, or possibly destroyed. Logical security is built into the software. The software permits only authorized access to the system and authorized processing once an individual is on the system.

Physical security is achieved by locked doors, fireproof safes, access badges, alarm systems, and other common security devices. Logical security for on-line systems is achieved primarily by "passwords" and authorization codes. An end user may use a global password that permits access to several information systems and their respective data bases or a password that limits access to a subsystem or a portion of the data base.

Security Analysis Procedures

The question that most corporate officers ask about the security of information and the computer center is "Is everything OK?" They should be asking "What are we doing about it?"

User managers should collaborate with IS managers periodically to conduct a security analysis assessing the level of risk that each is willing to accept. In short, this means deciding how big a "padlock" is desired. Unfortunately, some corporations are willing to accept an enormous risk and hope that no natural or premeditated disaster occurs. Some corporations have found out too late that "rarely" is not the same as "never."

In accomplishing a security analysis, user and IS personnel assess the adequacy of literally scores of checklist items. For example, under physical security the team might examine the number of access routes to the machine room or whether there is an authorized list for entry into the machine room.

The following steps constitute a recommended approach for a security analysis.

1. Evaluation of risk
   ♦ Identify and analyze vulnerable areas.
   ♦ Assign the probability of occurrence of a particular event.
2. Risk assessment
   ♦ Establish a level of acceptable risk based on the risk evaluation (information systems security is implemented in degrees).
3. Reduction of risk
   ♦ Minimize or eliminate threats to vulnerable areas.
   ♦ Repeat steps 1, 2, and 3 until the risk is acceptable.

COST ALLOCATION SYSTEMS

At some time during the growth pattern of the information services function, a corporate policy decision is made as to whether to charge end users for professional and/or computer services. The trend for medium and large organizations is to allocate cost of information services to the end users via **chargeback systems.** Chargeback systems are implemented to encourage the judicious utilization of the information/computer resource. The premise behind chargeback systems is that a department is more deliberate when spending its own money than with somebody else's.

There are many considerations to implementing a chargeback or cost allocation system. For example, should the end user be charged for the costs of feasibility studies? Should this charge be a fixed amount designated by information services, or should the charge be based on the actual time expended? Should machine utilization charges be based solely on processor utilization or should these charges be separated for each peripheral device (printer, disk storage, and so on)? Should price breaks be given for volume usage? Should price breaks be given for non-prime time computer usage?

There are four basic approaches to allocating costs to the end user. As one might expect, each has advantages and disadvantages. The following approaches are representative of those being used.

No Charge to User for Information Services

One approach is to allocate the corporate information services budget to the IS department and charge them with providing the best possible service to the user within the constraints of resources available. This method is administratively simple and service is available to everyone at no charge. The disadvantages are: The burden of priorities (without a steering committee) rest with information services; users do not appreciate the cost and do not fully analyze the benefit/cost ratio of their request; and invariably, the largest user gets the best service. This is, however, a viable option if and only if a strong and fair information services steering committee exists that can allocate IS resources based on corporate need.

Provide Each Requesting Department
with an IS Budget

An information services budget is allocated to each requesting department. In this approach the department simply requests that a certain amount of funds be allocated for information services. There is, in fact, no internal transfer of funds. In the trade, this type of budget allocation is known as "funny money" or "wooden nickels." The advantage of this approach is that it provides a limited amount of control over the information services budget and provides the user with feedback on IS expenses incurred. Again, the user does not appreciate costs and does not analyze the benefit/cost ratio. Budget allocations tend not to be taken seriously since the user need only request a greater allocation when the initial allocation is exhausted.

This is a viable option only when real dollar penalties are assessed for going over the initial budget allocation. This approach is helpful when a corporation makes a transition to a chargeback system where actual dollars are transferred between departments (discussed in the next section). This kind of chargeback system can be used to produce "memo charges." These memo charges are used for about a year to give user managers an idea of what to expect when IS services actually are charged to the functional area budgets.

Charge Directly for all Information Services

In a direct chargeback system user departments are charged for
all hardware utilizations, personnel services, and materials. The advantage to this system is that it encourages user managers to analyze the
benefit/cost ratio for their request. Therefore, only high priority and
cost-effective requests are submitted for information services, thus
allowing resources to be concentrated in areas more critical to corporate
operation. The most significant disadvantage of this approach is that
the cost may discourage potential users from considering computer-
based information systems as an alternative.

Combination Corporate Subsidy
and Direct Charge

User expenditures are matched with funds from a corporate information services pool. This approach requires the user to pay, through
internal funds transfer, a portion of the charges for information services.
For example, the user might pay 30%, 50%, or 70% with the remainder
being charged to the corporate information services account. The advantage of this approach is that it encourages reluctant users to invest in
cost effective computer-based systems. Even though the user is charged
only a portion of the total cost, there is still an awareness of cost. To a
lesser extent, the disadvantages of direct charge for services are also
applicable to this approach.

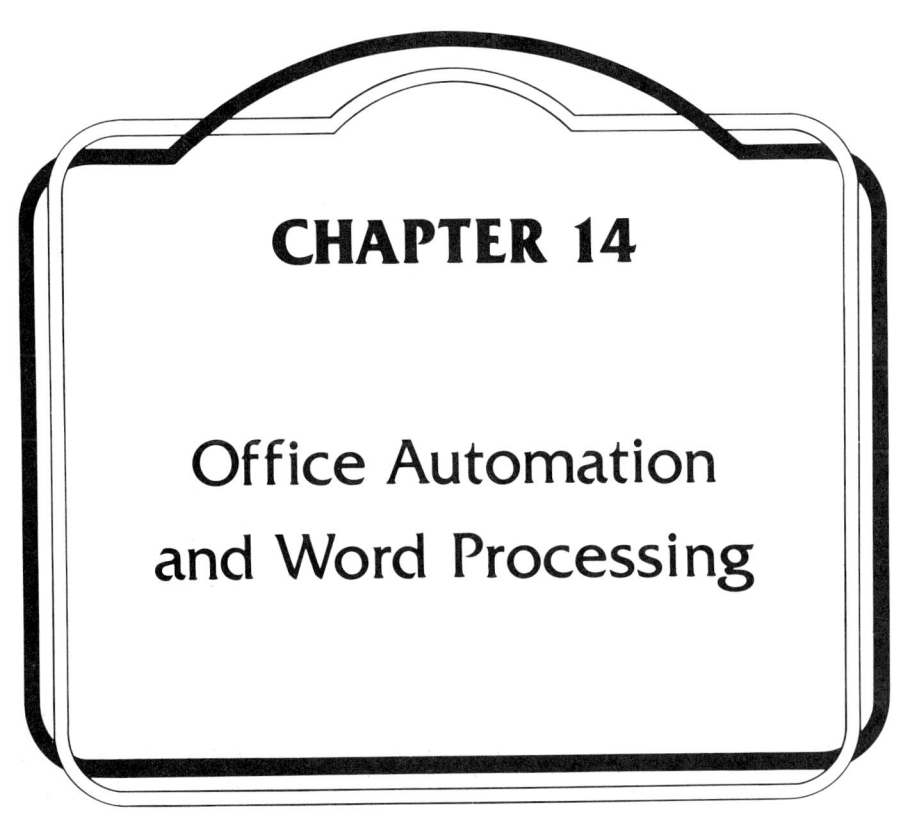

CHAPTER 14

Office Automation
and Word Processing

OFFICE AUTOMATION IN PERSPECTIVE

Every year white-collar workers are comprising a greater percentage of
the work force; yet only recently has any emphasis been placed on
using the computer to make their immediate working environment
more efficient and effective. Productivity among white-collar workers
has not kept pace with that of blue-collar workers. Surprisingly, professionals spend from 10% to 75% of their time on clerical tasks, and clerical personnel spend 10% to 50% of their time unnecessarily on tasks that
could be easily automated. Any corporation or office with a full-time
secretary can justify the purchase of a computer and support software.
Office automation and, in particular, word processing has significantly
increased productivity in many office environments. The payback period
for an investment in office automation is usually no more than two
years.

The benefits of office automation can be realized by executives

307

and clerical personnel alike. For example, secretaries have traditionally typed text generated by the managers through dictation or handwritten documents. Now the secretary uses word processing equipment to simplify the transcription process; moreover, a manager can make minor revisions on a VDU more quickly than the revisions can be explained to the secretary. It is not overly optimistic to expect a 50% increase in typing productivity, not to mention a commensurate increase in output quality.

WHAT ARE OFFICE AUTOMATION AND WORD PROCESSING?

The term **word processing** (or **WP**) was introduced by IBM in the mid-1960s and applied to their line of magnetic card/tape typewriters. The term *word processing* became very popular in the mid-1970s when it became commercially feasible to dedicate small computers to text handling. **Office automation** has evolved over the last 10 years and refers collectively to those computer-based applications associated with general office work. Although the terms are often used interchangeably, word processing is a subset of office automation. In truth, the scope and meaning of these terms has been, and is still, a source of confusion to IS personnel, user managers, and clerical personnel. Office automation includes such applications as word processing, data processing, data entry, electronic mail, facsimile, and voice processing. Assuming that these application areas are an accurate reflection of the scope of office automation, one might ask, Why all of this attention to office automation? In reality, office automation is simply another application for computer-based systems. The terms were coined to sell stand-alone hardware to support office automation, but word processing and office automation are simply extensions of the information services function.

Office automation is a good and cost-justifiable application of computers, but it is oversold (by vendors), undersold (by IS departments), and missold (by all) to functional area managers. For this reason the topic is treated in a separate chapter. The following sections describe the major application areas of office automation.

Word Processing

Word processing is the cornerstone of office automation. Therefore, the bulk of this chapter is devoted to this application area. Word processing is using the computer to enter text, store it on magnetic storage media, manipulate it in preparation for output, and print it. Text manipulation includes such tasks as merging name and address files with appropriate form letters. Any more sophisticated data manipulation would fall under the application area of data processing.

Data Processing

Certain data processing (DP) applications have been associated with office automation. The most common systems include office work scheduling, calendar, personnel scheduling, facilities management, and travel arrangements.

Data Entry

The data entry function is usually part of a more encompassing data processing or information system, but since it is a traditional office function, data entry is sometimes associated with office automation.

Electronic Mail

In the electronic mail application, the computer is a vehicle by which to route messages to persons within, and in some cases, external to the corporation. Electronic mail is discussed in detail in Chapter 10 with other communication-based applications.

Facsimile

Facsimile equipment can be used to transfer images (hard-copy documents) via telephone lines to another office. These devices can operate independently of word processing or data processing computers.

Voice Processing

Voice processing includes teleconferencing and voice message switching. The voice and video of teleconferencing are supported by the telephone network. Voice message switching (a store-and-forward "voice mailbox" system) accomplishes the same purpose as digital message switching or electronic mail, except the hard copy is not available. A sender's voice is digitized and stored on a magnetic disk for later retrieval. It is routed to the sender-designated destination(s) upon request by the intended receiver(s). Neither of these applications would be supported by the word processing or host computers.

WORD PROCESSING SYSTEMS

For whatever reason, vendors and word processing experts have elected to use such words as "logic" and "intelligence" to refer to word processing capabilities. The "computer" is seldom part of the word processing community's vocabulary. Perhaps this is an attempt to disassociate word processing from computers and information systems. Make no mistake about it, a word processing system is a computer system. Most stand-alone word processing systems are configured similarly to small business computer systems. The only difference is the software.

A corporation can choose from a variety of word processing systems. These options are described in the following sections.

Stand-Alone Word Processing System

The **stand-alone word processing system** is configured with minor variations, as illustrated in Figure 14-1, with a computer, video display unit, diskette (or floppy disk) magnetic storage, and a high-quality printer (probably with an automatic sheet feeder). The computer is usually housed in the VDU assembly. The disk drive(s) are usually in a separate unit, but are sometimes included with the same unit as the computer and VDU. Although the printer is usually a separate unit, a few vendors offer a single unit which contains all components.

Stand-alone systems are designed for use by a single operator. However, it is possible for two stand-alone WP systems to share disk space and a printer (see Figure 14-2). Most stand-alone systems have the capability to interface with the corporation's host computer. In medium-to-

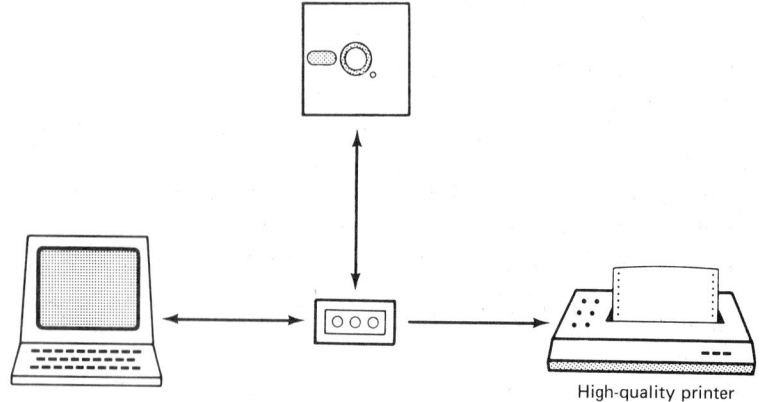

High-quality printer

FIGURE 14-1 A stand-alone word processing system.

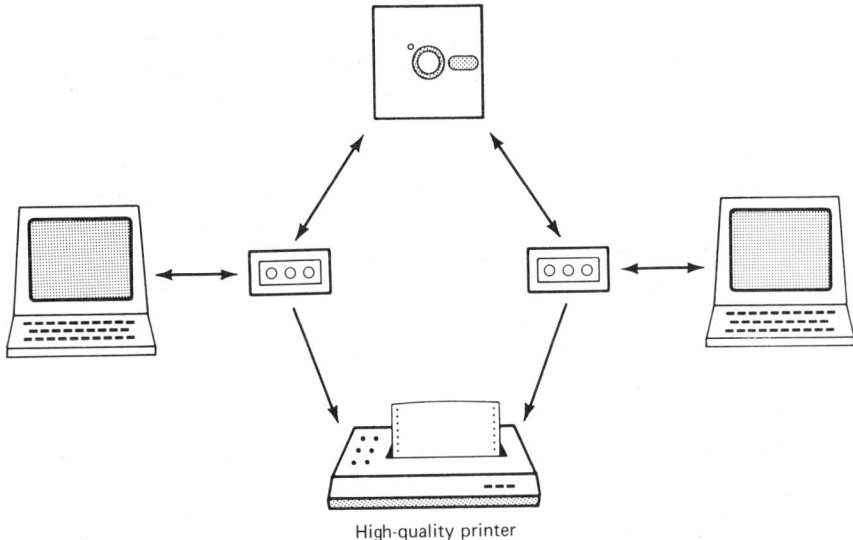

High-quality printer

FIGURE 14-2 Two stand-alone word processing systems with shared diskette and printer.

high volume typing environments, the rapid payback of stand-alone WP systems has made the typewriter almost obsolete.

Shared Logic Word Processing System

The **shared logic word processing system** can be likened to the star communications network. Multiple work stations (VDUs) are linked to a small computer and operators share disk storage space and printers. The number of work stations, printers, and disks that can be linked to a computer is dependent upon the size of the computer. These systems use "hard" disks, not diskettes. A typical shared logic system is configured in Figure 14-3. The primary disadvantage to the shared logic system is that all work stops when the computer fails.

Shared Resource Word Processing System

The **shared resource word processing system** takes the shared logic system one step further. Each work station has its own intelligence (small computer) and "local" disk drives (diskettes). In effect, each work station is a stand-alone word processing system without a printer. Work stations would normally share disk space, printers, and a computer. If any of the shared devices fail, operators at the individual work stations

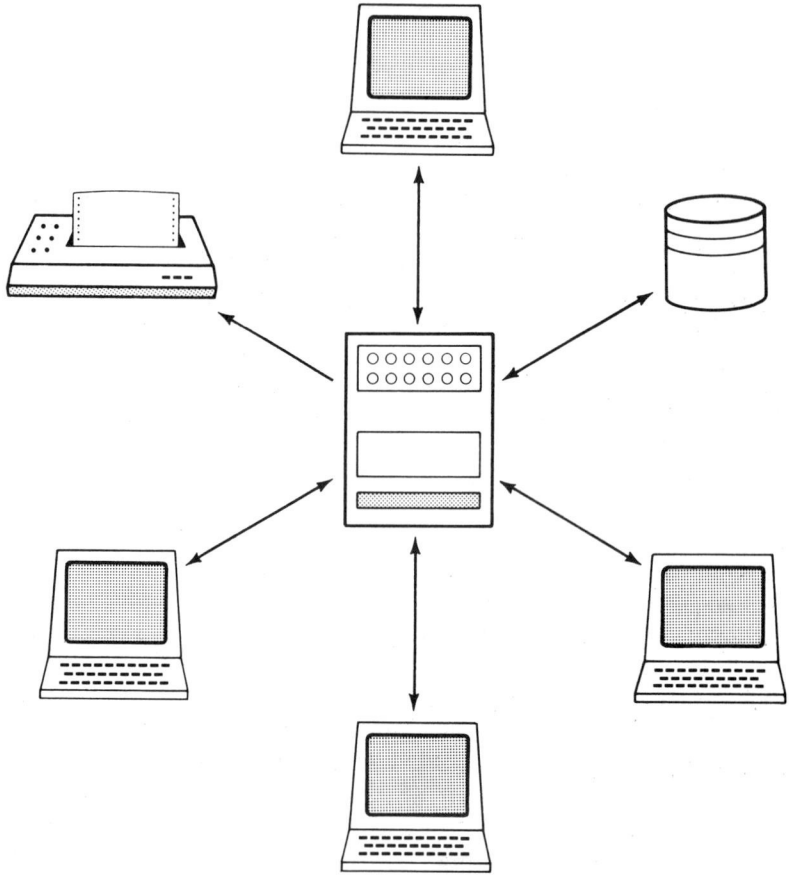

FIGURE 14-3 A shared-logic word processing system.

can continue in local mode. Figure 14-4 illustrates a shared resource word processing system.

Host Supported Word Processing System

The computer system(s) used to support the corporate information services function can also be used to support the WP function. This is called a **host supported word processing system**. Remote terminals (VDUs) in user offices that are normally used for data entry and inquiry can just as easily be used for word processing. The only other hardware requirement is a high-quality character printer. In a typical configuration, each work station would have a VDU and operators would share a high-quality printer(s).

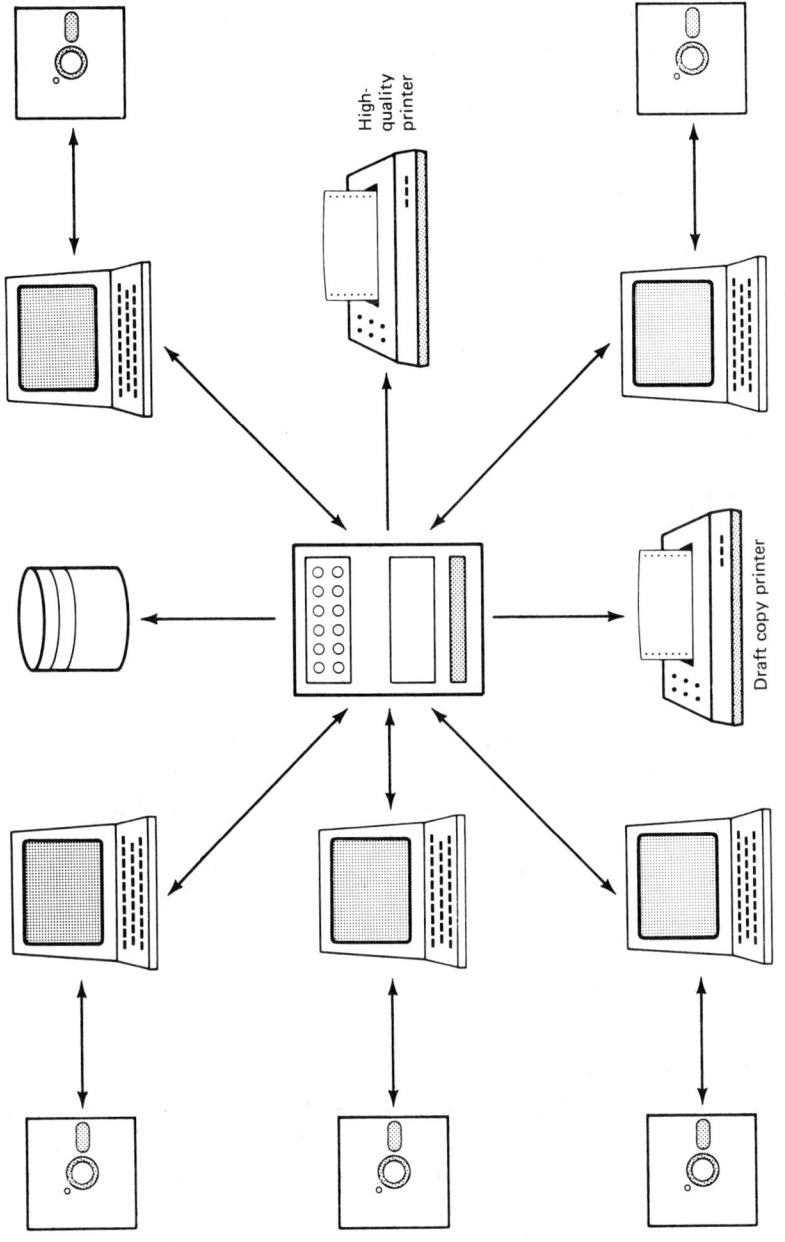

High-quality printer

Draft copy printer

FIGURE 14-4 A shared-resource word processing system.

Most stand-alone units have the capability to interface with the host processor. When stand-alone units are used as work stations, the host processor and the corporate data base are shared resources. The potential to use the corporate data base in word processing applications provides a significant advantage over those word processing alternatives discussed above.

With almost unlimited disk storage space and greater processor power, host supported word processing systems provide an overall greater capacity than other word processing systems. With increased processor power comes increased system capabilities. In the typical office, these higher levels of word processing sophistication would never be used. Host supported word processing systems are most appropriate where the user is the originator of the text, not the secretary. For example, these systems are particularly applicable in universities and research centers where research personnel and students routinely generate substantial documents. These users have a need for more sophisticated word processing features like automatic footnoting, table of contents, and index generation. Host supported systems also provide the user with the option to integrate graphics and word processing capabilities.

WORD PROCESSING SOFTWARE

Word processing software is available on all computer systems, from personal computers to large-scale computers. The design philosophy in virtually all word processing software is to keep it **user friendly**. That is, the end user with little or no experience should have no trouble interacting with the system. Appropriate prompts and "help" commands make using word processing software easy, even for the novice. Word processing software is either menu-driven or statement-driven. These design approaches are discussed below.

Menu-Driven Word Processing Software

Menu-driven WP software is standard on all systems dedicated to word processing. This includes stand-alone, shared logic, and shared resource WP systems. Each of these systems is functionally directed to the secretary as an end user. For this set of end users, menu-driven software is preferred because it is easy to learn and use.

The end user enters and manipulates the text by selecting operations from a "menu." The text is manipulated on the VDU until the desired output format is achieved. Typically, a primary menu lists all basic functions. The end user selects the desired function and a more detailed menu appears. The desired operation is then selected from the detailed menu.

Some VDU keyboards have special function keys that aid the end user in interacting with the system.

Statement-Driven Word Processing Software

Statement-driven WP software is designed such that the end user inserts format commands while entering the text. This type of software is programlike and is used primarily on host computer supported word processing systems and by a more sophisticated end user. It is more difficult to learn, especially for someone with no programming experience. However, this type of software has a greater range of capabilities.

Once the text and commands have been entered, the end user requests that the text be formatted according to the inserted commands. Only then does the formatted output appear on the VDU. If the end user desires to alter the text or format, the system must be returned to "edit" mode. The process is repeated until the desired output is achieved. This process is similar to "debugging" a program.

Typical Word Processing Software Features

Editing. The end user can use editing features to add, delete, change, and move words, phrases, paragraphs, and entire sections of the text. For example, a sentence can be deleted, a character added to a misspelled word, two paragraphs interchanged, an extra adjective added, and so on.

Formatting. Formatting options allow the end user to format the document. The margins can be adjusted. The end user can select such options as single or double spacing. Text can even be right-justified. A special command allows the end user to format "notes" differently from the body of the text. Another command enables lists of items to be automatically numbered. Two-column printing is an option on many WP systems.

Spelling. "Typos" can be eliminated with automatic spelling verification. Word processing software is usually accompanied by a dictionary file of 30 to 100 thousand words. These words are matched against the words of the text; any misspelled words are highlighted and brought to the attention of the end user.

Global search and replace. This feature allows the end user to search the entire text for a word or phrase and replace it with something else. For example, to save keystrokes, an end user might type "isx" (a unique configuration) throughout the text of a report and before producing the hard copy, change "isx" to "information services" throughout the entire text. This feature can also be used to go immediately to a specific portion of the text without having to scan the text visually.

Pagination. Word processing software automatically numbers the pages of a document. If text is added or deleted, page numbers are revised accordingly.

List/merge. Simple files can be automatically merged with the text. For example, a file containing the names and addresses of persons scheduled to receive the same letter can be merged with the text, making it unnecessary to key in the name and address or retype the letter. This feature is helpful when entering text that is standard except for a few entries (e.g., standard no-contest wills).

Highlighting. The end user can request that words or phrases be overprinted on output for highlighting. Those parts that are overprinted appear as darker, bolder letters. This feature is used for headings and subtitles, and to highlight key words.

Footnotes. Footnotes are entered in the text and automatically appear on the appropriate page.

Indexing. Key words noted by the end user will be included on an alphabetized list with cross-references, by page number, to all occurrences of the key words.

Table of contents. This feature is helpful when compiling reports, theses, or books. A table of contents is automatically compiled from major headings.

Computation. Some word processing systems provide the capability for the end user to perform certain basic mathematical computations.

Sorting. Word processing lists (or files) can be sorted. For example, a name and address file can be sorted, then processed by zip code.

RESPONSIBILITY
FOR OFFICE AUTOMATION

As with any other computer-based system, the responsibility rests with the person or department who will ultimately use the system. The same corporate policy applied to other computer-based systems should also be applied to word processing systems. Normally, the user manager desiring to implement a word processing system would submit a service request through appropriate channels. This ensures that system compatibility is maintained throughout the corporation.

Some have advocated that special "office administration" groups be set up to control word processing. This is, at best, a short-term, perhaps even counterproductive approach to word processing. As word processing (and office automation) become ubiquitous, each work station will be integrated into the corporate computer network. As part of an integrated network, a word processing system can take full advantage of the corporate data base and the power of the host, and can even serve as an electronic mailbox. Any organizational structure that promotes stand-alone autonomous word processing systems will be in direct conflict with the information resource management (IRM) concept.

IMPLEMENTATION
OF A WORD PROCESSING
SYSTEM

The key to successful corporate-wide implementation of word processing and office automation applications is to concentrate initial efforts on one office and make it a success. In no other computer-based application is resistance to change more acute. Wholesale implementation of word processing can result not only in failure, but chaos. By far, the best approach to full-scale implementation is via a successful pilot project and subsequent demonstration. The pilot department should be selected on the basis of visibility (number of departments affected by or aware of the pilot department's output), probability of success, and potential of recognizable economic benefits.

Compared to most information systems, the technology of word processing is not difficult. The major obstacle to implementation is the decades of tradition that have created oneness between secretary and typewriter. Invariably, the resistance persists until the end users learn how to operate the word processing system. Once the system is mastered, very few secretaries would trade their work station for a typewriter.

Having a successful pilot project to demonstrate minimizes initial resistance and encourages other managers and secretaries to understand the benefits of word processing.

OFFICE OF THE FUTURE

Tens of thousands of words have been written and spoken about the "office of the future." It is described as if managers will have to wait to realize its wonders. In fact, the technology for these so called "offices of the future" is available now. The whole area of office automation is at the infant stage of implementation. Willing IS and user managers can take these applications to maturity within the confines of existing technology.

Part IV

STRATEGIC PLANNING FOR INFORMATION SERVICES

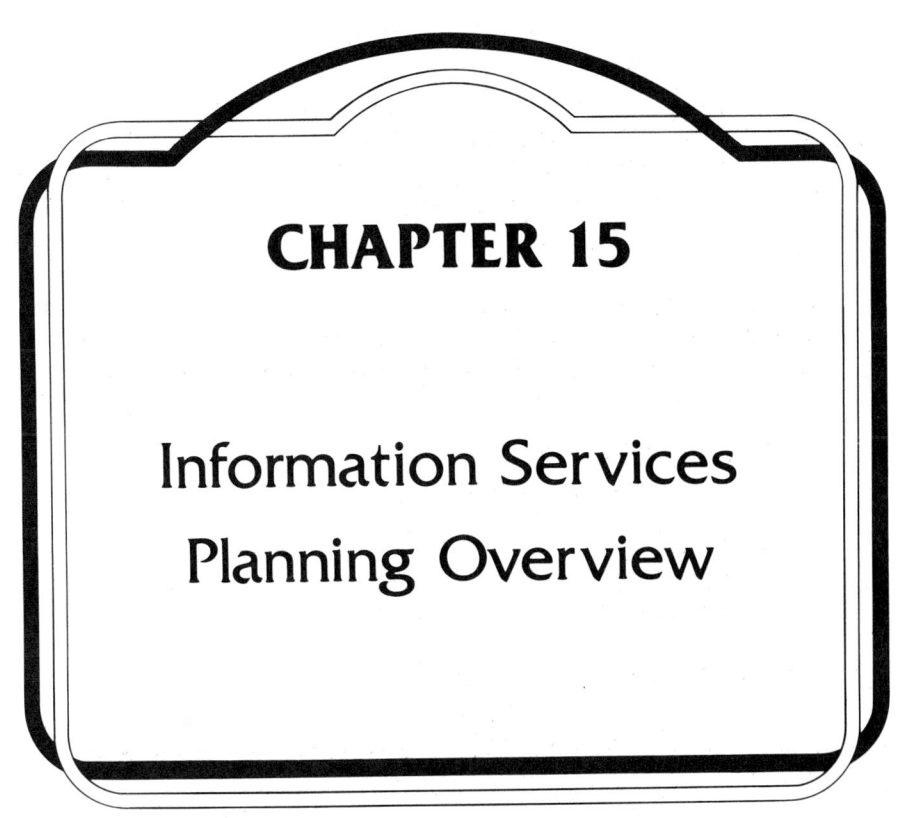

CHAPTER 15

Information Services
Planning Overview

With the emphasis on information resource management (IRM) comes the need for strategic planning for information services. For the last two decades any IS-related planning has been focused on hardware, with little attention given to information systems and to other areas of IS strategy. Strategic, or long-range, IS planning has evolved in recent years because of a desperate need for corporate coordination of the data base and information dissemination. Like any technical activity, the learning process is slow and several years may elapse before a given company can compile an effective **IS long-range plan**.

CORPORATE AND INFORMATION SERVICES
LONG-RANGE PLANNING

For whatever reasons, many corporate long-range plans deal directly with the corporation's product or service and often do not consider the plan's effect on the information services function. Whether corporate plans include a new product line, new warehouses, increases in personnel, or a new salary and wage structure, all have a substantial and direct effect on information services. Yet, information services is still avoided at some executive staff meetings. This reluctance to discuss information services can be attributed to the way it is perceived by top management. Information services is often relegated to a position several levels below other major corporate entities. This attitude is quickly changing, and IS considerations are becoming a major input to corporate long-range planning. Strategic planning for information services is subordinate and in support of corporate long-range planning and, to be successful, requires the full cooperation of users, top management, and IS personnel.

STATE OF THE ART
OF IS LONG-RANGE PLANNING

Only a few years back, IS departments were planning little more than one year in advance. Even large-scale IS projects (which were known to take more than one year) were planned, approved, and developed without a specific timetable for completion. Pressing deadlines from every corner of corporate endeavor became pressing deadlines for information services. These are the circumstances under which IS planning is introduced. The state of the art of strategic IS planning is well below that of the corporation and of sister functions (marketing, production, accounting, and so on). To make matters worse, expertise and experience are scarce in the area of IS planning. Only a small percentage of corporations have a viable IS long-range plan. This is also true of Fortune 500 companies. Since strategic IS planning is the key to integration via the data base and increased productivity via computers and information systems, those corporations not now involved in IS planning will be in the near future.

WHAT CAN BE ACCOMPLISHED

The implementation of an IS long-range plan will create an environment in which IS can realize a better relationship with users and top management. Systems that are not responsive result in ill feelings. Such ill feelings are irritated by ad hoc selection of internal priorities for information systems development and enhancements. Increasing responsiveness to users can be provided via a coordinated plan to integrate functionally adjacent application areas. Also, a strategic IS plan can instill cooperation among users, top management, and IS personnel by encouraging all to be active in the planning process. Continuous feedback from all levels of personnel and all functional areas is a prerequisite to successful IS planning.

An IS long-range plan will provide a more efficient allocation of precious corporate resources. By integrating systems and minimizing the need for system changes over a multiyear period, resources can be scheduled over a longer time horizon. This efficient mode of long-term scheduling will free resources and allow for an expanded scope of IS services. Too often the corporate information services function becomes involved, voluntarily or involuntarily, in activities that waste resources and do not contribute to corporate or IS goals. When resources are judiciously allocated well in advance and reasonable priorities are established for IS projects, IS is not obligated to respond to unreasonable requests. Even though most requests for service are justified, many are not well conceived nor are all the ramifications considered. The latter can be eliminated via an IS long-range plan.

Another aspect of an IS long-range plan is that it can be used as a benchmark for performance, both internal and external to the IS department. Since the plan identifies projects and milestones, it is a good vehicle for personnel and department performance evaluation.

A good strategic IS plan should make a significant contribution to corporate profit. This contribution is made in the form of better utilization of personnel and equipment and through systems which are more responsive to user needs. Such systems have an effect on the balance sheet through reduced inventory, better customer relations, and so on.

The IS long-range plan provides the foundation for the coordination of all future IS activities. Traditionally, corporate application systems have grown as autonomous units because of immediate needs. Information systems now and in the future should be integrated. Virtually all facets of corporate operation are linked by data and information passing through the computing center. Any company not undertaking an IS long-range plan is forfeiting a valuable opportunity to coordinate future information systems activities.

An IS long-range plan has another notable benefit to the corporation: the planning process forces management to think past routine activities to ways that existing activities can be improved. Too often managers are restricted by time to responding to routine activities. The IS long-range plan forces managers and planners to take a hard look at information processing. The results of this introspection are ideas and a better understanding for all.

SCOPE OF STRATEGIC IS PLANNING

An IS long-range plan should include events and activities which are affected by or under the control of the information services department. This includes all facets of IS which play on effectiveness and efficiency of IS operation, both internal and external to the corporation. The long-range plan for IS is more than just goals and objectives or hardware acqusition planning. It encompasses not only the peripheral activities internal to the IS department, but the long-range objectives of the functional area departments.

INTEGRATION THROUGH IS LONG-RANGE PLANNING

An IS long-range plan can be used to integrate the functional areas of a company. The typical corporate approach to better integration of corporate entities is to revise the structural organization of the corporation. Some corporations have been radically overhauled at each level of command with no improvement in overall integration. Corporate reorganization can be beneficial, but the real common denominator and the best vehicle by which to integrate corporate operations is information. The IS long-range plan can be a valuable aid in realizing an effective and efficient flow of information throughout the corporation.

PITFALLS IN IS LONG-RANGE PLANNING

The following potential IS planning pitfalls are noted so that user and IS management can take precautions to avoid making the same mistakes that others have made.

Ensure Recognition of the Need for IS Planning

One of the obvious pitfalls is that management may not recognize the need for IS long-range planning. In these cases, efforts to develop a plan are approached half-heartedly and the plan is not given the attention necessary to produce an effective end product.

Recognize the 80/20 Rule

User and IS personnel sometimes get carried away with the potential of a computer-based information system. Each should be aware that the 80/20 rule is applicable; that is, 80% of the necessary data and information can be obtained with only 20% of the effort required to realize the full potential of the information system. An information system has degrees of sophistication. Today, limited resources preclude the luxury of channeling all resources to a few select development projects. Assuming that the 80/20 rule is applicable, the implementation of a system at the highest level of sophistication would require five times the effort of simply attending to the critical 80%.

Rather than attack a few application areas with great intensity, perhaps a better planning strategy would be to get all critical systems operational, then attend to higher levels of sophistication as the availability of time and resources permits. The 80/20 rule is graphically illustrated in Figure 15-1.

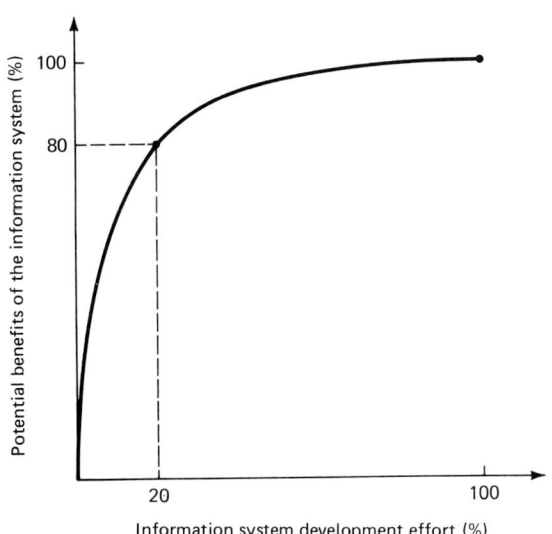

FIGURE 15-1 The 80/20 rule.

Involve those Persons Affected by the Plan

This IS plan cannot be accomplished in isolation, especially in isolation from user managers. The plan is a cooperative effort between functional area managers and the various operational units of the IS department. The planning process is iterative and requires continuous feedback from those entities and persons who are affected by the plan.

Be Conservative in Scope

An IS plan that schedules projects beyond the scope of resources of the corporation can backfire and cause more harm than good. If anything, the plan should reflect a conservative posture.

Emphasize Service, not Hardware

Too often there is an overemphasis on the latest technology. This overemphasis causes planners to overlook the fundamental need of providing cost-effective service to the users. That "more and better computer capabilities will solve the problem" is a myth. The constant planning for implementation of state-of-the-art technology will only compound existing internal problems. Hardware planning is only a small part of the total planning process.

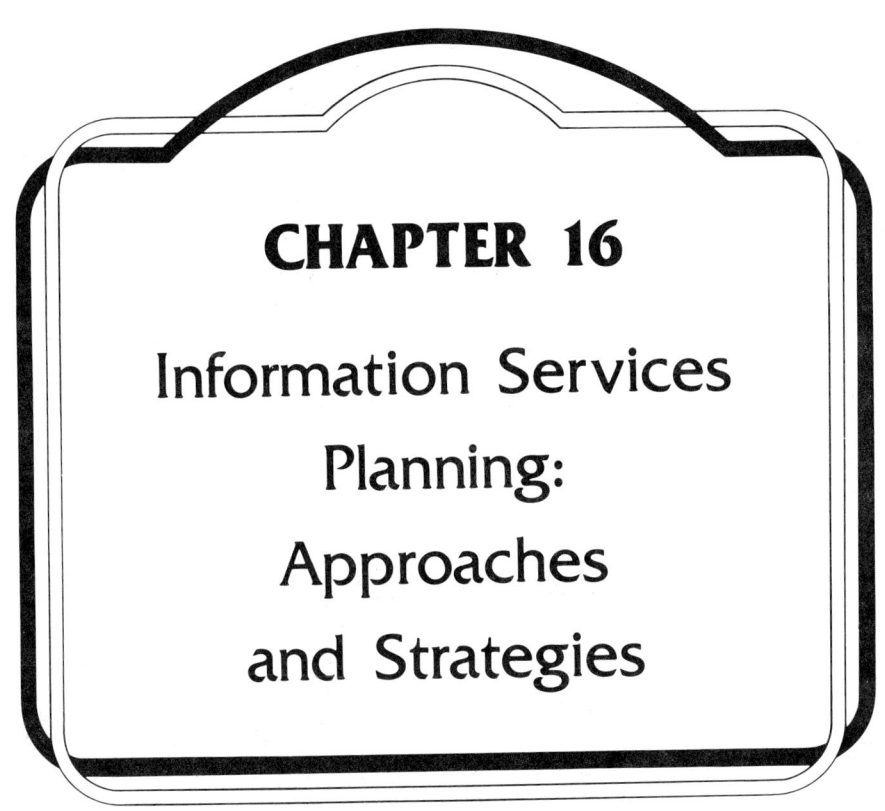

CHAPTER 16

Information Services Planning: Approaches and Strategies

There is no magic approach to strategic IS planning which, if followed, would ensure that all pieces would automatically fall into place. The IS planning function encompasses virtually every functional area within a corporation and requires the cooperation of representatives of these areas (user managers). Unless a certain amount of rigor is associated with the planning process, corporate, user, and IS personnel have a tendency to take shortcuts. This is true in any planning endeavor. Therefore, it is important to implement a planning methodology that outlines duties and responsibilities. The methodology should also provide a vehicle for those affected by the plan, especially the user managers and corporate executives, to have continuous input and some veto power over those aspects of the plan that affect their respective destinies.

This chapter outlines an approach to information services long-range planning. Those aspects of the planning process that require involvement by user management are emphasized. The *IS long-range planning methodology*[11] is discussed in three phases: *Phase I—Prepara-tion*; *Phase II—Development Process*; and *Phase III—Implementation and Maintenance.*

PHASE I—PREPARATION

Before an activity as encompassing as an IS long-range plan can be initi-ated, certain preparations must be made. These preparations involve attitudes, design, organization, education, and familiarization. The neglect of any of these preliminary considerations could make the de-velopment of an IS long-range plan unnecessarily difficult.

Recognition and Commitment

Those charged with the responsibility of IS long-range planning must assess whether user, IS, and corporate managers understand and accept the IS planning function as critical to meeting corporate objec-tives. Inevitably, an IS long-range planning project will require a signifi-cant commitment of personnel throughout the company. If managers and executives do not comprehend the scope of the IS planning func-tion, those responsible (usually the information systems policy com-mittee) should provide the necessary information to raise IS planning awareness. Less than complete acceptance of the merits of IS long-range planning will result in less than full cooperation.

Organizing for Information Services Planning

The manner in which the planning function is staffed depends on the size of the organization. In small computer centers the director of information services is the functionary and carries out the activities of the planning process. Computer centers with professional staffs of more than 25 people can easily justify a full-time coordinator of IS planning. Large computing centers having more than 175 professionals can justify a small planning group. The key persons or groups in strategic planning for information services are the director of information services, man-agers of the various operational areas within information services, func-tional area managers, corporate officers, the information systems policy committee (ISPC), and an IS long-range planning committee. The

---

[11] This methodology is condensed and edited for user managers from another book by L. Long, *Design and Strategy for Corporate Information Services: MIS Long-Range Planning* (Englewood Cliffs, NJ: Prentice-Hall, Inc., 1982).

IS long-range planning committee is a standing committee of IS and user managers formed to provide continuous input to the IS planning process.

Feedback and Approval

IS planning is an iterative process that requires a formal, ongoing feedback mechanism and well-defined authority for approval, both intermediate and final. Although IS and corporate organizational structures have well-defined lines of authority, approval authority for IS planning is often vague. A formal approval process should be defined by the information systems policy committee before planning commences.

One approach to formalizing the feedback and approval authority process is shown in Figure 16-1. This figure illustrates the ongoing interaction between principals in the IS long-range planning process.

PHASE II—DEVELOPMENT PROCESS

During Phase II a strategic plan for information services is compiled and approved. A suggested approach to development is illustrated in the *work flow diagram* of Figures 16-2. The diagram illustrates the sequence and relationship of major activities in the IS planning process.

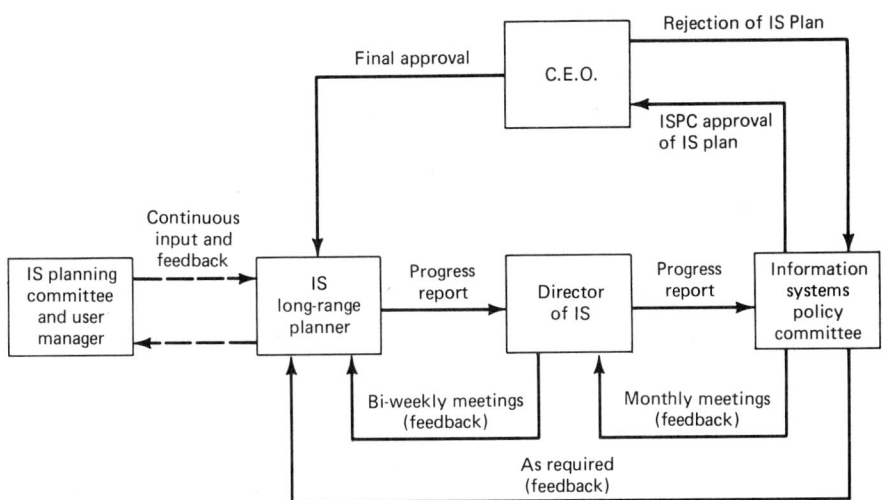

FIGURE 16-1 Interaction between principals in the IS long-range planning process.

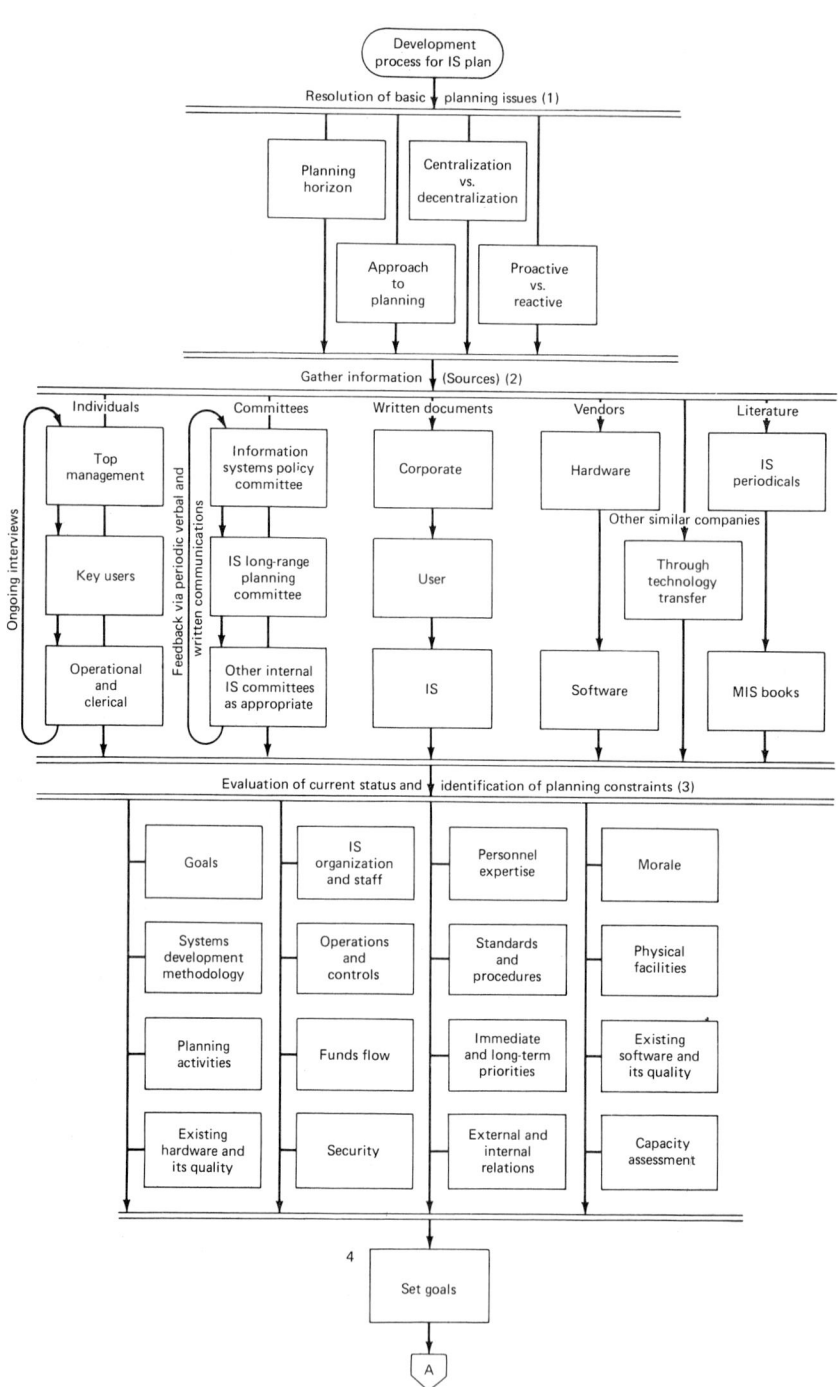

FIGURE 16-2 Development process for an information services long-range plan.

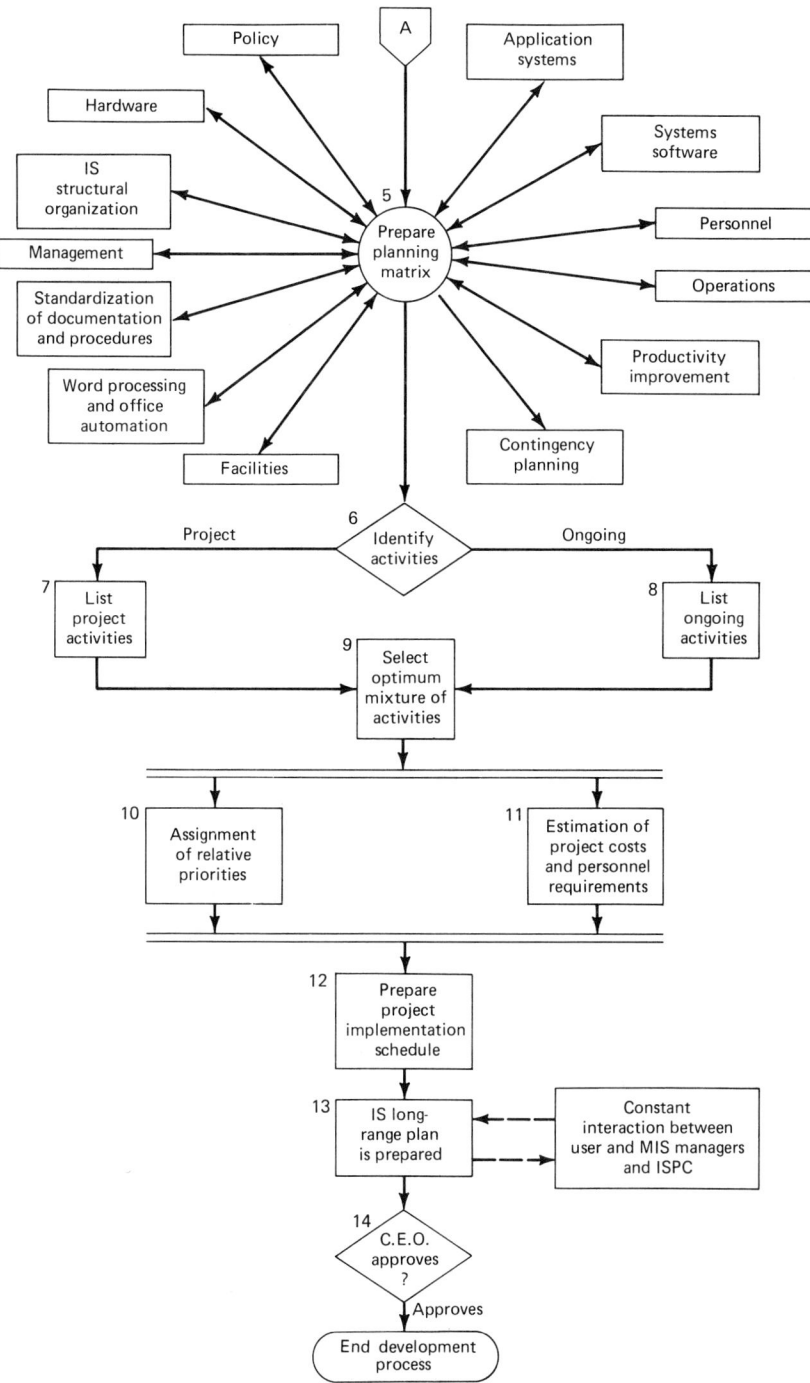

FIGURE 16-2 Continued.

Each major activity has a number placed outside the upper left corner of the *activity block* or in parentheses above a group of related blocks. These numbers do not necessarily depict the order of execution of the activities. They serve as a cross reference to the following detailed *activity descriptions*. The activity descriptions expand on personnel involved, responsibilities, criteria for decisions, considerations, approaches to a solution, and sources of information.

1. Prior to the commencement of the IS planning process, certain planning issues should be resolved, considered, or at least identified as having some effect on the planning process.

Planning—Centralized or Decentralized

Decentralized thinking has been promoted because of the growing emphasis on distributed data processing. In decentralized environments, certain aspects of the plan can be accomplished at the remote sites. This type of planning requires a more direct involvement on the part of user managers. Even decentralized planning should be coordinated at a central site.

Approach to Planning—Top-Down or Bottom-Up

The IS planning process is most effective when the planning team takes advantage of both the top-down and bottom-up methods of information gathering. In top-down planning, the input to the plan is a perspective on overall corporate goals, objectives, and trends. In the bottom-up method, information is gathered at the clerical and operational levels. From this vantage point, the input tends to reflect the "real environment" with all of its embedded constraints.

Planning Horizon

As a rule of thumb, the minimum planning horizon would be no less than 1 year, with a maximum of from 3 to 10 years. There is no typical horizon, but the average is between 3 and 5 years.

Planning—Proactive or Reactive

A fundamental question must be addressed: Should information services be reactive or proactive? There are advantages to each. Specifically, if a computer center reacts to situations, monies for education, systems development, and the like are funneled directly into approved projects. On the other hand, so-called proactive computer centers must commit funds to such activities as professional education and hardware upgrades in anticipation of future corporate information services needs. The proactive environment is generally more responsive to user requirements.

2. Those charged with the responsibility for IS planning have six primary sources from which to gather information: individuals, committees, written documents, vendors, similar companies, and the literature.

Individuals

Persons at various levels of the corporation who are directly or indirectly involved with information services are interviewed on an ongoing basis. These people can provide feedback to the planning process by suggesting alternatives, offering compromises, and/or discussing tradeoffs. The planning process is an iterative procedure that requires constant feedback from all involved or affected.

Committees

The ISPC, the IS long-range planning committee, and certain other internal IS committees (e.g., the hardware/software acquisition committee) have meaningful roles in the IS planning function. For example, the ISPC can offer input on applications systems requirements, systems integration, and priorities. The ISPC ultimately renders approval for implementation of the plan. The IS long-range planning committee, comprised of user and IS managers, is the primary source of ideas and serves as a sounding board for alternative planning strategies.

Written Documents

The typical information service department has numerous written documents that can be helpful in the planning process. For example:

♦ Approved service requests
♦ Previous IS long-range plans
♦ Internal directives and important memorandums
♦ Appropriate information systems documentation (including user manuals)
♦ IS department organizational charts
♦ Internal and external auditors reports
♦ Post-implementation reviews and periodic system evaluations

Similar printed matter exists at the corporate level and in the functional areas. Of particular importance at the corporate level are the corporate long-range plan, internal policy statements, and the corporate organizational chart. In the functional areas, user managers should make anything available that might aid in the planning process: an organizational chart, a statement of goals and objectives, an internal procedures manual, and so on.

Vendors

Hardware and software vendors are another valuable source of information. Most marketing representatives are more than happy to provide input to the planning process. Vendors can provide important information on their products and will usually work within the structure of the organization to propose what they feel to be feasible alternative solutions.

Similar Companies

Other computing centers in similar companies represent another source of information. The benefit of this type of interaction is the possibility of technology transfer, primarily systems design or software.

Literature

The volatile and growing field of computers and information systems has spawned many excellent periodicals: *Computerworld*, *Infosystems*, *Datamation*, *Data Management*, and *Interface*, to mention a few. (See page 361 for others.) These periodicals have numerous articles to spur the imagination of those involved in the planning process.

It would behoove the user manager to contact the information services liaison and request that they be placed on appropriate periodical routing lists or that personal copies be ordered. These periodicals serve a valuable function by keeping IS and user managers current. Many are offered free of charge.

3. At this point, the status of the corporate information services function is evaluated and the constraints that affect the scope and direction of the planning effort are identified.

Evaluation of Current Status

The purpose of evaluating the current status of the IS function is to provide the planning team with a definition, or "benchmark," of where the IS and functional area departments stand with respect to each area of information services planning. Of those areas listed in activity 3 of Figure 16-2, the user manager's primary input is in the areas of goals, IS organization and staff, operations and controls, physical facilities, funds flow, immediate and long-term priorities, existing software and its quality, security, and external and internal relations.

A number of questions would have to be answered to evaluate the current status of the IS function. For example, under operations and controls, questions like "Is operations meeting production schedules?" and "Is there a clear definition of responsibilities for control of systems?" must be addressed. Under immediate and long-term priorities, questions must be asked like "Have priorities been established for approved projects?" "Who sets priorities?" and "Are priorities followed?"

In the IS planning vernacular, this step is also referred to as a **situation assessment.**

Indentification of Planning Constraints

The identification of the *planning constraints* is actually a byproduct of the evaluation of the current status. Anything that would be expected to limit the scope or direction of the IS planning effort would be noted. For example, a corporate freeze on hiring over the next year would be a constraint, as would a finite and saturated office space.

The Resultant Product

The end product of the evaluation would be a written report depicting the current status of the information services function and enumerating IS planning constraints.

4. Perhaps the most important step in the process is to establish *goals* for information services over the planning horizon. Goals for information services should be established by corporate management and members of the information systems policy committee. Once established, the goals would provide the general framework for accomplishing the information services long-range plan. In order to establish goals, management must address such issues as scope and quality of service, policy, organization, personnel, and so on. At this point in the planning process, it is still premature to discuss information systems requirements.

5. This planning methodology advocates a "comprehensive" IS long-range plan. A comprehensive plan focuses attention on virtually all areas that affect the information services function. An IS long-range plan that encompasses less than the topic areas listed below will give less than adequate coverage to the considerations necessary for IS planning.

- Policy
- Information systems
- Hardware
- Systems software
- IS structural organization

- ♦ Personnel
- ♦ Management
- ♦ Operations
- ♦ Standardization of documentation and procedures
- ♦ Productivity improvement
- ♦ Facilities
- ♦ Contingency planning
- ♦ Word processing and office automation
- ♦ Others, depending on type industry (e.g., R&D)

A *planning matrix* can be used to ensure that interactions between the various planning areas are considered. IS and user management should be aware of how planning for one area affects planning for another. The planning matrix of Figure 16-3 illustrates which planning areas affect or overlap each other. Each planning area (discussed separately below) interacts with at least one of the other areas. For example, information systems may have a significant effect not only on IS operations, but on functional area operations. The interactions noted in Figure 16-3 are included primarily to illustrate the mechanics of preparing an IS planning matrix. They should not be construed as typical interactions. The scope of the IS planning effort, the planning areas selected, and the maturity and sophistication of the existing IS environment will significantly alter the complexion of the IS planning matrix from one corporation to the next.

The planning matrix ensures that "all bases have been covered" and encourages a structured approach that reduces the complex IS planning process to more intelligible and manageable modules. IS planning functionaries and advisors could use the planning matrix as an aid to developing strategies for each of the major IS planning areas. Possible strategies are discussed briefly in the following sections, with an emphasis on those areas that concern user and corporate management.

Policy

The topic of information services policy was discussed in Chapter 4. Particular attention should be given to the establishment of a high-level steering committee (ISPC) and a charter for the information services function.

Information Systems

Each facet of the IS long-range plan has far-reaching effects on all phases of corporate endeavor, but the driving force and common thread of strategic IS long-range planning is information systems planning.

X Planning for one impacts planning for the other

←↑ Prerequisite to planning area noted

	1 Policy	2 Application systems	3 Hardware	4 Systems software	5 Organization	6 Personnel (including education)	7 Management	8 Operations	9 Documentation and procedures	10 Productivity	11 Facilities	12 Contingency planning	13 Word processing and office automation
1 Policy	■	←	X		X	X		←					←
2 Application systems		■	←	X		↑		X	X			X	
3 Hardware			■	←		↑		X			←	X	←
4 Systems software				■		↑		X				X	X
5 Organization					■	←					←	X	
6 Personnel (including education)						■	X		X	X	X		
7 Management							■		X	X	X		
8 Operations								■	X		X		X
9 Documentation and procedures									■	←	X		X
10 Productivity										■	X		X
11 Facilities											■	X	X
12 Contingency planning												■	
13 Word processing and office automation													■

FIGURE 16-3 An IS planning matrix.

Therefore, this facet of information services is perhaps the most critical planning area. Virtually all other facets of the IS plan are in some way affected by information systems planning (also called business systems planning).

Most corporations are emphasizing increased productivity as a way to increase profits. But surprisingly, the majority have failed to realize the importance of tapping an existing corporate resource. This resource is information. Every corporation has the potential to obtain this information; however, careful planning and coordination is critical to tapping the information resource. Redundant, autonomous data processing systems are commonplace. This makes collection and dissemination of valuable information for managerial decision making difficult, if not impossible. To make the resource of information available, the central theme in information systems planning should be integration.

The information systems planning process provides insight for a better understanding of corporate operation. The documentation compiled and the knowledge acquired by those involved in the planning effort can provide valuable input to corporate managers whose scope of responsibility spans the gamut of corporate operations. Figure 16–4 graphically illustrates the activities for information systems planning. These activities are discussed below.

Systems Identification. The purpose of this information systems planning activity is to identify all existing automated systems, manual systems with potential for automation, and automated systems with potential for improvement and/or integration with other systems. In order to obtain a good understanding of existing systems and those systems proposed for the future, the following *intermediate system summary documentation package* should be compiled for each existing manual and proposed system:

♦ A brief summary that includes a discussion of the basic functions of the system, pertinent characteristics or features of the system, identification of other systems with which this system does or should have an interaction, and any future plans for enhancements or changes to the system.
♦ Identification of file types, sizes, and storage media (should be related to an integrated data base when appropriate).
♦ Relative scope of the present or proposed automated system.
♦ Equipment requirements if equipment is a significant feature.

The primary input to the documentation of the existing manual and proposed system is the documentation for existing computer-based systems, services requests, the list of approved projects compiled by the high-level IS steering committee, and the recommendations from periodic system reviews. After this documentation is compiled, the task of assigning priorities and suggesting areas of integration will be made easier.

Expected Benefits. An information system, like any other corporate investment opportunity, must be justified. The estimated cost must be paired with the expected benefits (1) to determine if the system should be implemented and (2) to establish a relative priority position.

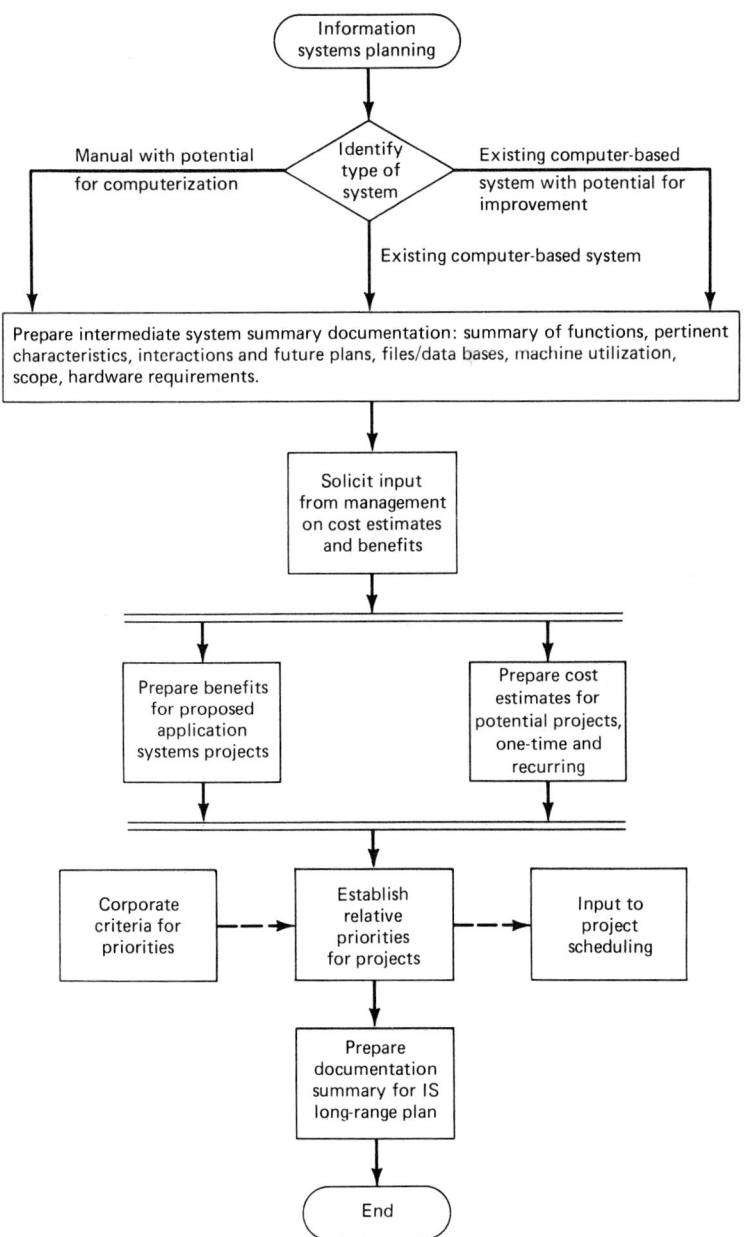

FIGURE 16-4 Activities diagram for information systems planning.

As IS departments mature, fewer systems are justified solely on the basis of tangible benefits. The scope of IS has transcended basic transaction handling and personnel reduction. Now, through information, systems can also provide insight into the decision-making process. The benefits derived from this type of system are often not reflected in direct or indirect savings in personnel and/or resources.

Some corporations have elected to associate dollar savings (or earnings) with certain intangible benefits to prepare a benefit/cost ratio and/or a rate-of-return analysis. In most cases, the dollar figures assigned to the intangible benefits are, at best, wild guesses. Therefore, benefit/cost and rate-of-return analysis for systems with many intangible benefits should be tempered with a certain amount of subjective evaluation.

Cost Estimation. Cost estimates are required for all systems being developed and/or proposed. The cost estimates prior to accomplishing a comprehensive feasibility study are ballpark figures based primarily on a concept, not a design.

For each system in development or planned for development, two cost estimates should be made, one for the one-time cost of systems development and implementation, and the other an estimate of recurring costs for production and ongoing maintenance of the system over the life of the system. The latter cost should be an estimate of yearly recurring costs.

See activity 11 for a recommended procedure for making estimates of costs.

System Priorities. Existing and potential information systems must be given a relative priority position for development and implementation. The typical IS department has a greater demand for services than a capability to supply the services. Therefore, systems must be given a priority.

Each corporation must set its own criteria for the establishment of system priorities. However, the following are criteria for consideration:

A *Federal regulation* or an *internal mandate* from the president or the board of directors must be addressed. If the Internal Revenue Service changes payroll withholding percentages, or the board of directors authorizes a change in procedures, there is no option but to address these system needs.

The corporate and/or IS department *cash* flow would affect cash availability and limit development efforts. However, if resources are available to generate the necessary cash flow, a positive cash flow can be generated by the implementation of certain systems, especially integrated systems.

Another consideration is the *interdependency* of the various systems. That is, some priorities are known a priori because one system must be completed and/or designed prior to the development of another. For example, an on-line personnel reporting system may supply the data base for the proposed upgrade to the payroll system.

The *return on investment*, benefit/cost ratio, and/or a subjective evaluation of cost versus the tangible and intangible benefits should be considered.

Some systems are obviously consistent with the corporate long-range plan whereas others' association with the corporate plan is less clear. Perhaps one criterion could be *consistency* with the corporate long-range plan.

System Documentation. A subset of the previously compiled intermediate system documentation package should be included in the IS long-range plan. The intermediate documentation was compiled for the purpose of making cost estimates and setting priorities. Within the text of the IS long-range plan, each existing and proposed system should have the following *documentation*:

- ◆ A brief overview of the proposed project (no more than one or two paragraphs).
- ◆ Cost estimates with breakdowns into very general categories. (Cost estimate categories should be the same for all systems).
- ◆ A summary of tangible benefits using dollars as a common denominator and brief explanations of major intangible benefits.
- ◆ A proposed priority position relative to other information systems projects.
- ◆ An optional implementation schedule showing no more detail than the feasibility study, systems analysis and design, programming, testing, and conversion and implementation (see Figure 16-5).

To illustrate the interaction between the various systems, an *overview corporate work flow diagram* as shown in Figure 16-6 can be

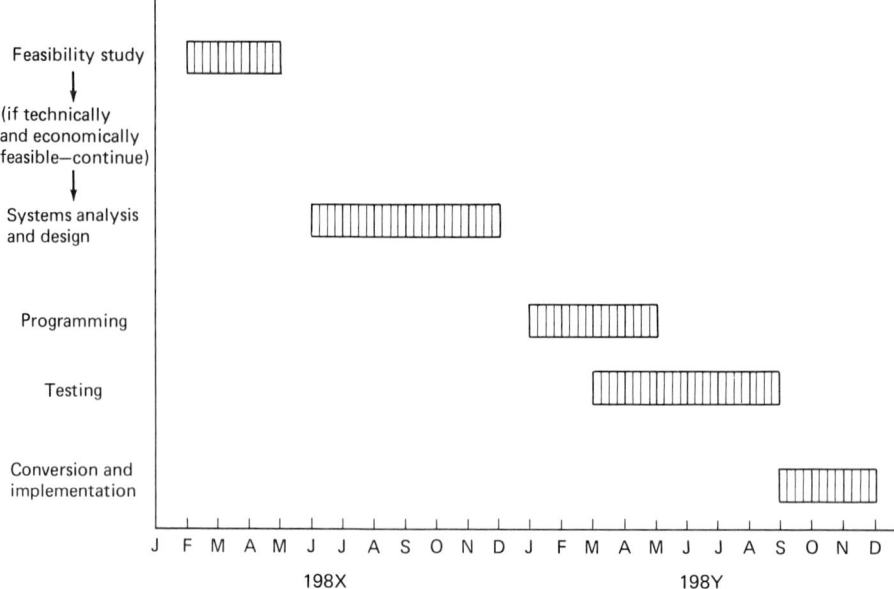

FIGURE 16-5 Information systems implementation schedule.

included. Such a diagram can be used to illustrate data and work flow interactions between all major systems of the corporation. The diagram should not be limited to computer-based systems because existing manual systems are often prime candidates for computerization and often interact with computer-based systems. The corporate work flow diagram can be used to designate manual and computer-based systems, if a system is being developed, if a system is planned for development, or the extent to which a system is computerized. In addition, the priority position for development can be indicated on the chart.

The corporate work flow diagram can be compiled in a variety of formats and at varying levels of detail. The purpose of including such a diagram in the IS long-range plan is to illustrate the fundamental relationships between the operational systems within the company. A more detailed diagram can be compiled later to assist IS in plan implementation.

Figures 16-7 and 16-8 are supplements, or perhaps even alternatives, to the corporate work flow diagram. As a preliminary step for corporations planning to implement an integrated corporation data base, those departments and/or functional areas that are data sources or have uses for information derived from the corporate data base are listed. For illustrative purposes, five such areas are noted in Figure 16-7. Figure 16-8 graphically illustrates which areas provide data input (are source of data) to other areas, thereby noting data dependencies. Con-

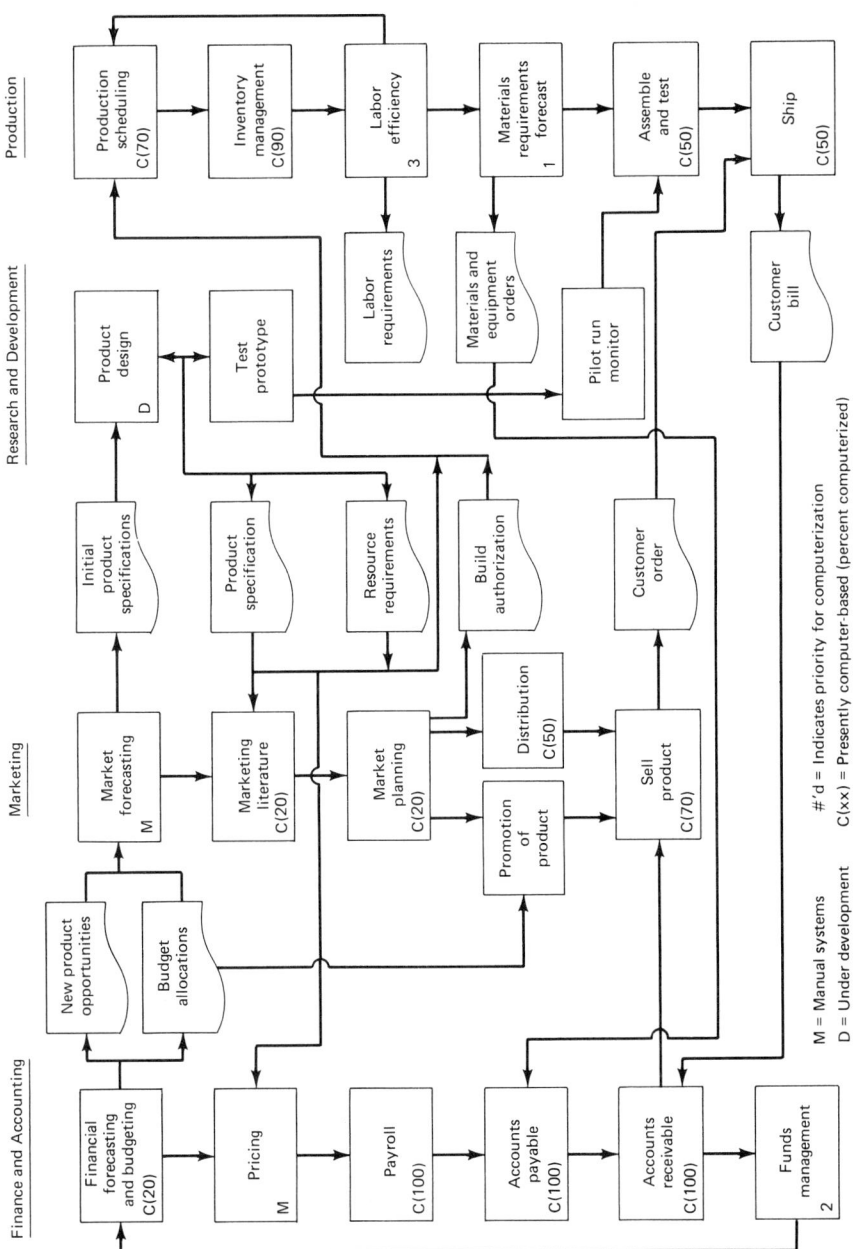

Finance and Accounting   Marketing   Research and Development   Production

M = Manual systems
D = Under development

#'d = Indicates priority for computerization
C(xx) = Presently computer-based (percent computerized)

FIGURE 16-6 Corporate work flow diagram.

343

necting lines with arrows at either end indicate a bilateral transfer of data between areas. Such an overview of data/information flow can be a valuable aid to those project teams working in functional areas, to the data base administrator, and in establishing priorities for systems development.

In summary, the documentation directly related to information systems planning that should be included in the IS long-range plan is:

A. An overview of each system that includes a description, benefits/cost analysis, recommended relative priority, and perhaps a suggested implementation schedule for each information system.

B. A corporate work flow diagram that illustrates the relationships

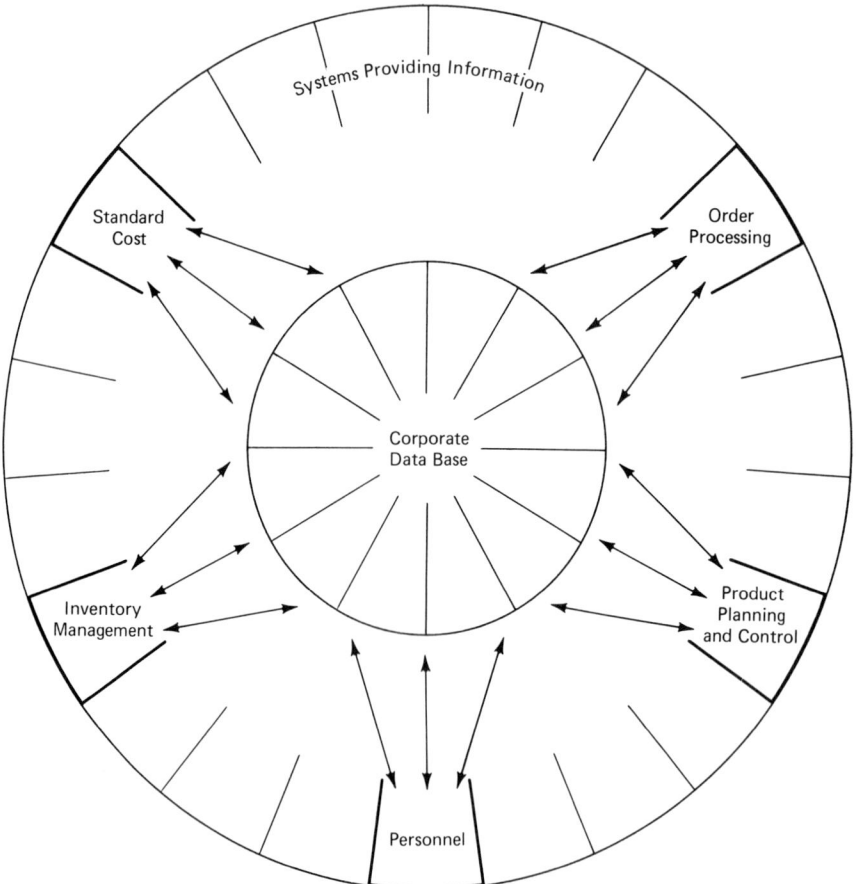

FIGURE ▬ Corporate data base and systems providing information.

between various corporate systems and the computerization status of each.
C. An information sources and uses chart.

This documentation provides a foundation for planning in the other areas that support information systems planning (e.g., hardware, personnel, facilities, and so on).

Hardware

The sophistication of IS methods, software, and hardware is increasing rapidly. This is particularly true of computing hardware. Computer systems have become more complex and require periodic upgrades to each of the devices configuring a computer system. Data communications is playing a greater role in information systems; therefore, the

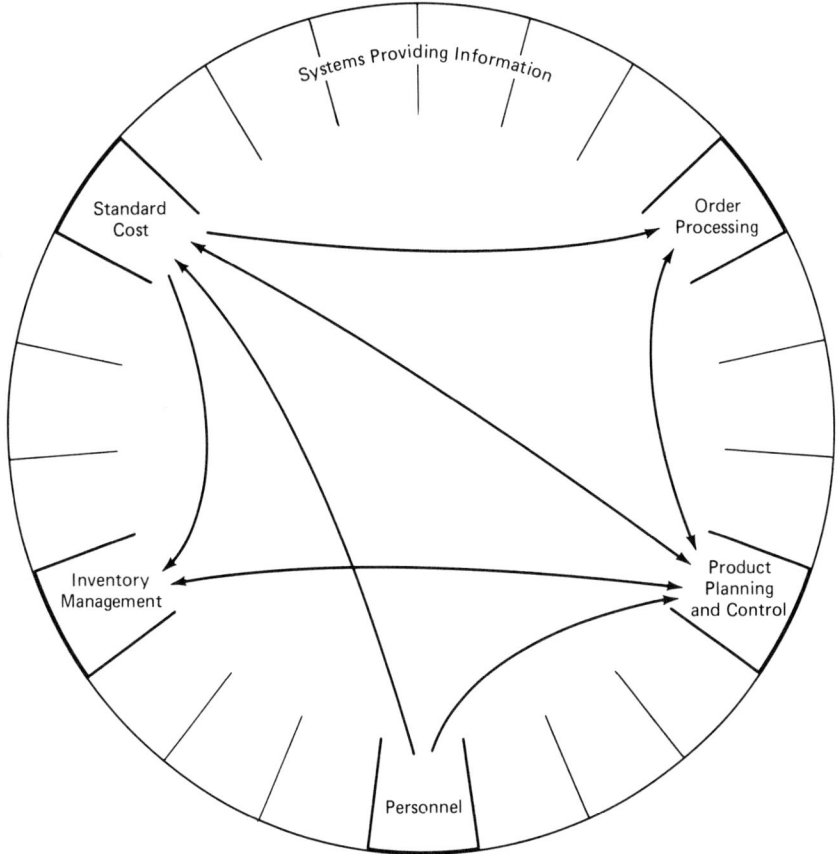

FIGURE 16-8 Information sources and uses chart.

hardware planning traditionally confined to a central facility is now expanded to include communications equipment, communications links, remote computers, and remote input/output devices. Hardware decisions involving data communications inevitably involve the functional area manager.

The advent of data communications technology has made possible the implementation of the distributed data processing (DDP) concept, which encourages the decentralization of computing hardware. Decentralization requires a closer control on hardware acquisition in order to maintain compatibility, thereby making short- and long-term hardware planning essential.

The availability of relatively inexpensive, small computer systems has prompted many user managers to purchase computers to support systems within their realm of responsibility. Word processing hardware has been upgraded to the point that word processing systems are no longer limited to text editing. Many word processing systems have data retrieval and manipulation capabilities and can perform some basic DP functions. These small computer systems and word processing systems are proliferating in many corporations. If not coordinated, these systems inevitably cause compatibility problems and redundancy in the maintenance of the corporate data base. Hardware planning is a vehicle by which to control this proliferation.

Information systems planning is the driving force behind hardware planning. When hardware planning precedes information systems planning (and it does in many corporations), systems must be developed to accommodate available hardware. Systems development is difficult enough without placing unnecessary hardware constraints on developers. Hardware planning is based on historical utilization statistics and the capacity requirements of proposed information systems. The end product is a configuration of all corporate computer systems, both now and over the horizon of the IS long-range plan. See Chapter 7 for systems configuration considerations.

Systems Software

Systems software, like hardware, can cause compatibility problems if not properly coordinated. Since systems software is for the most part applications-independent, the user seldom becomes involved in this area of IS planning.

IS Structural Organization

Information services is a dynamic corporate function. As applications and computer hardware change, the information services function must be periodically reorganized to accommodate new procedures, to develop specialty expertise, and to experiment with organizational alternatives which better serve the changing needs of the corporation. Since one of these alternatives is distributed data processing (DDP), the functional area departments will probably be affected by any IS organizational planning. Information services organization is discussed in Chapter 3.

Personnel

The current seller's market in the computer/information processing field is expected to persist for the next decade. IS and user management will continue to have problems recruiting and retaining IS professionals. The successful IS long-range plan will address these issues by focusing on personnel-related topics such as morale, education, career development, and salary administration.

Management

Since the first commercial computer was installed in the U.S. Bureau of Census in 1951, IS professionals have been more adept at solving technical rather than managerial problems. The lack of managerial expertise and/or interest still exists, but to a lesser extent. However, management of the IS function is still one of the most pressing problems facing information services. Over the last decade there has been a significant shortage of IS professionals, and the shortage is even more acute for IS managers. The lack of capable managers and the unwillingness of primarily technical people to accomplish the management function are only part of the IS management problem.

Many IS managers use the seat-of-the-pants approach to management. Management, like programming, requires highly developed skills and use of the latest technology to be effective. Tools supporting the programming function may be more highly developed than those supporting the management function, but management tools have been developed that are a significant aid to IS management. These should not be overlooked in the planning process. Possible projects regarding management of the information services function may include the implementation of a project management and control system, productivity measurement techniques, and a performance evaluation system.

Operations

The primary strategy consideration in the area of operations is that of production scheduling (see Chapter 13). The fundamental objective in the scheduling of production information systems is to utilize computing hardware in an optimum manner while meeting production deadlines.

Standardization

Standardization in the area of computers/information processing is a prerequisite to corporate integration. A variety of standardized procedures and conventions must be developed, adopted, and implemented. The corporate data base must be standardized. In order to maintain hardware compatibility, guidelines must be developed for the purchase of small computer systems and word processing systems. For ease of documentation maintenance, the contents and format of system documentation should be standardized. These and scores of other areas are typically standardized through corporate information services. Those areas that should be standardized and are not should be included in the IS plan.

Productivity Improvement

The user can play a significant role in increasing productivity in the development and operation of information systems. The following list presents several strategies in which the user can make a contribution to productivity improvement.

Use of a Standardized Methodology. The economics of and justification for implementing a standardized system development methodology are discussed in Chapter 12. A methodology establishes guidelines by which user and IS personnel can cooperate to develop and implement a quality information system. Higher quality on the front-end means less maintenance during production. A decrease in maintenance results in a net increase in personnel available for new systems development, thereby increasing productivity.

Collection of Data at the Source. By collecting data as close to the source as possible, the number of times a transaction has to be transcribed is minimized and accuracy is increased. In many companies, users complete a hard copy and physically deliver it to on-line operators at the computer center who transcribe the data to a machine-readable format. In most environments, data entry can be done more accurately and more efficiently by the user, thereby eliminating at least one step in the transcription process.

Use of High-Level User-Oriented Languages. Attention by IS professionals to one-time user requests for special reports is minimized with the existence of a high-level user-oriented language. With proper education, users can obtain their own one-time reports in less time than it would take to fill out a service request.

Information Systems. Each information system has a set of procedures that may or may not result in the most efficient use of personnel. The operational procedures of most information systems have the potential to be made more efficient, thereby saving personnel time and increasing productivity. These procedural deficiencies usually surface during the periodic system reviews through feedback from users.

Improved User Interaction. Companies have shown through improved interaction that productivity in system development can be improved by as much as 400%. The best approach to improving this interaction is to provide the opportunity for users to gain an understanding of IS principles and the local methods and approaches used to develop and maintain systems. A program of ongoing user education is one method of achieving user awareness (see Chapter 11). This book is another. Others include:

♦ A monthly IS newsletter.
♦ Involving the user in the systems development methodology.
♦ Establishing a high-level steering committee (ISPC).
♦ Rotating user personnel to working tours in the IS department (and vice versa).
♦ Providing a procedure for periodic user feedback relative to IS performance.

Implementation of a Chargeback System. A user chargeback system encourages user managers to appreciate the scope of their requests for services. The implementation of a cost allocation and control system prompts the user to consider the merit of the request more closely. See Chapter 13 for a discussion of chargeback systems.

Technology Transfer. A corporate policy encouraging the investigation of the possibility and/or feasibility of technology transfer for software will inevitably yield significant returns by saving personnel time. Rather than "reinvent the wheel" by channeling efforts of programmers, analysts, and users into fundamental application areas, corporations should concentrate on industry-specific applications for which there is no existing software. The software industry has become very competitive and hundreds of companies offer thousands of products that can save corporate resources.

Use of a Data Base Management System. Data base management systems provide a vehicle for systems integration and, therefore, the opportunity for efficient programming and systems design.

Facilities

As information systems, hardware, and personnel are distributed, functional area managers must become attuned to special requirements for physical facilities. Facilities must be made available for on-site IS personnel and for distributed hardware. Plans for construction or renovation must consider extra power requirements and communications links, plus security, environmental, and fire controls.

Contingency Planning

The contingency plan is actually a series of plans for each type of occurrence that has the potential to drastically disrupt IS operation. These occurrences can be a result of individual or group negligence, environmental disaster, or emergency corporate or government requirements. Contingency planning also encompasses planning for extraordinary occurrences (personnel strike, peacetime to wartime operations for military installations, sudden departure of all key personnel, and so on.)

Under normal circumstances, a corporation without a contingency plan can continue to operate indefinitely. However, the corporation not prepared for other than routine operation is courting corporate disaster. Corporations have gone bankrupt because of the computer center's inability to recover from a disaster and/or provide continuing services to the corporation.

A *contingency planning team* should be formulated as a standing team that meets periodically to develop contingency plans and revise those that become out of date. The team typically consists of operational managers in a variety of support areas throughout the corporation. Extremely close coordination is required for IS contingency planning. When a plan is placed into operation, not only is coordinated support critical, but so is timing. The contingency planning team would involve personnel with a direct interest in operations (user and IS), systems analysis, systems programming, applications programming, internal auditing, legal ramifications, security, data communications, IS management, building maintenance, fire protection, transportion, and insurance adjustment.

IS and user management should identify potential disasters and extraordinary occurrences to be considered in the contingency plan. The corporation should accept some risk, in that there are marginal returns for developing contingency plans for all possible occurrences. Those disasters and/or occurrences that are most probable and those with the greatest effect on corporate operations should be identified. The contingency planning team would work together to develop a contingency plan for each potential extraordinary occurrence. Each plan would outline the duties and responsibilities of each of the functions represented on the contingency planning team.

Office Automation and Word Processing

Chapter 14 is devoted to presenting the definition, scope, and strategies for office automation and word processing.

6. Since resources are scheduled and allocated by activity, specific activities necessary to carry out the planning strategies set forth in activity 5 must be identified. In every computer center there are essentially two types of IS activities: *project-oriented* (one-time) and *ongoing* (recurring activities.

7. The following are examples of project-oriented activities:

♦ Feasibility studies
♦ Information systems development
♦ Periodic system reviews
♦ Internal and external audits
♦ Security analyses or security audits
♦ Development of documentation and procedures manual (and other in-house manuals)
♦ Major system enhancements
♦ System software upgrades
♦ Education (group or individual)
♦ Construction or physical facilities improvement
♦ Hardware/software acquisition
♦ Equipment installation
♦ Benefit/cost analysis of a project

8. The following are examples of ongoing activities:

♦ Production and control of an information system (e.g., payroll, inventory, general ledger)
♦ Minor enhancements to information systems (e.g., general maintenance)
♦ Administration and management of the IS function
♦ IS long-range planning
♦ Writing, publishing, and distributing monthly IS department newsletter

Note that ongoing activities are often the result of project-oriented activities.

9. Limited resources preclude the implementation of all entries on a "wish list" of ongoing and project-oriented activities. Therefore, to optimize the mixture of proposed activities for the good of the corporation, some proposed activities must be deleted. This mixture can be determined by selecting the proper ratio of project-oriented and ongoing activities and the proper mixture of high- and low-risk activities.

Each existing and proposed project should be given some type of rating relative to risk. Risk refers to the validity of the personnel, money, and time estimates, and to the probability of project completion and success. To select and propose all high-risk projects would jeopardize the success of the IS department and the company. On the other hand, across-the-board selection of low-risk projects would probably eliminate certain needed projects from consideration. The best approach is to select an optimal mixture of high- and low-risk projects. Each project should be evaluated relative to complexity, level of technology required, and scope.

Those projects that are highly structured provide the project leader with a clear view of what needs to be done. These projects will have a low to medium risk, depending upon whether the project is of high or low technology and/or a small or large project. Similarly, the projects that do not have a clear beginning and end will have a medium to high risk. An example of a low-risk project would be the introduction of a series of in-house seminars on data base management systems. An example of a high-risk project would be the implementation of an integrated on-line manufacturing resource planning system.

10. In order to schedule IS projects for development and implementation, priorities must be established and cost estimates compiled. Unless extenuating circumstances prevail, existing projects and ongoing activities would be given the highest priorities. One proven approach to establishing priorities involves collective thinking and decision making on the part of the user and IS management. This approach assumes that each person in the group has a knowledge of the problem or task and the ability to provide meaningful rationale to support their opinion on a particular matter of discussion. This interactive approach results in a group concensus opinion. The steps are as follows:

A. A user manager serves as the leader and explains the objective (to set priorities). Possible considerations in establishing IS priorities are:

- ◆ Corporate need (compatibility with major thrusts of corporation and input from the Information Systems Policy Committee [ISPC])
- ◆ Availability of critical expertise
- ◆ Length and complexity of the project
- ◆ Systems dependencies and integration
- ◆ Availability of support hardware
- ◆ Corporate preparedness (physical, educational, psychological, etc.)
- ◆ Opportunity to increase productivity
- ◆ Portability (potential for use as a standard product in corporate entities with similar objectives)

If necessary, appropriate background information is presented.

B. The leader lists all proposed project and ongoing activities for all to see.

C. The leader may need to clarify why a particular activity is included in the list. If participants indicate that all activities are clear in their initial presentation, this step may be omitted.

D. In this step, each member of the group ranks the activities. Depending on the number of activities initially listed, an odd number somewhat less than the total of the list is selected. For example, seven might be selected from a list of fifteen activities. Each member of the group selects what they believe to be the top seven (in the example case) activities, then assigns a rank to each activity by starting with the extremes and working to the middle (i.e., first, seventh, second, sixth, third, fifth, fourth). For ease of tabulation, each person, including the leader, notes the rank for each activity on a separate card. The highest-priority item is given a "7".

E. The scores are tabulated. The group rank for each activity is the total of the individual rank. The activities are listed in order (most significant first) for all to see.

F. The leader coordinates an open discussion to debate personal differences with the ordered list compiled from accumulated individual rankings.

G. Repeat steps D, E, and F until it is apparent that further iterations will not significantly alter the priorities shown in the most recent ordered list.

11. The scheduling process requires that preliminary estimates of costs and personnel requirements be made for each activity proposed. These estimates are based primarily on a concept and not on a design or a comprehensive description of a particular activity.

The procedure described in Chapter 14 (system development activity 14) can be used to make estimates of costs, personnel, and time requirements.

12. The preparation of the project implementation schedule is an iterative process. The scheduling process is essentially a trade-off between maintaining the priorities set in activity 10 and minimizing the fluctuation in personnel requirements (work-load leveling). Given priorities, costs, and personnel requirements (activities 10 and 11), a preliminary project implementation schedule chart can be prepared. Several iterations of the project implementation schedule will be required to level the work load. Although personnel and dollar estimates are fixed, there is some flexibility to either lengthen or shorten the duration of a project and/or to shift the project completion date forward or backward in time. When the shifting of a completion date alters the relative priorities of projects, such changes should be cleared with the ISPC.

A preliminary project implementation schedule is shown in Figure 16–9. Project 1, a market analysis system, is presently underway and scheduled to be completed at the end of May. Project 4, the development of a manufacturing resource planning (MRP) system, is scheduled to begin February 1 and to be completed at the end of August. The MRP project will require 21 person-months of effort over the life of the project from February 1 to September 1. This is indicated by a circled "21." The estimated dollar expenditure for Project 4 is $550,000. This amount represents the estimated total one-time project cost—materials, machine time, personnel, and so on. The "1/2" in the square represents the estimated recurring costs in person-years per year over the life of the project. In most cases the recurring costs begin immediately after project termination (usually system implementation). The $50,000 represents the annual recurring costs (maintenance and production) of the proposed MRP system.

13. Once the high-level information systems steering committee (ISPC) approves the project implementation schedule, IS and user management can prepare the details for implementation of the proposed activities. The details are, in fact, the IS long-range plan. Throughout plan preparation, user and IS managers and the ISPC are constantly interacting. This interaction should be somewhat formalized. A suggested approach is presented in Figure 16–1.

The first step in the preparation of the written plan is to develop a general outline. An example outline is shown in Figure 16–10. The strategic plan for information services contains the details for accomplishing the proposed activities over the horizon of the plan. The plan reflects changes, approaches, potential problems and solutions, and implementation methods for the proposed activities.

14. The strategic plan is submitted first to the information systems policy committee for approval. Once approved by the ISPC, the docu-

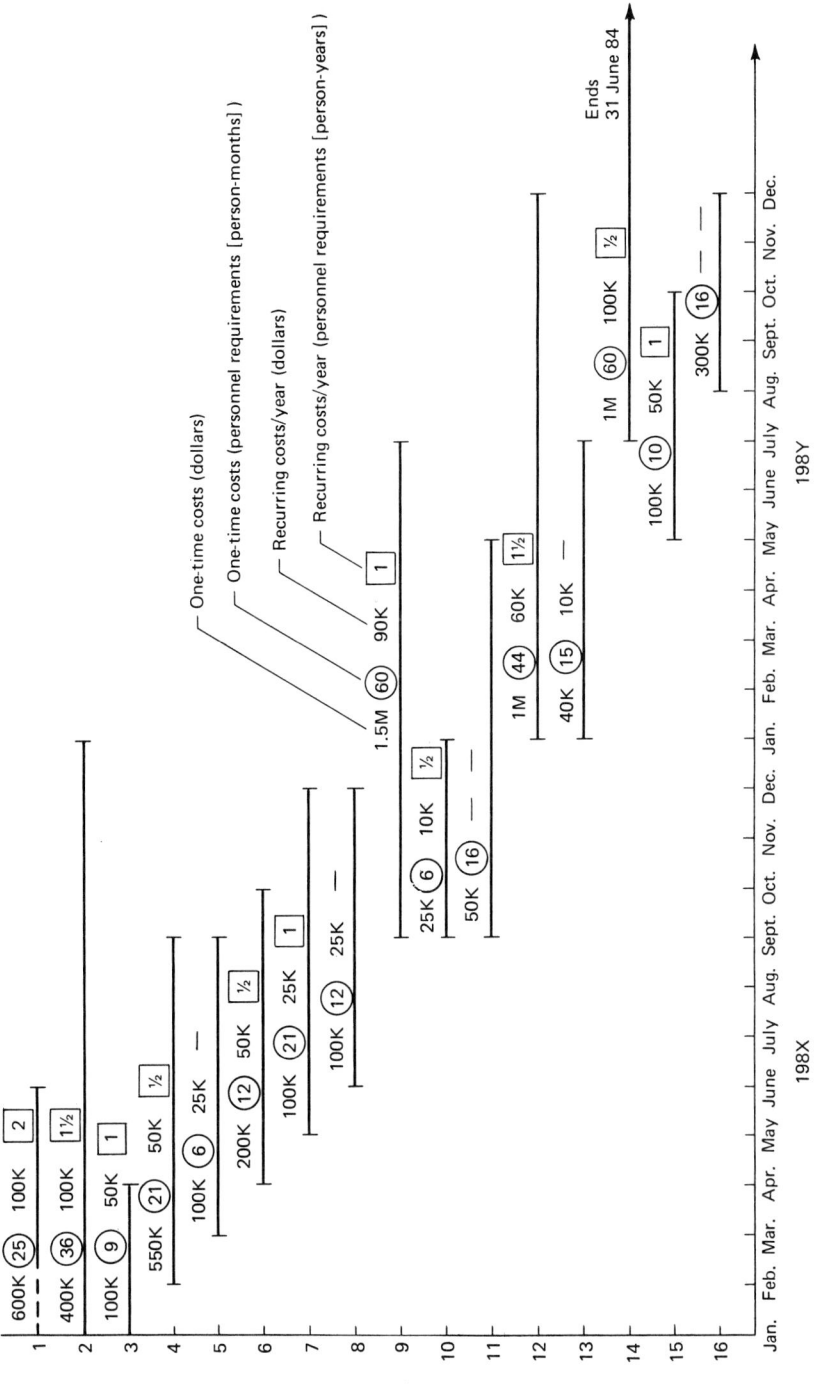

FIGURE 16-9 Initial project implementation schedule.

ment is then submitted to the chief executive officer not only for approval, but for support. Presumably, controversial issues would have been debated and resolved by the ISPC.

PHASE III—IMPLEMENTATION AND MAINTENANCE

Each segment of the strategic plan for information services should have been prepared in cooperation with the information systems policy committee and appropriate IS and user managers. If procedures illustrated in Figure 16-1 (interaction between principals in the IS long-range planning process) were followed, implementation of the plan should be smooth and present no serious problems.

Long-range plans, whether corporate or information services, tend to be neglected, or in some cases purposely overlooked, unless a formal periodic review is built into the planning methodology. Progress towards implementation of the strategic plan for information services should be reviewed no more than once per quarter and no less often than semiannually.

The initial information services long-range plan may take from six months to two years to develop. The process is then continuous. The plan should be completely revised at least once every one and a half years and no more often than once a year. Although the initial document may take up to two years to complete, subsequent revisions to the plan should take no more than six to nine months. If they do, staffing for the IS long-range planning function should be increased.

Executive summary
Introduction
Goals
Current IS status
Planning constraints
IS policy
Planning areas
    Information systems
    Hardware
    Systems software
    Organization
    Personnel
    Operation and production
    Standardization of procedures
    Productivity
    Facilities
    Office automation
    Internal relations
    Contingency planning
Summary of proposed activities
Benefit/cost summary
Implementation schedule and method
MIS long-range plan maintenance procedures

FIGURE 16-10 Example of the structure of an IS long-range plan.

SUMMARY

The common denominator in corporate operations is data; therefore, strategic planning for information services will have an effect on virtually every corporate entity. With the emphasis on integration and the trend toward decentralization of computers and information processing, the user manager will play a significant role not only in information services planning, but in the information services function in general.

Epilogue

The *user manager* is the future of information processing. In this era of information resource management, user and IS management have become partners in search of better information. There is a direct correlation between the quality of information and the user manager's willingness to become actively involved in information services activities. Because of the critical nature of user involvement in all facets of computers and information systems, user management's role in information services activities is expanding. Over the next decade the user's role will continue to expand, and user managers will ultimately become the catalysts for most IS activities.

Current trends support the premise that the future of information services is in the hands of the user. Managers have embraced the concept of information resource management. In so doing, they have accepted the responsibility to manage and control information as they have personnel, money, and physical facilities.

The high-level information services steering committee is a vehicle that users have adopted to enable them to decide their own destiny as it relates to information and automation. Information services managers welcome the direction and support provided by these user-based committees.

The trend to distributed data processing has caused processing and hardware to be moved closer to the people that use them. Managers, whose past involvement has been limited to the role of end user, are finding themselves managing their own information services department—including programmers, analysts, operators, hardware, and a few extra headaches.

Technological advances in both hardware and software are in support of distributed data processing and a more active user participation. Computing hardware, both small and large, is being designed to be "distributed" and physically located in the functional areas. This hardware orientation promotes the functional area organizations as the focus of an integrated data communications network.

The direction in software development is to even higher-level user-oriented application generators that will enable managers to create their own applications systems. The manager will need only to generate the design specifications. The application generator software will produce the programs necessary to make the system a reality.

The user's involvement, now and in the future, is further encouraged by standardized IS procedures. System development methodologies have made the user an integral part of every development activity. In many companies the functional area manager is appointed to manage the information system development team. The same extent of user involvement is apparent in strategic planning for information services.

The information center is a positive innovation which encourages users to learn and, at the same time, to take advantage of the information resource. The growth in the number and use of information centers is testimony to the user manager's increasing role in information services.

Every trend leads to the same undeniable conclusion—the user manager is the future of information processing.

For More Information

BOOKS

J. Burch, Jr. and J. Sardinas, Jr., *Computer Control and Audit: a Total Systems Approach*, John Wiley, 1978.

J. Cougar and R. Zawacki, *Motivating and Managing Computer Personnel*, Wiley-Interscience, 1980.

T. DeMarco, *Structured Analysis and System Specification*, Prentice-Hall, 1979.

C. Gane and T. Sarson, *Structured Systems Analysis: Tools and Techniques*, Prentice-Hall, 1979.

C. Finkelstein and J. Martin, *Information Engineering*, Prentice-Hall, 1983.

A. Gaydasch, *Principles of EDP Management*, Reston, 1982.

E. Joslin, *Computer Selection*, Technology Press, 1977.

L. Long, *Design and Strategy for Corporate Information Services: MIS Long-Range Planning*, Prentice-Hall, 1982.

L. Long, *Data Processing Documentation and Procedures Manual*, Reston, 1979.

J. Martin, *Design and Strategy for Distributed Data Processing*, Prentice-Hall, 1981.

J. Martin, *Principles of Data-Base Management*, Prentice-Hall, 1976.

J. Martin, *Telecommunications and the Computer*, 2nd ed., Prentice-Hall, 1976.

J. Martin, *The Wired Society*, Prentice-Hall, 1978.

K. Orr, *Structured Requirements Definition*, Ken Orr and Associates, Inc., 1981.

E. Yourdon, *Structured Walkthrough*, Prentice-Hall, 1979.

PERIODICALS

- *Byte*
- *Communications of the ACM*
- *Computer Decisions*
- *Computerworld*
- *Data Management*
- *Datamation*
- *Harvard Business Review*
- *Infosystems*
- *Interface*
- *Mini-Micro Systems*
- *MIS Week*
- *Today's Office*

Glossary

The glossary contains those computer/information processing terms that might be used during conversations between user managers and information services personnel. The definitions have been condensed to include only the essence of the meaning. The reader should refer to the index and then to the text of the book if a more detailed description is desired or needed. A few terms are not addressed in the text. Each item is defined within the context of computer systems and information resource management.

ACCESS TIME. The time interval between the instant when a computer makes a request for a transfer of data from a secondary storage device and the instant when this operation is completed.

ACOUSTIC COUPLER. A MODEM-type device that is used with a standard telephone headset to transmit data over telephone lines.

ADD-ON MEMORY. Supplemental primary storage.

ADDRESS. (1) A name, numeral, or label that designates a particular location in primary or secondary storage. (2) A location identifier for terminals in a computer network.

ADP (Automatic Data Processing). Same as Data Processing.

ALPHANUMERIC. Pertaining to a character set that contains letters, digits, and special characters.

ANALOG COMPUTER. A computer that operates on data represented in the form of continuous-variable physical quantities such as electrical current and temperature. (Contrast with Digital Computer. Related to Hybrid Computer.)

ANSI (American National Standards Institute). An organization that sets syntax standards for programming languages.

APL (A programming language). An interactive symbolic programming language.

APPLICATION. A problem or task to which the computer can be applied.

APPLICATION SOFTWARE PACKAGE. A prewritten set of computer programs designed for a specific application. (Related to Proprietary Software.)

ASCII (American Standard Code for Information Interchange). A seven-bit code.

ASSEMBLER LANGUAGE. A low-level symbolic language with an instruction set that is essentially one-to-one with machine language.

ASYNCHRONOUS TRANSMISSION. Data transmission in which each character is individually synchronized with start/stop bits. (Contrast with Synchronous Transmission.)

AUDIO RESPONSE. Recorded or synthesized voice output.

AUDIT, INFORMATION SYSTEMS. Functions to ensure the integrity of production information systems.

AUDIT TRAIL. A design procedure whereby processing can be traced to the original source document.

AUXILIARY STORAGE. Same as Secondary Storage.

BACK-END PROCESSOR. A host-subordinate processor that handles administrative tasks associated with retrieval and manipulation of data.

BACKGROUND. The processing area of primary storage dedicated to low-priority, usually batch-oriented, information systems. (Contrast to Foreground.)

BACKUP. Pertaining to equipment, procedures, or data bases that can be used in the event of system failure to restart the system.

BACKUP FILE. Duplicate of an existing production file.

BANDWIDTH. Pertains to the volume of data that can be transmitted per unit time over a data communications channel.

BAR CODE. A graphic encoding technique in which vertical bars of varying widths are used to represent data.

BASIC (Beginner's All-Purpose Symbolic Instructional Code). The primary programming language on small computer systems.

BATCH PROCESSING. A technique in which transactions and/or jobs are collected into groups (batched) and processed together. (Contrast with On-line Processing.)

BAUD RATE. The unit of measure for the speed (data transmitted per unit time) of a data communications channel. One baud approximately equals one bit per second.

BCD (Binary Coded Decimal). A six-bit code.

BENCHMARK PROBLEM. A problem or situation used to evaluate the performance of computers and/or information systems relative to each other.

BIT. A binary digit (0 or 1).

BLOCK. A group of data that is either read from or written to an I/O device in one operation. (Synonymous with Physical Record; compare with Logical Record.)

BLOCKING. Combining two or more logical records into one block.

BOTTOM-UP DESIGN. The technique by which analysis is initiated at the detail level and the system constructed in successive levels of greater generality.

BROAD-BAND LINE. Same as Wide-Band Line.

BUFFER. A storage area used to compensate for differences in the rates of flow of data or in the times of occurrence of events when transmitting data from one device to another.

BUFFERING. The act of using a buffer.

BUG. A logic error in program or computer system design, or a hardware fault.

BURSTING. The machine or manual process of separating the pages of continuous form paper.

BYTE. A group of adjacent bits configured to represent alphanumeric data.

CACHE MEMORY. High-speed limited capacity primary storage.

CAI (Computer assisted instruction). Using the computer as an aid in the educational process.

CARD, PUNCHED. A medium for off-line data storage.

CARRIER, COMMON (Data communications). A company which furnishes data communications services to the general public.

CATHODE-RAY TUBE (CRT). An electronic vacuum tube on which can be displayed printed and graphic information. A reference to CRT usually implies an attached keyboard for key input, i.e., a cathode-ray *terminal.* (Synonymous with VDU, Video Display Unit, Visual Display Unit.)

CDP (Certificate in Data Processing). The recognized certification for information services professionals. (Compare with CPA—Certified Public Accountant and PE—Professional Engineer.)

CENTRAL PROCESSING UNIT (CPU). The logical unit of a computer system that interprets and executes program instructions. (Synonymous with Computer, Processor, and Mainframe.)

CENTRALIZED ORGANIZATION. Hardware and personnel associated with the information services function are in one organizational unit.

CHANNEL. The vehicle by which data are transmitted from one device to another (e.g., host to terminal, CPU to printer).

CHARACTER. A unit of an alphanumeric datum.

CHARACTER-ORIENTED COMPUTER. Refers to a computer that can operate efficiently at the character level. Oriented to business systems. (Contrast with Word-Oriented Computer.)

CHARGEBACK SYSTEM. A method by which costs for information services are allocated to the end user.

CHECK DIGIT. A number derived through an algorithm. It is appended to a number (e.g., credit card account number) for security purposes.

CHECKPOINT/RESTART. A procedure by which the status of an information system is periodically recorded at various "checkpoints" such that processing can be begun at the last checkpoint. This precludes the need to accomplish all processing again.

CHIEF PROGRAMMER TEAMS. An organizational concept used to promote a structured hierarchical approach to the programming effort.

CLOSED SHOP. Pertaining to the operation of a computer center in which only designated specialists are permitted to operate the computers. (Contrast with Open Shop.)

COBOL (Common Business Oriented Language). A programming language used primarily for administrative information systems.

CODASYL (Conference on Data Description Languages). An organization that sets standards for applications-independent (generalized) data management software.

CODE. (1) The rules used to translate a bit configuration to alphanumeric characters. (2) The process of compiling computer instructions in the form of a computer program. (3) The actual computer program.

COLLATE. Typically a reference to comparing and merging two similarly ordered files.

COM (Computer Output Microfilm). A device that produces a microform image of a computer output on microfilm.

COMMON CARRIER (Data Communications). See Carrier, Common.

COMMUNICATIONS. See Data Communications.

COMMUNICATIONS LINK. Same as Channel.

COMPATIBILITY. Pertaining to the ability of one computer to execute the programs of, access the data base of, and communicate with another computer.

COMPILE. The process by which a high-level programming language such as COBOL is translated to machine language in preparation for execution. (Synonymous with Translator; compare with Interpreter.)

COMPILER. Systems software that performs the compilation process.

COMPUTER. Same as Central Processing Unit.

COMPUTER-BASED INFORMATION SYSTEM (CBIS). Same as Management Information System.

COMPUTER CENTER. (1) A collective reference to the organization accomplishing the information services function. (2) The physical facilities in which computing hardware is kept. (Synonymous with Machine Room.)

COMPUTER SYSTEM. A collective reference to all interconnected computing hardware, including processors, storage devices, input/output devices, and communications equipment.

CONCENTRATOR. A communications device used to collect data from a number of low-speed devices. It then transmits "concentrated" data over a single high-speed channel. (Synonymous with Multiplexor and Cluster Controller.)

CONDITIONING, LINE. Electronically enhancing the data transmission capability of a communications channel.

CONFIGURATION, SYSTEM. The type of hardware devices and manner in which they are linked in a computer system.

CONNECT TIME. Elapsed time between the time the end user "logs on" and the time the user "logs off."

CONSISTENCY CHECK. A control method wherein like data items are checked for consistency of value.

CONSOLE. That unit of a computer system that allows operator and computer to communicate.

CONTROL. Pertaining to the procedures used to ensure the integrity of the input to and the output from an information system.

CONTROL FIELD. Same as Key.

CONTROL TOTAL. An accumulated number that is checked against an established value for the purpose of output control.

CONTROL UNIT. An intermediate device between the central processing unit and one or several input/output devices. It is used to facilitate the transmission of data.

CONVERSION. The transition process from one system (manual or computer-based) to a computer-based information system.

CORE. An obsolete form of primary storage. The term is still used interchangeably with primary storage. (Synonymous with Main Memory.)

CPU. See Central Processing Unit.

CRT. See Cathode-Ray Tube.

CYCLE TIME. The elapsed time between successive accesses to primary storage.

DAISY-WHEEL PRINTER. A letter-quality character printer whose interchangeable character set is located on a spoked wheel.

DASD (Direct Access Storage Device). A random access storage device.

DATA. Representation of fact. Raw material for information.

DATA BANK. Pertaining to all available data, regardless of storage media or scheme. (Compare with Data Base.)

DATA BASE. An integrated collection of data that are stored on a secondary storage device with controlled redundancy.

DATA BASE ADMINISTRATOR (DBA). The individual responsible for the physical and logical maintenance of the data base.

DATA BASE, HIERARCHICAL. An approach to data base design whereby logical components are linked in a tree-like structure.

DATA BASE MANAGEMENT SYSTEM (DBMS). All software necessary for the creation and maintenance of the data base.

DATA BASE, NETWORK. An approach to data base design whereby any logical component can be linked to any other component.

DATA BASE, RELATIONAL. An approach to data base design that permits relationships to be established at the data element level.

DATA COMMUNICATIONS. The collection and/or distribution of data from and/ or to a remote facility. (Synonymous with Telecommunications; compare with Teleprocessing.)

DATA DESCRIPTION LANGUAGE (DDL). That portion of the data base management system (DBMS) software that describes the logical relationships of the data.

DATA DICTIONARY. A listing and description of all data elements in the data base.

DATA ELEMENT. The smallest logical unit of data. Examples are employee number, first name, and price. (Synonymous with Field; compare with Data Item.)

DATA ENTRY. The transcription of source data into machine readable format.

DATA ITEM. The value of a data element.

DATA PROCESSING (DP). Using the computer to perform operations on data. (Synonymous with ADP and EDP; compare with Information Services.)

DBMS. See Data Base Management System.

DEBUG. To eliminate "bugs." (See Bug.)

DECISION SUPPORT SYSTEM (DSS). That component of an information system that uses available data and technology to enhance the decision-making process.

DECISION TABLE. A graphic technique used to illustrate possible occurrences and appropriate actions within a system.

DECODE. The reverse of the encoding process. (Contrast with Encode.)

DENSITY. The number of bytes per linear length of track of a recording media. Usually measured in bytes per inch (BPI). (Synonymous with Recording Density.)

DESTINATION. The receiver station of a data communications message.

DIAGNOSTIC. An explanation of a program error.

DIAL-UP LINE. A telephone line used as a regular data communications channel. (Synonymous with Public or Switched Line.)

DIGITAL COMPUTER. A computer that operates on digital data. (Contrast with Analog Computer.)

DIGITAL DATA TRANSMISSION. The transmission of the original electronic signal produced by a computer device. Not all channels have digital capabilities.

DIRECT ACCESS PROCESSING. Processing of data and records randomly. (Synonymous with Random Processing; contrast with Sequential Processing.)

DIRECT ACCESS STORAGE DEVICE. See DASD.

DISK DRIVE. A magnetic storage device that records data on flat rotating disks. (Compare with Tape Drive.)

DISKETTE. A thin flexible disk upon which data are stored. (Synonymous with Floppy Disk and Flexible Disk.)

DISK PACK. A storage medium consisting of one or more magnetized disks on which data are stored. (Compare with Diskette.)

DISTRIBUTED DATA PROCESSING (DDP). An organizational concept in which various aspects of the information services function, including hardware, are distributed to the functional areas.

DOCUMENTATION. Permanent and continuously updated written and graphic descriptions of information systems and programs.

DOWN-LINE PROCESSOR. A processor at or near the terminal point in a data communications network that facilitates the transmission of data. (Related to Front-End Processor.)

DOWNTIME. The time interval during which a computing device or the computer system is not operational.

DUMP. The duplication of the contents of one storage device to another storage device.

EBCDIC (Extended Binary Coded Decimal Interchange Code). An eight-bit code.

EDP (Electronic Data Processing). Same as Data Processing.

EFT (Electronic Funds Transfer). A computer-based system allowing electronic transfer of money from one account to another.

EGOLESS PROGRAMMING. A programming philosophy that is based on the premise that a program is developed for the company, not the individual.

ELECTRONIC FUNDS TRANSFER. Same as EFT.

ELECTRONIC MAIL. A computer application whereby messages are transmitted via data communications to "electronic mailboxes."

ENCODE. To apply the rules of a code. (Synonymous with Code; contrast with Decode.)

END USER. The individual providing terminal input and using terminal output.

ERASE. To clear a storage medium of any data.

EXCEPTION REPORT. A report that has been filtered to highlight critical information.

FEASIBILITY STUDY. A study performed to determine the economic and procedural feasibility of a proposed information system.

FEEDBACK LOOP. In a process control environment, the output of the process being controlled is input to the system.

FIELD. Same as Data Element.

FILE. A collection of related records.

FILE ACTIVITY. The number of records in a file or data base that are updated or processed during a processing cycle. (Compare with File Volatility.)

FILE/DATA BASE MAINTENANCE. Adding, changing, and deleting data to keep a file or data base up to date.

FILE LAYOUT. The arrangement and structure of the data elements in a file.

FILE VOLATILITY. The rate at which records are added or deleted from a file or data base. (Compare with File Activity.)

FIRMWARE. "Hard-wired" logic for performing certain functions. Built into a particular computer.

FIRST-GENERATION COMPUTER. Computers characterized by vacuum tubes (1946–1959).

FLAG. A character that signals the occurrence of some condition.

FLAT FILES. A traditional file structure in which records are related to no other files.

FLEXIBLE DISK. Same as Diskette.

FLOPPY DISK. Same as Diskette.

FLOWCHART. A diagram that illustrates work and data flow via specialized symbols which, when connected by flow lines, portray the logic of the system.

FOREGROUND. High-priority processing area of primary storage that is usually reserved for software supporting on-line information systems. (Contrast with Background.)

FORTRAN (Formula Translator). A high-level programming language designed primarily for scientific applications.

FRONT-END PROCESSOR. A processor used to off-load certain data communications tasks from the host processor.

FULL-DUPLEX LINE. A data communications channel capable of transmitting data in both directions simultaneously. (Contrast with Half-Duplex Line.)

FUNCTIONALLY ADJACENT APPLICATIONS. Application areas whose data processing objectives and data base contents overlap.

FUNCTIONAL AREA. Pertaining to a corporate entity charged with accomplishing a specific objective (e.g., accounting, marketing, engineering).

GANTT CHART. A chart used to illustrate the schedule of a project by activity.

GRAPHIC DISPLAY TERMINAL. A video display unit (VDU) capable of alphanumeric and graphic output.

HALF-DUPLEX LINE. A data communications channel that can transmit data in both directions, but not at the same time. (Compare with Full-Duplex Line.)

HARD COPY. A visually readable printed copy of computer output.

HARDWARE. The physical devices that comprise a computer system. (Contrast with Software.)

HARD-WIRED. Logic built into a computing device that cannot be altered. (Related to Firmware.)

HASH TOTAL. Same as Control Total.

HEXIDECIMAL. A base 16 numbering system that is used in information processing as a convenience to condense binary output and make it more easily readable.

HIGH-LEVEL PROGRAMMING LANGUAGE. A language whose instructions combine several machine-level instructions into one. Still, the programmer must detail procedures describing both "what to do" and "how to do it." (Compare with Machine Language or Low-Level Programming Language; compare with Query Language.)

HYBRID COMPUTER. A computer capable of processing both digital and analog data.

I/O (Input/Output). Input or output or both.

I/O DEVICE. A hardware device capable of input and/or output from and/or to the CPU.

INDEX SEQUENTIAL ACCESS METHOD (ISAM). A direct access data storage scheme.

INFORMATION. Assimilated data that communicates knowledge or intelligence.

INFORMATION CENTER. A physical facility and organization established within a company to provide hardware facilities, technical support, and education to the user community.

INFORMATION PROCESSING. Pertaining to the processing of data and the production of information.

INFORMATION RESOURCE MANAGEMENT (IRM). A concept advocating that information be treated as a corporate resource.

INFORMATION RESOURCE MANAGER. The person charged with the responsibility for the corporate information resources.

INFORMATION SERVICES. The organizational entity or entities that develop and maintain computer-based information systems. (Compare with Data Processing, Information Center, and Information Resource Management.)

INFORMATION SYSTEM. A computer-based system that provides both data processing capability and information for managerial decision making. (Synonymous with Computer-Based Information System and MIS.)

IN-HOUSE. Pertaining to a local operation.

INPUT. Data to be processed by a computer system.

INQUIRY. An on-line request for information.

INSTRUCTION. A program statement that specifies a particular computer operation to be performed.

INTELLIGENCE. Computer-aided.

INTELLIGENT TERMINAL. A terminal with a built-in computer or microprocessor.

INTERACTIVE. Pertaining to on-line and immediate communication between the end user and computer. (Contrast with Batch.)

INTERPRETER. Systems software that translates and executes each program instruction before translating and executing the next. (Compare with Compiler and Translator.)

INTERRUPT. A signal terminating the execution of a particular sequence of program instructions.

IRM. (1) See Information Resource Management. (2) See Informaton Resource Manager.

JOB. A unit of work for the computer system.

JOB CONTROL LANGUAGE (JCL). The language describing tasks to be performed by the operating system.

K. (1) An abbreviation for "kilo" meaning 1,000. (2) A computerese abbreviation for 2 to the 10th power or 1,024.

KEY. The data element in a logical record that is used as an identifier for accessing, sorting, and collating records. (Synonymous with Control Field.)

KEYBOARD. A device used for key data entry.

KEY-TO-DISK. Keyboard to magnetic disk data entry.

KEY-TO-TAPE. Keyboard to magnetic tape data entry.

KEY WORD. A word that has a special meaning to a compiler.

KOPS (Thousands [or K] of Operations Per Second). A measure of computer capacity.

LABEL. A name associated with a data element, data base, file, or program for the purpose of identification and retrieval.

LEASED LINE. A permanent or semi-permanent communications channel leased through a common carrier.

LIBRARY. Functions to catalogue, monitor, and control the distribution of disks, tapes, system documentation, and computer-related literature.

LIMIT CHECK. A control procedure by which similar data elements in a file, or output, are checked against pre-established minimums or maximums.

LINE SPEED. The maximum rate at which data can be transmitted over a given channel, usually recorded in baud or bits per second.

LOG. A chronological record of all the jobs run on a computer system.

LOGICAL RECORD. A collection of related data elements (e.g., an employee record). (Contrast with Physical Record and Block.)

LOW-LEVEL PROGRAMMING LANGUAGE. A language comprised of the fundamental instruction set of a particular computer. (Compare with High-Level Programming Language.)

MACHINE-INDEPENDENT. Pertaining to software that can be used on several different computers without modification. Such software is said to be portable.

MACHINE LANGUAGE. The programming language in which a computer executes all programs, without regard to the language of the original code.

MACHINE-READABLE FORMAT. Pertaining to data that can be read via an I/O device directly into a computer system.

MACHINE ROOM. Same as Computer Center.

MAGNETIC DISK. Same as Disk.

MAGNETIC TAPE. Same as Tape.

MAINFRAME. Same as Central Processing Unit.

MAIN MEMORY. Same as Primary Storage.

MAIN STORAGE. Same as Primary Storage.

MAINTENANCE. The ongoing process by which information systems (and software) are updated and enhanced to accommodate varying functional and organizational requirements.

MANAGEMENT INFORMATION SYSTEM (MIS). Same as information system.

MASTER FILE. The permanent source of data for a particular computer application area.

MEGABYTE. Referring to one million bytes of primary or secondary storage capacity.

MEMORY. Same as Primary Storage.

MERGE. To combine two or more files into one.

MESSAGE. A series of bits sent from a terminal to a computer or vice versa.

METHODOLOGY. A set of standardized procedures, including technical methods, management techniques, and documentation that provide the framework to accomplish a particular function.

MICROCODE. Programs, written using low-level languages, that are embedded in the architecture of the computer and executed automatically with each use of the computer. (Related to Firmware and ROM.)

MICROCOMPUTER. A very small computer.

MICROPROCESSOR. A computer on a single electronic chip.

MINICOMPUTER. Those computers with slightly more power and capacity than microcomputers, still classified as small computers.

MIPS (Millions of Instructions Per Second). Measure of computer capacity.

MIS (Management Information System). Same as Information System.

MODEM (Modulator-Demodulator). A device used to convert computer-compatible electrical signals to signals suitable for transmission facilities and vice versa.

MODULAR DESIGN. Segmenting, then analyzing and designing a program or a system into intelligible modules.

MULTIDROP. The connection of more than one terminal to a single communications channel.

MULTIPLEXOR. Same as Concentrator.

MULTIPROCESSING. Using two or more computers in the same computer system to execute two or more programs simultaneously.

MULTIPROGRAMMING. Pertaining to the concurrent execution of two or more programs by a single computer.

NETWORK, DATA COMMUNICATIONS. Remote computer hardware devices interconnected by communications channels.

OBJECT PROGRAM. A machine-level program that has been compiled and can be executed directly.

OCR (Optical Character Recognition). Machine identification of printed characters through light sensitive devices.

OEM (Original Equipment Manufacturer). The supplier, not the manufacturer, of small computer systems. They add value to the system in the form of software.

OFFICE AUTOMATION. Pertaining collectively to those computer-based applications associated with general office work.

OFF-LINE. Pertaining to data that are not accessible by, or hardware devices that are not connected to, a computer system. (Contrast with On-Line.)

ON-LINE. Pertaining to data and/or hardware devices that are accessible to and under the control of a computer system. (Contrast with Off-Line.)

OPEN SHOP. A mode of operation whereby both user and information services personnel have physical access to the computer system. (Contrast with Closed Shop.)

OPERATING SYSTEM (OS). The software that controls the execution of all applications and system software programs. Also called an *executive*, a *monitor*, or a *supervisor*.

OPERATIONS. The information services function that encompasses machine room activities, primarily the running of routine production information systems and other nonscheduled system requirements.

OPERATOR. The person who performs those hardware-based activities necessary to keep production information systems operational.

OUTPUT. Data transferred from primary storage to an I/O device.

OVERHEAD. The hardware resource commitment required before any applications software can be executed.

OVERLAY. A technique by which a program that exceeds alloted main memory storage can be loaded to main memory in segments, "overlaying" that portion of the program not currently in use.

PACKAGED SOFTWARE. Software that is generalized and "packaged" to be used, with little or no modification, in a variety of environments. (Compare with Proprietary Software.)

PAGE. A program segment that is loaded to primary storage only if it is needed for execution. (Related to Virtual Storage.)

PARALLEL OPERATION. Refers to the simultaneous operation of an existing and a new information system. Performed during the system conversion process.

PARITY BIT. A bit appended to a bit configuration (byte) that is used to check the accuracy of data transmission from one hardware device to another.

PASCAL. A multipurpose high-level programming language.

PCM (Plug-Compatible Manufacturer). A company that manufactures I/O devices that are fully compatible with another manufacturer's mainframe computer, including the electrical connection.

PERIPHERAL EQUIPMENT. Any hardware device other than the central processing unit.

PERSONAL COMPUTER. An inexpensive microcomputer designed for the mass market.

PHYSICAL RECORD. Same as Block.

PL/I (Programming Language/I). A multipurpose high-level programming language.

PLOTTER. A device that produces hard-copy graphic output.

PLUG-COMPATIBLE MANUFACTURER. See PCM.

POINT-OF-SALE (POS) TERMINAL. A computer terminal similar to a cash register.

POLLING. The periodic interrogation of each on-line terminal to determine if a message is ready to be sent.

PORT. An electrical bus in a computer through which data can be transmitted or received.

PORTABILITY. The flexibility of a procedure or software to be used in a variety of environments.

POS TERMINAL. See Point-of-Sale Terminal.

POST-IMPLEMENTATION EVALUATION. A comprehensive system evaluation conducted three to six months after an information system has been implemented.

PRIMARY STORAGE. The memory area in which all programs and data must reside before programs can be executed or data can be manipulated. (Synonymous with Core, Main Memory, Memory, and RAM; compare with Secondary Storage.)

PRINTER. A device used to prepare hard-copy output. The types of printers, in order of increasing speed, are character, line, and page.

PRIVATE LINE. A communications channel dedicated to the exclusive use of one communications network. (Contrast with Public and Leased Lines.)

PROBLEM-ORIENTED LANGUAGE. A high-level language whose instruction set is specifically designed to address a specific problem (e.g., process control of machine tools, simulation, analysis of structural stress).

PROCEDURE-ORIENTED LANGUAGE. A high-level language whose general-purpose instruction set can be used to model scientific and business procedures.

PROCESS CONTROL. Using the computer to control an ongoing process in a continuous feedback loop. Output from the process becomes input to the computer. The computer then uses this input to control the process.

PROCESSOR. Same as Central Processing Unit.

PROGRAM. (1) Computer instructions structured and ordered in a manner that, when executed, cause a computer to perform a particular function. (2) The act of producing computer software. (Closely related to Software.)

PROGRAMMER. One who writes programs.

PROGRAMMER/ANALYST. A position title of one who performs both the programming and systems analysis function.

PROPRIETARY SOFTWARE. Vendor-developed generalized software that is marketed publicly. (Related to Packaged Software.)

PSEUDOCODE. Non-executable program code used as an aid to develop and document structured programs.

PUBLIC LINE. A communications channel offered for public use by a common carrier.

QUERY LANGUAGE. A programming language with English-like commands that is used primarily for inquiry purposes. The programmer need only designate "what to do" not "how to do it." (Contrast with Procedure-Oriented Programming Language.)

QUEUE. A waiting line. Used in data communications to refer to a message queue or a service queue at a terminal.

RAM (Random Access Memory). Same as Primary Storage.

RANDOM ACCESS. Same as Direct Access.

RANDOM ACCESS DEVICE. Same as Direct Access Device or DASD.

RANDOM PROCESSING. Same as Direct Access Processing.

RANGE CHECK. A control procedure used to ensure that the value of a numeric data element is within a particular range.

READ. The process by which a record or a portion of a record is accessed from the magnetic storage media (tape or disk) of a secondary storage device and transferred to primary storage for processing. (Contrast with Write.)

READ ONLY MEMORY (ROM). RAM that can only be read, not written to.

READ/WRITE HEAD. That component of a disk drive or tape drive that reads from and writes to the respective magnetic storage media.

REAL-TIME PROCESSING. Computer-based processing that at all times reflects the current status of the system. (Related to Process Control.)

REASONABLENESS CHECK. A control procedure used to ensure that the value of a data element or output is consistent with that expected.

RECEIVER. The individual or department receiving a message in a data communications network. (Contrast with Sender; related to Destination.)

RECORD. Same as Logical Record.

RECORD COUNT. A control procedure that checks the actual number of records processed against an expected number to ensure complete processing.

RECORDING DENSITY. Same as Density.

RECORD LENGTH. A measure of the size of a record, usually specified in number of bytes or characters.

REGISTER. A small high-speed storage area in which data pertaining to the execution of a particular instruction are stored. Data stored in a specific register have a special meaning to the logic of the computer. Registers contain such data as the instruction, the address of the value to be added, and the value on which an operation is directed.

REMOTE ACCESS. Pertaining to the ability to access a computer system from a distant facility.

REMOTE JOB ENTRY (RJE) UNIT. A terminal that permits jobs to be batched to a computer system for processing.

RERUN. A repeat of a run. A result of a procedural, software, or hardware malfunction.

RESPONSE TIME. The elapsed time from when a data communications message is sent to when a response is received.

REVERSE VIDEO. Characters on a VDU presented as black characters on a light background. Used for highlighting.

RFP (Request for Proposal). A formal request to a vendor to propose a hardware and/or software alternative that will meet specific requirements.

RING NETWORK. A computer network in which the data communications channel linking the computers completes a full circle through all computers.

ROM. See Read Only Memory.

ROUTINE. Loosely, the same as a Program.

RPG (Report Program Generator). A high-level programming language with special features that make report preparation easier.

RUN. The continuous execution of one or more logically related programs (e.g., print payroll checks).

RUN MANUAL. A manual describing how and when to initiate computer runs or to bring up on-line systems. The manual also contains instructions to operators for both routine and exceptional situations.

SATELLITE, COMMUNICATIONS. A radio wave-based data communications channel using earth station to satellite to earth station transmission.

SCHEMA. A graphical representation of the logical structure of a data base.

SCROLLING. A VDU function allowing the operator to move the screen display up or down, permitting display of subsequent or previous screens.

SECONDARY STORAGE. Magnetic disk and magnetic tape storage. (Synonymous with Auxiliary Storage; compare with Primary Storage.)

SECONDARY STORAGE DEVICE. A magnetic tape drive or a magnetic disk drive. (Synonymous with Auxiliary Storage Device.)

SECOND-GENERATION COMPUTER. A computer characterized by transistor technology (1959-1964).

SENDER. The person originating a message in a data communications network. (Related to Source; contrast with Receiver.)

SENSE PROBE. A device used to input data (usually relative position) directly on a VDU screen.

SEQUENTIAL PROCESSING. Processing of files that are ordered numerically or alphabetically by key. (Contrast with Direct Access or Random Processing.)

SEQUENTIAL STORAGE. Storage of logical records in an ordered sequence depending on the value of the key. (Related to Sequential Processing.)

SERVICE REQUEST. The formal vehicle by which a user requests any kind of service from the information services department.

SET. A data base concept that serves to define the relationship between two records, an owner, and a member. Each owner record can have one or more member records (e.g., faculty advisor [owner] and student record [member]).

SETUP TIME. The preparation time for a particular computer run.

SOFT COPY. Temporary output that can be interpreted visually (e.g., a VDU display). (Contrast with Hard Copy.)

SOFTWARE. The programs used to direct the functions of a computer system. (Contrast with Hardware.)

SOFTWARE HOUSE. A company whose primary product is the software and accompanying documentation for computer-based systems.

SORT. The arrangement of data elements or records in an ordered sequence by key.

SOURCE. The terminal or the computer used to send a message in a data communications network. (Contrast with Destination; related to Sender.)

SOURCE DOCUMENT. The original hard copy from which data are entered.

SOURCE PROGRAM. A program prior to being compiled, usually hard or soft copy. (Compare with Object Program.)

SPECIALIZED COMMON CARRIER. A company providing data communications services with enhancements to services provided by common carriers. (Related to Value Added Networks.)

SPOOLING. The process by which output (or input) is loaded temporarily to secondary storage. It is then output (or input) as appropriate devices become available.

STAND-ALONE COMPUTER SYSTEM. An independent computer system that is not linked to a communications network.

STAR NETWORK. A communications network configuration in which all terminals are linked directly to the host computer.

STATEMENT. Same as Instruction (in a computer program).

STORAGE CAPACITY. The amount of data that can be contained in a storage device. Measured in characters or bytes. (Related to Primary and Secondary Storage.)

STRUCTURED DESIGN. Pertaining to the modularization of a program or system into logical functional units using the top-down approach to design.

STRUCTURED PROGRAMMING. The modularization of a program into one of the three basic program constructs (sequence, decision, and loop) and applying the principles of structured design.

STRUCTURED WALKTHROUGH. A peer evaluation procedure for programs and systems under development. It is used to minimize the possibility of something being overlooked or done incorrectly.

SUBROUTINE. A logical unit of a computer program. It is stored and called (retrieved) as an independent program unit.

SUPERCOMPUTER. Pertaining to the largest of computer systems.

SYNCHRONOUS TRANSMISSION. Terminals and/or computers transmit data at timed intervals. (Contrast with Asynchronous Transmission.)

SYSTEM. The integration of people, procedures, software, and/or hardware to accomplish a particular function.

SYSTEM LIFE CYCLE. A reference to the four stages of a computer-based information system: birth, development, production, and death.

SYSTEMS ANALYSIS. The analysis, design, development, and implementation of computer-based information systems.

SYSTEMS ANALYST. A person who does systems analysis.

TAPE DRIVE. The secondary storage device that contains the read/write mechanism for magnetic tape.

TECHNOLOGY GAP. The gap between the state of the art of computer technology and management's ability to cope with the technology.

TECHNOLOGY TRANSFER. The application of existing technology to a current problem or situation.

TELECOMMUNICATIONS. Same as Data Communications.

TELEPRINTER. A hard-copy character printer. Typically used as a terminal.

TELEPROCESSING (TP). The integration of information processing and communication facilities. Originally an IBM trademark. (Compare with Data Communications and Telecommunications.)

TERMINAL. Any device capable of sending and/or receiving data over a communications channel.

TESTING. The process of eliminating errors in a computer program or system. (Compare with Debug.)

TEXT EDITING. The addition, deletion, changing, and moving of words, phrases, paragraphs, and sections in stored text material. (Related to Word Processing.)

THIRD-GENERATION COMPUTER. A computer characterized by miniaturized circuitry (1964–present).

THROUGHPUT. A measure of computer system efficiency. The rate at which work can be performed by a computer system.

TIME SHARING. Multiple end users sharing time on a single computer system in an on-line environment.

TOP-DOWN DESIGN. An approach to system and program design that is initiated at the highest level of generalization. Design strategies are then developed at successive levels of decreasing generalization until the detailed specifications are achieved. (Contrast to Bottom-Up Design.)

TRACK, DISK. That portion of a magnetic disk face surface that can be accessed in any given setting of the read/write head. Tracks are configured in concentric circles.

TRACK, TAPE. That portion of the magnetic tape that can be accessed by any one of the nine read/write heads. A track runs the length of the tape.

TRAFFIC. The volume of data flow through a communications channel.

TRANSACTION. A procedural event in a system that prompts manual or computer-based activity.

TRANSACTION FILE. A file containing records of data activity (transactions).

TRANSACTION LOG. A record of all on-line transactions, usually over a period of one day.

TRANSFER RATE. The rate at which data are transmitted from an I/O device to the central processing unit.

TRANSLATOR. Same as Compiler.

TRANSMIT. To send data from one device to another.

TRANSPARENT. Of little or no concern to end user.

TURNAROUND TIME. Elapsed time between the submission of a job and the distribution of the results.

TURNKEY SYSTEM. A system, both hardware and software, that is installed without modification, to perform a particular function.

UNBUNDLING. Pertaining to the separate pricing of hardware and other computer-related services.

UNINTERRUPTABLE POWER SYSTEM (UPS). A device placed in line between the computer system and the primary source of power. It supplies power for limited continuous operation upon failure of the primary source of power.

UNIVERSAL PRODUCT CODE (UPC). A 10-digit machine-readable bar code placed on consumer products.

UPDATE. To run transactions against a master file for the purpose of adding, deleting, and changing records to reflect the current status.

UPTIME. Time in which the computer system is operational. (Contrast with Downtime.)

UPWARD COMPATIBILITY. Pertaining to the compatibility of software and hardware throughout a particular line of computers. A company can upgrade their computer system without program modification.

USER. A name applied to any person who uses the computer or information services.

USER FRIENDLY. Pertaining to an on-line system that permits a person with relatively little experience to interact successfully with the system.

USER MANAGER. The manager of a functional area that uses computers for information processing.

USER MANUAL. A manual, written for end users, that provides instructions and explanations for the operation of a given computer-based information system.

UTILITY PROGRAM. An often-used service routine (e.g., a program to sort records).

VALUE-ADDED NETWORK (VAN). A specialized common carrier that "adds value" over and above the standard services of common carriers.

VARIABLE. A named quantity in a program that can assume different numeric or alphanumeric values.

VDU. See Visual Display Unit.

VIDEO DISPLAY UNIT (VDU). Same as CRT.

VIRTUAL MACHINE. The processing capabilities of a computer system created through software (and sometimes hardware) in a different computer system. The virtual machine does not exist, only the processing capabilities.

VIRTUAL MEMORY. The use of secondary storage devices and primary storage effectively to expand a computer system's primary storage (memory). Although the added memory capacity is not real, this is transparent to the programmer. The programmer can assume that "virtual memory" is real memory and use it accordingly.

VISUAL DISPLAY UNIT (VDU). Same as CRT.

VOICE GRADE LINES. Regular telephone lines used for data communications that range in speed from 600 to 9,600 baud.

VOLUME. Pertaining to a single magnetic tape reel or a single disk pack.

WALKTHROUGH, STRUCTURED. See Structured Walkthrough.

WIDE-BAND LINE. A data communications channel with baud rates greater than 9,600 baud. (Synonymous with Broad-band Line.)

WORD. For any given computer, an established number of bits that are handled as a unit.

WORD-ORIENTED COMPUTER. A computer designed primarily for scientific applications. (Contrast to Character-Oriented Computer.)

WORD PROCESSING. Using the computer to enter text, store it on magnetic storage media, manipulate it in preparation for output, and print it. (Compare with Text Editing.)

WRITE. To record data on the output medium of a particular I/O device (e.g., tape, hard copy, VDU screen display). (Contrast to Read.)

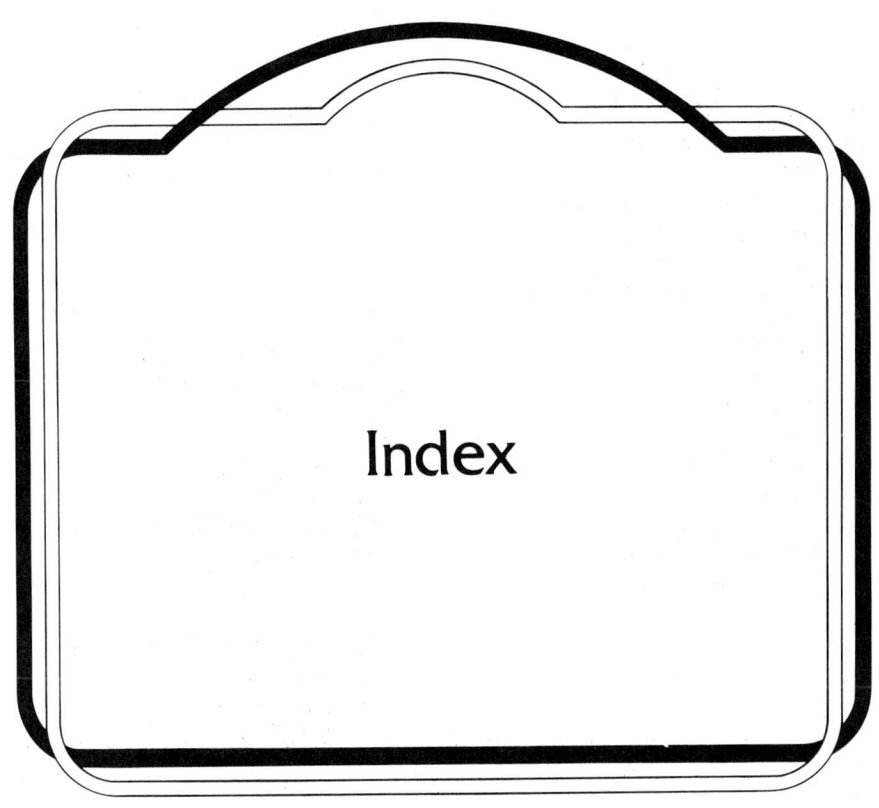

Index